BORN UNDER  THE SIGN OF ODIN

The Life & Times of Robert Bly's

Little Magazine & Small Press

MARK GUSTAFSON

NODIN PRESS

Image Credits
p. ii – Photo by Earl Seubert, with permission of the Minnesota Historical Society.
p. 59 – Photo by Carol Bly, courtesy of Robert Bly.
p. 83 – Photo by Earl Seubert, with permission of the Minnesota Historical Society.
p. 128 – Photo by Carol Bly, courtesy of the Lac Qui Parle County Historical Society.
p. 143 – Photo by Carol Bly, courtesy of Bridget Bly.
p. 193 – Photographer unknown, courtesy of Robert Bly.
p. 263 – Photo by Carol Bly, courtesy of Bridget Bly.
p. 300 – Photo by Carol Bly, courtesy of Bridget Bly.
p. 358 – Photo by Mike Hazard, with thanks to him.

ISBN 978-1-947237-33-9

Library of Congress Control Number: 2021943232

Acknowledgments can be found on pages 347-349

Published by
Nodin Press
5114 Cedar Lake Road,
Minneapolis, MN 55416
www.nodinpress.com

Printed in USA

For Sarah,

sweet love of my life

Contents

Introduction

A horse and rider dominate the front cover of *The Fifties*, which first appeared in the summer of 1958. This is no hayseed astride his favorite nag, but a bold and stylized representation of an equestrian figure armed with spear, shield, and helmet, two birds in flight, and a serpent rearing up in attack mode. If not exactly menacing, the image is unmistakably militant. Printed on the verso of that first issue's cover is one sentence: "The editors of this magazine think that most of the poetry published in America today is too old-fashioned." A simple credo that had been in Bly's mind for years, this first loud blast signaled that battle lines were being drawn.

The rider is the Norse god Odin, on his steed Sleipnir.[1] The god's mighty spear is Gungnir. His ravens, Huginn (Thought) and Muninn (Memory), tell him daily what's happening in Midgard (the Earth). Jörmungand is the formidable serpent who kills his victims by constriction.

Probably only a few readers made this identification. More of them would have had an inkling of Pegasus, the winged horse of Greek mythology who was associated with poetry and had long been the logo for *Poetry* magazine.[2] Bly first saw this motif on a pre-Viking, Vendel Era (c. 550-793) helmet, during his recent time in Norway, the land of his ancestors. It looms over every appearance of *The Fifties, Sixties,* and *Seventies,* and serves as the distinctive emblem for the Sixties Press as well.

A half-page advertisement in the February issue of *Poetry* had announced "a new literary quarterly, *The Fifties,* a magazine of poetry and general opinion," and invited contributions and subscriptions.[3] In retrospect, the notice seems innocuous and sober, but at the time it surely caused some puzzlement. What kind of name was *The Fifties*, especially near the end of the decade? What was "general opinion" doing next to poetry? Had anyone ever heard of the editors, William Duffy and Robert Bly? Were they professors? Or beatniks? Did they have some hidden institutional support or inherited wealth? (The promise of "payment on acceptance" was unusual for a little upstart.) The address, Briarwood Hill, concocted for the occasion, had an old-world ring. But the town where Duffy lived, Pine Island, was unheard of. As for Minnesota, wasn't that near Chicago? Something unusual was afoot.

After the third issue, when Duffy terminated his involvement, the business operations, such as they were, moved across the state, from southeastern Minnesota to Bly's hometown on the western edge. Bly knew it would not suffice to use the actual address, which was simply R.F.D. (Rural Free Delivery).[4] He wrote to his friend Donald Hall about the new name: "How do you like Odin House? (That is, the chickenhouse.) I...had to find some sort of address, since simply 'Madison, Minn.' looks too unreliable. Do you think Odin House is all right?"[5] "Odin House is great," Hall replied, in innocent deference to the deity.[6] Still, it would have been hard to make the whereabouts sound more outlandish and obscure.

To put *The Fifties* in proper context, to appreciate fully how it fit or didn't fit there, some broad observations are in order.

In the late 1950s, the so-called New York intellectuals were ascendant. Men such as Lionel Trilling and Jacques Barzun valued seriousness in literature specifically, and in culture more generally—high or highbrow culture, that is. They were determined to hold the line against any reduction of standards, destruction of values, dilution of taste—in short, against philistinism.[7]

Also, New Criticism, which had taken hold in the literary world of the 1930s and 40s, was still firmly in place. Poet-critics like Robert Penn Warren, John Crowe Ransom, and Allen Tate placed a high value on anonymity, self-sufficiency, and aesthetic distance in a literary work. They felt that the social, historical, and political settings of a literary composition were secondary concerns, if not entirely irrelevant. So too the writer's biography. Instead, they focused their attention on technique, attaching great importance to form, rhyme, meter, and other aspects of language, as well as to mythological allusions, irony, ambiguity, paradox, and other more or less semantic complexities.

More than a few young writers of the time found this program stifling and oppressive, considering it a retreat from the Modernist advances of the 1910s and 20s. The growing unrest became a literary revolution in the later 1950s, as the opacity and formalism of New Criticism was rejected in favor of a renewed interest in the radicalism and experimentation of Ezra Pound, William Carlos Williams, and other Modernist figures. Emerging *avant-garde* schools including the Beats and the Black Mountain poets, although certainly disparate, nevertheless had a common foe, and, in that sense at least, a common cause. More generally, this literary ferment, with its emphasis on freeing poetic language from academic restraints while also broadening poetry's responsibilities, played a significant role in the more widespread social and cultural upheaval of the 1960s.

Where does the literary magazine fit into this picture? *Partisan Review, The Kenyon Review, The Southern Review, The Sewanee Review,* and others, were the organs for the reigning literary muckety-mucks and their ilk. Sometimes called the "bigs," or the "big littles," these magazines were usually well established, had solid financial backing, and were destined for longevity. The so-called "little" magazines, on the other hand, were typically small, independent concerns with limited circulation and uncertain, though usually short, lifespans. Produced on a shoestring, with scant or no hope of making money, they were not subject to the same constraints of propriety, conformity, and predictability as the established giants. Therefore, little mags usually were (and still are, to varying degrees) idiosyncratic, experimental, impatient, and antagonistic. The same may be said for their editors.

To start such a publication requires audacity in any literary climate, for sure, along with a fervent conviction that literature is worth promoting, discussing, and criticizing. The editor's challenge lies in balancing the magazine's positive function of promoting new and original work outside the mainstream against its negative function of fostering discontent with the *status quo*. Some sort of manifesto or call to action is usually at least implicit in any such endeavor.

Early in the 20th century, little magazines had served as the vanguard of Modernism. Pound was the prototype of the little mag editor. "His early cultural complaints were various and extreme but almost uniformly against the going norm, whatever the norm was."[8] Pound wanted to save the world. He wrote to Harriet Monroe: "My problem is to keep alive a certain group of advancing poets, to set the arts in their rightful place as the acknowledged guide and lamp of civilization."[9] Poems in a little magazine, he thought, could and should teach and enlighten not a large general audience of readers, but a discrete audience of poets and writers. They in turn would disseminate and carry out the purposes of the ideas set forth. The academy was not to play a role. Pound said: "All the U[niversity] of P[ennsylvania] or your god damn college or any other god damn American college does or will do for a man of letters is to ask him to go away without breaking the silence."[10]

Thus it is not surprising that some American writers in the Cold War climate of the 1950s sensed that they were on the verge of something. Poet and translator Paul Blackburn, for example, writes to Bly: "This is the greatest age of transition since the renaissance. The western world, western civilization is finally dead. There's a future to build, for christsake let's make it human. Let's insist on certain human values and not just piss up a hot steampipe about how shitty everything is...."[11] To promulgate such views, new little magazines started appearing. Early on were *Origin* and *Black Mountain Review*; later in that decade came *The Fifties*, followed by *Yugen, Big Table, Kulchur, Poems from the Floating World*, and *Trobar*, as the trickle became a torrent.

As one of the more disgruntled and zealous leaders of the uprising, Bly felt a responsibility to be of service to the culture. While he plainly had a bone to pick with the establishment, he (at first in tandem with Duffy) did not want to change the world so much as to change the way American poets wrote, read, and thought about poetry. "I set myself up to be the teacher of my own generation," he says.[12] Bly built a platform from which he could both exercise his singular gifts as a public intellectual and gadfly and have an impact on the dramas that the next decade would bring. He called for "a sustained raid on modern life," and that, in retrospect, is what he helped to deliver.[13] Together with the Sixties and Seventies Press, the magazine's specific objectives were to foster "a new imagination" in American poetry, to demonstrate the need for honest criticism, and, with a sustained and unprecedented commitment to translation, to direct attention beyond the traditional confines of the English language, to poetry from South America, Europe, China, and elsewhere.

His efforts sometimes went beyond teaching and theorizing to preaching and proselytizing. He aimed to win the hearts and minds of the unenlightened, to convert them to a new way, a new aesthetic, a new poetic faith, with a concentration on the inner life reached and expressed via images from deep within the unconscious. Alongside this inner focus, a second campaign focused on the outer world, on the need for poets to be socially and politically engaged.

The magazine was tendentious, provocative, and dead serious, at the same time that it was fresh, playful, and wildly irreverent. Although it came to represent a community of poets, from start to finish it reflected the comprehensive vision of one impassioned and prolific man on a mission. Through his overlapping roles as poet, translator, critic, editor, and antiwar activist, for all of which the magazine and press served as staging ground, Bly attained an eminent position from which he wielded enormous influence and had a lasting impact. He made many friends, and many enemies. The rulebook he played by was very much his own; his candor was astonishing; he was not afraid to attack established poets; he insulted the editors of other magazines; he brought politics into the mix.

Eleven issues were published between 1958 and 1972. I have devoted a chapter of this book to each one of them, also taking into account contemporaneous press publications and other relevant writings, activities, controversies, and relationships. The output may seem meager at first—less than one issue per year. But once the individual numbers are examined—with their wide array of poems, translations, quotations, critical essays, reviews, satires, parodies, and comments—and Bly's personal responsibility for the contents is weighed together with his other pursuits, that output begins to look consequential indeed.

The connection between a little magazine and a small press is like a synapse. As Robert Creeley, who ran both *Black Mountain Review* and Divers Press, said: "There had to be both a press and a magazine absolutely specific to one's own commitments and possibilities. Nothing short of that was good enough."[14] In Bly's circumstance we see that the two literary enterprises had a symbiotic relationship; they were siblings, more like fraternal twins, conceived simultaneously, born in quick succession, raised in the same house.

From the Sixties and Seventies Press, which was always a more collaborative effort than the magazine, there issued: an initial broadsheet; seven books of twenty (and one of forty) translated poems of an individual poet; three anthologies, one of poems in English, another of poems from other languages, a third of writings against war; and a collection of critical reviews.

Throughout these years, Bly continued to live and work just outside the small farming town where he was born and raised. Nevertheless, his voice was not quite that of a rustic crying out in the Minnesota wilderness. It bore signs of his sophisticated literary résumé, which included Harvard College, New York City, the Iowa Writers' Workshop, and a Fulbright year in Norway. While Harvard and Iowa constituted extraordinary opportunities at top-notch institutions, his initial stay in New York in the early 1950s was comparatively grim and austere. Also, Norway could scarcely have matched other European locales for *belles-lettres* and cosmopolitanism. But, as will become clear, these non-academic experiences had a profound impact on his work.

It is no coincidence that Bly's appearance changed dramatically over time, from the sedate, everyman-in-1950s-America look of suit, white shirt, tie, with closely cropped hair, to the madly gesticulating, sarape-clad wild man with tousled hair, spouting surrealist images, chanting like a shaman, and ranting like a prophet against the power structures that were undermining the health of society. Poetry had changed, as had this poet.

This book gives an account of the dispatches, mostly in magazine or book form, that issued from Odin House. It is a Minnesota story, but one that had a seismic effect felt far beyond state lines, across the United States, and beyond. Some reverberations are detectable to this day. Although he was anything but insular, Bly's location in the hinterland, roughly equidistant from New York and San Francisco, worked to his advantage both as a haven and as a launching pad.

A chronological approach will allow us to trace the growth of a poetic community as well as the development and spread of Bly's ideas. As will become apparent, in assembling this account I have stitched together copious primary source materials consisting of the dispatches themselves as well as extensive correspondence, journal entries, and related evidence.[15] A few of the chapters consist of in-depth digressions that help to flesh out the larger story.

An additional thread running through the book connects to that cover image. Bly's spirited publishing project was launched, as we have already seen, not under the sign of Pegasus but under the sign of Odin. Setting out on what was to be a long, strange trip, this god proved to be a strikingly suitable patron and muse (of a sort). Four principal Odinic aspects, not always visible but always present, are reflected in the magazine and press and also in their editor.

As god of war, Odin here represents polemic and harsh criticism. No poet was immune: dead or living, young or old, friend or foe. Nor were institutions of any kind. Bly's weapon, equivalent to Odin's magic spear, was his sharp pen, which he used to attack, skewer, and deflate. As his provocations (some of them with his *nom de guerre*, Crunk) began to pile up, there was noticeable increase in the number and ferocity of skirmishes. He relished a robust battle.

A second aspect is Odin's role as foremost of the gods, often called Allfather. "Odin...rules all things and, no matter how mighty the other gods may be, they all serve him as children do their father."[16] When it came to criticizing contemporaries, Bly was utterly convinced that one must always be honest and direct, including, as appropriate, both praise and blame. All poets had faults and stood in need of some fatherly correction, some tough love. Bly began regularly seeing and sharing ideas with James Wright, James Dickey, Louis Simpson, Galway Kinnell, and Donald Hall, close friends who became like a poetic family. But Bly was the man with the megaphone, the chief theorist, and his predominance is undeniable. (Similarly, Odin was a member of the Aesir, a group of warrior gods, but he was also its leader.) As even younger poets came under Bly's sway, he became a strong father-image for many. Of course, the classic relationship between teacher and student is akin to that between parent and child.

Third, acting as a shaman, Odin "could send out his spirit... on journeys between worlds;...he could win wisdom from the dead."[17] There are many polarities highlighted in the magazine: inward and outward, feeling and intellect, unconscious and conscious, the live world and the dead world. One way to travel between these poles was, as Bly put it, by means of wild association, or leaping. Translation was comparable, another kind of voyage. He also journeyed between eras, occasionally seeking wisdom from antiquity.

In this same guise, Odin might evoke animals as spirit guides or message bearers. Therefore Bly speaks of "the interior animal life" and of using animal imagery "to penetrate down into an evolutionary part of the mind."[18] He identified with animals, most notably, perhaps, the badger and the owl. But Odin also likes human disguises.[19] Though attentive readers had little doubt of Crunk's true identity, fewer saw through the several pseudonyms Bly used to publish his own poems and translations.

Fourth, and maybe most importantly, Odin is the god of poetry and inspiration. When he asks for a drink of mead but is refused, he says: "I may be strong...But to be a poet: that's the finest calling." Eventually, he gets possession of the mead and drinks of it. "From time to time he offered a draught to...a man or two...; he offered them the gift of poetry."[20] The magazine and the books were mead enough, and more, for many poets in search of stimulus and example. But one crucial reason for their irregular appearance was that Bly was also drinking mead. He may have had the strength of nine men, but he held the art of his own poetry in higher esteem. It was the private work on which all of his other work was based.

This then is the biography of a literary magazine and press out of rural Minnesota that made a difference in the world. It entails the story of a group of poets looking for and finding a literary community based on a shared passion, common pursuits, and some healthy competition. Not so incidentally, it is also one perspective on the early career and maturation of an unusually charismatic and visionary writer.

Especially impressive is how vivid so much of the magazine still seems. Bly's global perspective is as important and relevant as ever, if not more so. The fresh impetus he gave to translation, both to transmit riches found in poems from other languages as well as to reap poetic benefits from the process of translation itself, has not let up. Seen over time, the consistency and interrelatedness of Bly's ideas is truly astonishing. The seeds and first fruits of many of the concerns for which he has since become even more widely known are discernible at or near the beginning.

Now let us move back to that beginning, to the middle of the last century, to watch it all coming to pass. American poetry would not have been the same without Robert Bly and his wild little magazine and small press, the news issuing from Odin House.

1

Making a Clearing in the

Forests of Convention

A new morning was dawning in American poetry, and Robert Bly employed Gunnar Ekelöf, a Swedish poet, to make the announcement. "In the Forests of Convention," the first poem in the first issue of *The Fifties*, begins:

> *In the forests of convention,*
> *Some men walk there with rough-shirts*
> *a sound of ax-blows in the morning air!*
> *Each eye is open there*
> *When the giants waver and crash.*
> *Each breath is deep there:*
> *A wonderful smell from the fallen trees!*
> *There it is always dawn!*

Bly has said: "I started my magazine to clear ground for myself and for other poets."[1] After the lumberjacks were done, the farmers would start planting, and soon there would be new growth stretching off into the distance.

Bly calls Ekelöf "Sweden's greatest poet in the twentieth century," who "single-handedly...introduced modern poetry into Sweden." In a clear indication of what Bly was up to, he writes that Ekelöf "is most interested in destroying the old logicalistic or European thinking, and often suggests that everything must be abandoned. Others have said before what he is saying, but what he really presents is a new kind of imagination." Five more of his poems followed.

Co-translator credit goes to Christina Bratt Duffy (then co-editor Bill Duffy's wife), a native speaker. She helped Bly to understand "what the meanings of the words were, the morphology and the grammar, the relationship between the words." Then her job was done. "He understood what the poet was trying to say, what the images were, what Ekelöf was after, and he would translate it not at all *verbatim*, but close to the intention, what a linguist would call the elocutionary force, of what the poet wanted to put across."[2] Bly sent Ekelöf the first issue, inviting comments and criticism, and the Swede happily complied.[3]

Other poems in the first issue are by Tom Kristensen, a Dane "of the generation of the Twenties," and his French contemporary, Henri Michaux.[4] All three of these poets Bly had discovered in Paal Brekke's Norwegian anthology, *Modernistisk Lyrikk fra 8 Land*.[5]

Attention next turns to, of all things, a *young* American poet. A critical essay, "The Work of Louis Simpson," is attributed to the critic known as Crunk (here Bly).[6] "Everywhere in [his] work there is the sense that an age of some sort has come to an end." Crunk says that Whitman, "whose theme was somewhat the same, namely the end of one age, and the coming of another, made the content and form say the same thing. When he spoke of a new age, his form was also new." Yet Simpson uses traditional forms. Crunk sees "a conflict between form and content…a conflict that tends to be self-destructive." Here a perennial Bly concern gets its first airing. Crunk praises some poems from Simpson's first book, *Arrivistes,* but he ends with a summary directive: "He should search for a form as fresh as his content."

Though they hadn't yet met, Simpson had invited Bly a couple of years earlier to contribute to *New World Writing* #11 (of which he was poetry editor).[7] Bly's ability to maintain a critical distance, and his apparently unfazed fearlessness in criticizing a peer's work and prescribing means for improvement, are remarkable. Simpson wrote: "Of course, I am happy to see your essay…I am happy about the good things you find in my work; and reasonably worried by your observations on my form—or lack of form, though the problems you point to there are such as I have been considering, myself, for some time, and will be trying to deal with for years to come."[8]

A measurable change in Simpson's poetry did become noticeable a few years later, when he told Bly: "I really think I am working in a new dimension."[9] In at least a few poems in *At the End of the Open Road*, which won the Pulitzer Prize in 1964, he moves away from his traditional orientation, experimenting with some new techniques. One cannot help but surmise that some of this change was due to his now regular encounters with Bly's views.

Next is a section of "Modern American Poems." The first two are by Charles Reynolds. "England: The Nation in the Sea," peppered with historical figures, presents a bleak view of the casualties of the Industrial Revolution.[10] "Voyage of the Hungarian Dead after Death" is more surrealistic, but still has a clear historical orientation. This poet, we are told, "lives in the Black Hills. He writes us, 'I think the most important book on the problems of art is the letters of J.B. Yeats to his son. Of every poem I write, I ask myself if it has a direct relationship to what is happening now, and if not, I throw it away.'"

Reynolds was a pseudonym. But Bly did, in fact, value highly that book of letters. Publishing one's own poems could invite accusations of running a vanity press. Although he already ran this risk, he wished to avoid giving the impression, especially at the start, that there was either a *Fifties* clique or a shortage of poets who met his requirements. At the same time, he was submitting poems to other magazines as Reynolds. He told Hall: "it enables you to get a fresh reaction to your own work without all the intermediate distortions of your name, etc."[11] Odin, we should mention, also used some aliases to avoid attracting attention when among mortals.

Next are two poems by Hall: "The Foundations of American Industry," about life in the post-war boom; and "Marat's Death – after Munch" with the first two lines of each stanza consisting of seven syllables, and the third consisting of eight. Hall was Bly's closest college friend and most regular correspondent. As poetry editor first for *New Poems*, and then for the *Paris Review*, Hall had published some early Bly poems. While he shared or would come to share Bly's vision for a new poetry to an extent, like Simpson he was not as radical or rowdy as Bly.[12] Hall wrote, somewhat cryptically:

> I am never going to agree with you about form. For me sonnets and talking lake are equally possible...You don't let poems come as they will; you tell them how they are going to come...I really think that your attitude toward form is puritanical, willful, proscriptive, Lutheran, and blasphemous to the Sacred Mysteries of the Unconscious.[13]

Bly responded, clarifying: "My eyes almost started from my head when you spoke of 'talking lake meter.'...Then I remembered it is a translation of Lac Qui Parle [the name of a lake near Bly's home in Madison, as well as of its county]; we have to figure out a better name for it than that..." He adds: "The sonnet is the worst, because the beauty of feeling there is destroyed by being in that hideous sonnet form, like jewels in a pig's snout."[14] This friendly antagonism would continue.

Then come two very different poems by Gary Snyder, who had been studying in a Zen Buddhist monastery in Japan, "First Shaman Song" and "Milton by Firelight – Piute Creek: August, 1955," which Philip Whalen had sent. Both contain striking images, and reflect Snyder's experience working in the mountains of Oregon and Washington. Although he and Bly had not yet met, and although he would never be linked with the Sixties group, it was the start of a decades-long mutual admiration club.

Last in this section are two poems by W.D. Snodgrass, whom Bly had met in Iowa City.[15] Both have traces of a rhyme scheme. Snodgrass's first book of poems, *Heart's Needle*, was forthcoming from Knopf, and would win a Pulitzer in 1960.

Bly's essay, "Five Decades of Modern American Poetry," is the first bit of extended prose clearly emblematic of the fledgling magazine and its reason for being. It opens with a condensed literary history of the twentieth century, beginning in about 1910 with the appearance of a remarkable generation of American, but also French, Norwegian, Italian, and German poets. "These men carried with them, as we know, a new imagination, and with the imagination, a content, and with the content, a style. The new style and the First World War came together; why is another question; the new poetry appeared, and what I am wondering here is what happened to it." In the succeeding decades, through the Great Depression and World War II, Bly says: "the iamb came back into poetry and settled itself with a vengeance, like an occupying army returning on a people that had temporarily evicted it."

He issues a call to the poets of the 1950s to recapture that lost opportunity. "An imagination, a content, a style exists that has a magnificence of suggestion and association." But the new movement will be different from the earlier modernism:

> Freud's ocean has deepened, and Jung's work on images has been done. To Pound an image meant "Petals on a wet black bough." To us an image is "death on the deep /roads of the guitar" or "the grave of snow" or "the cradle-clothes of the sea." Secondly, Europe and South America have continued to write poetry with the new association, and the poems are in no way related to Pound or Eliot, or to our own work.

This distinction between the old and the new kind of image would cause not a little confusion and require many future attempts at refinement. He mentions Neruda, Lorca, Vallejo, Ekelöf, Char, Michaux, Trakl, and Benn, "all of them writing in what we have called, for want of a better word, the new imagination, and making contributions to that imagination as enormous as Eliot's or Pound's and with a totally different impact, and on totally different roads."

To face openly "the Nazi camps, the terror of modern wars, the sanctification of the viciousness of advertising, the turning of everyone into workers, the profundity of associations" which comprise the whole of modern experience, is the work yet to be done by American poets of the 1950s. But the means are close at hand. "There is an imagination which assembles the three kingdoms within one poem: the dark figures of politics, the world of streetcars, and the ocean world." Bly ends with a clarion call: "We need poets now who can carry on a sustained raid into modern life, and in work after work, carry on the green and vigorous waters of this profound life."

Obviously, the ideas in Bly's first general critical essay were neither raw, nor half-baked, but fully cooked; they had been simmering for a long time. And Bly's penchant for sweeping comments would soon become well known. Finally, in his focus on generations of poets, a rationale for the name *The Fifties* is implied.[16]

So far, the combination of material is relatively normal for a poetry magazine. But then comes a satirical feature titled "Madame Tussaud's Wax Museum." As a response to young poets seeking advice, the editors delineate what to avoid: abstract language without images, four-letter words, and classical references. This exhibit of the wax figures Yvor Winters, Allen Ginsberg, and Longfellow brilliantly showcases not so much the poets as their poems, which, though at first glance apparently alive, are presented as lifeless, dead. While Longfellow was immune from such criticism, Winters and Ginsberg and their supporters may have been a little annoyed.[17] This deliberate and rambunctious offensiveness, in what was expected to be the somewhat elevated if not necessarily stodgy forum of a literary magazine, was unheard of.

As if the broad fun of the "Wax Museum" weren't enough, "Wisdom of the Old" immediately followed. First under this rubric is a parodic short essay, "The Writer as Teacher," by "Ray B. East, Jr.," skewering the academy. (Ray B. West, Jr., founder and editor of the *Western Review*, had been at the Iowa Writers' Workshop in the early 1950s.) Next is a sarcastic discussion of J. Donald Adams' attack on John Ciardi in *The Saturday Review*. After that, "Everybody" is quoted as saying: "America is in strong moral condition." Four lines go unattributed: "The group is the individual | Christianity is salesmanship | Consumption is production | Advertising is creation." Finally, William Blake's words resound, seeming to address Bly, Duffy, and those joining them: "O young men of the New Age! Set your face against the ignorant hirelings! For we have hirelings in the Camp, the Court, and the University who would, if they could, forever depress mental and prolong corporeal war."[18] Here, *The Fifties* augurs the 1960s.

In a report titled "Good News From Chicago," James Mc-Cormick comments on the Chicago police, racism, Mayor Daley, and newspaper corruption and obfuscation.[19] No explicit connection is made with poetry. This is surely "general opinion."

Last is the "Interview with the head of the *New York Times Book Review*." Bly talks to Francis Brown, who comes off as a fool. The rollicking success with this interview led him to seek another with Howard Moss, the poetry editor at the *New Yorker*, who refused, as he told Hall: "He said something like, Well... you can't just expect us to lie down in front of you & let you crucify us!"[20]

Ambitious plans for future issues are spelled out. There will be translations of twenty-four named poets, for which contributions are encouraged, "paid for at the same rate as original work." Second, "Our famous critic, Crunk, whose identity frequently changes," will write on W.S. Merwin, Edgar Bowers, Donald Hall, James Wright, David Wagoner, Thomas McGrath, Robert Creeley, and others. Calling Crunk "famous" was another bit of clairvoyance.

On the back cover were these few words:

AN EASTER MESSAGE FROM MR. STRAUSS:

STRONTIUM 90

BUILDS BONES FOR HALLOWEEN!

Lewis Strauss was chairman of the Atomic Energy Commission, pushing "peaceful use of the atom." Hall takes the credit for this.[21] Bly noted the subsequent fallout: "From the number of objections to a mention of the hydrogen bomb in a poetry magazine... I gather everyone is in the habit of compartmentalizing everything, and that is another reason I would like to unite... fire and water."[22]

Thus *The Fifties* had its debut. The editors shouldered the task of distribution, enlisting the help of friends and sending copies to bookstores, literary magazines, newspapers, libraries, potential contributors, and many writers, prominent and otherwise. The entire printing eventually sold out.[23]

While a failure in economic terms, the expressions of interest and encouragement indicated a much more important kind of success. Among the respondents were John Berryman, Edmund Wilson, Stephen Spender, James Laughlin, Dorothy Parker, Dwight Macdonald, Lawrence Ferlinghetti, Richard Wilbur, Malcolm Cowley, Alfred Kazin, Hilton Kramer, Babette Deutsch, Thom Gunn, Jonathan Williams, Archibald MacLeish, and Boris Pasternak. It was not only the image of Odin and the contentious statement of purpose that struck them. Bly says: "What caught everyone's attention was that I was printing great poets who had somehow escaped the notice of the Americans."[24] As Bly described to Hall:

> Letters are beginning to come back...All so far have liked
> the satires very much (except for one person who thought
> Longfellow was a pretty good poet, and was a little miffed)...
> I think on the essay, to the same degree it will be liked by our
> generation, it will be detested by those older, so you old bulls,
> the back o' me hand to ye![25]

Philip Whalen wrote: "It is very good to find out what's happening in Scandinavia & I look forward to the poems from Germany & Italy."[26] Richard Eberhart said:

> I like it because of the earnestness behind the Bright
> Intellection...The juxtapositions are excellent. And the humor
> is most appealing...Your own essay is rewarding because of the
> earnestness, the willingness to come to grips, not to fall into one
> camp or another, a daring to think for oneself...As a matter of
> fact, all your notions make a good deal of fresh sense.[27]

Bly's college classmate George Plimpton reported from Cuba: "I thought you'd be interested to know that prominent in a large magazine rack in Hemingway's living-room in San Francisco de Paula is *The Fifties*...He's read it, talked about it, and was in praise of it, though I can't remember whether the word used was 'lively' or 'provocative' or 'pro-Scandinavian'...one of them, at any rate."[28]

Notable too is the early contact with poets who would become close friends, co-conspirators, and important literary figures. Simpson wrote: "I like the informality of the essays and the general wildness of spirits...I will be delighted to send you poems..."[29]

Snyder said: "I had no idea *The Fifties* was to be such a lively & intelligent thing {perhaps the "old-fashioned" type-face on your letterhead fooled me} & it is delightful to see such opinions being vigorously expressed & used as a basis in editing a magazine."[30]

William Stafford wrote: "Certainly a part of me responds in harmony to what I sense as the general orientation of the issue…"[31] Bly rejected the poems he sent along, but with detailed comment.[32] Stafford says the rejection "set me to brooding…The real stinger in your letter was that about how the poems tend to start off all right but then begin to change toward we's and I's—'to somewhat vague descriptions of the poet's ideas about himself.'"[33] Then, a few weeks later: "I include a revision of the spider poem which you detailed some criticisms of: I changed all the ending, left myself out. As a result of your remarks I am slowly disappearing from my poems. Thanks for the liberation!"[34]

Jerome Rothenberg, who was starting a small literary press, Hawk's Well, in New York, wrote:

> the magazine has gotten a good reception almost everywhere I've shown it. The poetry is particularly good…. And of course the translations—I had expected them to be good and wasn't at all disappointed. As for the rest, I find the prose pieces and comments most striking where they are most brash. The… generally pugnacious and uncompromising tone are precisely what has been missing from the little magazines for much too long a time now.[35]

After Bly's response Rothenberg replied: "What you write about *The Fifties* and surrealism and all is more exciting to me than I can tell you. I have been trying to get certain ideas to fruition for a long time—ideas probably along certain of these same lines." He invites Bly to collaborate on "a sort of Surrealist-Dadaist anthology, possibly along the lines of your third issue but covering a greater range. I'd like to see this almost as a 'manifesto' piece—that is, pointed in a definite and presently realizable direction."[36]

James Dickey, the first but hardly the last to use the salutation "Dear Captain Bly," responded to the rejection of his poems: "I don't for one second agree with a thing you say, but there is a certain amount of liveliness in the way you say it." Still, he writes,

"I am interested in your magazine, and I think it has a good, hard-hitting future (whatever kind of future that is)." He signed off: "Yours in 'mutiny.' Fletcher Christian."[37]

Anthony Hecht unwittingly echoed Dickey in one particular:

> It's good to find again the audacious tone that made the old
> *Furioso* so good; especially when all the quarterlies now seem
> to be more and more learnedly earnest. And it's good to have
> some attention paid to the new young writers, who deserve
> more praise and thoughtful reading than they've gotten so far.
> And yet for all the vigor and life which is really there in your
> pages, I detect the shrill and hortatory tone of a man with a bug
> up his ass, a sort of literary Captain Bly.

Hecht was also confused, however, as were others: "The trouble is, what do the editors mean by an 'image'?" He names particular poems by Shakespeare, Donne, Herrick, Herbert, Chaucer, and Auden as lacking images and therefore suggests, supposing this an absurdity, that the editors would have to reject them.[38]

Robert Creeley, then editor of the *Black Mountain Review*, wrote: "I like the look of it very much, both format and tone. And I appreciate, I had better, the context you are trying to make." He lists some possible contributors and interested readers, including Louis Zukofsky, Charles Olson, Edward Dahlberg, Denise Levertov, Joel Oppenheimer, Robert Duncan, Ed Dorn, Philip Whalen, and Irving Layton. Bly admired some of them, but would intentionally distance himself from most.

Denise Levertov showed her favor:

> It's the most interesting & intelligent magazine I've seen in
> a long time…I wd. be really pleased to appear in *The Fifties*.
> It doesn't seem cliquey or stuffy or (thank God) "beat" &
> nowadays one has to search for an atmosphere in which one
> can breathe freely…The thing on Chicago was very good—the
> original plan for *Black M'tn Review* included such pieces but it
> never came off.[39]

The following spring she wrote again and submitted some poems: "Altho' I didn't like, or agree with, everything in the 1st one (naturally) there was a certain vigor, freshness, & cleanness of cut about the whole magazine that put it way above any others currently appearing."[40] She expresses the hope of getting together in New York, and offers to invite Paul Blackburn over at the same time.

A letter, somewhat pedantic in tone, came from Robert Duncan:

> My response to contemporary poetry is more narrow than yours—I do not get exactly what your ground is...
>
> The Wax Museum section would reproof my practice... I am a traditionalist (in a tradition that includes now even for the most conservative Stein, Pound, Eliot, Williams, Marianne Moore, etc.); and like Pound, H.D., Sitwell, Joyce, and even Williams filld [*sic*] with " classical references."[41]

From Allen Tate, who had been a teacher of Bly's wife Carol at the University of Minnesota, came this bit of condescension:

> I have had a great deal to do with Little Magazines, from the Little Little Ones to the Big Little Ones, like *Hound and Horn* and *The Sewanee Review*. The Little Little ones have one reason to exist—which is to put over a new group of poets. I take it this is your purpose in the long run.
>
> It strikes me as rather curious that a survey, however brief, of the poetry of this century could omit the names Ransom, Stevens, and Cummings. It depresses me to see one more member of the younger generation succumb to W.C. Williams' mystique of the non-iambic line. It seems to me that the thinking which can describe the iambus as a "convention" would also describe our walking on two legs as a convention...
>
> You are going to have to do better than this if you are going to convince the Old and the Tough.[42]

The friction between these two would continue.

Of all the responses Bly received, one would have a far greater effect than any other. It was from a lavishly praised young poet who was teaching at the University of Minnesota. James Wright had been a student of Ransom's at Kenyon. Immediately upon receiving the magazine, he gushes. "I had just about decided to stop publishing any verses—to force myself to stop publishing, really—for at least a year or two, and maybe even to stop writing altogether." Wright refers to his first book, *The Green Wall*, with its "'sincere' display of all the current cute tricks of meter and rhyme," and says it "may well be the most insipidly polite book of verses in the past twenty years... It could have been written by a dead man."

He provides a condensed account of his own life in poetry, telling how, on a Fulbright to the University of Vienna, he accidentally discovered Georg Trakl, "who had the grasp and shape of what you in your article called the new imagination... I only slightly felt, rather than understood, what in the name of God was crying in the miracles of those images that were sane to the depths of their being and which yet followed no rules that anyone else had ever dreamed of." Wright continues: "just this morning... I wrote my own 'Farewell to Poetry.'... I begged pardon (I really did, I mean it, and I meant it) of the Mother of Roots or whoever the hell she is who gets into Whitman, Trakl, Neruda, Lorca, Char, Michaux—into almost everybody, in fact, except me."

About *The Fifties*, he writes: "It is, to my mind, the finest little magazine to be started this whole decade. It is funny, honest, deeply compassionate and intelligent, and intolerant of the second- and third-rate which some American poets of genuine gifts are letting themselves be tricked into regarding as the real poetry of our time."[43] He praises individual components of the magazine. "My God! Why hasn't somebody created CRUNK before this? This essay on Simpson was one of the most profoundly searching works of literary criticism—of really living literary criticism...that I have read or even heard of." And, in a second letter written that same day, he starts to seek clarification on some points—image, meter, differences between the new style and the old. Near the end he says: "You've blasted open in me an abandoned cavern where the sacred mysteries used to be clumsily but reverently celebrated, before I found it was, upon the whole, somewhat more comfortable to be dead."[44]

Bly discerned at once the enormous value of Wright's interest. "Thank you immensely for the praise; your concern is the greatest compliment this magazine will ever receive... I am overjoyed that you feel the phrase 'new imagination' conveys something." To the question about the old style, Bly says: "I think there are only two ages of humanity—that before the Industrial Revolution, and that after." Then he moves to matters of form and meter:

> Every meter, iambic among them, carries with it subconsciously an entire group of attitudes, emotions, perceptions, even subject matter. If then a poet adopts the iambic…he becomes more and more absorbed in experiences natural to [it], most of which have been beautifully expressed in the past, and so more & more absorbed in the past, until finally he becomes incapable of any experience whatever in the present. I think so because I went through that myself, and breaking myself of it was like rising from the dead.[45]

This is an eloquent and wordy start to a vital friendship, one that captures and elucidates several of the themes that will be developed in the course of this book and that are fundamental to Bly's burgeoning aesthetic outlook.

Wright shot back another letter, simultaneously self-deprecating and powerfully serious. His engagement with the ideas that had been raised is deep and detailed. He heaps praise on various of Bly's ideas and formulations, not without constructive comment. He says, at one point: "you should know that my assistance is immediately available to you <u>if you should ever happen to need it or want it</u>."

He also includes the poem he had mentioned in the first letter, "His Farewell to Poetry." Regarding that, he says:

> I have got to learn how to open myself more and more to the imagery which is ours and only ours, and to crack the iambic shell which used to be—and usefully, I believe—a <u>mold</u>. It is as though a man who had broken his neck had asked a doctor to prop his head with a plaster cast, and had strengthened the muscles of his throat till he was sure he could hold his head up and look at the world in front of him, and then discovered that the doctor, whether mistakenly or not, had made the cast out of cement. I could have cracked the plaster with a blow of the hand; but now I must chip and claw the cement away with the few fingernails I have left.[46]

He ends with seven questions or points for discussion, and then signs off: "Thank you immensely for everything, <u>everything</u>. I, too, feel as if I had risen from the dead."

Bly writes about Wright to their mutual friend Hall, with no little excitement and a prediction:

> he feels there is definitely a revolution of some sort going on; and is very enthusiastic about the phrase "new imagination"; and from what I understand, wants to revamp his entire approach, and begin again!...If we can continue this revolution, we will be a generation as famous as the 10s! And we will have laid down some important ideas for poetry, and perhaps even some important poetry![47]

Once again responding to Wright, Bly takes up his points for discussion:

> If we say "there is an imagination which assembles (and reassembles) the three kingdoms within one poem: the dark figures of politics, the world of streetcars, and the ocean world"—I mean there are three worlds—above us, around, and beneath. Above us are the oppressors, those who keep us oppressed, just as politics is merely the way those who oppress others stay in power; and since we do not want to see this, we never look up; if we look out, we see streetcars, steel mills, cars, machines, etc.—few people ever see that either; but if we look within, we will see the ocean world, with salt and dark water, great green plants, giant leaves and dark seas: the world of our inner growth, which the ancients knew better than any other world, and which we are only beginning to touch, to see!...If a poem has any one of these worlds in it, it has some reality in it; but if it has all three, what a great poem then![48]

Bly invited Wright to come out to the farm, and he eagerly accepted, "since I have about five hundred more questions to ask you about everything in the universe except your opinion of the heroic couplet (which I think I can infer)."[49]

To Hall he wrote: "I swear to God I think I would have perished without...the correspondence with Robert Bly, whom I am going to visit next week...He is first-rate. His letters are honeycombs of ideas."[50] Wright's coming on board was invigorating and indispensable, and would both amplify and refine the plans already in place.

24

2

A Beautiful Crop of Corn
Down the Middle of Main Street

The Fifties seemed to come out of rural Minnesota like a bolt out of the blue. In later years, Bly became accustomed to saying that he conceived the idea during his Fulbright year in Norway. That may make sense when it comes to conceptualizing Odin on his horse, but the magazine's origins unmistakably lie further back, not only in Bly's previous experience as an editor and critic, but also in his even earlier development as a young overachiever.

For example, in 1937 he won first prize for his Shropshire lamb at the 4-H Club Achievement Day at the Lac Qui Parle County Fair; it was later discovered that he was only ten, two years younger than the minimum age. In high school, he won first prize in an essay contest sponsored by the Women's Army Corps and the American Legion. He wrote his first poem in Florence Puerner's English class, on Emperor Tojo of Japan. As his major project for that class, he assembled a poetry anthology including Longfellow, Poe, Stevenson, Bryant, Whittier, Kipling, and Whitman, and dedicated it to the same teacher, "whose untiring efforts to get me to like poetry were finally rewarded." The poems were in three groups: "Liberty and Patriotism," "The Door of Death," and "The Better Life."

ROBERT BLY
"Bob"
Rouser Staff
Student Council
F.F.A.
Band
Orchestra
Junior Class Play
Senior Class Play
Soph. Class President
Valedictorian
National Honor Society
Declamation
"A bad man is worse when he pretends to be a saint."

Bly's high school yearbook, 1944

Next to his graduation photograph in *The Rouser*, the Madison High School annual for 1944, is a list of Bly's involvements in music, drama, speech, student government, the Future Farmers of America, and the National Honor Society. In his valedictory address, also printed there, Bly suggests four means of ensuring a new world order, the first three pertaining to the newly-formed United Nations. His final prescription is that "the peoples of the United States must forsake their traditional isolationism...." It is hard to dismiss this as merely another proverbially earnest graduation speech when it invokes an internationalism that would be at the heart of his literary enterprises.

The annual also includes a "Senior Class Prophecy," written from the imaginary vantage point of twenty-five years in the future (i.e., 1969). "Well, the Bly boys—James, Robert and Mahlon. They started farming years ago and now own all of Madison and surrounding territory. They've got a beautiful crop of corn down the middle of Main Street." Actually, Bly's older brother Jim did shoulder much responsibility for the very successful family farm. Their cousin Mahlon became a dairy farmer. Robert, his talents fertilized with hard work, became a wild farmer of grand ideas planted in the midst of American consciousness.

A few months after graduation, Bly enlisted in the U.S. Navy. He studied radar and sonar technology, caught rheumatic fever, and spent periods in Chicago, Florida, and California. A friend from the naval hospital, Warren Ramshaw, remembered Bly as a "skinny, red haired, argumentative chap," and added: "Your venture into publishing is what I might have predicted for you if I had to guess."[1] Another Navy friendship, with Izy Eisenstein, the first person he ever saw write a poem, also loomed large.[2]

St. Olaf College in Northfield, Minnesota, a bastion of his own Norwegian Lutheran tradition, was the next stop, in 1946. When his Freshman English teacher read Bly's first paper, he moved him into Advanced Composition with the seniors. He was also a feature writer and columnist for *The Manitou Messenger*, the college newspaper. His pieces were comical and slightly barbed. In "Bly Bridges Barrier But Bungles 'Blisho'," he invents a new language as a solution to the problem that "foreign languages are treacherously draining the strength of our nation's youth...." Standard college fare, maybe, but it foreshadows what we've already seen in the first issue of *The Fifties*: an emphasis on translation and a keen sense of humor. Not everyone perceived his writing as harmless, however. The Dean of Academic Instruction, John M. Bly, a "shirttail" relative, summoned the young man to his office, acknowledged his intellectual talents, but made it clear that he was to rein himself in.

In April, Bly won first prize in the college's annual writing contest for "The Negro Problem: Its Solution." He was also assistant editor for *The Campus*, St. Olaf's literary magazine. His only contributions, both fiction, appeared in the Summer 1947 issue. "Misstep Before Noon" describes an incident of white prejudice and hostility toward blacks. "One Hundred and Eighty-four Grapefruit" is in a different vein. It begins: "As you probably all know by now, just last week in Orgonoli, that strange little country that floats around in the middle of the Darrhenian Sea, a terrible thing happened. Oggen the Great died." Bly displays his fanciful imagination in a political satire.

He remembers his departure from St. Olaf as being primarily due to the dean. "I saw the picture."[3] But his application letter to Harvard belies that, indicating his strong interest in creative writing and underlining the fact that he had already exhausted all that

St. Olaf had to offer in that regard. He also states his intention to pursue graduate work.

So he went to Harvard. There Bly studied Latin, ancient Greek, and German, with a major in English Literature. This was a "golden moment" in American education, when veterans on the G.I. Bill enrolled, men of different ages packed into the same classes. Writers and future luminaries John Ashbery, Kenneth Koch, Frank O'Hara, Harold Brodkey, Donald Hall, John Hawkes, George Plimpton, L.E. Sissman, and Bly (as well as Adrienne Rich, Alison Lurie, and Barbara Zimmerman Epstein at Radcliffe) all overlapped as students. Robert Creeley had just left.

Among their teachers were Archibald MacLeish, F.O. Matthiessen, Albert Guerard, and John Kelleher, Bly's tutor. MacLeish, a novice in the classroom, found himself facing a group of confident men who had survived boot camp and, in some cases, combat. "We were arrogant," Bly says. "MacLeish was used to yes men from his years as Librarian of Congress. We veterans treated him like a sergeant."[4] He adds: "He brought a poem of Ezra Pound and read it to us, making sure we understood that Pound was his friend. One of us asked, 'Do you have any friends that write better poetry?'"[5] Looking back, Bly says: "Our behavior was outrageous, and it took MacLeish a long time to get over it."[6] In a gracious letter responding to the first issue of *The Fifties*, MacLeish wrote:

> I wouldn't say I remember 'em all—students, that is. But
> some of them give me great joy and twinges of pride which
> I am not stern enough to reject though I know I have no
> right to them. No man has. I taught thee naught. Though
> the opposite wouldn't be true. Though, again, I couldn't say
> precisely what. Endurance at first, I suppose. I broke my teeth
> on that class you were in—and was nigh unto breaking my
> heart too.[7]

The reading list at Harvard was conservative and narrow. "It seemed like a natural thing at the time, but MacLeish knew it wasn't," Bly says.[8] Hall encapsulates their college instruction: "We were brought up on English language modernism, which is very different from the modernist tradition in Russia, in Spain, in Norway, in Germany even." He adds: "We didn't get Whitman or Hardy either. We got the seventeenth century and the twentieth century, pretty much."[9]

Hanging around were Robert Frost, Richard Wilbur, Richard Eberhart, John Ciardi, and Ruth Stone. T.S. Eliot, Marianne Moore, William Carlos Williams, W.H. Auden, and Wallace Stevens all read on campus during Bly's years. The literary atmosphere was further thickened by two Cambridge bookshops specializing in poetry, the Mandrake and the Grolier.

Soon after his arrival, Bly joined the staff of the *Harvard Advocate*, the nation's oldest and most venerable undergraduate literary magazine. His short story, "Strength is a Tower," is an unflinching portrayal of a marriage and the emotional brutality of a man full of anger and bitterness. It might not have suited the more staid literary magazine at St. Olaf.[10] The following year, Bly became the literary editor, called "Pegasus" after that winged horse of Greek mythology. [11]

Bly reviewed *New British Poets: An Anthology*, edited by Kenneth Rexroth (and published by New Directions, the house of James Laughlin, himself a former Pegasus).[12] Though he calls the book a welcome reaction to "the glib abstraction and impersonality of the old Auden group," and praises New Directions for publishing it, his appreciation is lukewarm. "Generally... there is a distressingly fuzzy definition of emotion, a watery sort of insight and the use of a vocabulary which is almost invariably ineffective and anonymous."

The last issue with Bly as Pegasus bears what would be a characteristic mark of *The Fifties, Sixties,* and *Seventies,* namely, that his hand seems to be everywhere.[13] He contributes a poem, a short story, and a review, as well as the usual unattributed editorial "Notes from 40 Bow." "Letter from a Wedding Trip," which consists of nineteen iambic rhyming lines, stands as his first published poem. The short story is titled "Fish, Flesh, and Fowl," an apparent allusion to Yeats' "Sailing to Byzantium." The two, as the editor's note says, "are essentially experiments on the same theme." As with "Strength is a Tower," fish, flesh, and the anguish of a marriage all figure in. His review of *Terror and Decorum: Poems,*

1940-1948, by Peter Viereck (who had published in the *Advocate* a decade earlier), is almost entirely negative.

In the next issue, with Hall as his handpicked successor, Bly, now a "Senior Editor," reviews Williams' *Selected Poems*. "Those who heard William Carlos Williams' wild tongue at his reading here last month will, I think, rub their hands to find his best verse now available in a single volume. Like all good poets, Williams fits no movement." This short review really has some vigor, and Bly does not lack the confidence to criticize: "In his less successful poems (generally the longer), his sense of form is however, at best, unsure." Williams was not exactly in the poetic mainstream at the time, and Bly admires his innovative style:

> He was brought up with the Imagists, for whom the past
> and its traditions were anathema: Williams himself speaks of
> "pimps to tradition," and repeats: "We must invent! invent!"
> Yet for one who felt it necessary to invent everything he used,
> Williams has done astonishingly well, and I highly recommend
> this volume. If he does not speak in the "grand style," he
> nevertheless is one of our very few adult American poets who
> is communicating anything.[14]

Bly had discovered Williams' poetry not in class but at the Grolier, and he had been inspired to hitchhike to his home in Paterson, New Jersey, earlier that year.[15] Bly says: "He understood that I just wanted to *look* at him. I drifted out, floating along the street. It was heavenly."[16]

Important lessons were learned. *Dulce est periculum* is the motto surrounding the *Advocate*'s monogram. A literal translation is "Danger is sweet," but "risk-taking is a delight" might be more in the spirit.[17] Hall recounts one of Bly's risky Pegasus adventures. The staff put together an issue highlighting an alumnus.[18] "When [the printer] read in our typescript that we were dedicating the issue to T.S. Eliot in honor of his sixtieth birthday, he decided that we had made a simple error in typing," and changed the number. Eliot could not have been happy to read that his undergraduate poems were reprinted for his "sixteenth" birthday.

Because the *Advocate* was in dire need of money, and because the issue had sold out quickly, they hatched a related plan: "One of us knew a pamphlet printer who volunteered to print up a thousand copies of the Eliot poems as a booklet which we could sell at a profit." Bly and his friends seem to have been ignorant of the publishing protocol of "permissions." When Eliot saw a copy of the booklet, "His letter dropped down on us like a wolf on the fold. ... We had perpetrated enormities: reprinting poems without asking permission, not considering his rights or privileges, and in addition botching every poem we stole." While this incident made clear the hazards of editorial carelessness, it would hardly be the last time that Bly raised the ire of some august figure.

Also, the task of judging the poetry of his peers was valuable. When Ashbery submitted "Some Trees," Bly remembers, "I was amazed that someone my age could write that."[19] He adds: "We had a lot to choose from, and we learned a lot arguing over poems and stories."[20] Hall puts it this way: "We worked hard... to keep standards high, which is to say that we worked hard at rejecting things. When there was an argument, the negative could be counted on to win."[21] Here is one of Bly's later critical stances in embryonic form.

Then there was Bly's growth as a poet. Hall observes: "Yeats was very important to both of us; he gave us rhetorical tradition." He adds: "When I first knew Bob, at the outset, he was known as a critic. He was writing poems in secret. But while we were still at Harvard together I began to see his poems, and they were very much [Robert] Lowell, and very much pentameter."[22] In 1958, Bly looked back: "I have been thinking that the publication of [Lowell's] *Lord Weary's Castle* in 1947 was an unfortunate event, in many ways, for us: I know it was for me. It urged me not to become a sensitive man, but to become a tough guy."[23] Also pertinent is Hall's characterization of Bly as Don Quixote to his Sancho Panza, a reflection on the dynamics of their friendship that shows Bly as the ever-undaunted and dreamy point man.[24]

As a senior he won the Lloyd McKim Garrison prize, comprised of a silver medal, $185, and the publication of his poem in the *Advocate*.[25] "The Indian Trail," blank verse concerning Minnesota's Dakota War of 1862, was lengthy, and only a thirty-five line excerpt, titled "Famine," was printed.[26] While it anticipates some of the psychological themes of American poetry in the 1960s, its style was still tied to Lowell. Bly also was named class poet, thus delivering the class poem, "Introduction to the Seasons," as he graduated *magna cum laude* in 1950.[27]

That fall and winter, Bly read and wrote, first at his uncle's cabin on Kabekona Lake, then on the North Shore of Lake Superior. He later reflected on that time: "I was...with my Milton, trying as hard as ever I could to write Miltonic sonnets up here on an Indian reservation!" He continued: "One reason I think I liked these poems so much is that the only experience I really recognized as mine through college was a sort of <u>martial</u> experience. I think I thought of myself through Harvard as a sort of warrior."[28] Shooting partridge illegally, the former or rather re-purposed warrior managed to sustain himself.

The next summer, Bly moved to Manhattan where he lived the solitary garret life—reading, working odd jobs, translating the odes of Pindar, and trying to write. As he has said: "I lived in small dark rooms, and that loneliness made clear to me my interior homelessness, my lack of respect for myself, and my interior starvation." Very few poems came of it. "Yet the misery had its own justice, because I was living my own life, and not someone else's. The stump of misery occasionally puts out a radiant sprig. After a year and a half of solitude, I experienced a subtle gift, and my serious poetry began."[29]

In somewhat more typical Harvard graduate fashion, Bly's close friend Donald Hall had moved on to a fellowship in Oxford. "Bob sent me a bunch of Shakespearean sonnets he had written, and then, before I could read them, another letter came: 'These are too old-fashioned.' We were all old-fashioned at the time, and that to me was the first indication that he wanted to go somewhere else."[30] This is the earliest expression of the statement that opened the first issue of *The Fifties*. But the transformation took a while. Two years later, in 1953, Bly wrote in his journal: "Today it seems to me inevitable that I shall have to give up the iambic line, for these reasons: 1) trouble with "modern" feeling; 2) expression of my own most typical emotion, which is a soaring sort of lift which implies more vowels than iambs can give; 3) doubt that there is any going back."[31] His own revolution was underway. Hall recalls: "The first terrific poem by Bly was 'the crow, the crow, the spider-colored crow.' We published that at Oxford, and I published it in the *Paris Review*."[32]

When Bly left New York, he went back up to Cambridge for a while, and was assistant director at the Poets' Theater for the first American production of Yeats' "Player Queen." He continued to churn, wrestling with his ideas, asking himself: "What kind of poetry do we wish from our young poets? Ten years ago I would have said 'patriotic poems,' but now what comes first to mind is this: poems that recognize the hideous materialism that is making a mockery of life in this country."[33] So he was moving forward.

While in Cambridge, MacLeish suggested the Iowa Writers' Workshop to Bly and recommended him for some Rockefeller money. Bly asked Wilbur for a second letter. Then he "bought a car for $65 and started west."[34] On the way, at Indiana University he heard Ransom lecture on the sixteenth-century writer, Thomas Nashe. Ransom read "Song" (from "Summer's Last Will and Testament"), which, Bly says, "gave hints of other possibilities besides the iambic."[35] Due to some mix-up, when he reached Iowa City he found no financial aid waiting. Nevertheless, he enrolled and, in order to support himself, taught two courses, "The Greeks and the Bible," and Freshman English.

The collection of quonset huts where classes were held was a far cry from Harvard Yard, not to mention New York City, and much closer to Bly's landscape of origin. Nevertheless, Paul Engle's workshop, one of only a few such programs in the country, already had a sizeable reputation.[36] Donald Justice, Karl Shapiro, Ray B. West Jr., Marguerite Young, and Berryman were among the teachers. Students that year included Constance Urdang, Robert Dana, W.D. Snodgrass, Henri Coulette, and William Dickey. Philip Levine arrived a year later. Bly notes the contrast between his college classes and workshopping: "At the end [Engle] would come in and say rather sensible remarks. Given my history with MacLeish, whose lofty pronouncements floated down from some earlier heaven, this workshop was my first experience of literary democracy."[37]

Williams came, and then the young acolyte encountered his idol: "How I trembled to meet Robert Lowell...He stood there, hunched, a weight behind his eyes."[38] But hearing Lowell and the others "mocking Williams and telling malicious stories about him," Bly dared to defend him and endured their withering glances. Eventually, he showed Lowell his poem, "With Pale Women in Maryland." The poet, in line with his own process, told Bly to go to whatever county they had been driving through, find the courthouse records of all the violent crimes that had taken place there, and then get everything into the poem. Bly says: "I thought to myself, 'If that's what's required, I may as well quit, because that is the last thing I'd ever do. That's not the kind of poem it is anyway.'"[39] He felt isolated.

Bly told Hall that "everything I learned there I learned from Marguerite Young, a fiction teacher."[40] But a fellow student also important to him was the fiction writer Kim Yong Ik. Bly remembers their discussions, and Kim's helpful criticism:

One day I brought to him a poem that I had begun in New York, and it said something like:

I wander down the streets, not knowing
Who I am, and I am lost.

Kim said, "Oh no. If you say you're lost, that means you're already partly *found*. If someone is...truly lost, he doesn't even know that he's lost."

I was stunned. "Well, what do I do then?"

"You just take out the phrase 'I am lost.' Then you compose some images that seem not to belong exactly, rationally. Then when the reader experiences those images, he will say, 'This kid is lost!'" I've been grateful for that for years.[41]

Shortly after the end of spring term in 1955, Bly and Carolyn McLean, a young woman from Duluth he'd met when he was at Harvard and she at Wellesley, married. They moved to Madison, Minnesota, to a house on a farm purchased by and adjacent to his parents' farm. That fall Bly met Duffy. They shared a love for poetry, and they both had a nutty sense of humor. Duffy says: "We were both farm boys, and we got into this literature not as professor's kids, steeped in it. We came at it new."[42] Duffy, his wife

Christina, and Carol had all been in the M.A. program in English at the University of Minnesota. The Duffys taught high school in Clara City, a farm town on the way to Minneapolis, and the Blys made several stops there in the ensuing months.[43] Paulston (now Duffy's ex-wife) recalls: "The two pairs of us were just starved for intellectual conversation whenever we met."[44]

Bly soon recorded in his journal what seems to be the first explicit indication of what was to come: "In bed I thought of gathering a first issue of the magazine, The Poet's Magazine, a Poet's Review, and inquiring about cost of publishing. This noon the first Pocket Poets Book came from San Francisco. I am excited, and enthusiastic about the future of not only the series itself, but American poetry as vested in this wild little group."[45] The book Bly had received was *Pictures of the Gone World*, by Lawrence Ferlinghetti, who initiated the project; fifteen years later, Bly's *The Teeth Mother Naked at Last* would appear as number twenty-six.

He returned to Iowa in February. His M.A. thesis, "Steps Toward Poverty and Death" (the title of section three of Rilke's *Das Stundenbuch*), was submitted in June 1956. This collection of poems had actually been several years in the making.[46] A short time before completing his program, Bly talked to Engle: "I told him I'd like to start a magazine and publish some decent stuff, but he wasn't very sympathetic. He thought I was simply confused."[47]

Bly then received a Fulbright grant to Norway, his project being to translate Norwegian poetry into English. That was a year of discovery from which he got much more than he expected; in fact, he experienced a sea change. In Oslo he met the young poet Paal Brekke (editor of the anthology mentioned in Chapter One). Through Brekke he found the poetry of, among others, Ekelöf, Harry Martinson, Trakl, Gottfried Benn, Michaux, and Kristensen; and through his own reading, Juan Ramón Jiménez, César Vallejo, and Pablo Neruda. About the last, he likes to say: "The moment is still clear to me. The lines were: 'Girls / Sleeping with hands over their hearts, / Dreaming of pirates.'" These discoveries had an enormous effect. He told Hall:

> I think it was in Norway that I first wrote a poem of any
> sensitivity, and then really because in reading Spanish and

Swedish poetry I suddenly realized that it existed!...I no longer have the same view of poetry as I once had, nor the same ambitions in life, and I think the ones I have now are closer to my own nature, and to joy, which I think is nothing else than sensitivity.[48]

Late in 1956 he wrote: "last night, cutting up my Baudelaire book, I thought of still another plan; namely a book of translations from poetry in several languages." He envisioned including Baudelaire, Pindar, Rilke, Olaf Bull and other Norwegians, and Chinese poets. "The other possibility, of course, is to do an entire book of Norwegian, or Scandinavian, poetry."[49] Bly's early designs on multilingual translating point even beyond the as-yet-nonexistent magazine, to the eventual birth of the Sixties Press.

The next summer, just before leaving Norway, he was determined to edit an anthology along the lines of Brekke's. Reading that book again, he "was struck with the possibility that what has been developed since 1910 is a new style." He continued: "The style involves much freer association than the old style, many more images, and emphasis on city life, not nature as such, a rejection of the old meters, and most important perhaps, the movement toward new experience rather than intellectual formulation of age-old experience, as in the Eighteenth and Nineteenth Century."

New formulations and growing ambition were coming to light: "I myself am not completely aware, as I know, of this new style; ... but the distrust of the intellect, even hatred of intellect, as in Pablo Neruda, is unmistakable; it is much more a poetry of instinct and impulse and sensitivity; and its attempt to grapple and pervade the fantastic grotesqueness of modern life is also unmistakable." These thoughts were leading him "to think that the tendency in America now to go back to conservatism is foolish." That earlier generation of the 1910s had moved in a new direction. Bly wanted his own generation to emulate and move beyond them, "to be humble students of a new way of writing, much greater than those few men, or anything they did."[50] It is remarkable how many ideas Bly throws out here, seeds that would germinate and then blossom.

He sent some early translations of Rilke to Hall, and explained them this way:

All my interest in translation comes from a single discovery in Norway—that, in translating Norwegian literature for instance, men were translating it into an Anglo-American idiom, which struck them as sort of classical, enduring, reachable by more people, dignified, "safe," etc.—but that language is insensitive to slang…and therefore they could translate the words, but not the feelings, which take a fine net to hold.

There were unrealized possibilities with modern American English which, "like the Spanish, is quick as a snake!" Again, Bly's ambition seems boundless. His generation, he insists, "can do the greatest translations in the world, now, before the language stiffens."[51]

All his talk about a book of translations did not mean that the magazine wasn't still on his mind. Other journal entries provide some previews of coming attractions:

– You cannot succeed in poetry without clear daring blasts (drives) as of trumpet sound, that spring from intensity and conviction, and absolute recklessness. Intensity of daring.

– For the magazine, this principle: that a poem or any art should not be the emotion of the moment (modern abstract painting), [but] the expression of emotions felt over many years…as many as possible.

– Remember: All forms of flying seem vague to the badger.

He also was brainstorming about essays "on the strengthening and nourishing power of strong rhythm in poetry" and "on the different directions [in which] Europe and America move, are moving, have been moving."[52]

Bly's enthusiasm for Pindar, commencing in college, persisted. One note reads simply: "First issue: a good Pindar translation." At the same time, he could not tolerate the continued use of iambic meter. He wrote:

To the poets, if you are writing poems in another meter than iambs, send those to me, instead of the iambic poems. It was possible we would print one in ten years, but….if you write in the horse and buggy meter, send your poems to a museum

like the *KENYON REVIEW*, where it belongs. Only sheer
habit keeps so many people writing in iambs....[53]

He was capable of simultaneously appreciating the ancient Greek
poetic tradition and abhorring modern metric traditionalism.
"The Greeks lie in the future, not in the past."[54] Pound's dictum,
"make it new," reverberates here. But in other respects, as we shall
see, Bly resolved that the Greeks *did* lie in the past and should
remain there.

Late in his Norway sojourn, he continued communicating his
expansive determinations:

> I am more and more convinced that our generation has a
> real destiny in the course of American poetry. But I think the
> destiny lies in an opposite direction to where it has been living
> so far, namely it lies in revolution. If the writers of the 30's
> think we are too tame, let them watch: I will take them apart,
> brick by brick! How could the time of advance and radicalism
> be over, when the imagination has hardly touched the density
> of modern life?

He declares that the quality of current poetry is "quite low; ...
most of the poems simply lack kick, life – they simply are not convincing. Moreover their timidity in technique is appalling." Once
again he calls "the steady decline in American poetry since the
poets of the 1910's, Eliot, Pound, Williams, Moore, Jeffers...ab-
solutely undeniable."[55]

When he got home, Bly was primed for a major undertaking.
He was not seeking glory: "I was not born for fame," he told
Hall.[56] Rather, he had both the zealous assurance as well as the
humility of a missionary, an advocate who eagerly prompts others
to see the light and join in common cause, in the belief that they
too will flourish.

As for the next step, Bly recalls: "So I said to Bill, 'Let's start
a magazine. Let's do this.' He said, 'OK, let's do it.'"[57] They each
scraped together $500. Duffy's wife at the time says: "There's
no question but that it was Robert's idea, and Robert's values
and driving force behind it all. But on the other hand, there was
Robert all alone in the sticks in Madison, and he found somebody—whatever else Bill Duffy was, he was an intelligent person

and had good instincts about poetry—to bounce ideas off of, like a sounding board."[58]

In an effort to improve his co-editor's credentials, Bly gave Hall, then poetry editor at the *Paris Review*, a poem of Duffy's. "He has never sent a poem off to any magazine, and I asked for this one to send to you."[59] Bly and Duffy soon were engaged in the nitty-gritty of getting the first issue off the ground, discussing the cover design, how much to pay contributors, whom they might solicit poems from, and where to place advertisements.[60]

At the same time, *The New Poets of England and America*, an anthology edited by Hall, Simpson, and Robert Pack, was published. Bly was more dismayed than tickled:

> Of course it is always a thrill, even of a sort of degenerate variety, to see your name blazing or bubbling out in a book for the first time, as, thanks to you, it is here; and one has a sad feeling too, as if part of one were already dead, and we were reading the epitaph. (God knows, my poems looked dead enough to me!)…The sameness of form in the book is horrifying to me. The number of rhymes in the book would make even Milton turn over in his grave…Moreover there is a ghastly lack of passion in the book.[61]

His thoughts were running so far ahead of himself that he also seriously considered publishing more than one magazine. For a while it was three, he told Hall, saying: "It's getting weirder all the time."[62] And then there were two. *The Nineteen Fifties* "is going to publish nothing but poems, and then articles of opinion on either poetry or politics. There will be no fiction whatsoever…Then there will be my own magazine, still called *The Dark Republic*, over which I reign in solitary glory."[63] Even before the first issue was put together, Bly understood the need for his own magazine.

In January, it was coming along; the cover was ready, and a few poems had been accepted. He said he would try to get a review from Berryman (whose new wife was a friend of Carol's) at the University of Minnesota. He again asked Hall to contribute: "I want you to do me a favor: write a poem with the freest possible association and let me see how it looks."[64] A possibility of teaching at the University of Michigan with Hall for the second term didn't pan out, so they were planning to go to New York instead. Bly told him: "I have some plays I want to try to sell…, and I think Marguerite Young, who is there now, can help us get jobs."[65]

On March 15 they started renting by the week at the Earle Hotel on Washington Square. The faint outlines of a literary community become visible in Bly's letters. At Young's they had dinner with Mari Sandoz. There was gossip about Tate, Lowell, Carson McCullers, and Delmore Schwartz, with Bly concluding that "everyone is either mad or going mad."[66] Soon he found a place to write in solitude. "I have rented, as I did at times in Oslo, a little room for $7.00 a week, to which I come in the morning, and leave at 5 or so in the afternoon, and no one, not even Carol, knows where it is! As Rilke says: 'No one in the city knows about me.' I am writing in it now."[67] He attended poetry readings at NYU, hearing W.S. Merwin, Charles Bell, Galway Kinnell, Paul Carroll, John Logan, and others.

In the wake of the initial advertisement for the magazine came some poems and subscriptions.[68] By April, the progress was more evident. Then the Blys visited Carol's brother John McLean, who worked for the *Gazette-News Press* in East Hartford, Connecticut, and with whom Bly, especially attentive to the magazine's appearance—to paper, typeface, layout, and binding—arranged for the printing of the first issue. The couple moved into an apartment in Greenwich Village, at 65 Bedford St.[69] Finally, in mid-May, Bly wrote: "The magazine is at the printers! Joy, O joy!"[70] This momentarily freed him up to concentrate on his own poetry, plays, and translations. "New York is wonderful to write in! Astounding! Everything is alive here, from anthropology to St. Francis."[71] There were also financial necessities. "I have been working this week and the week before as a painter! and I am tired."[72]

A few months late, the first issue materialized in mid-summer. To mix myth and history and metaphor, Odin and his horse had crossed the Rubicon, and engagement was inevitable. We have already registered some of the initial reactions and results. Now it was time to follow up with a second.

3

Finding a New Path

The satisfaction Bly felt in the wake of the first issue is not hard to fathom. "I…feel an infusion of energy, and never in my life have I enjoyed an autumn so much as this one."[1] But there was also a price to be paid, as Bly told his new correspondent, Wright: "After being for years absolutely worthless to everyone, I suddenly find myself with advice which is of help to other people, and this tends to throw me off balance. Like the hermit who has always lived in a shack, and then comes to the city, I hardly know what is useful and what is not."[2]

The Fifties was intended as a quarterly. In September, Bly optimistically said the second issue "will be out about November 1st."[3] But there were holdups. First, they needed to cut production costs, so they gave the job to The Kerryman, Ltd., of Tralee, Ireland.[4] Another factor was Bly's own poetry; he was working on his collection-in-progress, "Poems for the Ascension of J.P. Morgan." As he wrote to Wright, he felt that poetry needs solitude and meditation: "Remember, busyness and poetry are absolutely incompatible."[5] But it was a struggle, as a week later he continued in this vein: "After months of steady work, I suddenly wake up and see behind me weeks of grueling labor, as if I were a business man or a laborer, and then suddenly remember those Persian poets or Chinese poets wandering about on the mountains or under the willows all day." He concluded: "I think America is a spiritual nut-house, disliking all culture that suggests leisure, or the need of doing nothing."[6]

At the same time, he tried to maintain a strict work schedule: "Two days a week, say Tuesday and Friday, I will spend in the apartment, on letters, sending back manuscripts, typing poems and translating, writing articles for the magazine."[7] But his journal is partly a record of his failure to stick to such plans. The editor's responsibilities were clearly in conflict with the poet's. Odin's masks could not all be worn at once.

The literary social life in New York, where Bly returned for the second consecutive year, was also intensifying. There were parties at Plimpton's, poetry readings galore, and parties after those readings. In February 1959 he read with Stephen Stepanchev and Ned O'Gorman: "I read most of Morgan at the first session of reading, and the audience understood my attitude...I don't think they understood the poetry very well, but I couldn't tell for sure." Afterwards, "we had a big party at our house with about thirty people that went on & on."[8] One morning he and Simpson accompanied Hall on a visit to T.S. Eliot.[9] Soon after, he, Rothenberg, Willis Barnstone, Kinnell, and Sonia Raiziss read their translations at NYU.[10]

The contours of a coterie of poets were emerging, as he was regularly seeing and sharing thoughts with his new friends. This helped him clarify some of the ideas he was trying to get across in the magazine. He wrote to Dickey, "To me, a picture is something which never breaks the natural order of nature, and an image always or nearly always does." He added:

> I don't know if this is any clearer; but I feel as strongly as you do that the ordinary or iambic or "English" style is absolutely bankrupt, and the *New Poets*, etc. was evidence in that direction. In the Spanish and South American poets, in Trakl and strange places, I sense something else, which I call perhaps wrongly an "image," but I don't know what other phrase would be better.[11]

Dickey responded, "You talk about poetry as though you were the other half of my own mind."[12]

Kinnell was working on an article that included discussion of "the standard techniques of poetry," the need for "facing the fact that we cannot be Transcendentalists," and something about "the matter of poetic form, i.e., if we drop iambs and rimes what then?"[13] He discussed these matters with Bly, and was hopeful that the article might, in some shape, be suitable for *The Fifties.*

Wright continued to be enthusiastic about Bly, but not blindly so. He wrote to Hall:

> Bly…is a genuine and natural-born <u>editor, critic</u>…, and <u>propagandist of new ideas</u>. In short, he is a genuine <u>fanatic</u>.
> … He has an enormous intelligence, and moreover he has the weird talent for suspending everything in this intelligence from its characteristic catholicity in order that he might direct <u>all</u> of its extraordinary power along one channel—the channel of the new style.[14]

Despite some disagreements, especially over iambics, which Wright and Hall were loath to reject outright, Wright became more and more convinced:

> I really do think he is a great man…It's a fact that he *is* an innovator—you get one in a generation, if you're fabulously lucky. I really believe it's the duty of anyone who recognizes the original man to believe in him; and this belief consists, I have finally realized, not in discipleship, but in searching and serious questions, in <u>criticism</u>.[15]

Clearly, a company of lively minds was coalescing around Bly (in his role as Odin, Allfather) and the new magazine.

In addition to fostering the growth of this gang, Bly still needed to earn money, which took even more time away from editing. He started teaching two days a week at Queens College.[16] He told Hall, "Luckily I have no office hours (I have no office!), so I simply lecture and go away."[17] Bly would always keep classroom teaching to a minimum.

Finally, after a series of problems with Kerryman, including mislaid copy, a flu outbreak in the shop, and delayed ordering of a requested typeface and special paper, the second issue was published in mid-April of 1959, in outward appearance very much like the first.[18] Bly immediately sent a copy to Wright: "I am so anxious to know your feelings after reading it, also appearance, etc. Your poems look wonderful…I don't think my own translations of German are very good."[19] Before publication, Bly had shown much of the material in this issue to Wright.[20] The mutuality of their working relationship is clear almost from the beginning, unlike Bly's relationship with Duffy. Still, Duffy was thrilled: "It must be the same kind of feeling one has when he is notified by a nurse that he's the father of a newborn son...My prediction is that it will get more favorable responses than the first, but that from this issue we will get our first slaps of criticism, too."[21]

Later that month, Bly went to the customs office to pick up the bulk of the magazine.[22] This time it was sewn in signatures rather than stapled, a practical improvement. But now customs and freight charges had to be paid.[23] And the print run had been doubled to 2000 copies. In order to stay afloat and perhaps even build on their success, they placed advertisements in *Poetry, Hudson Review, The Nation,* and *Village Voice,* and added subscription inserts, all of which cost money. There was also additional postage to pay. Despite all this, total expenditure was a bit less than for the first. Income, however, fell short of expectations.[24]

Duffy's job was to take care of subscribers. Bly and his wife addressed and mailed 300 copies to colleges and universities. Again, other friends were helping out. The bother of self-distribution was substantial, and it was compounded by the need to get the magazine into the right hands. Wright had been spreading the word. He suggested that Bly and Duffy work with Melvin McCosh, the eccentric owner of a popular used bookstore in Dinkytown, adjacent to the University of Minnesota: "He is the non-academic," Wright wrote to Bly, "and also non-pasteurized, non-supermarketish kind of bookseller who nevertheless has a certain influence around this place."[25] Edith DeSort, a contributor, sent a list of bookstores in Chicago.[26] Gordon Cairnie, proprietor of the Grolier bookshop in Cambridge and a friend from Bly's Harvard days, had sold out his supply and requested more copies.[27]

Turning to the magazine's contents, where the first issue had a single salvo for the new poetry, now there were five statements, signaling this issue's themes:

"The only remedy is to break everything." – La Forgue

"My work is to paint pictures of the modern soul-life."
– Edvard Munch

"The sonnet is the place old professors go when they die."
– Old Saying

"There is a loveliness exists, / Preserves us. Not for specialists."
– W. D. Snodgrass

"They say such different things at school." – W. B. Yeats

The "old saying" was in fact new, part of a satiric poem Bly sent to Hall, vividly rejecting the sonnet as a viable form for modern poetry. It began, "The sonnet is the pig's snout." [28]

The issue formally opens with four poems by Gottfried Benn. As Bly translates, the first begins as a lament:

Ah, that land so far off,
where the heart-breaking sea
on round pebbles
or rushy land quick as a dragon-fly
continues to murmur,
also the crafty light of the moon....

Benn, Bly writes, was of "the generation of the Tens" and was, with Edvard Munch, "a founder of Expressionism, in which they used everything and whatever they could see in the world, trees, bridges, faces, in any way possible to express the new emotions they felt moving within themselves." He "felt that what could be gained by busy-ness, activity, was at an end, and he felt we should move toward solitude, aloneness, stillness." He was, Bly continues, "interested in a new movement of the imagination within a poem." Darkness, the sea, and their depths, figure prominently here. Thus Benn is presented as another avatar of the new imagination.

In the essay on Robert Creeley, Crunk calls the Black Mountain group, "perhaps for the first time in America, nearly a 'school', in the French sense." Creeley's *Black Mountain Review* is "an honest and intelligent review, and in some ways the most interesting magazine in America." Crunk mentions Charles Olson, Irving Layton, Robert Duncan, Louis Zukofsky, and Denise Levertov, and indicates their admiration for Williams and Ezra Pound. "These poets are somehow politically more mature than the usual poet in, for instance, *Poetry* magazine, and understand that some form of oppression today, even in America, is as common as beauty, for those who have the senses which can grasp it." Then he notes their associations with the Beats.

45

But there is, Crunk says, "a sort of American isolationism," evidenced by the lack of images in their poems. In teaching mode, he lists seven traits of the genuinely modern European poetry: 1) the heavy use of images; 2) the descent into the self; 3) the evocation of city life; 4) brave self-revelation; 5) the use of recently invented words; 6) the investigation of men and women as subject matter; and 7) "the increasingly…apparent oppression in all countries" as subject matter. Creeley gets mostly high marks, but Crunk is critical of his schoolmates. "The American Tradition is not rich enough; it is short, Puritanical, and has only one or two first-rate poets in it, and the faults of the lesser poets are always the same—a kind of barrenness and abstraction."

Creeley was pleased by the extended treatment, and that it came from a poet of a different circle. His letter to Bly begins: "Your kind and good note on my work (I take it as having been written by you) was a great pleasure to have. I.e., whatever differences of attitude or opinion might exist between us would god knows be vitiated by the term of your dignity, and care to read rightly what I'd written." He then calls Bly's attention to some matters for clarification.[29] He wrote again later with more discussion of translation, its influence American poetry and language, and his own focus as magazine editor. He also asked for Bly's help in finding a job.[30]

Bly had several suggestions, for which Creeley was thankful: "No matter what comes, so to speak, it will have been a pleasure to have known someone so completely willing to be of use." Bly had asked him to write something for *The Fifties* about technique, specifically about "the line." Creeley said he would.[31] Bly's concern and generosity on a personal level is evident, as is his eagerness that lines of communication and understanding remain open. But, as Bly wrote to Hall: "I continue to get blasts from the western crowd for having the gall to criticize Creeley."[32]

Ekbert Faas elucidates: "Denise Levertov, who had become a personal friend of Bly, felt positively about the piece. Not so Duncan, who thought 'The Work of Robert Creeley' was one 'crappo' job of insincerity." It also seems that Duncan and Levertov thought that Bly "had made a complete ass of himself by acting in

tactless and opinionated fashion in rejecting some of Duncan's poems...What he needed was *educating*."[33] Creeley eventually came
around to his friends' negative viewpoint.[34]

Other commentary in *The Fifties* 2 includes "Syllabics," a
short piece offering an alternative to iambic meter, signed "Abednego." Hall had wanted his contribution to be anonymous. Bly
told him: "Carol and I at the last minute decided 'A Young American Poet' looked stupid, so we chose a pseudonym for you! We
won't tell you what it is—oh will you be surprised!"[35] Abednego
explains that the number of syllables in a line is the only unit of
measure in syllabics, and says that iambic meter is "insidious,"
making all but the very best poets prone to "artificiality" and
"false feelings." Syllabics gives English a new sound, affords a
more intimate tone, and possesses the authority, motives, and
feelings of direct, plain speech.[36]

Hall had been looking for a way to make the transition from
iambic pentameter to free verse. Still, he wavered on this anti-
iambic stance. Wright wrote him about the similarities of their
position on the issue: "My criticism of Bob is that he wastes about
fifty percent of his time and intellect on attacking iambics, whereas
he ought to devote himself wholly to expounding the virtues of
non-iambic *possibilities*. God damn it, the trouble with the man
is that he won't *let* himself talk about possibilities—only *necessities*."[37] Two days later, Bly took issue with this charge: "You seem
to feel...that I am moved by a grudge or hatred of iambic meter.
But that is not true; I worked for three years, happily in nothing
but iambs...I think the meter is graceful, precise, and beautiful,
and in many ways I love it." But, he continues: "our poetry in the
English tradition has written poems now in the iambic meter for
650 years, since about 1300, and that is long enough. A poetry
dies if it cannot find a way to change. For our own sakes and those
after us, we should find a new path."[38]

Bly's repeated use in his letters of the phrase "iambic (blecch)
pentameter," with its echo of the then-current *MAD* magazine,
should be seen in light of this love-hate relationship. Yet, for the
good of other poets, he felt it was important to establish an un-
equivocal position. Wright's marginalia on Bly's letter include two

remarkable comments. First: "This letter has genuine human great-ness in it. Robert Bly is a genius, possibly one of the two or three really crucial poetic geniuses of our century." And: "That does it. By God, I'll try anything now!"[39] This is testimony to the powerful effect that *The Fifties* and Bly were having on more than one poet.

The main figure introduced in the second issue is Juan Ramón Jiménez, who writes "only of solitude, and the strange experiences and the strange joy that come to a man in solitude." In exile from Franco's Spain, he received the Nobel Prize in 1956 and died in 1958. The seven translations here are by Carlos de Francisco Zea, a Columbian student in Chicago. One example, in "Zenith": "I shall not be I, death, / Until thou, in thy turn, shalt dress / My soul with pale bones." Is this the language of the new poetry? Not likely. Bly wised up, and he did not recruit Zea for the book he published later on Jiménez's work.

"Reply to Cecil Hemley" is Duffy's sole prose contribution to any issue of the magazine.[40] Hemley, then the editor at Noonday Press, had written that "the modern movement no longer appears capable of producing significant work." Duffy mockingly likens him to "a crippled old uncle at Kitty Hawk, who says to the Wright brothers, 'It won't fly.'" He goes on to speak of poetry in terms of decades, connects Nazi camps with suburban indifference and apathy, predicts the end of Western dominance, notes the acceler-ating changes that are a part of the Industrial Revolution, proffers the work of Benn as a refutation. The expressions and opinions of Duffy's co-editor are unmistakable here.

A few months earlier, Bly had written to Wright:

The old style, with the iamb, its caesuras, its rhymes, its thousands of reminiscent rhythms, its delicate ways of indicating slight feelings, its stanzas, its old tested devices of meter, is like a man speaking who gestures too much. The audience, watching, sees a dozen gestures every minute, and finally becomes lost, unable to relate the gestures to the emotion being expressed or the subject, and finally, in despair, must ignore the gestures entirely, and simply listen to the flow of words—and now <u>many more words are needed</u>. But in the new style, there is no necessity for continual gesture, by rhymes, etc.—therefore, if you raise your little finger once, slowly, it has tremendous meaning—[41]

Wright was so impressed that he urged Bly to put the comments in print.[42] They appeared in the second issue, with very slight changes, as "The Possibility of New Poetry."

The next piece, "A Paragraph of Valéry," derives from a letter Wright wrote to Bly describing his own experience on coming into contact with him:

> The same man may change his tastes and his style, burn
> at twenty what he adored at sixteen; *some kind of inner*
> *transmutation* shifts the power of seduction from one master
> to another... These defections, these sudden accesses of love or
> of grace, these conversions and substitutions, this possibility of
> being successively *sensitized* to the work of incompatible poets,
> are literary phenomena of the first importance. Therefore no
> one ever mentions them.

Wright added:

> I find it interesting that Valery should have used the word
> sensitized, because the word also occurred to you in your
> intense and, I might add, entirely convincing argument (in your
> recent letter to me) about the ascending vicious circles: "We
> construct, but the great poets are merely sensitive—" Nothing
> could be finer than that formulation of yours.[43]

Bly, wanting to print it, asked Wright for a short introduction, but ended up writing it himself. It includes this remark: "Valéry... suggested that it is not as the bourgeois world would have it, namely, that we understand and love radical work in our youth, and as we grow more mature, understand classical work, but the other way around."

In the section "American Poems," two in Wright's new style appear. "In the Hard Sun" begins: "Mother of roots, you have not seeded / The tall ashes of loneliness / For me." In his second letter to Bly, still before they had met, Wright sent a 91-line version of this, which he was then calling his "farewell to poetry." Bly responded:

> There is no question that you have within you the dark water of
> a new life, and when I see the images in this poem, I see I have
> very little or nothing to teach you! The images are strong and
> firm... I'm glad the articles helped with such a change, but as

they say around here, "cow tracks in a pasture means cows only to somebody who has already seen a cow." However, the poem is still a kind of mixture of the old style and the new style, I think.[44]

Bly went on to indicate the reasons why he cut three-fourths of the poem and provides some "random thoughts":

> In the new style, where the tension and density of the emotion is everything, you have to, like a good gambler, agree to stake everything on one throw, and agree to let only one of the images stand for the whole idea... Since the drama, the density of the emotion is everything, whatever explains too much, gives too many details, weakens the poem, and makes it sag like one of Dali's watches over a tree branch.[45]

Wright responded with a plea: "if you don't continue your present strategy of direct, ruthless, pointed criticism, I will be not only personally disappointed but also—at this stage of whatever it is that's happening—handicapped... I hope, indeed, that some day I will have really grasped this wild and strange new world into which I have been born."[46] When Bly told him that they had a final version of the poem, Wright demurred:

> I'm startled at the idea of its being published at all, to be perfectly frank. For, as you know very well, I didn't write that poem at all—you did. In so far as it is a poem and not a huge blast of yawping hot air filled accidentally with two or three phrases that by mere chance are like the translations of Neruda that I have read, it was entirely your work.[47]

Bly said: "That is absurd. Pound cut 2/3 or 1/3 or something of 'The Waste Land,' cutting the middle section from over a hundred lines to 8 or 9, yet Eliot nowhere says that Pound wrote it; and I added not a single line or a single word, but simply cut, and typed up in a row what wasn't cut."[48] Wright's second "new" poem, just seven lines, is "In Fear of Harvests." After more back-and-forth, Bly wrote back: "It is lovely!...I know you think of yourself as timid, etc., but really you are one of the guttiest of us—you; and when you cast off, you throw the ropes. These poems will give courage to those others, perhaps not so daring, who must still walk the extremely painful road out of the old meters."[49] Once more Bly clearly enunciates the teaching function of the magazine and each piece in it.

Wright continued to send his poems to Madison, and Bly's responses are lively: "The sudden appearance of really good lines in a poem that fails means that you had mistaken which poem it was that was to be written from the start—and the good lines are from the real poem—they are nothing more nor less than the seeds of that poem, which you then take and put in a quiet place till it grows the entire poem." He added: "Remember that a poem is not many thoughts, but only one thought. Pure, like a life devoted to only one thing.[50] Both men felt the new poems represented something important.[51]

Other poems for this section were initially to come from David Ignatow, Louis Simpson, and possibly Richard Hugo, a friend of Wright's. Bly acknowledged:

> You were right about Hugo—his poetry has a lot of interest, and he really has an astonishing sense of the image; the lines with images in them simply rise off the page, but in almost all cases are weighted down by the "thirties" type of factual detail or intellectual rambling which surrounds them, so I cut five or six of them right down to the images, and sent them to him, explaining what the principle of my cutting was, and asking to print a couple of them in the magazine. I should hear soon.[52]

But the other two American poets who appeared in the second issue were Thomas Parnell and Bly himself. The first of Bly's poems is "The Army of Advertising Men," which begins:

> *The merchants of death come*
> *Swimming through the air*
> *On mahogany boxes and leaves of China tea.*
> *They come in ornate galleons of false pity*
> *Or on the red wagon of a child*
> *Through the solid and sordid rain.*

His second, a late entry, is "Poem in Three Parts," which begins: "Oh, on an early morning I think I shall live forever! / I am wrapped in my joyful flesh, / As the grass is wrapt in its clouds of green." This remains one of Bly's best-loved early poems.[53]

Parnell, says the contributors note, an ex-Marine from West Virginia, had lived in France. "He published a small book of poems there called *The Auctioneer*. In the fall of 1957, he returned to the United States and is now working in Washington." The two poems, "La Dame France – 1958" and "The Bataan Death March," fit well. The first refers to the ongoing Algerian war against French colonial rule, with a bow to Keats' "La Belle Dame Sans Merci." The second finds memories of the ignominious defeat of American and Filipino forces in 1942 hidden just below the surface of 1950s America. Parnell, it turns out, was actually Duffy, who fabricated the pseudonym and author's bio.

When, late in 1958, Bly, Wright, and Duffy gathered at Duffy's house for a final push on the second issue, it was the first time the three poets had been together in the same room.

In another brief article, Bly recommends some new books, including several Italian translations, and he also refers to Jerome Rothenberg's Hawk's Well Press, which had recently published Seymour Faust, Thom Gunn, and others. "Mr. Rothenberg is without question one of the best translators of German in this country," Bly says, mentioning his anthology, *New Young German Poets*, forthcoming from City Lights. Their friendship had begun in the spring of 1958.[54] Rothenberg would soon include Bly and Wright in the first issue of his own little magazine, *Poems From the Floating World*, another specimen of the new poetics. Finally, Bly cites Gaetano Massa's publishing house, Las Americas, and its plans for more translations.

Next, in "On English and American Poetry," Bly attacks abstract language, and points a finger: "England has always been proud of her subjection of the emotions to the intellect, or to put it another way, her control of the dark passions. She is proud of her ability to go on quietly with plans for Empire despite the suffering of the dark natives on whom she imposes." He continues: "Intellectualism and abstraction are so fatal to poetry that the English poets of this generation seem the poorest of the sixty-five generations of English poets since Chaucer's time." Such hyperbole is characteristic of Bly's criticism: it makes a strong impression, but, resisting proof, it does not—nor is it really meant to—bear careful examination. Then he backs off a little: "The poets are not to be blamed—they can write nothing else, and perhaps no poet could in their situation." Nevertheless, he states: "The effect of English poetry of the last hundred years on American poetry has been disastrous."

Bly's effort to deflect North American poets from the stale English formalism and direct them toward the imagination evident in many European and South American poets was a rescue mission. "For every poet, such as Whitman, who breaks free of its influence, a thousand succumb and are destroyed. It is no accident that the three most daring and massive poets in the American language in the twentieth century—Wallace Stevens, T. S. Eliot, and Ezra Pound—have all immersed themselves in French, not English."

Bly then criticizes all sorts of American poets, both those in the universities and those "on the loose in Los Angeles or San Francisco." Although the Beats had, more extremely than the poets of *The Fifties*, rejected effete English standards of decorum, they still used abstract language. Bly saw himself somewhere between these two extremes. "Both are as far from the modern tradition of the deep images of the unconscious as possible."

Eureka! Here is Bly's first published use of the term "deep image," the basis for his association with a type of poetry that many call by that name. This essay, written in 1958, pre-dates the discussions of Robert Kelly and Rothenberg.[55] Although the poetic image was never a very clear concept to begin with, at first the three poets found much to agree on. But soon Rothenberg felt himself in an "intermediary position" between Bly and Kelly. Then a permanent fissure formed, largely over surrealism, and whether the Spanish or the French poets had primacy.[56] While the phrase may have originated with Bly, for him these words were *obiter dicta*; Kelly and Rothenberg made it into the label it became, and Bly never liked it: "The phrase...suggests a geographical location in the psyche. It misses...the physicalness of the image."[57] But, like it or not, it would stick.[58]

Bly concludes this essay with a summons for poets and readers to be students of European poetic traditions, and to translate:

If we have vigorous teachers we can write strong, vigorous poetry, but those teachers, those poets, write, as they always do, in other languages—not our own. They write in the Spanish tradition, suddenly reborn in the last fifty years, or in the French tradition through Char, in which so much sensibility is nourished, or in the German tradition of Rilke and Trakl, poetry which is not dying, but growing—poetry which has found a way to include not only more of the mood of modern life than any before, but also more of the joy of the unconscious.

Issue Two's installment of "Madame Tussaud's Wax Museum" calls attention, with some humor, to the deadening effect of classical references in poems. It includes lines from "The Greater Music" by Theodore Weiss and Mark Van Doren's "Tourist," followed by "suggested resolutions for young poets":

– I promise I will neither write nor read another poem on the death of Orpheus as long as I live.

– I promise I will never describe the sad fate of Oedipus in a poem again, on pain of losing my eyes.

– I promise I will never capture poor Perseus and drag him into my poems, nor Aeneas, nor good Achilles, nor Telamon, nor Penelope, mainly because no one knows who Perseus is.

One might object to unwarranted assumptions and conclusion-jumping here, but these funny resolutions are one more means of getting across this issue's message: if American poets of the 1950s were going to save themselves and not go down with the old poetry's sinking ship, they would have to jettison their fondness for classical allusions.

Two other insulting features follow. "Wisdom of the Old" begins: "We have grave doubts about the intelligence of most, if not all, the older men in the country." The editors explain that "one of our readers" has charged that Leslie Fiedler sees hints of homosexuality everywhere. In this brief parody, "Wiedler," reviewing Winston Churchill's *History of the English-Speaking Peoples*, notes: "he often describes large groups of men going out in the field with guns—that is his favorite subject, in fact—sometimes two or three thousand of them. *Why don't they take their wives with them?* I think the conclusion is obvious."[59]

Next is "The Order of the Blue Toad," a first-time satiric feature which quickly gained notoriety. Gilbert Highet is the august

54

honorand "for continual degradation of the literature of Greece and Rome. He finds all literature best if easily understood and a little jolly. He carries on the incessant academic war against modern poetry." Alongside Bennett Cerf, he is implicated specifically for his dismissal of Pound's *Cantos*. "We therefore award him The Blue Toad on a background of Doric pillars and nursery rhymes."

There is also a "Meditation Page," headed by words of D.H. Lawrence: "Freedom is, above all, freedom from lies." Underneath are six examples of various kinds of idiocy:

"You graduates of West Point are all crusaders for Peace." – Eisenhower

"The more you buy, the happier you are." – All Advertisers

"The fallout from H-bombs is no more dangerous than a radium wrist-watch." – Teller

"Soap operas give the people what they want." – Defense Secretary McElroy

"We only exploded 12 bombs in the recent tests." – The Pentagon

"Going to church is good business." – Sunday School

Not long after the McCarthy hearings, and in the midst of an unprecedented economic boom, potshots freely aimed at so many sacred cows—and in a literary magazine, to boot—may have shocked some. But most readers welcomed the unexpected dust-up as a kind of relief.[60]

Despite Bly's anxiety over how much time the magazine stole from his own poetry, he was also energized by it. He continued to develop its aims, such as that it "should be a searcher itself (not to present a *fait accompli*, or laying down rules)."[61] And in the end, he was gratified by his efforts: "What work! I have spent at least two entire weeks, full time, on this issue, but I think it is better than the first. Tomorrow, Friday, it will all be done."[62] Of course, making an end meant a new beginning.

4

Choosing the Door to a Secret Life

What the second issue lacked in surprise it made up for in other ways. More people now were paying attention, talking about it, anticipating what might come next. Thus its cumulative impact was greater. Wright said: "A great improvement over the first, especially in the clarity and force of the essays, yours and Bill's both. I especially liked your poem about waking up in the morning."[1] Likewise, Dickey said: "You are doing what I have always rather timidly wanted to do myself: to prove, by doing, that the magnificent imaginative approach of the Europeans and the Latin-American poets is just as possible in English...I hope you live for a thousand years."[2] He kept submitting, admitting that he was under Bly's sway: "I just wanted you to see what influence *The Fifties* is (are?) having on at least one American!"[3]

Bly was always soliciting reactions; others came unbidden. John Haines, a future contributor, wrote: "It's very heartening to me to think that you and your magazine are managing to do something there in an apparently insignificant part of the U.S."[4] Bly and Wright visited Williams in Paterson, who was pleased when they read poems aloud from the second issue.[5] Boris Pasternak, recent winner of the Nobel Prize, wrote: "The poems of Gottfried Benn (just as your translations) were beautiful. I liked also your own 'Poem in Three Parts.' ...But give up your friendly intention to spare me a place in the *Fifties*... It would lead you too far astray. More than anyone I am deviated from my former direction and become out of date."[6] Merwin offered his opinion: "Do you mind if I say that I've liked poems of yours that I've seen, and your magazine...May I also say I <u>agree</u> with you, and what you're after...If I could do translations for your magazine I'd be glad to lend a hand."[7]

If the reactions had all been positive, the magazine would have failed in its purpose. There were some sitting ducks whom Bly wished simply to blast out of the water; others needed only to have their feathers ruffled. Hearing Wright's account of meeting Tate at a New Year's Eve party, and the fracas over *The Fifties* that erupted, Bly wrote: "It is very interesting that Tate got so mad—by now he will have received the third issue—he subscribes—and be even madder! I like to think of him there, rolling out old Southern curses, as the Union cavalry refuses to obey!"[8] Donald Justice reported from Iowa City: "*The Fifties*...had some of the poets around here pretty excited—miffed might actually be the most accurate word. I find it interesting and entertaining, which is how I hope you want it to be, though there's a good deal I don't agree with. So what? Keep it up."[9]

Hugo said it was "stimulating" and appreciated its "good sound unproven prejudicial utterances." But he added his biting assessment, saying the writing—Bly's writing, that is—was "appallingly bad." He challenged Bly's hard-line stance on meter, insisting that "true originality lies in the personality," which will make itself known "regardless of the writer's attempts to pervert it, force it or forget it."[10]

Bly's capacity for accepting criticism and, as long as it was offered with integrity, not taking it personally, helps explain his success as an editor and a critic. As for the ideas he expressed, some he had been developing for years; the half-baked quality of others displays his zest to provoke any kind of response whatsoever.

Bly was now director of the reading program at NYU, a position he had inherited from Kinnell.[11] Among others, he scheduled H.R. Hays, Rothenberg, Clayton Eshleman, and himself all doing Neruda,[12] and, a short time later, Wright and Dickey.[13] Bly's first face-to-face meeting with Dickey was at the airport: "There he was, a man with a blank face and a green hat! Courteous and Southern, bold and confused."[14] The reading went well, and the three had a rollicking time.[15] Dickey wrote to Bly:

> the experience...has been so precious to me that I did not really want to talk about it, even to you. But talk I must, and it may be that I can let you know how I feel by saying simply that for two or three days I lived as I have always wanted to live, and the way I believe people should live. As Jim said before he left, it is terrible to have to go back to a kind of half-life after something like that.[16]

Dickey wrote to Wright: "I love Bly. He is one of the most marvelous men I have ever seen, and yet a human being like all of us, too. But *what* a human being!"[17] Wright was similarly affected: "I can't really describe what it meant to feel free to emerge into that tremendous, ample sunlight of noble and heroic men with whom I spent those three days, drinking the green waters of the first and last seas."[18]

Then Bly scheduled Justice, Simpson, and Duffy, "as unlikely a threesome as I have ever heard of!"[19] And he invited E.E. Cummings for a "wonderful poetry reading," driving him himself.[20] January saw Richard Wilbur; February, Anthony Hecht and Robert Hazel; March, Levertov, John Logan, and Charles Tomlinson, also Lowell; April, Roethke and Kenneth Rexroth. He told Hall: "I am dickering with Tate too, who is said to be furious at *The Fifties*, but speaks very politely to me."[21]

In December, Bly read at Harvard.[22] The next night he did a reading at the YM-YWHA Poetry Center (run by Betty Kray) with Simpson and David Wagoner. The "outstanding members of America's new, distinguished generation of poets" that year were chosen by Isabella Gardner, Frederick Morgan (*Hudson Review* editor), and Henry Rago (*Poetry* editor), among others. The roster of readers also included Eliot, Cummings, Sandburg, Graves, Tate, Frost, Rexroth, Eberhart, MacLeish, Spender, and Untermeyer (along with new poets such as Paul Carroll, Dickey, Logan, Anne Sexton, George Starbuck, and Mona Van Duyn). Bly was now in distinguished company.

Bill and Christina Duffy visiting with Denise Levertov and Bly in New York, 1959.

Eight months after number two, the third issue was on the way. In the summer of 1959, Bly wrote Hall:

> We finally got the issue done at Pine Island, with less screeching and hollerin' than usual at my syntax... We also sent back a good 800 manuscripts, and are now keeping a file, on 3 x 5 cards, of all the advice, etc., we give to poets who have sent in MSS. Some of them start a correspondence with us on points we make, so we have to remember exactly what we said![23]

Maintaining a quarterly publication schedule was proving untenable. The primary problem seems to have been Bly's multiple pursuits. Another was the time it took to have it printed in Ireland. Separate shipments of the third issue reached the New York docks in December and January, as Bly told Hall, "after arguments with [Customs] officials there as to whether it was Communist propaganda or not."[24]

He sent fifty copies to Hall who was in the U.K., urging him to give them "to all the poets that seem to have a grain of sense. #3 has fewer insults to England, so maybe they can eat it without their faces puckering up quite so much."[25] In New York, the good news was that they had found a real distributor.[26] Back in Minnesota, Duffy was trying to manage the subscriptions and exchanges with fifty-seven other little magazines, and doing legwork among the local bookstores.[27] The issue was selling "like mad," so Bly ordered a second printing.[28]

The theme is again hinted at inside the front cover, this time a single line from Jung: "Only what is really oneself is able to heal." For a couple of years he had been reading deeply in psychology—Jung especially—thus the heightened attention to inward life and, more indirectly, the role of the unconscious in the new imagination.[29]

The first two issues had opened with European poems in translation; this one begins with a group of American poems written in the new style, that is, *not* from the English tradition. Margaret Scheinin was a New York friend with whom the Blys would occasionally stay.[30] Her poem, "The Gates Parted," begins: "Inward and downward was the way," with images of the underworld, darkness, death, and blood. Bly told Dickey that he had cut this poem "from a prose dream of hers."[31]

Bly's own contribution is "Poem":

The wild bull is bleeding on the mountain.
But it is green, dark green,
In the wild cave of the Virgin.

In the cave of the Mother of Joy,
From a bed of hot coals
The odor of rosemary and thyme is rising.

When the smoke touches the roof of the cave,
The green leaves burst into flames,
The air of night changes to dark water,
The mountains alter and become the sea.

Many of these archetypal images resonate with others found in contemporary writings of his.[32] He was giving the unconscious free reign.

In part one of Rothenberg's "Three Landscapes," a "dark

bull" wanders on the beach under the moon. The brief second part evokes a warm river and the rain. The last part begins, "White monks are climbing hills / inside her skull," and has more blood, cinders, and another moon. It is clear once more how much the ideas of Bly and Rothenberg had been dovetailing.

The third issue had a deep red cover.

A brief aside: later that year, the Rothenbergs and the Duffys unintentionally visited Madison farm at the same time. It was not a good occasion. The city-folk were already leery of sleeping out in the screen house. Bly wrote to Hall: "One night about 2 in the morning Bill, drunk as a coot, went out, creeping through the grass, and pretended to be a 'stubble bear,' and scared them into the house; it was very funny, but consequently they hardly spoke again."[33] While the differences in Rothenberg's and Bly's understanding of surrealism and image had been gradually growing clearer, this incident marked a definite cooling off of the relationship.[34] Bly quite successfully straddled the disparate worlds of rural Minnesota and urban New York. But this had been a disastrous clash of cultures. "This was Endsville. Nowheresville. I am only recovering now."[35]

Another poem in this section, "The Second World War," is by a newcomer, George Kresenky, who "makes his living as the gardener of a fruit orchard on the Eastern shore of Lake Michigan." But this was one more Bly pseudonym. Images of the war in Europe abound. It begins: "Bull horns swallowing / The sea, in gardens of lettuce and green pools / Among barbed wire …"

Wright's two poems, "The Dream of the American Frontier," and "On an American Girl's Marriage," open and close this section. Bly had done some editing, as usual. In the margin of a letter of his, Wright scrawled: "Robert's daring suggestion...is perfectly accurate—I haven't learned this art of <u>final</u> cutting yet enough to breathe it. I "think" too much." He addressed Bly directly:

> So please <u>go on</u> cutting as pitilessly as you can. I am <u>not</u> beyond instruction. The <u>essence</u> of the art of the new style is in <u>cutting</u>. Everything depends on finding the inevitable image, and having sufficient faith to <u>let it stand alone and grow like a sapling</u>. I am astounded at your final version of "Marriage." It defines several crucial problems at one stroke![36]

A requisite characteristic of Bly's poetics is apparent in the process of peeling away the outer layers, the record of the conscious, rational mind, until the germ, the unconscious image, stands revealed.

This symbiotic poetic relationship between Wright's foremost editor and Bly's foremost contributor is impressive. In that same letter, Bly wrote: "I am very grateful, Jim, that you give me the first choice for *The Fifties*—that way I can not only have beautiful <u>poems</u> in these first issues, but I can suggest certain ranges of the 'new style' that are perhaps best done in a confined space." More of Wright's marginalia reads: "I too am grateful. I feel as if I had just wakened from a dream of desperate comfort, and refreshed myself on a drink of clear, cold water. *Fifties* gives me an occasion to identify the devotion I always wanted to give, and it also teaches me endlessly, in the most <u>usable</u>, stylistic terms."[37] Here are the first two stanzas of the poem as it finally appeared:

She dreamed long of waters.
Inland today, she wakens
On scraped knees, lost
Among locust thorns.
She feels for
The path backwards, to
The pillows of the sea.

In this entire introductory grouping, the reader cannot fail to notice the striking recurrence of images such as "bull," "the sea," and "waters." It is more than mere coincidence, even Lorca-esque. While we should reckon that they arose from the unconscious minds of poets intent on breaking the old rationalistic images, surely the editor's mind, as he gathered and trimmed them, was operating in a consciously symbolic mode.

In "Some Thoughts on Lorca and René Char," Bly declares that there is a widespread enthusiasm for these poets, "and everyone would like to leap, at one bound, into their heaven." As he outlined earlier, "we have had no bold new poetry" since Eliot's *Waste Land*, Williams, Stevens, and Crane's *White Buildings*. Again, "how is it that…in America…poetry has been getting older and older every year, like a running down clock, until today even the younger poets are dissatisfied with their own work?" And why has poetry in Spain and South America and France flourished in the meantime? The answer is simple: "these other poetries have passed through surrealism; we have not." Bly explains:

> Beginning with Baudelaire, French poetry went through a dark valley, a valley filled with black pools, lions, jungles, turbid rivers, dead men hanging from trees, wolves eating the feathers of birds, thunder hanging over doors, images of seas, sailors, drunken boats, maggots eating a corpse with the sound of a sower sowing grain, endless voyages, vast black skies, huge birds, continual rain. This immersion has given French poetry its strength, its rich soil, whereas our soil is thin and rocky, and the poetry of the 30's and 40's increasingly resembles a flower cut off above the ground, slowly withering.

The link between this essay and the previous series of water-soaked poems becomes visible. Surrealism is the door to the unconscious, to the inner life that American poets so desperately need.

Once more, Bly praises Eliot and Pound and "the astonishing revolution of imagination" they effected. Unfortunately, however, their "Puritan streak…prevents their sinking deeper into the mind. They both win the victory over the unconscious so easily. They somehow skip over the passions which Freud has described so well."

The bell is rung again for the third issue's theme. Bly adds:

> The Imagists were misnamed: they did not write in images from the unconscious, as Lorca or Neruda, but in simple pictures, such as "petals on a wet black bough," and Pound, for instance, continues to write in pictures, writing as great a poetry as is possible, which in his case is very great, using nothing but pictures, but still, pictures are not images. And without these true images, this water from the unconscious, the language continues to dry up.

Spanish poetry is "a sea poetry, a poetry of the unconscious, a poetry of water." We are once more submerged. "As Lorca says, 'Green, green, go deeper, green.'"

Next, Rothenberg translates the Romanian Paul Celan. His poems "are sunk deeply into an inward world, and in many ways they seem much stronger than the French surrealist poetry of twenty years ago, and in many ways represent an advance on them." So, of course, there are lessons to be learned. "Corona" begins: "Autumn is eating a leaf from my hand; we are friends. / We are picking time out of a nut, we teach it to run: / and time rushes back to its shell." The sea is here, in the lines: "we sleep like wine in a sea-shell / like the sea in the moon's bloody rays."

The last and longest poem, "Death Fugue," is about the death camps, where some of Celan's family died, and thus connects with outer life as well as inner. It begins:

> *Black milk of morning we drink you at dusk*
> *we drink you at noontime and dawntime we drink you at night*
> *we drink and drink*
> *we scoop out a grave in the sky where it's roomy to lie.*

The next essay, provocatively titled "The Necessity of Rejecting a Shakespeare Sonnet," has an interesting backstory. After *The Fifties* 1, Bly received "an extremely discourteous letter from Thom Gunn, enclosing 'The expense of spirit' sonnet of Shakespeare and asking if I would turn that down too ... I must answer, of course, I <u>would</u> turn it down; the style is too old fashioned."[38] Wright called this "one of the happiest, most truly funny things you have ever written to me ..."[39] Actually, the personal letter

Gunn wrote to Bly praised the "handsome new magazine" and expressed admiration for his poetry. It is the accompanying letter to the editor that has a caustic tone.[40] Although Gunn probably knew he would respond tit-for-tat, he might have been surprised by the form it took.

Bly says that Shakespeare's language was interesting when he wrote it, that it was "striking and new," but now such language is "exhausted, dead." The answer to Gunn's question is "Yes": If Shakespeare submitted one of his sonnets to *The Fifties*, he would reject it (probably with a pointed, rejection-slip comment along the lines of: "This horse died 350 years ago. We think it's time you found a new horse."). "But, of course," Bly is quick to say, "he wouldn't; he would write today in a language as fresh as his was in 1600. What that might be is hard to estimate, but I would guess it might resemble the language of Lorca or perhaps Neruda." There's the rub, and it fits beautifully with Bly's program as elaborated in the first and second issues. "When one language dies, or is worn out, another must be used."

Bly then quotes a portion of Neruda's "Gentleman Alone" dealing with the same subject as Shakespeare's sonnet, sexual love. And on the subject of death, Bly quotes the first lines from sonnet 60 ("Like as the waves make towards the pebbled shore / So do our minutes hasten to their end ..."), followed by part of Neruda's "Death Alone."[41] The essay stops there; Bly figures his point has been made. The original shock value of this short piece is not easy to gauge. One might emulate but never surpass Shakespeare's English. Still, at least in Bly's company, few writers could seriously sustain the argument that such an antiquated mode of expression, however brilliant, inventive, and, in one sense, timeless, would be acceptable in the mid-twentieth century.

There is another matter to note here, one of great importance to the life of the magazine. The translated excerpt of "Gentleman Alone" has a couple of ellipses in two successive lines, printed as follows:

And the hours ... when the bees have an odor of blood,
and the flies are buzzing in anger ...

This was not the copy that Bly submitted to the printer. The first ellipsis left out:

> *after lunch, when the young male students*
> *and the young women students, and the priests are masturbating,*
> *and the animals are riding each other frankly*

and the second ellipsis omitted:

> *and cousins play strange games with their girl-cousins,*
> *and doctors look with rage at the husband of the young patient,*
> *and the morning hours, when the professor, as if absentminded,*
> *performs his marital duty, and has breakfast...*[42]

Kerryman's typesetter made the arbitrary, unannounced decision to bowdlerize. Bly likened this to "a warning shot," and started thinking about finding another printer.[43]

Next come two poems by the Czechoslovakian Mirko Tuma, translated by Bly. Tuma had spent time in a concentration camp; after the Russians took over, he left Prague. The two poets met by chance at the New York Public Library.[44] "Letter," the first poem, "was written to a visiting nurse in one of the large hospitals in New York."[45] Here is the second, "Poem," in its entirety:

> *Closer than the night...and flesh...throwing off sparks*
> *Blood boiling from holding the voices in,*
> *My poetry,*
> *A bee who lost his way and wound up on the halo of a light bulb,*
> *On a naked breast sparkling*
> *In the middle of the sea.*

Once again we are at sea, after a brief surrealistic journey. Before publication, Tuma, who had shown them around, wrote: "Everyone by the way admires your brilliant translation."[46]

Crunk then launches into his distinct orbit: "I am never able to read the poems of Donald Hall without having many thoughts about the middle class, and it is possible that it is just such thoughts that the poems are intended to evoke." This essay is loaded with stuff that the two friends had been thrashing out over several years.

Crunk reflects on the concept of the poet in America, in contrast to Ireland, France, Spain, or South America, suggesting that here poets are connected somehow with the middle or business class. Even if they're not, the critics put them there; that way they become non-threatening and worthy of consideration. Pound and Eliot, instead of yielding to this, exiled themselves. He blames Ransom, Mark Van Doren, and John Ciardi for sustaining the concept of "the poet as a useful citizen and family man." He says:

> Poetry, at the beginning of the fifties, had slipped back to the old situation before Baudelaire, when poetry and the middle class were living in an uneasy bliss. Poetry was writing itself in nice iambic lines, which the middle class in America had always loved, and with which it was long familiar; in rhymes, the absence of which in poems makes the middle class very nervous; and in content, it tried to be modern without offending anyone.

But positive movement is afoot. He notes the efforts of Snodgrass, Snyder, Creeley, Simpson, and Wright "to pull themselves out of this soggy ground."

Crunk is harsh on Hall's first book, *Exiles and Marriages*, summarily dismissing its "light verse" section. Furthermore, the "triumvirate of Father, God, and middle class society are the three great giants in this book, and toward all three the poet has the same mingled longing and loathing." But he sees progress in Hall's newer book, *The Dark Houses*, though it is not without its faults, including over-reliance on iambs.

The "little tour" ends; Crunk says it could be called "adventures of the American poet trying to imagine himself." A new idea of the poet is needed, neither the middle class representative nor the "homosexual hipster." (Crunk thus alludes to the Beats in the broad strokes of caricature. Later in this issue, Bly comes to their defense.) Poets need to be independent from the middle class and from the academy, and to be critics of the same, like Thomas Mc-Grath, Ferlinghetti, Merwin, and Rexroth. At least ideally, "the poet is one who devotes his whole life to poetry; it is not merely to bring poetry into one's life, but to change the whole thing into poetry, and it is possible that to do that one must leave the middle class entirely, and all its ideas and securities."

The essay ends with the last stanza of a new poem, "The Long River":

The musk-ox moves
when the boat stops,
in hard thickets. Now
the wood is dark
with old pleasures.

"This poem seems to me by many times the finest poem he has written, and at the same time the poem of his which is most completely a poem. It also suggests that the way out of the middle class is by a door the middle class cannot find—a secret life."

Hall has spoken of Bly's influence on him: "I was getting stuck in the pentameter line, and it was limiting my subject matter... The first poem I remember which really moved elsewhere was..., after a lot of talk with Bly, called 'The Long River.' And I had no idea what I was talking about." He continues: "His essay about me made me partly uncomfortable." At the same time, he admits: "There's some truth to it. *Exiles and Marriages*... had poems in it that were sort of written to be approved of, not entirely, but to be a good boy."[47]

Their deep-rooted and durable friendship was based in part on mutual criticism. They made a bargain in 1958, as Bly sent a bogus form at the bottom of a letter:

Sign this and return:

I HEREBY SWEAR TO ANSWER ANY LETTER
CONTAINING POEMS WITHIN TWO DAYS OR RUN
THE RISK OF BEING CUT OFF FROM MY SUPPLY OF
HOP. (GOOD ALL OVER THE UNITED STATES.)[48]

Many letters in the ensuing years would invoke the 48-hour rule, and many would chastise the addressee for failing to honor it.

This is not to say that one would always take the other's advice. Hall went ahead and published *The Dark Houses*, despite Bly's resistance. And Bly let him have it. He lists seven poems that "should not have been published" because they "are nothing but talk, talk, talk; the words are abstract, the situation intellectual, the mood distant and attenuated;...the poems never get anywhere."

The form of another five poems "is too old-fashioned." Seven more are seriously flawed. "This leaves 10 poems…But 10 poems are not a book…If you are publishing a book only to become famous, you will destroy yourself."[49]

The third issue's emphasis on the unconscious image is advanced by "Four City Poems." The subject matter also recalls a statement from the second issue: "A third great movement of modern poetry, and an invention horrifying to the bourgeois, is the simple description of life in modern cities, life after the Industrial Revolution, life exactly as it is." These poems display the reality of city streets and sidewalks. Simpson contributes "Chamber of Deputies," a vision of Paris during World War II. The first stanza reads:

Do you remember the
Sleeping city
Street of the Skeleton
Red gutters of
The grand butchery
Odors of love?

On David Ignatow, with whom Bly had recently become acquainted, the note says that he "has never left New York for more than three months in his life."[50] The grittiness of real urban living competes with equally authentic inner visions. In "The Dream,"

Someone approaches to say his life is ruined
and to fall down at your feet
and pound his head upon the sidewalk.
Blood spreads in a puddle.

Ignatow wanted Bly to move to the city. "You're missed here very much. You made things happen. Maybe one day you'll want to settle down here and keep a steady fire boiling under that black, grimy kettle of N.Y."[51] He called Bly "a rare friend, out of the Minnesota sky, a kind of wild duck."[52]

Lastly, in "February Evening in New York," Levertov evokes the end of the working day in Manhattan: "As the buildings close, released autonomous / feet pattern the streets / in hurry and stroll..." The oxymoron in "released autonomous feet" neatly captures the ordinary truth of the daily grind.

These poems are followed by "A Note on Hydrogen Bomb Testing." The "Strontium 90 builds bones" remark from the first issue, and a couple of remarks on the "Meditation Page" in the second, had hit their target. Bly writes: "We have received letters asking why, if we are *poets*, we concern ourselves with the activities of the Atomic Energy Commission. We believe that artists above all are not exempt from fighting in national issues." He mentions Yeats as a model. "Americans as a whole have been too much trained toward *tolerance*; when a false shepherd calls, they follow along like sheep." The fact is that the A.E.C. "has lied directly" about a number of things. "We believe that poisoning and mutating children who aren't even born yet, in this country and elsewhere, is an immoral act, regardless of the circumstances. Yet no major stand on the part of any mass medium or by any church in the United States has been made against the A.E.C."

This is a powerful statement, especially given the usual view of the 1950s as a conformist, complacent decade. The time for being silent was over. The harmful effects of radiation, the failure of the media and the church to call prevailing norms into question, *Life* magazine's honoring of Edward Teller (another liar), a freshly misplaced respect for "the scientific mind" and its influence on public policy, the indifference of scientists to human suffering—all of these and more called for speaking out and for active opposition. "Unless these men are fought, in their inquisition millions will die."

Just as serious, in its comic way, was "Madame Tussaud's Wax Museum." This installment inveighs against "academic poetry," the grandchild of the old "poetic" poetry. The academic poets "are now the judges and sponsors for the new poetry in America. The Lamont Poetry Prize is becoming more absurd every time it is given, and with respect to John Hall Wheelock, the poetry he publishes is for the most part archaic and decrepit." Three sets of quotations follow, the first in each set from a poetic grandparent, the second from a poetic/academic grandchild. The paired poets are Edward Coote Pinkney and John Crowe Ransom, Elizabeth

Akers Allen and Louise Townsend Nicholl, and Ella Wheeler Wilcox and John Hall Wheelock.[53]

Bly's rude public persona did not mean he was entirely devoid of manners. He told Hall: "The other day I wrote Wheelock…and told him beforehand of the insult in Wax Museum…. He wrote back…arguing but not violently and ending: 'As you grow older, you will learn a good many things. In the meantime, I wish you great success with your own beautiful work. Stick to that.' Now that was a sweet letter."[54]

In somewhat the same vein as the Wax Museum is "The Other Night in Heaven, by Diana Tilling." This was a take-off on Trilling's piece in the recent *Partisan Review*, titled "The Other Night at Columbia: A Report from the Academy." That article, an account of Allen Ginsberg's reading at his alma mater (where her husband, Lionel, had been his teacher) was itself almost a self-parody.[55] Trilling describes Ginsberg as a sensation-seeker, a self-promoter, a difficult and troubled boy who refuses to toe the line. She recalls the good old days of the 1930s, and drops names. She notes that "the auditorium smelled fresh…I took one look at the crowd and was certain that it would smell bad. But I was mistaken…The audience was clean and Ginsberg was clean and Corso was clean and Orlovsky was clean."[56] Her condescension continues, until finally, almost as an afterthought, she gets to the poetry:

Ginsberg heard himself announcing that no one at Columbia knew anything about prosody; the English department was stuck in the nineteenth century, sensible of no meter other than the old iambic pentameter, whereas the thing about him and his friends was their concern with a poetic line which moved in the rhythm of ordinary speech; they were poetic innovators, carrying things forward the next logical step from William Carlos Williams.[57]

Bly had also been in the audience, and his account—as "Tilling"—is briefer, and intentionally ridiculous:

How different it might have been for Ginsberg and his friends if they had been born ten or fifteen years sooner!…That they weren't born before the thirties was a real loss; they should at least have tried to. If they had, they could have sung union

71

songs, played mah-jong, and been great rebels like us! They could have criticized Freud, and ended up running the *Partisan Review*, like Lionel and me. They could even have looked down on Frost!

Names are dropped in vast profusion, and then: "All these people, my friends, were wearing new clothes. All intellectuals do this. It is one of the rewards of being a successful writer in America." Befitting her remarks about poetic tradition, she says: "The biggest thrill of the evening came when Ginsberg read a poem for my Lionel. It was entitled 'Go Home, Lionel,' and it nearly moved me to tears. The poem had all the passion, goodness, sympathy, thankfulness, the wonderfulness, the hopefulness, the Thirties-quality, of any decent poem." Tilling's words are self-congratulatory, inflated, duplicitous, ridiculous, and, finally, empty—just like Trilling's words, in fact.

Simpson looked this over in advance. "There's a style all of your own—a kind of innocence that kills—and I don't really see how it could be improved." But he was concerned about a lawsuit. "I think the Trillings and their clique quite capable of being very nasty, especially as they have a vested interest in their reputation, and no humor."[58]

This was a parody positively begging to be written, and it revealed the common cause of Bly and his comrades and Ginsberg and his. Both camps were reacting against and seeking an antidote to the hide-bound, fusty traditionalism of the academic poets who still controlled the way poetry was taught in the universities and disseminated in established literary magazines. Compared to the academy's exasperation, Bly's criticisms of the Beats were relatively measured. His journal entry, written the day after the reading, gives an indication of this and his own preconceptions: "Surprised throughout at prosiness. Also all more intelligent and rational than I had guessed. Some warmth."[59]

Bly's magazine was gaining notoriety for slicing humor, and also using it in advertising. He placed an ad in Columbia University's *Columbia Spectator*: "We celebrate the new decade with a parody of Diana Trilling's article on the Beats' Reading at Columbia from the recent *Partisan Review*. Let the era of literary flattery be over." Even in the *Partisan Review* he placed an ad for his parody.[60] Also in the *Village Voice*: "*The Fifties*: Our publications are not chosen by Jacques Barzun, Lionel Trilling, or W.H. Auden! Amazing!" The *Voice* set this just above an ad Harper & Brothers took out for *The House of Intellect* by those very three.[61] A second *Voice* ad took a swipe at all sorts of poets: "*The Fifties* / Soon to become *The Sixties* / 'American poetry today is too old-fashioned.' / A poetry magazine opposing Ransom, the Universities, the junkies, the isolationists, the buggy drivers, and the rationalists."[62] A third consisted solely of three paragraphs excerpted from the Tilling piece.[63]

Bly wrote to Hall:

> We hear more rumors that Diana Trilling will sue, but I doubt it. At a party a few nights ago, a man rushed up saying, "I want to congratulate you on that article on Mrs. Trilling, etc.! I am Norman Podhoretz [editor of *Commentary*]." That was weird. I told him flatly that among the people I knew he was considered as a Trilling stooge and nothing more—he seemed to consider that reputation unfair, and swore he had never slept with Diana Trilling. It's all fantastic. [64]

A final major attack follows. "The Order of the Blue Toad is herewith awarded to Norman Cousins, editor of the *Saturday Review*, for putting out a boring, stupid magazine. His list of reviewers is enough to make anyone die of boredom.... Why waste paper on such junk?" While that magazine's attention to Albert Schweitzer's atom-test appeal, John Ciardi's blast against Anne Morrow Lindbergh, and Cousins' opposition to the A.E.C. are all acknowledged positively, they are insufficient, for "the magazine itself bends to every wind." The consequence is "that if Cousins wants to bore people to death and still get rich, he will have to accept insults. We therefore award him The Blue Toad, painted on a background of bedroom slippers, couched and rampant. The Toad is riding a fast turntable, and croaking scientific maxims." Bly's good humor and fanatic heart sometimes hit their mark to good effect. He told Hall: "Norman Cousins wrote an insane letter saying that he agreed with us, and was going to try to make the *Sat. Review* better!"[65]

Ciardi, that magazine's poetry editor, on the other hand, was peeved. Although his complaint is not extant, Bly's response is:

> You may not like what stands on page 57, but believe me, the *Saturday Review* and your part in it recently has been pure junk. Those quarterly roundups are so insipid they're painful. Also, I could hardly believe your recommendations for poetry this last year: in a year when both Simpson and Wright, for instance, published good books, as well as Gary Snyder and Snodgrass, you recommend that wilted flower, Hollis Summers. You're out of your mind.[66]

This is an unbridled retort that fits with Bly's increasing sense of his own Odinic power.

The list of contributors ends with an extended comment starting as a response to feedback on the second issue and then circling back to this issue's theme:

> In arguing that the poetry of the Black Mountain group is not avant-garde, we do not claim that the poetry in *The Fifties* is; on the contrary, we believe there is no real avant-garde in American poetry. The term avant-garde or modernist movement, or new literature movement, has, we believe, an overlooked meaning: it has been used in Europe and South America for nearly a century to describe *poetry heavy with images from the unconscious.* ... Pound and Williams have consistently looked for a poetry of clarity and reason; the poets who have learned from them have accordingly aimed for a spare, bare poetry, and one result is a poetry of very few images. This neglect of the unconscious and absorption in reason we interpret to be the stamp not of modern French or Spanish movements, but of our own Emersonian or Puritan, American isolationist tradition. It is a great tradition, but it has dominated too long.

While Bly seems to distance himself from the label avant-garde, the magazine itself controverts that. As usual, he tips his hat to some major figureheads of modernism, but he urges their followers to break free of traditional routine and answer the call of a new imagination.

Finally, the back cover reads:

REASSURANCE FROM THE GOVERNMENTS OF
RUSSIA, ENGLAND, AND THE UNITED STATES:
Only one percent of the new-born will be deformed.

Negative reactions to such comments only fanned the flames of Bly's penchant to incite in this way.

Meanwhile, demands continued to mount. He wanted to spend more time with his poetry, and he would. There were other opportunities as well. For example, Hall asked Bly to interview Williams for the *Paris Review*. He declined, saying: "I have promised myself not to do any prose or criticism etc. of any kind for anything other than *The Fifties* for at least two or three years. ...whatever prose I do, I want it to help *The Fifties* to accomplish its purposes...."[67] Nevertheless, this pledge would be transitory. And there was another important development—a new decade had begun.

5

Wringing the Swan's Neck

Wright was honored at the Poetry Society of America's dinner at the Waldorf-Astoria on January 21, 1960, and the Blys were his guests.[1] Despite eager anticipation and the presence of Robert Graves, Robert Frost, Marianne Moore, Delmore Schwartz, and others, Bly described it as "a horrible, depressing banquet of low intelligence, and pitiful egoism and ambition, after which everyone was depressed for hours."[2]

There were less formal and less upsetting New York social events. At a cocktail party hosted by the art critic Harold Rosenberg earlier that month, the Blys met Norman Podhoretz again, critic Alfred Kazin, cartoonist and illustrator Saul Steinberg, painter Philip Guston, Frederick Morgan, editor of *Hudson Review*, and his assistant William Arrowsmith. A few weeks later, Bly told Wright that he and Levertov had visited Williams, that he was planning to take the Williamses to see Ingmar Bergman's *Wild Strawberries*, and that in April, Jackson Mathews, Hecht, and he would read with Yves Bonnefoy at an event organized by Betty Kray.[3]

Bly was now teaching part-time at NYU, and overseeing the reading series for Kray at the YMHA Poetry Center. He was still working on his "Morgan book." He contracted to translate, from Danish, Hans Hvass's *The Illustrated Book of Reptiles and Amphibians of the World*. This effort netted $800, "which keeps us here on the farm for five or six months."[4] He was also translating Trakl, Jiménez, and Vallejo.

In the spring, Bly wrote to Hall: "It was reported to me that John Hollander didn't like the third issue of *The Fifties* so well! Do you still write to Gunn? What did he think of it? Please send one to old T.S. Hellalot, or mention it to him, if you happen to write him, and I'll send him one."[5] Hugo thought it "a true improvement." He affirmed Bly's speaking out with "a nasty voice on public issues," and urged him to continue. "This has almost died out in America, and I say, let's bring back the nastiness of Mencken."[6]

Kinnell wrote: "I liked all but Ignatow. The Hall piece, after all, very good. It is clear at all times you are moved by justice, & you can be as biting as you like."[7] Dickey also weighed in on the *Fifties*: "It is lively; it is outspoken; it publishes good European and South American writers. Its articles are refreshingly unacademic. It seems to me to go a long way toward restoring the sense of the necessity of poetry: its interaction with the lives of all of us. And as a subject for controversy!" He did, however, advise Bly to drop Crunk: "You are not going to further your 'cause' by lengthy commentaries on the dead-heads like Edgar Bowers and others you project articles on."[8] Soon Dickey would realize that Crunk's work on contemporary poets was essential.

Anselm Hollo said: "It is wonderful to come across a magazine that corresponds with/to one's own preoccupations and opinions to an astonishing degree." He found #3 in a bookshop in London, "and after reading Celan's 'Death Fugue' and your editorial I knew that 'this is it,' that the *Fifties/Sixties* are truly part of 'it,' the ohsonecessary renaissance renewal and free flowering of poetry and life, the voyage to jungles and caves and to the eternal sea—." He ended: "Believe me: your magazine is, or at least this issue I have is, the very best of its kind I have seen for years."[9]

George Hitchcock, an editor of *San Francisco Review* (later founding editor of *kayak*), wrote: "Believe me, it is the only poetry magazine in the country that makes sense...Keep it up—it's a refreshing wind out of Pine Island."[10] Hilton Kramer, the *New York Times*' art critic, said: "Like a lot of other people, I suppose, I had wondered how the magazine happened to emerge from Pine Island, Minnesota." He praised the piece on Lorca and René Char, and, making his stance clear, continued:

The point about Surrealism in relation to American poetry is a very important one, and I think a lot of "responsible" poets and critics have been afraid to face it for fear (among other things) that they might be giving comfort to the enemy—O'Hara, the Beats, and that crowd—who carry on such a heavy traffic in fake Surrealism. I am altogether grateful to you for pursuing such a clear course between the Beats and their phony freedom and the academics with their empty rectitude.[11]

Logan, another poet and new friend, was teaching at Notre Dame. "I read the Donald Hall essay you wrote and found it (as well as the note on Char and Lorca) very provocative and in fact profound. The problem of the lack of an image has deeply wounded me I realize—like looking in a mirror and seeing only other people."[12]

Then Lewis Turco reported from the Iowa Writers' Workshop on the cumulative effect *The Fifties* was having in the poetic trenches: "The new elegance is dying hard here, but it is dying... I've been writing nothing but syllabics and free verse for months now. They work well for me. About everyone in the workshop is trying them both. No one listens to Engle when he hops in and starts shooting. Don Justice is writing syllabics too."[13] This was good news.

Not everyone was so positive. Dan Langton, in the Bay Area, admitted that he, "a poet of order & reason & intellect," had been thrown off balance by the third issue. "I would never be satisfied with a poem if I had not absorbed it completely, was <u>consciously</u> certain of everything I said...I am afraid of the dark, of anarchy, of blood."[14]

Transatlantic recognition came with John Wain's write-up in London's *Observer*. "This is a magazine with a programme.... whether one accepts the initial thesis or not,...the editors make it livelier still by accompanying the poems with a button-holing critical commentary on the situation in general, with particular reference to poetry but bringing in many other things." He added that he found the polemic mostly unconvincing, and he was "particularly skeptical of one of Mr. Bly's pet theories, which is that English poetry had led American poetry into a desert."[15] Bly wrote Hall about Wain's comments: "I was very pleased with it.

He is smart, and gave his own opinion, and saw the difference between this little two headed baby and the other tree stumps. Naturally I didn't agree with the third & fourth paragraphs, but one could hardly expect an Englishman to swallow the old dry cowpie I offered them."[16]

Many respondents focused on the potent humor. Cultural critic Dwight Macdonald wrote: "The parody of D.T. was masterly (alas, for she is a good woman and a friend) and terribly funny…It was so good, in fact, that I'm enclosing $2 for a year's sub, lest I miss something similar. (I also like the Blue Toad awards to Fiedler and Cousins.)"[17] Elizabeth Hardwick, Lowell's wife and a frequent contributor to *Partisan Review*, said much the same.[18] Michael Rumaker, a recent graduate of Black Mountain College, called the parody "delicious," and added: "You're (your mag is) excellent at this sort of <u>much</u> needed satire—and the pungency of the Blue Toad award! Such a pleasure, yet so strange that the deflating of solemn asses is so rare (& yet so necessary!)."[19] Hiram Haydn, editor of *American Scholar* and at Atheneum said: "The piece on Diana Trilling had me in stitches. I laughed till the tears came home…You're doing a valuable work. Keep it up."[20] Gene Frumkin, editor of *Coastlines* (in Los Angeles), appreciated "the demolition of Mrs. D.T. for which I kiss your cheeks… *The Fifties* has seemed to me one of only two or 3 mags worth reading for the pleasure of it."[21]

Erik Wensberg, editor of the *Columbia University Forum* (on whose Editorial Advisory Board sat Diana's husband), was not at all pleased. Bly responded to his "nasty letter," saying: "Your attempt to evade the criticism of Mrs. Trilling by maintaining that we wrote the satire only because we cannot bear the sight of success does not carry much conviction." Furthermore, he says, "You admit that the attack on the *Saturday Review* has a firm intellectual ground, and then are forced to maintain the attack on Mrs. Trilling's piece was sheer spite. This is ridiculous."[22]

Wright thought it "the fullest and soundest issue yet to appear."[23] He agreed that something was wrong in American poetry, yet he was getting more uncomfortable with Bly's approach: "You yourself very vigorously recognize the need for change, and your mention of the possibilities available to us in other literatures is a great, a major statement—or it would be, if you offered it as a possibility (the opening of a door) rather than as what you still too often seem to make it: a despotic command."[24]

Bly tried to address some of Wright's concerns and defend himself at the same time:

> In your last letter, you were troubled that the magazine was trying to force writers to write in one way only—but how can that be, when the first issue described the problem as getting nearer to modern industrial life, streetcars and so on; the second, according to [Stanley] Kunitz certainly, talked of iambs and leaving iambs as the way, and the third talked of nothing but the unconscious! Every issue suggests a different way of growth...The fourth issue will emphasize something else I think. But certainly strong ideas are best, at the beginning?[25]

For such an idiosyncratic publication, the need to rest on the shoulders of one person is plain. Bly sought and accepted advice and comment, but his own vision rarely wavered.

Later that year, just before the appearance of #4, Wright struck a more affirmative note, urging Bly to publish forthcoming issues more frequently:

> You must surely realize how very many editors and reviewers are noticing the magazine, and noticing it with the deepest interest...I may be wrong; but I have the impression that a very large number of American writers of hitherto "established" position...are finally being forced to realize that something is wrong, and—this is the best point—that there are resources of imagination in ourselves and in the places where we live now that are tremendous. You have started this fire of response.[26]

Alas, the magazine was unlikely to appear either more often, or regularly. Also, from Bly's perspective, this "fire of response" was still too limited. His persistent disillusionment with the preponderant poetic ethos is clear in his critique of *Paris Review* 21, which he offered to Hall, its poetry editor: "Of the poems as a whole, which are very likely the best you received, I think they show that American poetry now hardly needs *The Fifties* or anyone else to whisk it away; it is already dead on its feet."[27]

Hall was involved with the second edition of the *New Poets* anthology, to which Bly had been asked to contribute. He told Hall: "I wouldn't appear in [Donald] Allen's anthology if he asked me, and I don't want to appear in [Ronald] Pack's either. I don't despise Pack, nor Allen, but Pack is so conservative that the sense of poetry begins to disappear, just as Allen is so obsessed with the obvious that the sense of poetry begins to disappear with him also."[28] A couple of weeks later he added:

> Did you see Richard Foster's article in the new *Perspective*? It is a great blast of the *New Poets of England and America*. It takes Pack apart with accuracy, speaks of [Robert] Mezey with contempt, and even ventures on forbidden ground in pulling Wilbur's nose. (How is that for a mixed metaphor!?) ... At the end, he blasts *The Fifties* also, and calls me a jackass, but I like the article as a whole. He tends to be a nay-sayer, but that is the first step toward sanity, after all.
>
> More and more I am struck by the incredibly poor criticism in this country... The reviews show timid and provincial ignorance of the most squalid sort.
>
> The "new criticism" should be called the "no criticism," to fit with "no directions" [= *New Directions*] and "pig table" [= *Big Table*]. And don't tell me England is any better—they remember what criticism is like—the same way one remembers a bad-mannered cousin, now fortunately dead.[29]

In sum, there was much encouragement and much that needed fixing.

Given the magazine's higher profile, the number of submissions kept increasing.[30] Bly wrote Hall in early August: "The 4th issue has been postponed horribly... but that will burst from its eccentric cocoon one day."[31] Later that month, Simpson and his wife stayed at the farm for two weeks on their way back to Berkeley, and Louis lent his assistance.[32]

Advertising efforts increased as well. Preceding election day, as Eisenhower's term was coming to an end and Nixon and Kennedy were running neck-and-neck, this appeared in *The Paris Review*:

> Thoughts in an Election Year: Leslie Fiedler is the Nixon of the literary world. John Ciardi is Jim Hagerty, and Yvor Winters is

J. Edgar Hoover. J. Donald Adams is Mamie. Jacques Barzun is Chiang Kai-Chek.

The academic poetry of the last twenty years, moreover, resembles the results of the Republican Farm Policy: we now have huge surpluses of poems. These poems cannot be used to help anyone to live, however, and are stored in anthologies and libraries for which the government is paying rent. The good that could have come from the ground has been lost by determined isolationism. The Beat poetry is equally isolationist and resembles the filibusters of Senator Long.[33]

Another full-page ad ran in the *Hudson Review*. Its tone is more restrained, with a matter-of-fact description of the contents, and then this: "Satire on assorted old fogies such as Gilbert Highet, Diana Trilling, Norman Cousins, Leslie Fiedler, etc." It also mentioned that the Order of the Blue Toad award "for intellectual mediocrity, was given last time to Norman Cousins, [and] is awarded this time with appropriate inscription to Jacques Barzun."[34] A similar ad was published by the *San Francisco Chronicle* and *The Nation*, but rejected by *The New Republic*. Thus Bly complained to Gilbert Harrison: "It is precisely because of editors like you, who will allow the truth to be said about figures in politics, but not about similar figures in literature, that the literary world gets into dull states, as it is in at present."[35]

In early December, advance copies of *The Sixties* (so renamed) went out, as usual, to Simpson, Hall, Wright, and Duffy.[36] The rest arrived in New York at the end of the month, handed over to Bly duty-free, as before. But soon the Bureau of Customs caught up with him. The main reason was that he had changed "quarterly" to "occasionally" on the masthead.[37] That change was necessary, however, for it's easy to imagine both the irritation of subscribers who kept checking their mailboxes for "quarterly" issues that never seemed to arrive and the unpleasantness of responding to their persistent complaints. Bly said later: "My wife's idea is that when someone subscribes to *The Sixties* we ought to ask for the next of kin, because the subscriber may die before he gets his next issue."[38]

Another change was the place of publication, from the Duffy house in Pine Island to the Bly farm in Madison; that is, from

Carol Bly as business manager of The Sixties Press in Madison, MN.

one side of the state to the other. Duffy's primary roles had been to help finance the magazine and to take care of business matters, although his involvement extended further. A St. Paul newspaper reported: "Headquarters for *The Fifties* is 'the pig room'—Mrs. Duffy's name for the upstairs bedroom where she and her husband 'lived like pigs' the winter they remodeled the rest of the house. Piled up on a maple desk are manuscripts from all over the country and a card file listing their date of arrival and final disposition."[39] Another local newspaper said they received "an influx of manuscripts at an average rate of 200 per day."[40] Either that reporter made an error, or Duffy was pulling his leg. The following description of his workload may be at least slightly less exaggerated:

> Most manuscripts come to Duffy at Pine Island. He works after school evenings and 15 to 20 hours a day Saturday and Sunday reviewing at least half the manuscripts. Then he bundles them all up and sends them off to Bly in New York. Bly reviews Duffy's choices, edits the rest and the two get together on their selections for publication. The two take pride in the fact they use no printed rejection slips, but will return all unwanted manuscripts within three weeks with notes telling the poets why their work was rejected and what might be done to improve it.[41]

Such super-efficiency, had it existed, would have made the magazine something other than what it was.

Duffy offered opinions on submissions as a matter of course, and the two batted ideas back and forth, though Duffy inevitably deferred to Bly's judgment. But Duffy's carelessness with subscribers was finally too much. Bly adds: "I went to [his] house and found checks falling out of drawers...."[42] A letter from Carol reveals part of the process of handing over the reins. She writes: "Thank you for the clear, wonderful list of subscriptions. No complaints. Except half those libraries you listed as wanting a subscription beginning with #3 were simply renewing. But who cares, for cat's sake."[43] From then on, assuming the title of Business Manager, she dealt with subscriptions and related correspondence, did a lot of typing, and occasionally worked at securing copyright.[44] As noted in the introduction, Odin House now became the official mailing address.

In the summer of 1960, Duffy and his wife left to teach at the American School in Tangier, Morocco. Before their departure, they spent one last weekend in Madison, which was marked by typical craziness. Bly wrote:

> Chris and Bill went back Sunday on the bus, Bill wearing a
> French foreign-legion hat, with a veil down the neck to keep
> off the sun—which Carol had made for him—and Chris was
> so mad she didn't want to be seen next to him at the hotel in
> Madison, and begged him not to wear it. He wore it, with dark
> glasses, much to the astonishment of the ticket seller, and would
> occasionally say to Chris in a loud voice: "What are you going
> to tell your husband, darling?"[45]

Tangier in those days was a destination of many writers.[46] As Duffy wanted to stay involved, Bly asked Kerryman to ship him 95 copies, but they never arrived.[47] That left Duffy even further out of the loop. He returned home in 1961, after which came the formal dissolution of their partnership.[48]

Three quotations, fruits of Bly's reading and reflection, serve as this issue's thematic signposts. First, from Octavio Paz: "Poetry either leaps into the unknown, or it is nothing." The notion of "leaping," eventually a centerpiece of Bly's poetics, here reiterates the importance of the unconscious and of flight from the tyranny of reason. "Nothing," moreover, is applied by Crunk in this issue to some prose, and to some prosy poetry. Second, from Harold Rosenberg's *The Tradition of the New*: "Revolution in art lies not in the will to destroy but in the revelation of what already is destroyed." This sounds like the kind of revolution that Bly intended. Echoing this idea, but in imagistic language, is the final line, from Jiménez: "Roots and wings—but let the wings grow roots and the roots fly!"

The fourth issue opens with Bly's translation of "The Swan" by Enrique González Martínez, "one of the finest poets of Mexico in this century." The great Nicaraguan poet, Rubén Darío, founder of Modernismo, had used the swan as the emblem of his very formal poetics, but Martínez was signaling the advent of a new poetry. If *The Fifties / The Sixties* ever had a programmatic poem, this is it:

> *Take this swan with puffy plumage, and wring his neck,*
> *Who gives his white touch to the blue of the fountain pool;*
> *He displays his elegance only, but does not understand*
> *The soul of creatures, or the voice of the silent fields.*
>
> *Keep away from all forms, and all styles of speaking*
> *That do not change quickly to follow the secret rhythms*
> *Of the life that is deepest...and adore life*
> *Intensely, and make life grasp your devotion.*
>
> *See the intelligent owl, how he lifts his wings*
> *Abandoning the Greek mountain, he leaves the shelter of Pallas,*
> *And finishes his silent moody flight on that tree...*
>
> *He does not have the elegance of the swan, but his troubled*
> *Eye, which pierces into the darkness, reads*
> *The mysterious book of the silences of night.*

Here is a perfect illustration of how non-English poetry could be instructive for young American poets. It is as if Martínez steals the owl of Athena, the manifestation of reason, and adapts it, as the bird of darkness, to the cause of the irrational, the unconscious, the new imagination. Bly wrote Hall the following summer: "we have a new subscription brochure complete with a new emblem! How do you like it—that old owl with his claws around a vulture? (That's me! The vulture is Ciardi who has just eaten [Robert] Hillyer.) Do you think we should substitute it entirely for the horse and rider, or use both?"[49] Was Odin to be upstaged by an owl?

Next are seven poems by Antonio Machado, four translated by Bly (one of those as Charles Reynolds). Anne Sexton responded almost breathlessly with 'deep thanks' for the second, "From the Doorsill...", saying she'd "write Hitler a fan letter for that translation," and adding "you are not Hitler, but a reasonable young man who writes poems and lives in Minnesota (I think)." She then suggests that Bly forward her praise to Machado, "which consists of reading it and gasping oh my god!"[50]

The other three are translated by Willis Barnstone. Norman Thomas di Giovanni had previously suggested to Wright that Barnstone could use his and Bly's help.[51] Bly relays his first impressions: "He has had, maybe, one too many foreign languages at a good school, but he has nothing of the charlatan, or the publicity-hound; he has a true devotion to poetry, there is no doubt of it."[52]

In "A Note on Antonio Machado," Bly says: "Poetry is related to sensitivity; almost every poet agrees to that, but poets in this country tend to be sensitive to ideas and intellectual formulations...and the Spanish poets...are actually sensitive to owls, darkness, and the sea." Bly quotes the Spanish poet Pedro Salinas on Machado: "he said, 'kill your words and listen to your soul.'" In the present context, we might restate this as "kill the swan and listen to the owl."

Six poems by Lorca are next, two translated by Bly, two by Wright, and two by J.A. Cottonwood, who, according to the note, "lives in Salisbury, North Carolina. This is his first published translation." (Another fib; it's Bly again.[53]) "Song of Málaga" includes this surrealistic image: "Black horses and dark / People are riding / Over the deep roads / Of the guitar." Bly had first quoted this in "Five Decades of Modern American Poetry" (*The Fifties* 1) to distinguish the new imagism from Pound's.

Although in previous issues Bly had translated from Swedish, Danish, French, German, and Czechoslovakian, Spanish was new for him. He wrote to Hall in early 1959: "I am learning how to pronounce Spanish, and have started to learn by beginning on Vallejo's poem *The Spider*, which I am crazy about—I think it is one of the greatest poems I have ever read."[54] A short time later he said about Spanish Poetry: "Everything I see indicates it is a real treasure lost in the sea."[55]

The essay "On Current Poetry in America" is surprisingly brief. Bly says: "Our poetry in English for the last two hundred years suffers from continual overstatement." He also comments on the disproportion between humble emotions and the vast edifice of form, "developed by centuries of passion":

> This is a strange situation…we are no longer sensitive to form, and to what form *says*. Form speaks, just as the inner content speaks, but what if they don't say the same thing? Often in America, the poem grunts, and the form speaks in highly polished Cambridge English. Or the poem sails over the horizon as a huge fluffy swan, and when we look beneath, we see a small scrawny chicken.

These metaphors are distinctively Bly's, and new, but he has expressed the underlying ideas before. Still, it was important to keep up the pressure, not only because resistance continued strong among the entrenched formalists and the younger poets under their influence, but also because there were many others who had not yet gotten the message.

In the new installment of "Madame Tussaud's Wax Museum," Bly returns to "The Swan." He points to Rosenberg's essay on "French Silence and American Poetry" and the need to quiet the rhetoric that persists among even the most "modern" of American writers. He quotes poems of three poetry editors, Ciardi (*Saturday Review*), Howard Moss (*The New Yorker*), and John Hollander (*Partisan Review*), plus Jack Kerouac, and, in an absurd finish, Lascelles Abercrombie (who had been a poet, scholar, and teacher at Oxford, influential among British poets of the 1920s and 30s). Despite their obvious differences, these five writers have one trait in common: they are all swans. The inference is that they should be—metaphorically—strangled.

As promised, Crunk considers "The Work of W.S. Merwin."

Earlier, Merwin had written: "I see by your prospectus that you plan to write a piece about my dead hands. I can tell you that they had no rings on them, ever. That, at least. And that they wore out their gloves. Palmist, they were taught not to tell teachers anything."[56] As usual, Crunk is almost brutally direct.[57] "Mr. Merwin's best poems...show a strange kind of genius; still, the most striking characteristic of his work seems to me to be wastage of words." He stays too much on the surface, instead of diving "to the core of the emotion."

Crunk presents a hierarchy of literary intensity. Poetry is at the top; then "fiction like that of Salinger, Hemingway, Bellow;" followed by "essay and newspaper prose;" and last, "a level of writing empty even of information, which would have to be described as *nothing*." All of these levels are evident in Merwin's poetry. He quotes from his first book, *A Mask for Janus*, and says: "These lines have no emotional meaning, no intellectual meaning, no political meaning, no religious meaning, no dramatic meaning, nothing." Then about a poem in his second book, *The Dancing Bears*: "This parade of nothingness is frightening, and gives us a sense of emptiness like that of hell."

Merwin has too many set poems on classical and biblical themes: "Of all the infinite subjects for poetry, why should these chestnuts be hauled out of the fire again and again?" Also, his focus on things leads to "flat and stale poetry."

> We have endless poems on railway stations, urinals, aunts, Beat subway cars and dead cats. The absorption in a poetry of things is shared by almost all the poets in America today, regardless of "school." It is the quality that the poetry of Lowell and of Merwin has in common with that of the Beats, as well as with the poetry of the Black Mountain group...[58]

Crunk intrepidly takes on just about everyone, it seems.

"The main stream of poetry, however, in my opinion, moves in another direction." By "main stream" Crunk means (taking the widest possible view) Tu Fu, Baudelaire, Jiménez, Rilke, Vallejo, Neruda, and Blas de Otero. "Here the use of unconscious imagery is not intended to shock, but is merely an extension of the personal." This is the direction in which poets like Merwin should move. The summation of the negative criticism is that Merwin's poetry shows "a lack of inwardness."

Crunk becomes more positive, noting the power of some of Merwin's poems, including selections from his forthcoming book: "The new poems exist in a real landscape and the people are real, not shadows out of books…He has actually a wonderfully resonant imagination, which senses depth everywhere." Our guide then announces, in his customary metaphorical way:

> This must be the end of a short tour through Mr. Merwin's work…Behind his poetry, he presents the picture of a genuine, enduring, and graceful man, marred by a reluctance to be extreme. He lives on earth as though in a warm room, surrounded by a world of smiling objects, all of which he sleepily understands, as if he had known everything once and then forgotten it, like a great general born into the world again as a member of the animal kingdom.

At journey's end, we tourists gaze in wonder at this remarkable scene.

As mentioned earlier, Bly had first heard Merwin in the spring of 1958. He told Hall about it:

> Merwin…read fine new poems…sharp as tacks, and is terribly charming…I couldn't place this strange lazy charm, and it wasn't until he read a new poem about watching sparrows, carefully, on Boston Common that I realized, of course, the fellow is an incarnated cat! A wonderfully sleek Persian with electric hair, bright cat eyes, quiet feet like a tabby, and a lover of wing chairs and laps! It is curious how, in his poems, he slowly prowls around and around the subject matter in the poem, and then suddenly, in the last line, pounces on it![59]

Merwin had also offered his services: "if you…would like me to help out let me know. This goes for other translations of Spanish—or French, Portuguese or Italian."[60]

A few months after this essay, Simpson told of meeting Merwin, "a very nice fellow, and not at all pleased with your article on his work."[61] Bly became concerned, and eventually Merwin responded:

All the criticisms you made of my work I'd levelled at myself, not at the time perhaps, but since, and fairly thoroughly. Please don't feel that I was or am offended by your piece. And the respect and interest which prompted it were apparent to me. What happened was—I was puzzled. Not by your piece itself, but by the combination of that and the card you sent me to tell me of its imminent appearance. Never having met you it struck me that the latter was an attempt to be diplomatic, to be critical on the one hand and smooth on the other, and it was the combination that put me off. Sorry; I've realized since, from reading things of yours, and from talking to mutual friends, that such behavior would have been out of character and that the card must have been a simple gesture of goodwill in the circumstances.[62]

It is interesting to see Crunk's slicing criticism juxtaposed with Bly's almost disarming anxiety that the object of that criticism not think it unfair. Their mutual friend Kinnell offered his opinion: "The Merwin piece…was just, & of all criticism of him is the only piece likely to force him to think over his art. My guess is he will do something tremendously good next time, & very new."[63] This is exactly the kind of salutary effect that Bly the critic was after.

A section of "Some New Poems" follows. Two are by Levertov, whom, Bly tells Wright, he was seeing "maybe once a week or so," since she lived a block and a half away. "Nude Kneeling in Sand" is by Logan, "a wonderful man," who was starting his own little magazine, *Chicago Choice*.[64] Both Levertov and Logan would be specimens for Crunk's dissection. Duffy, erstwhile co-editor, is the third poet, with "Love Poem" and "The Horse is Loose." These may have been among those for which Bly thanked Wright: "Some of them are wonderful, incredibly good, with wonderful leaps of imagination. Some of them, also, you evidently found by yourself, on old envelopes, etc., since I had certainly never seen them before."[65] Also there is "Rain," by Benjamin Clemenson, "born in Caldwell, New Jersey. He took a law degree, and is currently running for sheriff of Erie County, New York." (A pseudonym, this time for Wright.) Finally, a marvelous poem by Bly himself, "Restless in the Fall Afternoon":

I

I cannot wait for the night to come again,
And the huge stars to come –
All over the heavens! Bowls of cradles and black pools
And the blue to fade away.

II

You must be alone six hours before you look at the stars –
Then coming out into the dark heavens
You will be like a drunkard returning to his table.

III

There is a huge star that stands alone in the Western darkness:
Arcturus. When I read that the Arabs called it
The Keeper of Heaven, I felt a strange joy. I think
It was in the womb that I received
The thirst for the dark heavens.[66]

There are still more American poems in a section titled "Four War Poems."[67] The first, by Hugo, is a 70-line excerpt from a long poem, "Mission to Linz." Initially he had resisted, though he appreciated Bly's taking the time to cut it down, calling it "very generous." As he explained, "I got the idea for writing the repeated phrases etc. from Mozart's Linz symphony."[68] Eventually they hammered it out, and a portion of two movements appears here. The excerpt describes both the mortal fear of those on board the bomber and the aseptic barrier between them and their victims. (Hugo had been in the Air Force over Germany.)

Although remarkably strong-willed, Hugo is another poet who submitted to Bly's instruction and reading suggestions. Apparently, Bly sent him a copy of the mystical treatise, *Theologica Germanica*. And he was reading Rilke (which he said was "like seeing Spring come again"), Blake, Buddhist works, and Ernst Cassirer's *The Myth of the State*. He admits his continuing hesitance at so much reading. "It is as if I am walking around looking at the flowers when suddenly I realize I am a flower." Yet he persists, he says, "purely upon your insistence," revealing that, if nothing else, "it takes me away from my loneliness."[69]

The second poem in this group, "A Dream of the Second

World War," is by a repeat contributor, Kresenky (aka Bly). Seymour Faust, whose first book had recently been published by Rothenberg, contributes the third. Last is Simpson's "Carentan O Carentan." It was very important, in Bly's view, for his generation of poets to write about the grim realities of World War II.

A new feature is "Books of Poetry Published in 1959." According to Bly, the five most interesting books were Snyder's *Riprap*, Simpson's *A Dream of Governors*, Creeley's *A Form of Women*, Snodgrass's *Heart's Needle*, and Wright's *Saint Judas*. (All these younger poets had been published or written about in *The Fifties / The Sixties.*) Among the older poets, new work by Berryman and Lowell is cited as worthy of note. "Among poets older still, Pound brought out new cantos," that is, *Thrones*. "This is an impressive group of books for one year." It is interesting how, despite his sharp criticism of the latter three elsewhere, in this context Bly is quite positive about them. He mentions some recent translations, but, he says: "There was no good Rilke, Lorca, Jiménez, Alberti, Guillén, Hernández, Baudelaire, Montale, Paz, or any of the South Americans. As usual, the translations of the Nobel Prize winners were horrible." Finally, a word about magazines: "*The Quarterly Review of Literature* brought out a fine issue devoted to Hölderlin. The issue shows great editorial care and intelligence."[70]

Another new feature is a review of Simpson's *A Dream of Governors*. Crunk signals his intention to follow up regularly on new work by former subjects of his. He still complains: "The poet is describing new experiences and inner sensations, for which there is no extensive precedent in English poetry, with a rhythm and diction developed in another century for totally different moods and events. Because the poem is divided against itself, a prosiness comes in." But he appreciates Simpson's description of the ugly truth, which needs to be stated. In a pleasing simile, he says: "Mr. Simpson's poetry at times is like a man who sits in a living-room quietly talking, and gradually smoke begins to come out of his ears, and to gather over his head. This sudden shift from one kind of reality to another seems to me one of the major qualities of his poems."

Then it is back to barbed fun with "The Order of the Blue Toad," awarded to Jacques Barzun, author of *The House of Intel-*

lect, "for his middle-class hatred of art and poetry disguised as a defence of intellect." Bly tars Auden and Lionel Trilling with the same brush, since they have joined forces with Barzun to oversee "The Mid-Century Book Society," which he views as a crass, money-making book club. They are like the three monkeys, Hear No Evil, See No Evil, and Think No Evil. Bly again deplores the co-opting of writers. "O Swift, where art thou?" he asks, acknowledging a need for even more pungent satire.

Yet another *Sixties* novelty comes in selections from "Stories of Cronopios and Famas" by Julio Cortázar of Argentina, translated by Paul Blackburn. These two little tales (almost fables, but without the explicit moral) involve three groups: the *famas*, or important ones; the *esperanzas*, or middle class; and the *cronopios*, the poor, artistic types. This is social commentary, to be sure, but also comment on the role of the poet. Blackburn, whom Bly had met in New York, had a Black Mountain pedigree.

Then there is "A Note on Miss Irita Van Doren," one more demonstration of the necessity for *Sixties*-style criticism. Bly plays a by-now-familiar tune: "It is strange that elsewhere—in France and Spain, for example—book reviews in the leading newspapers contribute to the intellectual life of the country, whereas *here* the *New York Times Book Review* and the *New York Herald Tribune Book Section* lay down vast mists, praising virtually everything; they surround the whole world of books with a neutrality like a fog." Hall had told him that he had reviewed Babette Deutsch's new book of poetry for Van Doren, editor of the *New York Herald Tribune Book Section* (since 1926).[71] His assessment, apparently not positive enough, was rejected. Bly, upset more in principle than on his friend's behalf, wanted to make an example of this incident. He first sent Hall a draft of this note: "I thought reasonableness was the best tone, and thought it best to...center the issue squarely on the details of 'fixed' editing, which are very interesting and very serious."[72] Hall made some changes, and expressed a worry, to which Bly replied: "I'll check with a lawyer, but I'm sure they won't sue."[73]

In the note as published, Hall is unnamed. Bly complains: "Behind such chicanery lies the typical American fear of harsh criticism, as well as a certain lack of intellectual honor... This is a sure way to kill the country's intellectual life." Deutsch responded, saying that Van Doren had never "suggested that I alter a review to flatter the author, nor rejected one of my reviews because it was unfavorable." Bly wrote back: "Of course she prints some unfavorable reviews; no one could deny that. But, in this case, she was protecting you. In doing so, she violated her own honor as an editor... This help may be flattering to you, but surely it is the kind of help that you should reject."[74] Bly could not make such charges and expect to go unchallenged, but he felt the need to defend intellectual and editorial integrity. This strong sense of mission was surely behind his feud with the *New York Times Book Review*.

"A Quotation from Tolstoy" has a brief preface: "Some readers feel we are too extreme, and that writers should be more respectful, etc. If you think we are extreme, you should read *The Kingdom of God is Within You*, by Tolstoy." The excerpt includes:

> [T]he hypnotization of the people...on which the power of the governments is based...is at the present time organized in the most complex manner, and beginning its action in childhood, continues over men to their death... The children are instilled with world-conceptions which were peculiar to their ancestors and are directly opposed to the modern consciousness of humanity.

The stress is explicitly political and social, though it has literary implications as well. Outspoken critics are needed in every time and place.

In "Ideas by Which We Live," Bly—lumping together a variety of denominations, unless he was primarily thinking of what he knew, Lutheranism—takes on what he calls "the Protestant Church," which "every day bends more and more to business and to flattery of the people... It helps very little in any spiritual life." "The American Protestant's Handbook" has quotations from advertisements, the clergy, and other sources, such as: "Christianity is Good Business!" "Christ was a businessman, too: he advertised the Word," and, "We should all be like Jesus and obey our fathers and mothers." This preposterous assemblage ends with words of the mystic Jacob Boehme: "And yet they always cry out: Here is the true Church, here is Christ, flock all hither!"[75] Although Bly had not abandoned the Norwegian Lutheran tradition in which he was raised, he always sought more avenues to spiritual growth.

A report: "The Longview Foundation announces that it has awarded a grant of $300.00 to Robert Bly for his contributions to *The Fifties* #1 and #2." This was one of thirty-three awards chosen by a committee that included Saul Bellow, Louise Bogan, Alfred Kazin, and Charles Boni. Rosenberg was behind it. He had written to Bly: "You certainly have managed to put together a lively magazine—there's no explanation for it except as a projection of the editor himself."[76] Bly welcomed the recognition, as long as it came from an acceptable source, with no strings attached, no implicit obligations, and no taint of co-opting by the middle-class.

Then more momentous news: "*The Sixties* announces the establishment of a small press for the publication of European, South American, and American poetry. We intend to publish five books a year." Bly had been thinking about this for a while.[77] The books planned for 1960 are: *Forty Poems of Juan Ramón Jiménez*, translated by Zea; *Twenty Poems of Georg Trakl*, by Wright and Bly; *Twenty Poems of Cesar Vallejo* and *Twenty Poems of Pablo Neruda*, by "various American poets;" and *The Continent Rising from the Sea*, "an anthology of the younger generation of American poets." (Of the titles mentioned in this ambitious announcement, one would never appear, and the rest trickled out over the next decade.)

"Wisdom of the Old" (last seen in #2) quotes Robert Penn Warren (in *Newsweek*, a middle-class magazine if there ever was one) on "meaning" and "structure," both serious matters. Bly's piling up of various comments—"structure of meanings," "structure with meaning," and the "meaning of structure"—results in something so convoluted as to be nonsensical. Thus the "wisdom" of the older generation, and also of the professoriate, is presented as ridiculous. With this, the swan's neck is given one final, partially self-induced, twist.

6

The Voyage into the

Sea of the Imagination

That Bly's literary universe continued to expand is due to the magazine's widening influence, his increased efforts on behalf of poets and editors, his use of vehicles other than *The Sixties* to convey his ideas, and his leap into book publishing. As usual, responses to the fourth issue were mixed. Pals like Simpson and Wright, of course, were enthusiastic.[1] Other young poets, Michael Benedikt and John Haines, were getting on board.[2] Adrienne Rich, a friend from college days, said with some clairvoyance: "The magazine is immensely alive and refreshing and valuable. Perhaps you will really succeed in giving this generation of poets an important part of its education."[3] Anne Sexton wrote about Crunk: "he is changing my life, whoever he is." She adds that she finds the magazine "a work of immediate genius."[4]

Among other contemporaries, Robert Hazel said: "Now, without qualm, I am ready to declare your magazine the best we have."[5] Roger Shattuck was encouraging, as was Howard Nemerov, though with a bit more ambivalence.[6] Members of an earlier generation such as Stanley Kunitz, Marguerite Harris, and John Hall Wheelock heaped on the praise—not without qualification.[7]

Ted Hughes expressed his admiration for the magazine's translations in particular, and asked Bly to send him others to be published in England. "I would like to see heavy doses of it coming out over here regularly—it's probably the only salvation, uproot a few of these oracular dry bodiless heads, & give the poets still in school a little courage."[8] Hardie St. Martin in Madrid offered to help with Spanish: "It would be a pleasure but, above all, please remember that I'm not trying to intrude on your property."[9] He became a long-time collaborator. Bly told Wright about meeting Octavio Paz (who once had an avant-garde magazine, *Barandal*) who "likes the *Sixties*, and gave me the names of some South American poets whom he liked."[10]

The noted translator Dudley Fitts was condescending and "full of hostility," as Bly's irascible response indicates. Bly begins, politely: "You have done an enormous amount, in your anthology of South American poetry, as well as elsewhere, to bring this Spanish-American and Spanish poetry to public attention in this country, which knew nothing of it." He also acknowledges a noted mistranslation as "an absurd error but one quite possible for people such as Wright and myself who have learned the language purely out of enthusiasm for the poetry, and who still know it very imperfectly." But, he adds, this "is not made more shameful because we criticized Jacques Barzun…Why should a writer who criticizes the mighty on intellectual grounds be more perfect in his own work than the writer who licks every literary boot in sight? This licking of literary boots has been the typical expression of the last ten years."[11]

Some present and future editors of little magazines were paying attention. John Logan, whose *Chicago Choice* was on the horizon, wrote: "You are doing an absolutely unique piece of work in these essays chockfull of intelligence, feeling, oracle. I don't know anything to compare them with."[12] Jim Harrison, still in college, was motivated to make a connection with Bly. In part, he was taken by the observation that academic verse is so highly rhetorical. "You aren't likely to wring a swan's neck if the swan provides your living. That's why most professors I know act, talk, look like, write like, insurance adjusters—coroners to the truly fated."[13] Felix Stefanile, editor of *Sparrow*, writes: "For some time now I have considered your magazine the very best by far of all the independent literaries."[14] The most interesting such exchange, however, was with Paul Carroll, editor of *Big Table*. He wrote:

> Congratulations! ... I admire yr guts & yr courage to stick out
> a critical neck, putting a plague on both houses, Academic &
> Beat...
>
> ...I think yr magazine is the most important, live
> contribution on the poetry scene today (*Big Table* excepted,
> of course!). What I most admire about *Fifties/Sixties*—in
> addition to gratitude for having the chance to read poets like
> Tuma & Machado...is the type of muscular, good criticism you
> produce.[15]

He sent Bly his two latest issues. Bly responded, "put[ting] a
plague" on Carroll's house:

> The best poems I thought were those by Logan, Creeley,
> Wright, Levertov, Hunt, and Snyder; your own poem was
> interesting also. I like the poems by [LeRoi] Jones and Duncan.
>
> The rest of it was the worst hogwash ever invented, in my
> opinion! I am serious. These "poems" by [Michael] McClure,
> for instance, Diane Di Prima, [Philip] Lamantia, [Bill] Berkson,
> [David] Meltzer....
>
> Among the others, Ashbery, O'Hara, and Koch are all
> intelligent men, in their ways, but the artificiality of their
> surrealism, which is really a kind of "false surrealism," puts them
> into the Nineteenth Century...
>
> Charles Olson's poetry is one of the worst hoaxes ever
> played on an unsuspecting public.[16]

Carroll's catholic tastes, his blurring of boundaries between various poetic schools, presented, in Bly's view, some real problems.

But Carroll was uncowed: "I appreciate & have learned from
yr thoughtful, good letter. Such a letter, with its care & concern,
is only one more proof of yr commitment to the art of poetry...
I will continue to publish Ginsberg & Burroughs & little Corso
whenever they send a good ms. Do not be so parochial as to feel
that they are incapable of writing a good poem. That simply isn't
so."[17] Such an open exchange may seem even more remarkable
now than it did then. Surely it exemplifies Bly's ideal. But the
intensity of his vision and the relative narrowness of his focus did
leave him vulnerable to charges of parochialism and other such

sins. After all, most of the poets he admitted to liking in *Big Table* had either been published or "Crunked" (or both) in *The Fifties / Sixties*. Were these the only good poets in the U.S.A.?

There seems also to have been an increase in the number of letters out of left field, from daft readers who sensed a kindred spirit. Yes, Bly was wild at times, and a risk-taker, but he was not unhinged; he was a rebel with a cause, his ideas and intentions were absolutely serious, well thought out, and woven in a fairly intricate design.

In late 1960 and early 1961, Bly was verging on a confrontation with a giant. While the antagonism had been festering, he explained the reason for the newest flare-up in a letter to Hall: "That damn *New York Times Book Review* reprinted a poem of mine in the July 24th issue without my permission, and I am going to send violent objections…That review is like fungus on the north side of trees."[18] Bly tried to rouse other poets to take collective action, reflecting his conviction that the poet is not a romantic recluse, insulated in an ivory tower, but a citizen of the world with a responsibility to speak out.

But the response was underwhelming. Kunitz, for example, wrote: "I am a dissenter from way back and no friend of the dreary *NY Times Book Review*, but I can't work up enough enthusiasm to sign your letter…It might be argued that for the sake of gaining an audience a poet ought to be willing to suffer a degree of insolence among fools."[19] Wheelock also rejected Bly's request: "Good grief! You must be hard up for a subject. Can't we get another one?…When I can spare the time, I enjoy quarreling—but I think I'd rather quarrel with Carlos Williams, or Robert Hillyer, or W.D. Snodgrass—oh, and yes, with Ezra Pound! There's another cantankerous guy, with a lot of time on his hands, who dotes on grievances."[20] Thus the letter was never sent.[21] Bly would find other means to vent his frustration.

In the spring of 1961, *The Nation* published Bly's critical essay, "Poetry in an Age of Expansion."[22] It was as provocative and quirky as any of Crunk's. "We can see the tracks of iconoclasm today, but the animal itself is rarely seen. We live instead in a time of praise…The flaccid affirmation of *The New York Times Book*

Review extends also into the fields of fiction and poetry." Furthermore, "a feeling of constriction" characterized the nineteenth century, which had a few iconoclasts (Jane Austen, Rimbaud, Whitman). But now, Bly continues, the problem is "a mood of infinite expansion." By that he means

> that we are half-conscious that too many babies are being born on earth, that cities are expanding, businesses are joining, publishers are merging, corporations growing bigger and bigger. Even ideas expand: industrialists become interested in Negroes and have liberal ideas, Continental Can supports Plato, old-time radicals believe in free enterprise—the living room of the thought expands to include everything. This expansion dominates morals, cool music, the mood of the country.

He also chews on that perennial bone of contention, form, faulting the academic poets for attempting to deal with expansion by imposing old forms on new material:

> I am thinking of Richard Wilbur, John Hollander, Thom Gunn, Allen Tate, Robert Penn Warren, Howard Nemerov, Yvor Winters and others. The comparison may not be entirely fair, but this group arrives at a position seemingly opposite, though in reality similar, to that of the Beats. Their position might be roughly stated as the belief that form is the same thing as spontaneity, reason is wildness, Apollonianism is Dionysianism, meter is breath, and at last, order is chaos.

No caution here; Bly names names, putting Academics and Beats in the same boat. He was fighting both the long-standing scholastic establishment and the newly-formed Beat one from a position he had staked out somewhere between the two.

The problem, Bly adds, is that "no one has yet figured out how to approach" this expansiveness in American life. "If America were truly iconoclastic in thought, the ideas suggested by the names Ransom, I.A. Richards, Eliot and Warren would long ago have been replaced by other ideas. Such supplanting is natural."[23] This is his called-for "raid," which consists not only of identifying the ideas and persons that are the problem, but of uprooting and replacing them.

The essay concludes on a more positive note: "Today, as the

mood becomes more and more expansive, the poem will grow shorter and more intense. I think one can also say that it is not the form of the poem that will be changed, but the poet's life." Bly suggests reading Wright, Creeley, Levertov, Logan, Snyder, Robert Hazel, Simpson, Haines, Hall, and Benjamin Clemenson. "It is not a matter of iconoclasm; poetry is beginning again."[24] There was new life in a new poetry.

The translator Di Giovanni responded: "Your remarks on great work, Lawrence, vision, etc., touched me to the quick and make me proud to be associated with you even in the very little I have been...Now of course I understand what you are doing and even why you have reacted to certain work of mine as you have."[25] Also Haines: "You keep presenting the problem of the poem from different angles, and after reading, one does have the feeling that something really is beginning to happen in American poetry...But what you said about the instinctive quality, the reaching toward thoughts as yet unthought—that's the exciting part."[26]

The first publication of the Sixties Press was a small pamphlet titled *A Broadsheet Against the New York Times Book Review*. It reprinted an interview with *NYTBR* editor Francis Brown from *The Fifties* 1, but the new four-page introduction packs the bulk of its firepower.[27] It begins: "How long is the farce of the *New York Times Book Review* to continue?...One doesn't realize how bad the [*NYTBR*] is until one notices that in other countries such reviews are written by the greatest living writers there." In the U.S. "the reviewers are uniformly a group of second-rate academics—absolutely indistinguishable from one another—who, having no ideas, are unable to make a review even interesting, let alone bring any vigor or authority to it." He continues: "These timid and vapid men [are] perfect mirrors for the editor of the *Book Review* himself." Its readers "are asking for bread and receiving stones."

Bly goes on: "Succeeding to a tradition of poor editors, Mr. Francis Brown is probably the worst the *Book Review* has ever had... Why should it be impossible to have an intelligent man as the editor of such a book review section?" Then he lists some possible candidates for the job, including Rosenberg, M.L. Rosenthal, Dickey, Macdonald, F.W. Dupee, Wayne Burns, Mary McCarthy, Stanley

Burnshaw, Rexroth, Robert Hatch, Kunitz, Gore Vidal, Jackson Mathews, and Edmund Wilson. "The failure of the *New York Times* to print distinguished and intelligent criticism is a national disgrace in itself. It leads, moreover, into a decline in the standards of book reviewing throughout the country. Those interested in literature should not stand by." On the one hand, Bly's assault probably made little if any difference to the *NYTBR*. On the other, it certainly solidified Bly's reputation as a cantankerous character.

Responses poured in. Benedikt, Merwin, Rich, Ignatow, and David Ray were mostly positive; Wheelock mostly negative.[28] The magazines paid attention, too. James Boyer May (editor of *Trace*) and Rob Cuscaden (*Midwest*) mentioned it.[29] Another reviewer thought Bly hadn't gone far enough:

> The Sixties Press is admittedly a band of noble Israelites and the NYTBR a Philistine giant; but if Mr. Bly means to play David for our good (and I surely thank him for doing so), his Broadsheet seems a very light pebble to sling at Goliath...I wish he had worked a little harder, gathered as many stones as he could, and hurled them with all his might.[30]

Victor Navasky, at that time editor of the satirical *Monocle*, later of *The Nation*, said: "I have been buying the 8th Street Bookshop out of your *Broadsheet*..., so restock them."[31]

Reed Whittemore's magazine, *The Carleton Miscellany*, sponsored a symposium on *The New York Times Book Review*, for which Bly was the closing speaker. Among other remarks, Bly admitted that "everyone agrees on its actual importance...This symposium is concerned with suggestions to increase its range and quality."[32] Dickey wrote in response: "You kicked up a good war against the *Times*; I notice that big guns like Dwight Macdonald [in *Esquire*] and Edmund Wilson have jumped into the fray; well, maybe something good will come of it."[33] If something did, it was short-lived.

Another sign of Bly's increasing visibility in the community of letters was the formation of ALMA (the Association of Literary Magazines of America). Whittemore was the prime mover, concerned with "the sad economics of the little magazine." He envisioned an association that would avoid "the aesthetics and politics if possible" and "would work on ways of getting the magazines distributed, getting them out of our respective closets."[34] Nineteen magazines and other publishing organizations sent representatives to the first meeting, which was held in St. Paul on November 11, 1961.[35] Bly was among the attendees, and the minutes reveal no timidity on his part. He expressed his "dislike of the principle of exclusion" which was being pushed to the disadvantage of the smaller, newer magazines. A membership committee was formed to consider this further, made up of Robie Macauley (*Kenyon Review*), Andrew Lytle (*Sewanee Review*), and Bly, representing two long-established magazines and one prickly, independent upstart. Allen Tate, co-editor of the *Sewanee Review*, who was then teaching at the University of Minnesota, was named honorary chairman of the association.

Bly later told Hall that the meeting had been "very interesting." He added: "Both Carol and I confronted Tate with these reports of ugly remarks he has made about me—calling me 'a bastard,' etc., & various four letter words—he denied it entirely! —that is, he said he didn't <u>remember</u> having said them."[36] At a second meeting held the following spring in New York, the rift between the established magazines—*Partisan, Quarterly Review, Hudson, Sewanee,* etc.—and the newer, smaller, less well-heeled ones became obvious.[37]

In 1961, a year later than announced, The Sixties Press published *Twenty Poems of Georg Trakl*. Three years before, when Bly and Wright first met, they had almost immediately begun to translate Trakl together,[38] and they continued to send translations back and forth for the next two years or so. Near the end of that laborious process, Wright wrote: "I'm convinced we were right in waiting so long over these poems. They ripened into meaning for us…We were like Lewis and Clark, tracing out the delicate strange dark places inside Trakl, all alone without anything from the <u>past</u> to guide us."[39] As an example, here is "Sleep" in its entirety:

Not your dark poisons again,
White sleep!
This fantastically strange garden
Of trees in deepening twilight
Fills up with serpents, nightmoths,

Spiders, bats.
Approaching stranger! Your abandoned shadow
In the red of evening
Is a dark pirate ship
Of the salty oceans of confusion.
White birds from the outskirts of the night
Flutter out over the shuddering cities
Of steel.

The cover illustration, a detail of the "Garden of Earthly Delights" by Hieronymus Bosch, depicts a man embracing an owl larger than himself. As I mentioned in an earlier chapter, Bly took the owl as a symbol of the new poetry.

In Bly's introduction, many of the usual themes are on hand. He speaks of "the magnificent silence" of these poems, how Trakl rarely speaks, but rather allows the images to speak, although most of them, too, are "images of silent things." He highlights Trakl's "darkness without roads," and says: "As his poems grow, more and more creatures live in his poems—first it was only wild ducks and rats, but then oak trees, deer, decaying wall-paper, ponds, herds of sheep, trumpets, and finally steel helmets, armies, wounded men, battlefield nurses, and the blood that had run from the wounds that day."

Wright's introduction tells of wandering into the wrong class-room in Vienna in 1952, and hearing Trakl for the first time:

> It was as though the sea had entered the class at the last moment. For this poem was not like any poem I had ever recognized: the poet, at a sign from the evening bells, followed the wings of birds that became a train of pious pilgrims who were continually vanishing into the clear autumn of distances; beyond the distances there were black horses leaping in red maple trees, in a world where seeing and hearing are not two actions, but one.

It's obvious that Bly and Wright shared a deep love for this dark, brooding, imagistic poet. Their subsequent poems clearly bear his marks.

The book was another advance for Bly's reputation. Kinnell, Merwin, and Harrison were lavish in their praise.[40] Burnshaw wrote: "I want to tell you how much I appreciate your new Trakl book and how highly I value it... The book is a major piece of poetry publishing, for which you deserve the warmest admiration."[41] H. Arthur Klein wrote in *The Nation*: "The present translations are readable and devoted, even when marred by minor misunderstandings and a few infelicities of phrasing. Trakl's... power and amazing precision of imagery do come through memorably. Readers of this book should include poets, for here is certainly a poet's poet."[42] Another reviewer wrote: "Mr. Wright and Mr. Bly have handled his lyrics with new subtlety and precision. Without losing a 'translated' flavor, the words do make good, native expressions. Since the originals rely heavily upon the sequence of their images, much of their mood can be preserved. It is a mood of awe, hush, decay, nature at peace, man in anguish."[43] Still another review ended in this way: "The work that the Sixties Press is doing in Madison, Minnesota, is an important contribution to American culture, and should receive greater attention."[44]

Of course, not all the reviews were good. One academic publication, *The German Quarterly*, said the book "demonstrates how amateurishly some poet translators go about their task. Those who know a language only through the dictionary should keep their hands off such an arduous undertaking."[45] Another negative notice came from John Simon in the *Hudson Review*: "It is most commendable of James Wright and Robert Bly to offer us *Twenty Poems of Georg Trakl*, but would it not have behooved at least one of the translators to learn some German?" He cites four mistakes that "are beyond the pale, even if in every other way the translations are most competent, which they are not." Bly told Hall: "I took an ad in *Hudson* [*Review*] quoting Simon's entire review of Trakl as if it were a blurb!... It looks rather strange, but I'm sick of everyone quoting favorable reviews. Louis thought it was a wonderful gag."[46] Bly and Wright didn't claim to be Germanic scholars, but they knew something about poetry, and they had worked hard. Simon's barb failed to draw blood.[47]

Then Malcolm Cowley, at Viking Press, proposed to publish one large book with the various translations Bly was intending. The offer presented him with a dilemma:

If I do the Viking thing right away—boom—there go a lot of sales. No one is going to buy 10 small books at $2.00 each, if they can get them together in a Viking book for $6 or $7...It would be good to get these poets introduced by a larger house, that is certain—good for them, since they wouldn't have to combat the disadvantage of the scorned House of Sixties. But I like good amateur publishing too.[48]

At the same time, Simpson, who had been pressing Bly to finish his proposed anthology, *The Continent Rising from the Sea*, wrote to Hiram Haydn, an editor at Atheneum, suggesting that Haydn publish it instead:

In a few years, the new ideas about poetry that Bly is expressing in his magazine and in the volumes of verse that the "Sixties" press is putting out, will be as influential in America as, say, the ideas of Eliot, or the Fugitives, were some thirty years ago...I believe that a large publishing house which allied itself with this movement would find itself in the avant-garde, rather than in the undistinguished mass, of poetry-publishers.[49]

Hall, in England, continued to do his part to spread the word about *The Sixties*: "I wrote Eliot and mentioned your magazine, so now you should send it to him. Also, please send copies to Stephen Spender at *Encounter*, to whom I have praised it."[50]

Amid all this activity, Bly was still looking for ways to remain solvent. "I got an excellent job in New York translating Scandinavian novels for Signet Classics. The first one will be a Strindberg novel, any one I wish, then a Hamsun. The royalties will run between a thousand and three thousand on each, I think, so that will take us through the rest of the year easily!"[51]

Issue #5 of the *Sixties* also appeared in the Fall of 1961. The cover indicates, simply: "Fourteen Poets of France." The previous numbers each had a thematic focus; this is the first to settle on poetry from one country, in one language.[52]

There are four epigraphs: two from René Char, one from Jules Supervielle, and this synesthetic statement of E.T.A. Hoffmann:

It is not only in dreams, or in that mild delirium which precedes sleep, but it is even awakened that I hear music—that perception

106

of an analogy and an intimate connection between colours, sounds, and perfumes. It seems to me that all these things were created by one and the same ray of light, and that their combination must result in a wonderful concert of harmony. The smell of red and gold marigolds above all produces a magical effect on my being. It makes me fall into a deep reverie, in which I seem to hear the solemn, deep tones of the oboe in the distance.

The creative act, unveiling and clarifying, is not a process of rational explication, but rather of heading into mist, dreams, the imagination, eagerly and with confidence.

The nineteenth century section begins with Gérard de Nerval, Théophile Gautier, and Charles Baudelaire, in whose "Dusk Before Dawn" are these lines:

> *It is the time of night when hordes of insane fancies*
> *Torture on their beds the sun-burned adolescents;*
> *When like a bleeding eye which throbs and rolls*
> *The lamp makes only a red bruise against the daylight,*
> *And the soul, borne down under the gross and sodden body,*
> *Repeats the struggle of power of the lamp and the daylight.*

"The natural world is a spiritual house," says Baudelaire in "Intimate Associations;" Bly sees a "mood of trust in the animal world" in the poem. Stéphane Mallarmé, Arthur Rimbaud, Tristan Corbière, and Jules Laforgue round out this section.

The twentieth century part begins with Paul Valéry's "A Room," which leaves behind "the devices of pure logic." It continues with St.-John Perse, Supervielle, and Paul Éluard's "Max Ernst," translated by Bly, which looks at the four corners of a canvas.[53] The same poet's "To Go By" has images like the following: "Thunder has hidden behind black hands," and "The rain has run through all the roads of blood / Rubbed off all the blueprints which showed the road to the living." Four poems by Char and one by Yves Bonnefoy conclude the French portion.

A remarkable statistic: out of twenty-nine French poems, Wright, Hall, Simpson, Kinnell, and Benedikt translate one each, Charles Guenther two, and Bly the remaining twenty-two. This torrent of production, including the books of Trakl and Lagerlöf (not to mention his work on Strindberg and Rilke), is noteworthy.[54]

"Some Notes on French Poetry" serves as a guide to the issue. Bly writes: "The French poets in the early nineteenth century start off on a voyage into the sea of imagination." He continues: "French poetry has exactly what American poetry has *not*: a true interest in the life below the "world." Rimbaud is not admirable because he took dope, as the Beats believe, nor because he shouted *Merde!* during contemporary poetry readings, though that was admirable also—but because he grasped the deep interior life flowing beneath the reason." The problem is that "the older American and English poets have not been interested in the sea, nor in the unconscious, in the animal world, nor in the kindness and gentleness that often mark those who embark on such a voyage." Although French poetry had not suffered the neglect of previous generations to the degree that Spanish poetry had, Bly contends that much had been ignored or missed.

The fear of the unconscious, Bly says, is "an old Puritan emotion," which "has multiplied in American poets after Eliot and Pound."[55] Hart Crane refused to succumb to that fear, but Bly sees it in Tate and Winters, passed on to Lowell. Then, Bly says:

> Ginsberg's work has the same fear of the unconscious and the same unkindness. Ginsberg's attacks on himself and attempts to degrade himself are no more valuable than his attacks on "Mammon." It is the same Eliot or Pound self-depreciation. Even though Eliot and Pound hate the Jews and Ginsberg hates the squares, it doesn't make any difference: it is all the same thing.

Bly goes out on a limb, and he brings his own saw, when he equates anti-Semitism and anti-squarism. It's an example of what can go wrong with such scattershot generalizing.

Moving on, Bly remarks that one reason American poets have not embarked on the voyage into the imagination is that they "do not live enough in solitude," a situation that could easily be remedied. "Yet the life of voyage is not impossible in the English language. The poems of John Haines, Richard LaFuze, Louis

Hammer, and E.D. Blodgett in this issue, three of whom have never been published before, show suggestions of the same kind of life. Older American poets also—Whitman, Hart Crane, Theodore Roethke—have contributed to the little genuine poetry we have." And thus it ends, neatly tying together (with some strain) the French portion of this issue with the American portion, and with the two subsequent short bits.

The first is "On Solitude," prose by Odilon Redon: "The seriousness of art moves those whose attention and disposition are inward. Even the creative artist realizes very well that of all his works, the one which reflects and reveals him best has been done in solitude." The other is a poem by Wei Ying-Wu (translated by Soame Jenyns), titled "At Hsi Chien":

> *I love to gaze alone at the dark grasses growing beside the river,*
> *When the orioles are calling in the thick woods.*
> *The spring tides come swiftly down swollen by the rains,*
> *By the deserted ferry the boat swings to and fro.*[56]

Five American poems follow. In Haines' "If the Owl Calls Again," the speaker identifies with the owl, with animal life, and makes a nighttime foray. Haines had recently moved from New York to a cabin in Alaska, after which *The Fifties* became a lifeline for him. He wrote later:

> I sensed, even at the distance I lived then, that there was
> something in the air, the first faint shock of a new energy. ...
> The new poetry enlarged and deepened that space; there was
> an unmistakable feeling of freshness—a new expressiveness
> and emotional depth...Between Bly and myself there followed
> letters...regarding this new poetry that was beginning to be
> written. My own views were often uninformed and openly
> skeptical; his were knowledgeable and for the most part
> persuasive...It would be difficult to exaggerate the importance
> of that contact for me at the time.[57]

Blodgett, a poet in his twenties living in Minneapolis, contributes "Fragment from a Mole's History."[58] "Return to Flight" by LaFuze, whom Hall had steered to Bly, is next. After the subterranean mole, here the poet is airborne, as a bird. Bly also used

Duffy's "Poem on Forgetting the Body," which begins:

Riding on the inner side of the blackbird's
Wings, I feel the long
Warm flight to the sea;
Dark black in the trees at night.

One might see this as a quintessential example of a "Sixties" poem.[59] Last was Hammer's poem, "Expansion is the Secret of Life," ending with these lines:

We watched elephants rise from the earth
And walk far out into sea;
We all rejoiced with the earth
That was happy building large beasts.[60]

All of these poems, obviously, involve close connection with animals.

Crunk's essay is on poet and editor John Logan. Bly had first heard him read in 1958. A year later he told Hall: "I think he is a fine man, with great power in his character, and a 'straight tongue'...and also without question one of the best poets of our generation."[61] Bly had published Logan's "Nude Kneeling in Sand" in issue #4. Logan taught at Notre Dame, and had just started up a new magazine, *Choice*, in February. For that first issue he had requested a poem from Bly, who not only sent him one, but also loaned him $50, shared *The Sixties'* mailing list with him, and recommended poets from whom Logan might solicit work. Logan wrote: "Cummings gave us a poem I like, which pleased me no end. He...mentioned how much happiness he has had remembering something Carol said...once when you three were crossing Washington Square."[62] Because of Bly's help, Logan wanted to list him as a patron.[63] He requested a note in *The Sixties* about *Choice*, and asked: "Would you be interested in collaborating with me on an anthology of Poetry of the 50's with critical introductions?"[64]

Crunk begins in typical fashion: "The first thing that strikes the reader about John Logan is that he is a very strange man.

Reading his poems, one often stumbles on something totally unexpected." Crunk noted that Logan was often pigeonholed as a Catholic poet. "Logan has a sense of grandeur." But, he adds, alluding to Gerard Manley Hopkins, "it is not the grandeur of God...; he has a sense of the greatness inside certain human beings."

He singles out "A Short Life of the Hermit," about an Egyptian mystic, from Logan's first book, *Cycle for Mother Cabrini*: "Most people act responsibly. John Logan, for example, supports his wife and nine children with a regular teaching job and occasional extra jobs." But "instead of defending his domestic position, as most poets do, he spends his energy understanding the opposite position—that of the anchorite! And he understands it better than any other American poet." Crunk sums up the first part of the essay: "Content is something that can be defined or agreed with. Logan's content obviously grows from his own thought and it is expressed with economy."

"The second power...is a certain lucidity, a certain clarity of eyesight." Instead of writing poems about baseball, to show he's a regular guy, Logan has a rare kind of emotion, "the kind of memory that Whitman was interested in." This puts him in good company. "Logan's poems have a content, then, and the impulse behind them comes from unusual experiences. The poems are not empty 'performances,' but evidently spring from what might be called an obscure experience of light."

As for Logan's faults: "At times the voice is too loud, as if he were shouting over the heads of many people... Force is visible. There is a tendency to use four-letter words, or to be temporarily the tough-guy, which is nothing but an embarrassment at being a poet. Occasionally the poems are cluttered with biblical or classical references." Nevertheless, "Mr. Logan is a poet of authentic vigor and originality. The originality cuts through the poetic habits of the last ten years." The essay concludes as our tour guide signs off with a simile. "He is a strange one, the possessor of great energy and power. He continually stands in the water on one foot, like some long-legged heron."

Again, Bly was worried over how his subject would receive it.

But Logan replied:

> I like the article very much, I learned from it about myself,
> I would rather read it than anything else that has appeared
> about me. I'm deeply indebted to you for your intelligence
> and sensitivity and for your generosity in applying them to me
> in print…I am much taken with your use of the concepts of
> energy and light in my work. I feel that you are aware what as a
> poet I attempt.[65]

It bears repeating: poets were learning from Bly.

Of "Books of Poetry Published in 1960," the six most interesting were by—no surprises here—Dickey, Kinnell, Snyder (who also made the 1959 list), Logan, Levertov, and Merwin. He trashes the book by Robert Mezey that won the Lamont Poetry Prize, calling it "junk." Sexton's highly praised book is "interesting," but "mostly…prose." Others are mentioned in passing, and then this:

> The worst book of the year was probably Charles Olson's
> *Maximus Poems.* This is Babbitt in verse, and it is painful to see
> intelligent men defend it. Donald Hall, Adrienne Rich, and
> John Hall Wheelock all deserve a kick in the rump for giving
> the Bollingen Prize to Yvor Winters, particularly since men such
> as Robinson Jeffers, whose imagination is a thousand times
> stronger than Winters', still has not received it. Eberhart also
> deserves it. Considering the whole drift of his work, Winters
> is not a poet at all, but a policeman. The force of his life has
> gone into opposing the imagination. A light verse poet, Phyllis
> McGinley, was given the Pulitzer. All in all, it was a good year
> for poetry, but a fantastic year for judges.

Odin's aim was true. This is tart, juicy, merciless stuff; the kind that endeared Bly to many and earned him the undying hostility of many others.

The Order of the Blue Toad award is bestowed on Robert Penn Warren and Cleanth Brooks' popular textbook *Understanding Poetry*, which, since its original publication in 1938, had probably been the most effective means of spreading New Critical doctrine. Here Bly really lets it rip. He accuses them of an academic bias for poetry that is "understandable," rational and readily explained, rather than highly imaginative and associative. Since the book includes eight poems by Housman, none by Whitman, and completely ignores French, Spanish, German, and Chinese poets, Bly says it "should have been called *Understanding A.E. Housman*." As usual, a final ridiculous image: "The toad, wearing A.E. Housman's moustache, is painted on a scarlet background. It is turning a meter machine with its left foot, and correcting term papers with its right. Above its head is the motto: *The Ghost of Criticism Past*, and under the toad's feet a banner that reads: VOTE FOR CALVIN COOLIDGE."

"Wisdom of the Old" features the words of Randall Jarrell accepting the National Book Award, roasted on his own skewer:

> Sometimes I read, in reviews by men whose sleep I have troubled, that I'm one of those poets who've never learned to write poetry. This is true: I never have learned. Sometimes a poem comes to me—I do what I can to it when it comes—and sometimes for years not one comes. During these times the only person who helps much is my wife: she always acts as if I'd written the last poem yesterday and were about to write the next one tomorrow. While I'm writing poems or translating "Faust" I read what I have out loud, and my wife listens to me. Homer used to be led around by a little boy, who would listen to him; all I can say is, if Homer had ever had my wife listen to his poems, he would never again have been satisfied with that little boy.

No comment necessary. Frederick Morgan, editor of *The Hudson Review*, had alerted Bly to this.[66]

It was an important year in Bly's writing career. He had, all along, been submitting poems and manuscripts, receiving many rejections and some acceptances. Among the latter, notably, was his translation of Selma Lagerlöf's novel *The Story of Gösta Berling*.[67] But in October Bly received a letter from Wesleyan University Press, possibly the premier American poetry publisher of the day, accepting his manuscript titled *Getting Up Early*. It would be published as *Silence in the Snowy Fields*. He was excited, and he reflects with Hall (not coincidentally, one of the editors of that series):

I am pleased to have a book of my own coming out. I have always had to spend so many hours of labor proofing, planning, typing, etc. to get said whatever I had to say that it seems strange that someone else will do all that, and all I have to do is turn over the poems! I'm liable to write more books at this rate. As for the Wesleyan series, I'll bet you'll have a book by Dickey (in spring 1962 group) then by me (fall 1962) then by Jim W. (spring 1963) then by Louis (fall 1963).[68]

This is as clear a picture of the "Sixties poets" as one might hope to find.

7

Rude Awakenings[1]

From the very beginning, *The Fifties* had actively solicited poems. As the magazine became more well known, and its opinions and ideas more influential, more poets wanted to appear in its pages. Because of Bly's (and, for the first three issues, his co-editor Duffy's) dim view of the current state of American poetry, and given the narrow set of criteria for the kind of poetry he wanted, almost all incoming poems were rejected.[2] The magazine swiftly became notorious for its personalized rejection slips, which were usually sarcastic and often just plain rude:

"This sounds like car-bumper poetry."

"This should go someplace where they have a tendency to like "cute" poems."

"These poems remind me of false teeth."

"This poem is like lettuce that's been in the refrigerator too long."

Duffy seems to have had a special knack: "We feel that these poems float too much on the surface like a boat on the water. Poems must either fly or be like the roots of a tree. These are transplanted trees without any roots."[3] And: "Your poems remind us of a huge bird who wanted to talk, but listened to the wrong records."[4] Bly showed his awareness of the notoriety when he wrote a friend: "I have a hundred envelopes of MSS to send back tomorrow. Carol is going to file my teeth tonight, and give me some wolfsbane."

Bly told Hall that all the rejections really said the same thing: "Written with the intellect, not the feeling."[5] This could manifest itself in many ways—in stilted, antiquated, or written (i.e., not spoken) language, or in traditional poetic forms, meters, and rhymes. And that was just the beginning, not even touching on subject matter or Bly's interest in images, surrealism, inner life, the modern world, etc. On top of all this, as he was making plain in one essay after another, Bly was convinced of the need for criticism that was subjective, harsh, and constructive all at the same time, and of the deleterious effect of anything less. Poetry could not be made new without it. The rejections, though they were often not constructive themselves, reflected this fundamental article of faith. The humor and sarcasm, while affording some comic relief for the editors amid the drudgery of reading piles of bad verse, also had a serious purpose.

No doubt many submissions arrived at first from poets who assumed that a new magazine, especially one from an unheard-of backwater, would be glad for almost anything. Many of the rejections were intentionally nasty, in an attempt to put a stop to repeated submissions from poets whose work would never be suitable. As time passed, however, it became clear that many submitters were just not paying attention to what Bly was about.

Some recipients sent testy responses suggesting they were ill-equipped to withstand a mordant rejection like: "[Your] poetry reminds me of pigeon shit dissolved in sherry."[6] Some insist that the rejection is unjustified, others lash out in anger, belittling the editor for his naïve audacity or chastising him for bad manners; more than a few admit to being devastated. Quite often, those who responded angrily would return the offending rejection slip.

Whatever the precise tenor of the rejection, many submitters were grateful for the personal touch, knowing it was an act of generosity far from the norm, and took the comments in stride. Although his rejection said "These poems are anally oriented," one poet recounts, "at least the notes were handwritten. There was a human on the other end doing the work of reading."[7]

To begin with, there were several variations on the charge of a poet being too "traditional." One clueless submitter—had he not read "The Necessity of Rejecting a Shakespeare Sonnet" in *The Fifties* 3?—imagined that his old-fashioned sonnets might pass muster. Bly said, "We believe that all people who write sonnets should be hung from the nearest lamppost." The response was a sheet with ten identical drawings of a stick-figure man hanging from a lamppost. Under each is a different name: Spenser, Sidney, Shakespeare, Donne, Wordsworth, Keats, Robinson, Frost, Cummings, and finally, the submitter's. He added: "To be hung in such company is an honor."[8]

Bly had also emphasized the point, early and often, that the long-dominant iambic pentameter would not do for the new poetry; he quickly tired of those who sent iambic poems and arranged for a printed note which began: "We think that the iamb is oddly unfitted for modern life, somewhat like the horse and buggy. However, if you wish to write in this old horse and buggy meter, don't send the poems to us—send them to some museum like the *Kenyon Review*, which has set aside special rooms." He also made up a small card which read: "This entitles you to buy the next book of Alfred Lord Tennyson as soon as it appears. A Public Service of the Sixties Press."

Bly had lambasted the use of classical references in "Madame Tussaud's Wax Museum," and he rejected one poem heavily laden with such allusions as follows: "We hate Troy, and academic poetry; and academic poetry about Troy—that's the end!"[9] While such references may have dwindled over time, academicism itself was more difficult to shake. Duffy wrote: "We must be frank and use a dirty word. This poem is academic."[10] Ten years later, Bly responded to another: "The truth is these poems are too academic. You refer to yantras, dhyini-buddhas, but there is no sense that you have experienced them. So it's no better than the old references to Achilles. You need more experience, in short, before the talk."[11]

Bly had other complaints. He told Gerard Malanga that his poems had "an artificial complexity and too much rhetoric...It is not a matter of finding another style, but of ending the rhetoric."[12] He wrote in a friendly note to Andrew Wylie: "These poems of yours have a lovely crisp English, but...they are too abstract at the same time…These words won't root down into the unconscious, and so the senses don't leaf out."[13]

There was a sub-category of academic poem. "This belongs to the odious genre called 'the workshop poem' in which you talk wittily on a subject you care nothing about, in 19th century language. Cut it out!"[14] And another: "I find these to be 'workshop poems,' a horrible genre. They are well written, but somehow off the top of the head—it's always others' lives, not your own, that they talk of." This rejection was returned, with the following words typed over Bly's script: "Thank you very much but what's a workshop? I've never been in one. Thank you for saying they're well written—they took me three minutes each. Maybe the pot helped."[15] Occasionally, those who had been rejected were able to be snide and funny, too.

One rejection said, simply: "Terrible! These corny rhymes are straight out of 1825." This was returned with the following bitter note, similarly direct, but using an Anglo-Saxon derivative, and some German for good measure: "Thank you for your recent comment on my poems. In plain, honest English, Mr. Bly, you are a prick. *Nicht wahr*?"[16] Bly received a similarly antiquated submission from Donald Junkins, a poem in three parts on Ahab, the Pequod, and Ishmael. Bly told him that a poem on another person's literary work was incestuous, and that he "should let Melville have his thoughts in peace. Respect his privacy. You can find your own whales."[17]

Most of the responses to rejections, some of which appear in the "Letters to the Editor" section of *The Sixties* #6 and #10, fit into a small number of categories. First, there are those who respond creatively. "To the Editor of the Old Fashioned Fifties—I did not submit the poems to be insulted by a fly-by-night upstart still wet behind the ears, ignorant of common courtesies. What an impertinent little heel you are." This came in 1958 from R.W. Stallman, an established critic and scholar at the University of Connecticut, Storrs. He had sent five poems, all published in other magazines. Duffy's rejection said: "We only print unpublished poetry. Even so, your poetry seems to have a very old-fashioned tinge."[18] Remarkably, Stallman's angry note was accompanied by more poems, daring them to turn him down again. The second rejection slip said: "Again, too traditional. Thank you." On the back, Bly wrote: "I did not write the rejection slip, but I did read the note you sent with your poems, which was extremely arrogant. Consequently, I think you deserve what you got." Bly also thought the response deserved to be exposed in the public square of the magazine. Stallman, in high dudgeon, responded with an Italian sonnet, "The Recollection," by John Peale Bishop:

> *Famously she descended, her red hair*
> *Unbound and bronzed by sea-reflections, caught*
> *Crinkled with sea-pearls. The fine slender taut*
> *Knees that let down her feet upon the air,*
> *Young breasts, slim flanks and golden quarries were*
> *Odder than when the young distraught*
> *Unknown Venetian, painting her portrait, thought*
> *He'd not imagined what he painted there.*
> *And I too commerced with that golden cloud:*
> *Lipped her delicious hands and had my ease*
> *Faring fantastically, perversely proud.*
> *All loveliness demands our courtesies.*
> *Since she was dead I praised her as I could*
> *Silently, among the Barberini bees.*

In case the poem was not recognized as an acrostic, an elongated circle was drawn in red crayon, encompassing the first letter of each line, and with an arrow pointing to Bly's name.[19] So much for ivory tower decorum.

More recipients of rejections saw fit to respond not with another's poem, but with their own, written just for the occasion. One rejection slip said, in typical fashion: "These are too traditional in what we conceive to be a worn-out tradition."[20] The addressee's response, which includes her measurements, was accompanied by a photograph of herself in uniform. It began:

> *Dear Mr. Bly, your curt reply*
> *On my first venture and I am shy.*
> *Let Mr. Duffy handle my rejects*
> *He's Irish—won't mind my defects.*

You say I'm worn out tradition.
38-29-38 is good addition.

It ended: "Keep my picture as reminder / To make your rejects all the kinder."[21]

Another person, resenting his rejection (which included "people don't talk that way"), sent the following:

Screw you Robert Bly
Do "people...talk that way"?
Check Picasso
Early or late,
Do people look "that way"?
The poem was bad
But not why you said.
Pity you think "that way."

The last stanza of this poem reads, memorably: "You are a sty / In the publication eye. / Screw you to pieces, Robert Bly."[22] Yet another respondent kept his poem to two lines: "Enjoyed your rejection. Thought perhaps you'd want to see my newest: 'I'm Robert Bly; / Cockadoodledoo!'"[23]

Two women, mindful of the magazine's regular satiric feature, "The Order of the Blue Toad," sent a joint effort, in multi-colored calligraphy so as to look like an official certificate: "The award of the Green Hippopotamus is benevolently bestowed on Robert Bly for his suburban defence of poetry as being the prattle of middle aged myxedemic women disguised as the perfect union of absolutes in the dissipated craft of modern poetry." This opaque statement is followed by the poem, "A Bly Line":

Robert Bly, you have kissed us off
With a flip of your pen.
You say we don't write poetry; you scoff
At our attempts as you would at a purple hen.
You laugh and call us sophomoric.
You say we are too literary
For talking about love in stale rhetoric.
To you our poems are hairy

Monsters. We don't write like we talk—that makes you sigh.
Well, to employ common slang, Mr. Bly—
You won't miss your water till the well runs dry.[24]

At least the gist of the rejection slip had been understood, as had the relative dearth of the "water" (or was it mead?) that Bly thirsted for.

One infuriated poet speaks of Bly's "bogus rejection." He adds: "I don't know why in the hell I <u>ever</u> thought you had anything to say to me as a younger man or poet. You're mostly a pile of shit in an impoverished field, Bly. And rest assured, I've read the last piece of poetry or prose I'll read of yours. You've nothing to say to me again." He includes a signed poem, "Ego Bird's Fall," which ends: "Bly, Bly, Bly away foolish bird, / Corn Mother rejects your featherless dance!"[25]

Others responded creatively in fanciful prose. On stationery under the letterhead "The Rejected Generation" is this piratical piece:

Ship ahoy, matey…steer aft or get blown down from the mizzen-mast… Hey there, barnacle Bill, clear the poop deck, sweep down the galley! Be alive now—turn to, full battle garb. Gunners, man your pieces. Ship in the two fathoms deep, sir. Aha! She flies the jolly roger! Tis Bly and his cut-throats sir, a black-hearted crew if ever was. Look at 'em a-swinging from the jib. But, Captain, sir, that's Bly, the scourge of the Barbary Coast, he is, sir. An' ye can't outrun his sloop, THE BLACK BUGGER. Aye, a trim craft she is, but we'll cut him down to measurable size, WON'T WE LADS? Hurrah for the Captain. Do in that Bly with one quick slash of the cutlass. O, 'e got me, Sir. Where are you hit, me boy? A…rejection…slip, sir…in the back, I…. Poor lad.

A page later, Gilbert Highet, Edmund Wilson, and Clifton Fadiman condemn Bly to walk the plank: "Justice, my friends, is done."[26]

Second, there were responders who disputed, unable to take "no" for an answer. Here's one: "Dear Mr. Bly, Thank you for your criticism: 'The poems seem to us to have a diction that is artificially complex.'" He then goes on, for three long pages, in a doomed effort to convince Bly otherwise.[27] Cynthia Ozick took issue with Bly's criticism at great length: "So infrequently do editors in their notes of rejection take the trouble to make critical comments, that I feel obliged to express my surprised thanks—mixed, I hope you won't mind my adding, with extreme puzzlement." She argues for her poem for several paragraphs, and concludes: "I am disturbed that you should have been willing to take the simple for the simplistic; the motivated for the uncontrolled obtuse; the artfully ingenuous for the idiomatically insensitive; the design for the cliché…In poetry, not all failures are caused by naïveté, though some successes are."[28] Her defense of her poetry may hold a clue as to why she gave it up in favor of fiction and essays.

Bly wrote to another: "Terrible! They are all imitations of 19th century English verse—'silvery caresses,' 'sighs unsighed'—awful!" The recipient, all high and mighty, reacted: "Rude rejections, like yours, are more amusing than annoying. You are obviously very young; you haven't had a chance to learn the fundamentals of good manners…I have published dozens of poems in very reputable journals, and will undoubtedly continue to do so!"[29] This complaint represents a common variant of the argumentative response, with statements such as: "Others like my poetry. You'll see; you'll regret it." Duffy asked one poet to forget their address. That poet responded: "I will only too happily comply with your request." Then he lists his accomplishments and names those who have praised him.[30] Here is another:

> If your rude note was intended to hurt me you failed abysmally!! I have been paid $5.00 a line from some of the most beautiful magazines in the world. A folder crammed with the nicest notes and letters attest to the opinion that your opinion is worthless. I actually laughed when I read it. I'll sell every one of the ones you rejected and will send you the proof…In all my writing career yours is the first of its kind!!![31]

There were the supercilious, scornful responses. Donald Kuspit wrote: "You seem to be a rather banal representative of Lumpenkultur, to say the least. You ought to know an editor should be humble and open-eyed and keep his place, and not display his stupidity, let alone claim to define poetry."[32] The one from Paris

Flammonde answered a rejection which seems to have said "these are not poems":

> Of course the submissions were not poems, they were verse. Having seen your publication, it never occurred to me you might revise your policy and publish actual poetry. However, since poetry, like civilized behavior, derives from the cultured, it should have been immediately apparent that it was as foreign to the Sicksties realm as were good manners.[33]

The "Sicksties"—that's precious!

Another would-be contributor, Burton Raffel, attempted to turn the tables: "I've just come across three of your poems... They're very disappointing, exactly the kind of half-trite flaccidity I expected, having received some of your belligerently inane rejection slips." He concludes: "Your poetry is bad enough, but as an editor you ought (but obviously will not bother) to be ashamed of yourself."[34] He was right about one thing: Bly would not bother.

Norman Moser (in #10) really tries to take Bly head-on. He faults Bly's dogmatism, as did some of Bly's close friends, from time to time. The letter begins "Dear God," though he probably wasn't thinking in Norse terms. He continues:

> So nice to hear from you. Poetry is serious, you are right, and the poem must be good in itself. But must it be only what you say it is, you silly pedantic slob? That's right, I said pedantic. I know you pride yourself on not being that dirty academic sounding word, but do you have any inkling what it means? It means one who refuses to believe anything but what he thinks or feels can have any truth, charm, power, insight, validity, etc., etc.

He goes on to defend each poem submitted in some detail, suggesting that the editor misunderstood them, and that he was likely to send some more eventually.

After Bly had met Moser, and after he asked for and received permission to print Moser's letter, he revealed part of his editorial outlook:

> I decided to publish a group of insulting letters in order to try to break the air of impeccable dignity—over-dignity—that hovers about the literary magazine. Editors usually preserve

an utterly smooth surface on the magazine, like unruffled water. This is reassuring, but not very interesting. One would think there were no reactions, or that the reactions were all favorable—everyone agrees...The purpose is to enjoy the criticism we receive as much as the praise (if any)—and if the criticism is more interesting, publish it, whether we look "undignified" or not. What's the difference? No one knows how a magazine "ought" to be run anyway.[35]

Most rejected poets were not so high-handed, but some would still shoot back. Bly wrote: "These poems remind one of the nightmare of a philosopher who had been reading *Finnegan's Wake* to try to get to sleep." The recipient answered: "This feeble sarcasm MUST be the waste product of a SMALL mentality. Your unbounded admiration and adoration for Robert Bly is exceeded only by your holier-than-thou snottiness. So glad I shall never find it expedient to cultivate your waspish fellowship. With a total dearth of respect."[36] Another used a scolding tone:

Perhaps you are not sterile, but your imagination certainly is, that is, if you are not completely bereft of one. Voyeurs like yourself, who wish to peep via their poems are murderers of literature. You demand adolescent phantasy, and I, fortunately, no longer have the need to masturbate. As the editor of a responsible magazine, Mr. Bly, I think it is high time you ceased wetting the bed.[37]

One young poet wrote to complain that another (whom she omits to mention is her husband) had been mistreated by Bly's rejection:

It comes to my attention that your tactics, when regarding the work of young poets, are both insulting and destructive. P____ H___ recently sent you works. You replied with a note that stated as follows: "It's all capitalist stuff, without any concern for the suffering of others, or even awareness of it—boring." ... Being a poet is difficult enough without people like you making it even more frustrating. You are in a position to offer meaningful support to young poets. Your rejection note reads like something I would have written when I was sixteen and sure that I was the most righteous and politically sensitive person in America.

She signs the letter "Respectfully…"[38] It seems legitimate to ask how respectful it is to compare Bly to a sixteen-year-old.

For poets who had been attracted to Bly's ideas, a harsh rejection could be especially difficult to stomach. For this rejectee, the days of admiration were over: "I wouldn't deign to drop you this note had I not, at one time in the remote past, admired greatly your poetry…Your rejection of my three poems…evinces poor enough critical ability on your part, but your observation 'it's clear it's wiseguy poetry,' betrays a critical shallowness as shallow as any 'wiseguyness.'"[39]

Finally, one poet attempts to out-think the editors, or at least to trip them up with their inconsistency. The letter says: "My first rejection slip from your publication was sent by Mr. Bly—noting that my poetry 'move(s) at such great speed that many of the words are wasted.'…My second rejection slip from your publication was sent by Mr. Duffy—noting that my poems 'lack the certain intensity needed in good modern poetry.'" Bly and Duffy respond to the third batch in unison: "These poems are too busy—all sorts of things are running around inside them."[40]

A third type of response was the denunciation. Bly wrote, bluntly: "You ignore everything that is said, and cannot even deign a reply, but merely go on sending long, long poems. Please send no more." (It is noteworthy that Bly wanted dialogue.) Herbert Morris seems to overreact in willful ignorance:

> Your intemperance and ill humor shake me. All this because I "ignore" everything that is said (should I have changed my life and style in conformance with your literary tastes?); because I do not "reply" (reply to what?). I return your words to you; their occasion lies, I know, in you, not me. I hope for you only that, somewhere, you can know the fundamental immorality of what you have done.[41]

Bly wrote to another aspiring poet in relatively gentle terms: "I don't have the feeling of a person behind these—you write about things, but we don't really have the sense that you are revealing much—or anything—about yourself." She wrote in a self-revelatory manner on the returned slip: "I got good & drunk when I read this and I cried & cried, so go to hell. Some people are sure

blind. I'll feel better after mailing this to you."[42] One unrecep-
tive writer tried to forestall the inevitable, and asked Bly not to
waste her time with a personalized rejection: "If you reject some
or all of them, none of your snappy comments, please. Just use the
generously stamped, enclosed envelope. Please don't construe my
request as lack of appreciation for the time and thought that went
into your previous comments. It's just that I don't think they (the
comments) do much good."[43]

Some take anger a step further. One writer was perplexed and
bitter: "Your little comments calling my poetry 'abstract' and now
'rationalistic babble' have been baffling." He asks for Bly's reaction to yet another poem, and then adds: "if it's too much of a
drag for you why not take a long walk in the woods sucking on
cyanide."[44]

Another rejection was brutally short and direct: "This is really
bad poetry." The response shows how crushing such a judgment
could be. At the same time the aspiring poet's wish to join the
ranks of *Sixties* poets is palpable:

> I disagree… Still a letter from such a recognized poet, a source
> of authority if you're into it, even a few words carries weight
> particularly to a "fledgling" who hasn't even published her first
> major book… I would be less than honest if I didn't say that
> your prestige notwithstanding, you blew my mind. I mean I
> really took you seriously and you caused me a lot of pain…
> Keats lost 6 months of work time in his 25 years because some
> pompous asshole, soon to be forgotten except in other poets'
> and writers' biographies, said his work ("Endymion," I think)
> stank. I make no aspersions on you or myself here… So, in a
> sense, fuck you.[45]

The last words would seem to bring matters to a close. But she en-
closes another poem—just in case! d.a. levy also responded with
the customary phrase of some of those who were convulsed with
rage at Bly's rejection: "dear robert bly, pertaining to yr criticism
of my poetry which i sent you—fuck you. language is not forced
and of course no one talks like shelly, blake, crane, stevens or peter rabbit either. IF YOU MUST CRITISIZE [*sic*] MY POETRY
PLEASE HAVE SOMETHING VALID TO SAY."[46]

126

Sometimes, when he detected even a glimmer of hope, Bly's rejections offered encouragement. For example: "There's liveliness in these poems, which is rare, but you're not even trying to be serious. 'Oh, juice of immortal loveliness' etc.—'silver filigree of gelatinous being'—you don't expect us to go along with that, do you? Humans don't talk that way, only books do, or over-cheerful inhabitants of late capitalist nations."[47] To another Bly wrote: "The very close of '1970' is moving. But most of the poem, to tell the truth, has the ring of nature observed through a car window. There's nothing wrong with that, except that the thoughts are neither as complicated as 'car thoughts,' nor as complicated as 'pure nature thoughts,' but a simplified mixture.'[48] This note gives specific advice: "The trouble is that your feelings are too cloudy to you. You don't see into them, they loom like a mist. When you hear bluejays, you're not sure what it is you feel. So you need to spend more time by yourself."[49] Often Bly would suggest that the poems be sent to a particular magazine that he thought likely to take them. In other cases he prescribed a reading list: "We like the one on women best, 'Amenities.' The technique seems somehow a little backward and awkward, and I would suggest a study of Alberti and Jiménez, perhaps even the Argentine woman poet, Alfonsina Storni, in the original Spanish."[50]

Bly's rejections, if not totally dismissive, were often received with gratitude. "Thank you for your note. I've never been called a 'word-teaser' before and it's something I shall ponder. At any rate, I thought I'd try again."[51] So also this one: "I think I am beginning to see your point about the limitations of iambic verse... Please accept my thanks, as always, for your time and trouble in looking my work over—and in taking up the very involved question of prosody with me. I can assure you that <u>that</u> is further than most editors would bother to go."[52] Another acknowledgment has a fitting simile: "Thanks again for the ferocity of your rejections. I've come to see you as a kind of sumo wrestler whose tactic is to toughen other wrestlers by driving them, skull first if need be, into the mat. It's probably the best technique around."[53] Hank Malone said: "This will undoubtedly be the finest rejection slip I will ever receive, if not the most defeating."[54] Another, if not unequivocally grateful, wrote: "By God, it's refreshing to get an honest rejection slip even if it is a kick in the ass."[55] There were many more responses like these.

Of course, a good number of established and up-and-coming poets (including Eberhart, Sexton, Duncan, Levertov, Stafford, Rich, and Leslie Woolf Hedley) submitted poems and were rejected along with the rest. Bly wrote to Dickey: "To us, this poem, though in form it is more or less free, in content it is still in the old pastoral tradition…If I were you, I would cut out everything but the images. You must forgive me for being so bold, and so on, but I like the poem, and I think boldness is no crime."[56] Bly and Dickey would become fast friends (for a few years, anyway).

Louis Zukofsky (a second-generation Modernist and co-founder of Objectivism) had sent something after *The Fifties* 1. What the editor(s) said is unknown, but it must have been relatively respectful. Zukofsky graciously replied: "Your note is fair enough to this old man. Get yourselves published—i.e., the young."[57] Theodore Enslin also took criticism fairly well: "Your last letter was about as fair a repudiation of what some of us are trying to do, as I've yet seen." He defended himself, saying: "I'm not aware of being particularly influenced by Pound." Finally, he said: "Well you're honest at any rate. Forgive my trespasses, and I hope you enjoy this poem, whether or not you want to publish it."[58]

Gil Orlovitz, on the other hand, was boastful and bitter: "Who in hell wants your gratuitous opinons? Certainly not Orlovitz. I know of no Spanish poet aside from Lorca worth talking about … If you take a long gander at all the Orlovitz you've seen, you may discover he has no peer since the Elizabethans…In brief, don't tell me what to do—just give me a yes or no—that's all I'm interested in."[59]

Wright was not submitting poems in the same way as most; Bly was soliciting them. Still, this critical activity is relevant here. Bly worked hard with Wright to cut what he had written and to reveal the true poem deep inside. Years later, Wright recalled the importance of that effort:

How helpful those old letters were to me, how humanly encouraging, how full of life and inspiration your ideas were and still are!...Your generosity toward other writers, especially young ones, is so instinctively deep, that your impulse must certainly be toward answering all these requests in detail...I remember one such remark of yours: "This poem is asleep. Wake it up!" That... set me free of all sorts of rhetorical clutter that I'd got myself tangled up in, and I could find my way to a clear, new path.[60]

Surely Bly's comments to other poets aimed at getting as many as possible on track.

Duffy rejected Charles Bukowski's poems as follows: "This *Evergreen Review* sort of thing is the new orthodoxy, and getting to be a school like the academics." Bukowksi objected: "In answer to rejection charge: I have only read the *Evergreen R.* once, and that halfway, if that...and if I wrote something like they write something, I apologize...Well, anyhow, it was nice to get a written reject from you for a change."[61] Bly then also responded in a manner remembered later by Bukowski:

last I heard from you was 5 or ten years ago when you rejected some of my poems and told me your buddy editor was going to join the F[oreign] Legion and when I told you bullshit I got back a photo of you and your buddy (he was dressed

Bill Duffy and Bly, in Madison, in costumes made by Carol Bly.

in his Legion wartogs) hovering blithely over a small table without wine by some tall trees in an expanded Minnesota breakfastnook.[62]

This was a bit of fun-making taken to an extreme.

Finally, Ted Kooser (appointed U.S. Poet Laureate several decades later), wrote:

> I know that it must be frustrating to you to receive frequent submissions of poems from poets whose work you don't like. Although it is an imposition, I persist in giving you things to reject because I hold your criticism in high esteem. I have been writing and publishing poems for 12 or 13 years now, and I still have not found what I think is my natural voice. I believe that if anyone will point it out to me, it will be Robert Bly.[63]

Late in the 1960s, having reached an early peak of fame, Bly was besieged with requests and burdened with expectations. A young poet, Mark Wilson, was assisting with many tasks, including reading and responding to submitted manuscripts. This fierce remonstration from Alexander Karanikas followed one of Wilson's rejections:

> When you read my poems you must have been either on some kind of trip, drunk, or insane. I am familiar enough with *The Sixties* to know how you try to rile up poets so they provide you with letters that make superb reading when you print them. Well, I'm not going to fall for that kind of crap... If you don't see meaning in my poetry, then you are just plain stupid. Odin House indeed! I hope your dour Nordic gods betray you when you most need them; and I hope that moment is when my rational Greek god Zeus anoints you with a jet of holy piss.[64]

Odin and Zeus at odds. Bly liked this letter so much that he flagged it for a third "Letters to the Editor" section (which never appeared).

There was at least one other assistant in writing rejections, Bly's first child, Mary. In the early 70s, when she was around ten, he would pass the poems to her, tell her what to say, and she would write the note. One early rejection slip from her says: "My fater askes me to tell you that...[h]e likes some of your lines but thinks you are to tied to the world. [*sic*]"[65] Some twenty-five years later, Bly says, "a man came up after a reading in California, and said, 'I have a rejection slip signed by your daughter.' I said, 'Really? What did she say?' The note goes this way: 'My father says to tell you that your poems don't have enough images in them. Don't pay any attention; he says this to everyone. I think your poems are wonderful.'"[66]

Almost predictably, in 1972, Bly wrote to Hall: "A couple of days ago I decided to bring to a halt my long time practice of writing notes to every one who sent me poems—there's no end to them, and the volume increases!"[67] Thus the editor prepared the last official rejection slip, not handwritten, but printed, impersonal, and certainly sent to many. It began: "The Ms. coming into *The Seventies* have increased in the last months to thirty or so a day, and I am absolutely unable to read and comment on them any longer." A breaking point had been reached, and so ended an important chapter in the life of the magazine. But this is getting ahead of the story.

8

Reaching Out to the Universe

with a Gloved Hand

That an identifiable "Sixties school" existed was becoming more apparent, but Bly wanted to steer clear of such an impression. This explains why, for example, he omitted Hall's name from a list of poets who had been, or would soon be, Crunked on the jacket of the Trakl book. When Hall expressed concern about the omission, Bly put it this way:

> I will take turns, in various brochures, etc., leaving out this one and that one, because I want to avoid the sense that the magazine is partial to anyone. That is why I left Louis' name off the list of persons who were mentioned as good *NYTimes Book Review* editors in the *Broadsheet*, and why I have urged Jim to publish large groups of his poems in *Hudson*, etc., rather than in the *Sixties*. Jim's dignity has been somewhat affected, at least temporarily, by statements like that of Thom Gunn's in *Yale Review*, implying that he is my disciple or something...The value of the magazine lies in its independence from the older generation, and its belief in the significance of what the younger ones are doing, not in any single association or in the printing of a single sort of poem.

By this stage in his career, Bly's influence was undeniable, but its purpose, he insisted, was not to control but to enable, to instill confidence: "That is why, contrary to what Allen Tate believes,

I have not attempted to keep Jim Wright in personal chains, or to prey on him; his poetry is fresh, but I can imagine many other sorts of poetry which would be equally fresh."[1]

Wright touched on this in describing his preparations for a reading circuit: "My plan was, and is, to begin my readings…by saying about ten tiny poems in a row. … Then, and only then, I'm going to reveal the authors. The point is to make it impossible for some fool to pipe up with the inevitable cliché ('Oh, you and Bly just imitate each other, etc.')."[2] Wright had written to Snodgrass about this same concern:

> I have a couple friends out West who mutter to one another
> that I am getting corrupted by associating with Bly, but that
> is absurd. I don't even agree with Bly (who is constitutionally
> incapable of reading an American poem that is iambic). God
> damn it a poem is a poem. But Bly is not afraid to leap into the
> dark and wrestle with strange animals.[3]

Not only Wright, but Hall, Simpson, Haines, and others were insisting on their independence from Bly, despite their close ties.

About *The Sixties* 5, Logan wrote: "I thought your comment on French poetry was terrific—one of the best things you've done. I sat back and learned, which is rare for me…It's the only magazine I read every word of."[4] Kinnell had one particular point to make: "I agree with you French surrealism wasn't true surrealism. I'll put it the other way. It was too much the true surrealism, it lived by intellect, wit, & formula—in the name of automatic expression. When it was ground into the earth of reality it was true poetry—your surrealism."[5] Haines wrote: "In the past I have always been put off from French poetry by what I saw in English… But…these translations give me something I never got before."[6]

Simpson's critique was more detailed, prodding Bly to make *The Sixties* realize its potential:

> The magazine is becoming what it should be…About the
> business of the subconscious always being regarded as evil…
> you have a major point here…I think you should write a big
> article on the subject, using your essay on the French poets as a
> point of departure. I think this article would be a manifesto, and
> reason for, the "new poetry of imagination."[7]

In the first sustained negative review *The Sixties* received, Le-Roi Jones mischaracterizes Bly as an academic, and an academic poet who "has now chucked it all...to become the poetry diva of the great north woods."⁸ He briefly praises the magazine, the apparent purpose of which is "to pick holes in the flimsy garment of American Academic Poetry," mentioning the "highly derogatory" Blue Toad, and saying "Bravo" to Bly's comment that Brooks and Warren's *Understanding Poetry* "was really written by Joe Friday."

But he complains that, instead of young French poets, or obscure ones, he finds an irrelevant selection no different than in numerous other anthologies of "modern" French poetry. Jones quotes Bly's equating anti-Semitism with anti-squarism and says: "Which is a mouth full, no? (Though I suppose it is understandable that Mr. Bly is so sensitive about square-haters.)" He suggests that the section of five American poets be presented as "The Rustic's Revenge." Bly and company were not only squares but country bumpkins, the latter a persona that Bly, despite his habit of living in Greenwich Village for half of each year, sometimes wore by design and to vex.

The Sixties, Jones writes, is the "most articulate" of those journals with a heavy emphasis on translation. (Again exaggerating for effect, he invents a silly title for a special issue, "The New Poets of Wake Island.") He sees this as "suggesting, somehow, that there is no poetry, new or otherwise, in our motherland." To him, surprisingly, such an emphasis constitutes colonialism, rather than what is most certainly was, internationalism.

He seems personally offended at Bly's denunciation of Olson's *Maximus Poems* as the worst book of the year. Given his web of comrades, Jones reacts predictably, saying that, if that were the case, it was because neither Bly nor Duffy had published a book that year. He concludes: "I suspect Mr. Bly and Mr. Duffy are ignorant fools."⁹

Jones does score a few legitimate points, despite some misapprehension. But while Bly's statement about hating squares is problematic, Jones' assertion of the pre-eminence of American poetry smacks of isolationism. The reasons for his defense of

Olson are transparent, and the American poets praised by Bly in the same article that attacked Olson—Dickey, Kinnell, Snyder, Logan, Levertov, Merwin—all had or have had long and remarkable careers. In any case, Bly, a practitioner of polemic and all-around feistiness, was pleased to have elicited some of the same.

In November 1961, Bly said: "#6 is already in type, and will be out January 15, #7 on March 15, and #8 on May 15."[10] Considering that #6 did not appear until June (and #7 in 1964, and #8 in 1966), we may surmise that this was wishful thinking and brash talk. Readers were always eager for the next installment, as was Hugo, looking forward to "another snarling, unreasonable (sometimes), cruel, nasty issue…always so damn much fun, and so often on the side of the angels."[11]

First, the opening quotations: "People always talk of the study of the ancients; but what does this mean, except that it says, turn your attention to the real world, and try to express it, for that is what the ancients did when they were alive."[12] This further clarifies that the prohibition of classical allusions or, for that matter, the necessity of rejecting a Shakespeare sonnet, does not entail a disregard of or disrespect for the past. The second is from Darío's *Prosas Profanas*: "Poetic expression was stiff-jointed, *anquilosada*, to the point that the mummification of rhythm had become an article of faith." And last, Yeats: "You can no more have the greatest poetry without a nation than religion without symbols. One can only reach out to the universe with a gloved hand—that glove is one's nation, the only thing one knows even a little of." By now these are enduring concerns of the magazine: to make it new, to break constraints, and to speak from one's own experience and circumstance.

The germ of the idea for the first section, "Some Poems Touching on Recent American History," seems to have been Wright's.[13] From his "Eisenhower's Visit to Franco, 1959":

Franco stands in a shining circle of police,
His arms open in welcome.
He promises all dark things
Will be hunted down.

135

But in the center is a poet really searching out the dark things:

Antonio Machado follows the moon
Down a road of white dust,
To a cave of silent children
Under the Pyrenees.

Finally:

Clean new bombers from America muffle their engines
And glide down now.
Their wings shine in the search-lights
Of bare fields in Spain.

In the second poem, "Twilights," Wright remembers his grandmother and his childhood. It ends with an isolated line: "A red shadow of steel mills." Last, "Autumn Begins in Martin's Ferry, Ohio," looks incisively at Wright's hometown, and the social and familial wreckage that results from living in that shadow.

The next poet, Durward Collins, Jr., had been a student of Hall's in Ann Arbor. Appended to "Temperate Belt (Reflections on the mother of Emmett Till)" is a grim explanation of the historical background. Collins thanked Bly for his editorial revision, which "certainly clarified the sequence of events as well as the tone."[14]

Bly then has three poems. "After the Industrial Revolution, All Things Happen at Once" is inhabited by businessmen. The next, "Sleet Storm on the Merritt Parkway," begins:

I look out at the white sleet covering the still streets,
As we drive through Scarsdale—
The sleet began falling as we left Connecticut,
And the wet winter leaves swirled in the wet air after cars
Like hands suddenly turned over in a conversation.

As it continues, the tone becomes clearer:

What a magnificent place for a child to grow up!
And yet the children end in the river of price-fixing,

Or in the snowy field of the insane asylum.
The sleet falls—so many cars moving towards New York—
Last night we argued about the Marines invading Guatemala in
*   1947,*
The United Fruit Company had one water spigot for 200 families,
And the ideals of America, our freedom to criticize,
The slave systems of Rome and Greece, and no one agreed.

Insightful, with a holistic connection between nature, society, and politics, this poem is partly reminiscent of Neruda. The classical allusion is historical rather than mythological, and therefore, apparently, permissible.

With "Condition of the Working Classes: 1960" we move down the social ladder a few rungs, but with similar effect. It begins: "There are bricks trapped in thousands of pale homes, / And pale children who in time will vote Republican." Associative leaps take place, some of them rather startling transformations:

Driving down the streets, we see the faces of children
Change suddenly into the doors of aircraft factories...

...

And the extricated axles change to missiles with warheads
Climbing up, and the stages change into the aisles of a church,
And the church-doors change into the faces of children standing beside
*   the new trees.*

So the poem ends, having come full circle back to the children, indicting society, the military, and the church. These three poems harken back to "Poems for the Ascension of J.P. Morgan" and to various statements from earlier issues, and anticipate *The Light Around the Body* (where the first two will appear) and *The Teeth Mother Naked at Last*.

"American history" is not limited here to North America. Neruda's "The Dictators" (from *Canto General*), translated by Bly, again foreshadows some of Bly's later work. And finally, in this group, is Charles Reynolds' "Thoughts on Alger Hiss."[15]

A comment from Haines indicates one hazard of the *nom de plume*: "I've had some funny thoughts about some of the people who have appeared in *Sixties* from time to time—Reynolds, Hammer, Blodgett, LaFuze, Clemenson. They seem to write so much alike."[16] He had discovered that Reynolds was Bly, and then mistakenly concluded that these others might also be.

Next is "A Note on Blas De Otero" by St. Martin, who speaks of Lorca, Aleixandre, Hernández, and Machado, and of the rebirth of poetry in Spain in the mid-1940s. "This new poetry is one of anguish and protest. De Otero and the other interesting young poets write human poems. As they begin to grow, they turn from purely personal problems and private thought to the sufferings and oppression of their country."[17] St. Martin also translates three by De Otero. In "Mundo" ("World"), St. Augustine appears repeatedly, juxtaposed with references to bombing, rape, and degradation in World War II. "Cap. 10 Lib. 11" ("Chapter 10, Book 11"), ends on a note of despair: "when these memories jolt me, I suddenly realize how hideous everything is and I resign myself to being ashes, lonely ashes damp with tears."

In "On the Necessary Aestheticism of Modern Poetry," Bly says that the ideas in Ransom's essay, "Poets Without Laurels," seem to him "quite mistaken." He continues: "Mr. Ransom characterizes the modern poet as one whose poetry, unlike the poetry of the past, takes no interest in moral questions or in the great issues of public life. This whole view is, to put it frankly, untrue. The idea is incredible when we think of poets of this century in other languages." He mentions Darío, Unamuno, and Machado, Benn and Brecht, Apollinaire and Éluard, all of whom Ransom should have known. Furthermore, "Neruda, to take a single example, is many times more 'modern' in style than the people Ransom mentions, yet his work is marked by exactly that same absorption in the issues of national life that marked ancient poetry." Mayakovsky, Pasternak, Brecht, and Rimbaud also show that absorption. "Modern poetry is not restricted to the English language, or to purely 'aesthetic' poems, and a description that so implies is not true."

On a tangent, Bly compares poetry to painting:

In several languages, poetry has gone far beyond what painting has been able to accomplish in this century. Poetry has taken

138

a path exactly opposite to that of Abstract Expressionism. The greatness of modern poetry is that it is able to describe the sights and sounds of modern life, as well as the powerful ideas, such as self-interest, dictatorship, colonialism, and political chaos that lie beneath it. Painting cannot do it.

While he may have a case for poetry, and even against the Abstract Expressionists, the last statement is wrong. What about—to pick only one obvious example out of many from the twentieth century—Picasso's "Guernica"?

Finally, regarding Ransom's vision of the modern poet as one whose work has only aesthetic considerations, Bly says: "This misdefinition, which is now accepted as a truism in the Universities, and the workshops, must be rejected if we are to see clearly what has been done." This short essay reflects a natural progression in Bly's thought, and, in part, his reaching out with a gloved hand.

Wright, who had been a student of Ransom's at Kenyon, protested beforehand that "a snippy little piece on Ransom would not be a revolutionary gesture...it would be a silly mistake."[18] Bly replied: "The world is not going to fall over if one magazine attacks Ransom! I intend to continue with plans for it, since I think it is just in its essence. Nevertheless I am glad you brought out, by pestering me, points at which he deserves praise—I will, when I redo the piece, make sure he is praised more."[19] Wright wrote back:

> I believe, if I believe anything, that *The Fifties* (I mean *The Sixties*) has several crucially important things to say to intelligent men in this country; and that is precisely why it must not (I mean I think it must not) give those intelligent men a chance to evade its point by calling *The Sixties* article on Ransom a piece of boorishness, bad taste, infantilism, etc.... Robert, you are a courageous, resourceful, and witty polemicist; but you ought to heed me, because I have a criminal's instinct in these matters of style: the style of the most effective revolutionist is always marked by balance, moderation, and decorum.[20]

Wright, a professor, was more respectful of academicians, and much more moderate.

"The Work of Gary Snyder" was assigned, for the first time, to an unidentified "guest Crunk." Wright, late as usual, vowed to visit the farm "and spend two entire days writing, rewriting, discussing, and revising the Snyder essay," not leaving until it is ready to print.[21] Years later, he describes what happened:

> Carol Bly...made sure that I would finish the essay, or at least work on it, by employing the simple and effective expedient of a Napoleon at the height of his career. She locked me into the chicken house, including the door and the windows...To this day, I remember those afternoons...as a curious combination of a pleasant study, Yaddo, and Devil's Island...In those days, by the way, I was a drunk; and...my realistic friends made sure that the chicken house contained no booze whatsoever.[22]

It was as though Frigg, Odin's wife, was confining him temporarily in Odin House.

Crunk begins: "Gary Snyder is an original man. He has written a poetry which is quite unusual and very different from most poetry written in the last years." In *Riprap* he notes the "sense of worth in lives of all human beings" which recalls Whitman, "with whom Mr. Snyder has other powers in common." There are images "of utter clarity," and there is "meditative power." Snyder "might be called devout, or religious in the most elementary sense. He regards life with a seriousness so profound that he is able to experience and express the inner life without resorting to the worn-out abstractions which so often nullify the public discussions of spiritual matters." Looking at *Myths and Texts*, Crunk says Snyder is always "'hatching a new myth,' in the sense that he is always seeking for a way to embody his celebration of physical life in some form that will reveal its religious meanings."

In part two, Crunk posits three ideas about Snyder's work. "First, his is essentially a Western imagination. His poems are powerfully located—sown, rooted—in the landscape of the far Western states." The second idea is that Snyder's poetry is distinct from Beat poetry "both in imagination and in style." Crunk finds in Snyder's work a "certain gentleness and care for civilization," and goes on to note that "instead of merely talking about Zen he went to Japan and entered a Buddhist monastery in Kyoto, where he still remains." This leads Crunk to his third idea: "The influence of the orient on Snyder is interior: it is the desire to overcome vanity and ambition." This also affects "the method of construction of the poem."

Crunk adds: "It is distressing to have to say it again, but...what Walt Whitman accurately called 'British literature' is not the only tradition from which American writers can be permitted to learn anything." Snyder is a good example, because the Chinese poets mean so much to him. He has courageously undertaken "the exploration of living traditions...for the purpose of claiming America itself—by which I mean literally our own lives and the people and places we live among day by day—for the imagination."

Furthermore: "His recording of solitude in his poems is another striking feature of his work." The final paragraph: "Mr. Snyder has courage and an air of faithful patience. He keeps his voice low, not out of timidity but out of strength."

Although he speaks from the *Sixties* platform, and although we may often detect the editor's voice, the prose of Wright's Crunk is less quirky, more professorial, and, most noticeably, lacking in harsh criticism. Snyder wrote to Bly from Kyoto: "Mr. Crunk is much too nice." At the same time Snyder offered a "moon poem" and adds: "Don't see much stuff otherwise but have seen a few of your poems here & there; hear you've got a cracking good book out. Like what I saw."[23] He was still glad to participate in *The Sixties* venture, if mainly from the sidelines.

Bly translates five Norwegian poems by Paal Brekke, whose work "shows connection also to the more modern poets of Sweden." "Mine, Though Bitter—," includes these lines:

> *But I will stand here in the shadows—*
> *the darkness can drink from me*
> *on the shore of the great light*
> *which bends about your hair.*
> *The hour is mine, though bitter.*

"The Weight of Boughs," ends as follows: "Boughs, heavy as nights that last a thousand years, are sighing, there is a sighing also / From birds in chains that try to rise from the earth." These poems are rich with many by now familiar images.

"Some Parodies and Satires" includes "A Fable," which essentially reiterates the reason for the magazine's existence, telling of a new generation: "Some of the farms were named, from the fathers who had founded them, the Eliot Farm, the Pound Farm, the Apollinaire Farm, the Rimbaud Farm, the Jeffers Farm, the Surrealist Farm, etc. Everyone here farmed just as their fathers did. Then something terrible happened." They had to sell much of what they had, and then they retired, turning everything over to another generation. "These younger farmers soon held their first exhibition, called *The New Farmers of England and America*. To this exhibition all the old farmers came to visit, and said, 'My, what poor farmers! They are only raising chickens!'"

The introduction to the next parody invites further contributions on "certain 'set' poems in magazines, for example, the dead dog poem, the foreign statue poem, the Troy poem, the public lavatory poem." The projected series begins with a parody of the "My Guggenheim to Italy" poem. "Definitive work in this field has been done by Jean Garrigue, Richard Wilbur and Anthony Hecht." Titled, "A Walk in the Gardens of Italy," by I. M. Baroque, Bly and Wright wrote it one weekend at the farm.[24]

> *The ultimate composition of the plaza,*
> *Empty of tourists, leads us to this abstract stair:*
> *Mozart and Tartini would have loved this plaza, where*
> *Soloppi, like Adonis, whispered Tutti Frutti*
> *Mal y Pense. The stone nipples of the buxom cherub, caro,*
> *Bronze and circumstantial, give license to our desires*
> *For inexpressible flesh, and so it is with a sigh of regret*
> *We say farewell to the gardens of the American Academy;*
> *The chaste expectancies of the evening, and the statues,*
> *Lead us to one overwhelming question: Where are the wops?*
> *There are no human beings in sight.*

Then, like the "I was a 98-pound weakling" ads from the back of magazines and comic books, comes a parody (of "A Note on Syllabics" from *The Fifties* 2) titled "True Testimonials."[25] And Simpson contributes "Keeping Abreast, or Homage to Pablo Neruda Perhaps," a parody of Bly. Lines include:

Yesterday I met Thomas.
He was wearing a cloak and smoking marihuana,
and in his hip pocket he carried a volume
of Pablo Neruda.
"What is this, Thomas?" I said.
. . .

"I have cast off my old ways," he answered,
"and I advise you to do the same.
It is all testicles nowadays and light,
and a series of ecstatic exclamations."
Whereon he struck the guitar
which he produced from his briefcase,
and began to sing of various mountains
in Chile. . . .

"Thomas," I said, "is this the new poetry?"

"It is the new world," he replied.

This kind of answer always leaves me feeling foolish.

Alas, I am outmoded.

Simpson has written: "My tastes in poetry were frequently different from Bly's. I thought that some of the South American poems—maybe as a result of translation into English—were just a series of ecstatic exclamations."[26] More recently, speaking of Bly and Wright, he put it this way: "I'm not knocking Robert's translations of Vallejo and Neruda and all those people, because he did a beautiful thing...a wonderfully useful thing, he and Jim between them at that time. But there was always that barrier for me, between my poetry and theirs."[27]

Before the next parody, "The Art of Talking," by Eleanor Rockwell, the editor writes, tongue in cheek: "We decided we should print interviews, just like *The Paris Review*." The first is with Gérard de Nerval. The interviewer makes a convoluted comment, including: "The nuances, the implications, the meter, are all, in my critical opinion, perfect." And: "I speak frankly, you understand, but from a literary and objective point of view rather than a subjective one." The poet responds in one sentence: "Al-

143

Bly, James Wright, and Louis Simpson, in Madison.

ors, je ne comprend pas l'anglais." The entire second interview, with Henry James, follows: "Interviewer: Mr. James, you wrote to William Dean Howells that 'the faculty of attention has utterly vanished from the general Anglo-Saxon mind.' Can you elaborate upon this? Henry James: Would you repeat the question?"

Last in this section is "Clocks" by Julio Cortázar, another from the series of Stories of Cronopios and Famas (two were in *The Sixties* 4), again translated by Blackburn. This is not a parody exactly, but more a fable in which the cronopio, that is, the laborer, the artist, the underdog, the insouciant, comes out ahead.

The Sixties 6 ends with five poems by Eugenio Montale. "His intense, almost harshly compressed, poems have had a great influence on Italian poets after him."[28] Bly translates the first four. "On a Letter Not Written" includes these lines:

> *...The red furnace*
> *of night is late*
> *coming, the evening goes on,*
> *prayer is torture, and not yet among the rocks*
> *that are rising have you received*
> *the bottle from the sea. The empty wave*
> *breaks on the point, at Land's End.*

144

The fifth poem, "The Sunflower," is translated by di Giovanni, who "has just finished a book of poetry of Cesar Pavese. His poems and translations often appear in the *Nation*."[29]

The notice about future issues includes solicitation of translations of Miguel Hernández. The back cover has "Wisdom of the Old." Senator Dodd of Connecticut "a sort of McCarthy who subscribes to *Horizon*," had, in 1960, asked Kenneth Tynan (the British theatre critic and author) what Bly here calls "one of the great questions of the last ten years." It was: "Do you think you have the right to hold opinions that differ from those of President Eisenhower?"

After issue #6 had been prepared, but before publication, Bly wrote, at the request of Frederick Morgan, editor of *Hudson Review*, an omnibus review of twenty-three books of poetry. The "Morgan mess" is an apt label for the imbroglio which ensued.[30] Ultimately, as Morgan insisted on cutting and Bly refused to yield, the piece was withdrawn and published in Logan's *Choice* instead.[31] While Bly liked some of the books, his unbending principle of honest judgment meant that much of the criticism was sharp and dismissive. He concluded by castigating New Criticism and its exponents for treating poetry as if it were prose. The effects, much rancor and sniping, reverberated far and wide.

Curiously, issue #6 contains no mention of *The Lion's Tail and Eyes*, even though its publication by The Sixties Press was imminent. The first trace of the idea is found in Bly's journal from 1959. Eventually the participants were boiled down to Wright, Duffy and Bly, with ten poems each. Some titles with connections to Minnesota history were tossed about, such as *Past the Days of Ramsey*, *Past Pillsbury and Ramsey*, and *The Source of the Mississippi*.[32] By later the next year, the decision had been made, as the book's introduction explains: "When Kate Skattebol saw some of the poems in this book, she said that they seemed very strange to her, as if an artist had drawn a lion, but had only drawn in the eyes and the tail. We have to understand that the rest of the lion is there."[33]

Bly wrote to Hall: "Carol designed the cover! I found the lion head, which is a Dürer lion I have liked for a long time, and she did the rest." He added:

Two years ago when I announced it, few or none of these poems had been published, and the purpose of the anthology was to show a poetry without direct statement. Now much of it has been published, and it seems more like beating my own drum. I dislike that. Yet I had announced it, and people have already paid for it. I had to go ahead and print it, I thought, and keep my word on it.[34]

The author's copy of *Silence in the Snowy Fields* arrived just two days later.[35] Wright's third book, *The Branch Will Not Break*, would be published the following spring. Duffy may have been the only one of the trio especially eager for this book to appear.

Bly's brief introduction is one of his better attempts at encapsulating what he meant by "image." Hall's reaction to the book as a whole: "I don't really like Duffy's poems. Most of them seem to me specious, to have false feeling in them, and to be strained or affected... Jim's poems hold up very well. Yours, of course, are beautiful. And I like very much the introduction and the copy on the jacket."[36]

Following its release in 1963, Logan reviewed it:

My objection to the number of horses... constitutes but a cavil in an unusual, exciting volume which serves ideally to lead readers into the extraordinary creative world of three Minnesota poets who are familiar with the contemporary poetry of several nations and who together are bringing to American poetry a powerful new direction away from academicism. These three artists are presenting what I would like to call "organic" poetry, poetry which experiments with content rather than with form and whose life does not depend upon the metrics but upon the life of the poet himself.[37]

X.J. Kennedy wrote:

This book...offers a fair taste of the kind of poetry Bly is after in *The Sixties*, our brashest little magazine and one I'd gladly read oftener...Neosurrealists—Georg Trakl, recent poets in Spanish—are supposed to be who Bly got it all from; but I'd reckon his own practice less willfully unconscious. In his poems...Bly is lucid, sweet-tempered, and articulate...If his theories have aided the wonderful transformation that has taken place in the late work of James Wright, they are well justified...

> As for William Duffy, who also contributes his quota of ten poems, does he exist or is he sprung full-loined from the brain of Robert Bly?[38]

One gets the sense that Bly's intentions were becoming clearer all the time, and the Sixties Press, as a complement to the magazine, had a lot to do with that.

Other reviewers found more to dislike. Dabney Stuart had some sour comments:

> It is a strange book...Wright has the best poems...Duffy's poems...don't seem true, they exaggerate beyond belief, they make one suspect what he says...Bly is not well represented in this collection. He has written some very good and influential poetry—satisfactory enough to affect quite a few poets' lines, in spite of all his preachments issued from The Sixties Press. But here his lines are complex, his images tend to be pretentious, and even his rhythms are off.[39]

Colin Falck, from across the Atlantic, was somewhat skeptical: "These poems nearly all avoid modern civilisation and retreat into a natural world of leaves and butterflies, and too many of them end up in a kind of Japanesey preciousness devoid of all intellect and personal emotion: when the whole animal does appear it is often anything but a lion." Nevertheless, he continues: "In its free verse-forms, its low moral pressure and its purely imaginative approach which gives no foothold to rationalism, this new kind of poetry promises a real breakthrough for the modern tradition."[40]

Lastly, a major attack by Gilbert Sorrentino came in the same magazine as Jones' attack on *The Sixties*:

> I think it's about time we stopped taking potshots at Mr. Bly and Company, and let them have the full strength of a broadside—for if there is one group of critic-poets in this country which has more consistently manifested its arrogant stupidity, I am unaware of it. Mr. Bly, as all readers of modern poetry know, is the man who has daringly proved to us, in his many critical excrescences, that American poetry is not *avant-garde* at all, since it is "Puritan," "afraid of its subconscious," "devoid of images," and so on. What we need here is a pick-up on the glorious verse that has been coming out of Spain, France, Germany, Somaliland, Rhodesia, and Freedonia.[41]

His disdain for Bly's effort to broaden the focus to poetry in other languages is in line with Jones' comments. Sorrentino says: "I'll try to confine my contempt for these cornshuckers to remarks on this glittering collection of platitudes." As the sophisticated city-slicker sneering at the Midwestern yokels (and having been effectively duped by the camouflage), he berates Bly's attempt to define an image and to distinguish it from Pound's "pictures." "...I can hear Mr. Bly yelling it to the chickens—'The *Cantos* ain't nothin' (cluck! cluck!) but them fool images just all mixed up with them statements (cluck?)!'"

Bly's insistence on the origins of the only real poetry comes in for ridicule. "That good old inward world shuffle is, of course, the poetaster's excuse for his manufactures. Since it is a difficult task to dig out the forms that are buried in matter, these fools insist that these forms do not exist, and they make up an 'inward world.' Then, anything goes." He wraps up: "The Sixties Press threatens to survive, leading us decadent and old-fashioned Americans and our gauche 'poetry of pictures' out of the wilderness and into the corn." Sorrentino made the most of mockery and caricature, a tactic not exactly unknown to Bly.

The critic also has a problem with the "hundred black-and-white Holsteins" in Wright's poem, "From a Bus Window in Central Ohio, Just Before a Thunder Shower":

> He saw these things from a bus window, the idea is that the bus was travelling past all this bucolic glory, yet he says a "hundred" —that's what you call a speedy eye, to be able to count them cows! But this is really an image, right? He doesn't mean that he really counted them, right? He only says a "hundred," right? That's all language is good for in poetry—imprecision, right? As long as you get a kind of "feeling," Charley, that's all, a kind of good "feeling" about things.

Wright, giving literal for literal, wrote to Sorrentino: "I counted the tits and divided by four."[42] Bly relished it all, as he wrote to Hall: "In New York, be sure to buy the new *Kulchur* (Eighth St. Bookstore). Has wonderful attacks on everything *The Sixties* stands for—only thing they didn't attack is the paper!"[43] John Ridland put this in the context of the brouhaha with Morgan, and saw them as parallel: "It's a funny thing that those people on the one side, and the strictest traditionalists on the other, are both screaming the same watchwords: Accuracy, Clarity, Transparency; the Poem is an Artifact...You have got *Hudson* & *Kulchur* on the same side, where they belong, throwing tin cans at you."[44] Again we see Bly not in a moderate position between two extremes, but rather in a separate spot, off to the side and in conflict with both.

The other Sixties Press book to appear that year was *Twenty Poems of César Vallejo*, translated by Bly, Wright, and John Knoepfle. Wright recalled: "When Bly showed me Hays's *Twelve Spanish American Poets*, I had never even heard of Vallejo and had scarcely seen anything by Neruda."[45] He began studying Spanish: "Not a day passes but I spend a beautiful and enriching hour or so with my grammar."[46]

When Bly announced his initial plans for The Sixties Press, Wright said: "I think your idea of a series on Spanish and S. American poets is superb, and I have ideas exploding like pollen in my head already, though I just received your note about ten minutes ago."[47] About Vallejo, he grew even more exuberant:

> What a noble man, what a sublimely courageous and miraculously living poet! I can honestly say...that I can no longer doubt that I do indeed know what real poetry is. And it is not argument, nagging and so on, that convinces me: it is the living evidence of Vallejo's book: why, the book is like a grove of wild, new, beautiful trees.[48]

So he persevered: "I swear, translating him is beyond question the most beautiful experience in writing that I have ever had in my life."[49]

The next winter, when Wright came to New York, he and Bly worked over their versions.[50] At first, the book was going to be translated by "various young American poets." Next, it was going to be Bly, Wright, and Hays.[51] But then, out of the blue, John Knoepfle, a young poet who had been reading the magazine, surprised them with some impressive translations. They decided to use them instead of Hays's, and Knoepfle was thrilled.[52] The book was released in early 1963. Once again the cover illustration is Carol's (in part), for the owl in the center is the very one she had drawn for an earlier subscription brochure.[53]

Predictably, friends' reactions were positive. Barnstone wrote: "Nothing could be closer to my heart. What a tremendous service you are doing to modern poetry."[54] Later that year, Dickey, then using the Trakl and Vallejo books in class at Reed College, wrote: "they went over great out here...I don't believe the current scene would willingly do without your operations, now that they exist."[55]

Among the reviewers, Victor Perera called the book "an excellent introduction to the Peruvian poet, whose work has been eclipsed in recent years, and especially in this country, by the growing reputation of Pablo Neruda."[56] Henry Gifford said: "The Sixties Press translations are in the main pleasing. To begin with, they read like something real, and the idiom has vigor without crudity."[57] Charles Guenther wrote: "I have read no poet, even Yeats, more personal, more conscious of his own flesh and blood and sensibilities than Vallejo, except perhaps Whitman or Antonin Artaud...a path-breaking book."[58] Colin Falck quotes from Wright's preface: "Current poets in the United States seem to be perishing on either side of a grey division between century-old British formalism on the one hand and a vandalism of anti-poetry on the other. In Vallejo we see a great poet who lives neither in formalism nor in violence, but in imagination." Falck says: "The voice here is not only Wright's but that of the whole Sixties Press enterprise, a new and very self-conscious movement which has taken its main inspiration from modern Spanish and Spanish-American poetry. It is a voice we could afford to listen to in this country."[59] There had been other books of Vallejo's poetry translated into English (by Hays, Muna Lee, and Donald Walsh), but this was a fresh approach.

Once again, the most negative review came in *Kulchur*, from Clayton Eshleman (whose Vallejo translations were in the same issue). "What Bly, Wright and Knoepfle have done is to sip off the easy cream of Vallejo and freeze it, as was done with Trakl and will probably be done with Neruda—20 poems to the batch—in the *Sixties*' format: a kind of 'instant' mysterium." He calls the book "practically useless, even if it were adequately handled, in revealing anything about Vallejo's work." He adds: "Wright is the best which isn't saying much…But the errors! Simple errors that anyone with a 25¢ dictionary can see!" Eshleman also considers Knoepfle's contribution, briefly, and then gets to his (and apparently *Kulchur's*) *bête noire*: "For some years now Robert Bly has been translating from five or six languages, many little anthologies, generally three to five poems each. These poems are always somewhat sweetened, very loose and talky. Bly does not gum up a translation in thick rhetoric as does Ben Belitt; Bly has no rhetoric. Nor ability to model." His summary judgment is tinged with jealousy:

> Considering the quality of his work, Bly has received far
> too much attention. I almost feel it would be best to have
> disregarded this book. Yet there is something about Bly that
> gets under my skin. I have read him carp for the past few years
> about "Puritanical" and "imageless" American poetry, and
> have read his own work garnished with the images of Neruda,
> Vallejo and other South Americans. And seen him botch them
> constantly, those who have given their best to him.[60]

The noticeable increase in the number and the ferocity of clashes was a good sign for the magazine and the press. As Bly had said to Norman Moser about issue #6, he wanted "to enjoy the criticism we receive as much as the praise."[61] There was a renewed vigor in American literary life, and *The Sixties* was in the thick of it.

In 1961, Bly had listed in his journal some ambitious plans for the Sixties Press beyond those already mentioned: *Thirty Political Poems* edited by himself and Ignatow; *Machado*; *Whitman*; *Twenty Poems of Miguel Hernández*; *Forty Brief Poems*; *Twenty Poems of Rimbaud*; *Thirty Poems of Rainer Maria Rilke*; *Twenty Poems of Lorca*; and *The Letters of Antonio Machado to Juan Ramón Jiménez*.[62]

In August he wrote: "The general schedule then is this: every third day I spend wholly on *Sixties* work. Business of all kinds."[63] A month later: "Monday and Tuesday for *Sixties* work, Sixties Press, preparation of books, proofs, business letters, essays; otherwise do not enter that room."[64] His own drumbeat was getting more insistent, and it all started to feel overwhelming, as Bly wrote in his journal a year later: "Just as my time as translator came to an end two years or so ago, now I want to end my editing 'life'—let all that be utterly secondary. The magazine is begun, and going well, one day a week should be more than enough for it and the Sixties books, the first ten of which are very close to finished."[65]

Would he succeed? Well, yes and no.

9

A Rising Flow of Imaginative Energy

C lose on the heels of the Morgan mess came a similar episode.[1] Bly had first met the formidable literary and art critic Harold Rosenberg in 1959.[2] A short time later, the Longview Foundation (on whose board Rosenberg sat) awarded Bly a grant "for his contributions to *The Fifties* #1 and #2."[3] Subsequently, Rosenberg revealed to Bly his plans for "a journal of art and literature ... essentially a magazine of ideas." He proposed "a terrific article on the limits of American poetry, what it lacks <u>at its best</u> ... Here, you could take the subject into a hard analysis of the modern 'ancestors' and the yes and no of their esthetics and content."[4] But he allowed that Bly might want to do something different.

Bly set to work, and then sent a draft of "A Wrong Turning in American Poetry" to Hall, who responded: "This is an extremely important essay, the most important one in modern time for poetry."[5] But soon the matter began to turn sour, as Bly clashed with Rosenberg, who was equally strong-willed and twenty years his senior. Rosenberg insisted on extensive changes, first involving dropping out references to inwardness and the unconscious, then wanting more discussion of Pound and Eliot. Bly refused to comply.[6]

He subsequently withdrew the article and ended the friendship. "I really admired him in many ways, and liked him, but it went too far."[7] Another friend, Saul Galin, editor of *Odyssey Review*, called it "the sharpest and most important statement about poetry and about so much more than poetry to come out of this country since World War II. Last two pages brilliant and prophetic." But he added a warning: "Be prepared for a frontal assault by panzer divisions. You've found the American poets out—a bunch of mannequins; you've poked your finger through them and found nothing inside but a little loose dirt."[8]

Simpson wrote: "you are making a name for yourself, and at the same time it is the kind of reputation that is throwing a fright into the conventional editors." He urged Bly to make *The Sixties* stronger, either by expanding it, bringing in other guest editors, or by continuing on his own—but regularly. He added: "What will not work, I'm pretty sure, is to continue trying to get your revolutionary ideas into anti-revolutionary places...A man like you cannot be at the mercy of editors."[9] Simpson makes a convincing case for his pragmatic vision of the magazine's potential. But Bly had even broader aspirations.

He gave the essay again to Logan's *Choice*.[10] In it he considers the first generation of Modernists, their movement "outward rather than inward," and then examines specific poems written by poets of the next generation. The essay concludes:

> American poetry took a wrong turning years ago. Some centuries have a profound spiritual movement; poetry, when vigorous, always is a part of it. We know ours is a century of technical obsession, of business mentality, of human effort dissipated among objects, of expansion, of a destructive motion outward. Yet there is also a movement in the opposite direction which is even more powerful. The best thought in this century moves inward...The weakness of our poetry is that it does not share in this movement.

Haines wrote: "you are giving American poetry the criticism it has needed for some time. No one else is doing it."[11] Thomas McGrath wanted more: "it's good jazz; more power!"[12] Bly also received a number of what he called the typical "'Now wait a minute...' letters."[13] And Richard Hugo chastised him for attacking poets like Eliot and Pound who were already *passé* in the minds of the new generation. "They seem so ancient, like getting pissed off at Xerxes."[14]

In any case, the piece was another boost to Bly's renown as a singular exponent of the new poetry. But his own magazine was still the primary vehicle. Hall went over the sixth issue and concluded: "This may be the best one—or the most enjoyable."[15] Bly's other favored reader, Simpson, commented: "The first section of poems, by you & Wright, is so far above the usual poetry in magazines that this alone would make the issue. In the Snyder article I was absorbed by your comparison of Western imagination and Eastern abstraction. The ideas are much larger than one hopes to find in criticism nowadays."[16]

Bert Meyers, a younger poet, had started a correspondence with Bly. After #5 he found himself "arguing with your notions about the value of surrealism, animals and kindness for American poetry...I do respect your opinions more than those of anyone else I know involved with American poetry."[17] Then, after #6, he wrote: "My argument with you is beginning to melt like spring ice—soon, a torrent of acquiescence."[18]

George Hitchcock wrote: "The last issue...has been an immense pleasure from beginning to end, with particular praise (from me anyway) for the political poems by you & James Wright & the excellent study of Gary Snyder."[19] Di Giovanni said the issue "seemed the best yet to me. I enjoyed the letters immensely and your Montale translations. It pleased me no end after so long a time to see my own work on your pages and to be in the fold at last."[20] Rob Cuscaden said: "As always, I was greatly stimulated by being introduced to a poet I had never heard of (de Otero), was encouraged by Crunk's sensibility, and fascinated by the 'Wisdom of the Old.'" But, he wondered, "where was my long-time favorite, the Blue Toad Award?...This feature MUST be reinstated."[21]

Ginsberg was moved to write from India with praise, a request, and recommendations:

Received late forwarded *Sixties* with Snyder essay which I thought was rare early perceptive. Otero poems very fine. I would like to see *Otero Trakl Vallejo Sea History* books you are publishing but have not enough money to order them properly; I am living very poorly here. Can you send me a set of the books, I will read them and pass them on to Hindi & Bengali & Marathi poets here (the Indian writers won't otherwise see them for years). When I get back to the US ten months from now I'll pay the debt.

155

He appended a postscript: "Other XX cent poets who might interest you—Nerala... Jevananda Das... V. Huidobro—I guess you know. Actually more interesting to younger Chileans than Neruda. More a poet's poet."[22]

The more general, cumulative impact of the magazine and its ideas was also evident. Hitchcock told Bly of his plans to start *kayak* (which became, probably, the most important offspring of *The Sixties*). "I am going to eschew eclecticism & evidence a vicious bias in directions you can well guess, but probably very little translation & a strong weighting (though not programmatic) toward the Pacific Coast." With a nod he made a request: "Since *kayak* is going to owe a <u>great deal</u> to the critical leadership you have given so many poets, myself included, I am extremely anxious that you be represented in the first issues, either by an article (e.g. a more detailed study of any one of the problems discussed in *Choice?*) or by poems or both."[23] Bly sent poems. Eventually, he would raise a critical ruckus there, too.

Harry Weber, editor of *The Minnesota Review*, said: "It's hard to believe that the most influential magazine in the country, at least as far as poetry is concerned, comes from Madison, Minnesota, which somehow makes me believe in God."[24] Richard Hadden of Wesleyan University Press said: "Who knows? Perhaps you are publishing the *transition* of this generation."[25]

Bly was working on a new book (then called *A Book About America*) and still rewriting the "Morgan book."[26] Tyrone Guthrie had approached him about translating a Strindberg play for his new theatre in Minneapolis. A book of essays on poetry was in the planning stages, as well as one he was calling *Seven Norwegian Poets*.[27] Furthermore, as he told Hall: "I am also nearly done with *The Continent Rising from the Sea*. I am writing brief <u>impressions</u>, highly personal in tone, of the poetry of each poet...."[28] A little later, he had more news: "I have finished a book of translations of which I am very proud—it is the old anthology Brekke began—10 'modern' poets of each country since 1910—all translated by me. I have added sections myself for Spain, South America, & Italy. So there are 100 poets represented—a sampler!"[29] But this whirlwind of activity took a toll.

Bly's self-admonitions to pull back and focus on his own poetry were increasing in frequency and intensity. "I think I have been mingling too much with the massive, turbid world—with the sour beehive...Also with the magazine—I have participated too much, and it is no longer my own magazine against everyone else in the world!" Thus he resolved: "no more reviews for *Hudson*, and all that...Let your whole participation in public life be yea and nay."[30] At the next ALMA meeting he resigned from the executive board.[31] Carolyn Kizer, editor of *Poetry Northwest*, took his place.[32] She then wrote: "I know perfectly well who the 'Queen-maker' (an unfortunate phrase in some ways) was, and wanted to say thanks, thanks. My sleeve is wet, as the Japanese say. You are an extraordinary man, in all sorts of complicated ways."[33]

Since *Silence in the Snowy Fields* had been published, Bly was doing more readings. In 1963 he did the Midwest circuit of colleges and universities, as well as the Guggenheim Museum in New York for the Academy of American Poets, with Wright. The next spring he read at the University of Massachusetts, Amherst, with Stephen Spender and Robert Fitzgerald.[34]

David Ray, soon to be a close associate, shared how he saw the influence of the new poetry: "That is the terrible impact of you & Wright. It will result in so much imitation, even on the part of people who don't want to be derivative in any way."[35] Haines, anticipating his first book, *Winter News*, wrote: "If the book ever comes out, I'm going to have a little note on the title page—coauthored by Robert Bly!"[36] Furthermore, and more importantly, Wright's *The Branch Will Not Break* (1963), Hall's *A Roof of Tiger Lilies* (1964), and Simpson's *At the End of the Open Road* (1963), which won the Pulitzer Prize in 1964, all manifestly exhibited the fecundity of Bly's ideas.

In an essay in the first issue of *kayak*, "Inventors & Diluters," Haines wrote that "poetry in America has been in a state of paralysis for over a generation." But he found some basis for optimism in

the renewed interest in translating the great modern poetry of other languages, particularly that of France, Spain and Germany, where most of what we now know as modern poetry originated.

This has been best represented by Robert Bly and his magazine...Since 1958 Mr. Bly has made an intelligent effort to present the work of the great moderns of Europe and South America, and also the work of some younger American poets who seem to be moving in a new direction. More than anyone else he has tried to create a climate in which a new poetry could be nourished and get a hearing. He has also written some of the best criticism American poetry has received. In fact, it is the only new criticism we have had since Pound began sending out his blasts from London around 1912.[37]

The Sixties 7 appeared two years late. Simpson wrote, grudgingly: "I suppose there is something to be said for the way you put out the magazine—when it <u>does</u> come out, it is such a surprise."[38] Inside the front cover are three quotations. The first, from the Danish poet Paul LaCour's *Fragments of a Diary*, ends with a question: "But what if the image contains that which thought can never discover?" The second is Machado's: "The intellect does not sing." And last, from Montale: "No one would write poems if the problem of poetry consisted in making oneself understood." This issue's focus is on the irrational, associative, emotive image, as over against intellectual, conscious abstraction.

The opening fanfare is five poems by Neruda. First is "III (From Alturas de Macchu Picchu)," from *Canto General*, translated by Wright. It begins:

The human soul was threshed out like maize in the endless
Granary of defeated actions, of mean things that happened,
To the very edge of endurance, and beyond,
And not only death, but many deaths, came to each one:
Each day a tiny death, dust, worm, a light
Flicked off in the slime of the suburbs, a tiny death with coarse
wings....

We might be reminded, awkwardly, of Simpson's parody in the last issue.

A love poem is followed by "The United Fruit Co." (tr. Bly), which includes these lines:

When the trumpet sounded, it was
All prepared on the earth,

And Jehovah parceled out the earth
To Coca Cola, Inc., Anaconda,
Ford Motors and other entities;
The Fruit Company, Inc.
Reserved for itself the most succulent
The central coast of my own nation,
The delicate waist of America.

Issue #6 had promised two Neruda poems. One of them, "Sólo La Muerte," is here translated as "Nothing But Death," but the other, "Caballero Solo," is absent. We recall that, in issue #3, these two poems were excerpted, minus some "offensive" lines in the latter censored by the typesetter. Bly had insisted on the complete poem in this issue; but the printer refused.[39] Without question a new printer would have to be found.

Bly's short essay, "The Surprise of Neruda," implicitly illuminates Neruda's role as a model for him:

In Neruda's poems, the imagination drives forward, joining the entire poem in a rising flow of imaginative energy... His imagination sees the hidden connections between conscious and unconscious substances with such assurance that he hardly bothers with metaphors—he links them by tying their hidden tails. He is a new kind of creature moving about under the surface of everything.

Bly's combativeness then comes into view:

The conventionally wise assure us that to a surrealist the outer world has no reality—only his inner flow of images is real. Neruda's work demolishes this banality. Neruda's poetry is deeply surrealist and yet entities of the outer world like the United Fruit Co. have greater force in his poems than in those of any strictly "outward" poet alive.

His dispute with another established viewpoint would become increasingly relevant as the decade continued: "Once a poet takes a political stand, the wise also assure us that he will cease writing good poetry. During the Spanish Civil War, Neruda became a Communist, and has remained one; most of his great books, one must admit, date after that time."

Next is a quotation from Yeats, which includes the following:

[The artist] can only convey [delight in beauty] in its highest form after he has purified his mind with the great writers of the world; but their example can never be more than a preparation. If his art does not seem, when it comes, to be the creation of a new personality, in a few years it will not seem to be alive at all...This is because art, in its highest moments, is not a deliberate creation, but the creation of intense feeling, of pure life; and every feeling is the child of all past ages and would be different if even a moment had been left out.[40]

This is a variation on a message the magazine consistently conveyed, and yet it could be lost as some over-enthusiastic young poets, skipping the necessary first step of becoming deeply familiar with their native literature, went straight to Bly's favorite Spanish poets (for example) and thus built their houses on sand.[41]

A selection of "American Poems" includes seven poets, four of whom are new to *The Sixties*. In Russell Edson's "A Chair," a personified chair waits for "the animate one" to sit down. The note says Edson "writes in a form he invented himself—a strange kind of prose-poem that fits none of the current categories." Second is "Cold Water," by Lewis Lipsitz, "a political scientist by profession." Third, Bill Knott, a real character whom Logan had discovered, has three poems.[42] Bly and others worked hard on his behalf.[43] The first "Poem" is as follows:

> *On nights like this the heart journeys to other islands.*
> *Beaches rise and dance naked under moonlight.*
> *Inland, asleep, you see*
> *The stone faces of your solitude being piled slowly ...*

After his poems were accepted, Knott wrote that he was "going around bragging to everyone about being published in the best magazine in America."[44]

Ignatow's "Earth Hard" is followed by three poems from Simpson. First is "The Inner Part":

> *When they had won the war*
> *And for the first time in history*
> *Americans were the most important people—*

...

Priests, examining the entrails of birds,
Found the heart misplaced, and seeds
As black as death, emitting a strange odor.

That vision of postwar America is remarkable. So too is "American Poetry":

Whatever it is, it must have
A stomach that can digest
Rubber, coal, uranium, moons, poems.

Like the shark it contains a shoe.
It must swim for miles through the desert
Uttering cries that are almost human.

These are in line with what Bly had espoused in the magazine from the outset.

Haines's "At the Foot of October" is the longest of the bunch. And Thomas McGrath, editor of *Crazy Horse* and author of the book-length poem *Letter To An Imaginary Friend* (the first half of which had already been published), makes his first appearance here. Bly and Wright first met McGrath at North Dakota State University in Fargo in 1962.[45] Shortly thereafter, Bly and Hall succeeded in getting a manuscript of McGrath's selected poems accepted by Wesleyan, but, out of a loyalty which Bly thought misplaced, McGrath let Swallow Press in Denver have the manuscript.[46] Here's the first stanza of "Hoot!":

Something lights my way
In the soft country of the future—
Like one hundred sixty acres
Of buried
Owls.

The section "Ten Brief Poems" draws from a wider variety of languages—Italian, Arabic, Spanish, French, German, Norwegian, and English—than are to be found in any previous issue. Bly writes: "One of the forms of poetry almost entirely overlooked by poets in the English language is the brief poem of three or four lines." The section includes poems by Salvatore Quasimodo, Ibn Hazm, Al-Muntafil, Apollinaire, Char, Hölderlin, Jorge Carrera Andrade, and Werner Aspenström; most of the translations would appear again later in *The Sea and the Honeycomb: a Book of Tiny Poems,* which the Sixties Press published in 1967. The only poem here originally written in English is "Snow" by John Kelleher, who had been Bly's tutor at Harvard.

The issue's major critical piece is Crunk's "The Work of James Dickey." Dickey had once told Bly: "I think you should consider dropping the series of articles on contemporary American younger poets (that is, unless you see fit to do mine, which I, like Walt Whitman, will be glad to write myself!)."[47] When Bly told him of his plans, Dickey replied: "I look forward to what you are going to say about my 'Southern eloquence' with great anticipation, believe me. What you say in your letter about my being a 'great poet' is very heady wine for me, believe me."[48] A short time later he wrote: "Naturally, I'll be glad to go over it with you (naturally!), make suggestions, and so on."[49] His pressing interest chafed with the slow motion of the issue's coming together. In Bly's "Prose vs. Poetry," Dickey's *Drowning with Others* got the first and the longest review (of twenty-three books), and it met with the most unqualified praise. So Dickey must have been feeling fairly safe in Bly's hands.

But Bly's opinion of Dickey had been changing. Dickey's characteristic swagger was becoming more pronounced, and Bly's initial excitement was now tempered by growing distaste. Bly commented to Hall on the most recent issue of *Poetry:* "Dickey has a long poem comparing himself to Jesus—an absurd thing called 'Folk-Singer in the Thirties'—full of lies."[50] Hall thought he was wrong, and said, "I think that your change of mind comes from thinking about Jim more than from reading his new poems."[51] Bly sent him a draft. "I know you don't agree with my sentences on his recent poems—and Dickey will come at me with a mace for it—but I can't run out on a fight, and pretend I hadn't read them at all."[52] Hall, still on the editorial board at Wesleyan, which was putting out Dickey's new book, liked the essay, with reservations.

In January, the Crunk essay was done, and Bly again wrote to Hall: "He's getting hopeless! I read a review he had in the *NY Times* for Dec 12th—four books, praised them all!...Dickey reminds me of those post-war descriptions of the Czechoslovakian parliament: one half absolutely incapable of anything, and the other half capable of anything."[53] He then sent the finished essay to Simpson, whose response sheds more light:

> Once an ad-man always an ad-man. I never went for that rough-hewn Southern charm—you know, the Bourbon laugh and the joke about negras which is intended to be taken as really pro-negra, maybe. Or the charming admission that deep down, one is prejudiced against Jews or Catholics...I don't trust grossness in any form, because it always goes hand in hand with a love of violence and corruption. And before you know it, you've got a reactionary on your hands.[54]

Apropos of this, Bly had written elsewhere: "A poem grows from a man like an ear, or a hand."[55]

The article begins: "The poems of James Dickey describe a spiritual struggle...the struggle of an animal to become a man." In his first book, *Into the Stone*, Dickey's imagination "seems to flower when he moves among the dead." The poet's own "doubt that he really exists penetrates all the poems, and leads to the idea of kingship. From believing himself nothing, he believes himself a king." Dickey's "weird obsession with kings" becomes clear in his second book, *Drowning with Others.* "The Owl King," Crunk says, is "as strange as a Grimm brothers' tale. It is a narrative of some hidden events of the psyche and also, incidentally, an explanation of the poetry we are reading. The poet is trying to tell the reader that...the poems were written by a blind child and an owl sitting up on a pine tree! This is a good idea. It's an idea that would drive a rationalist mad."

The criticism then takes a negative turn: "James Dickey embodies more of the South in his poems than any Southern poet ever has. Not only does his content remind us of the South, but the style seems Southern: it is quite plainly rhetoric, and a ghastly rhetoric is the worst weakness in these poems."[56] Crunk goes on: "Rhetoric exists here in a twisting of rhythm and language.

The lines are forced, whether they like it or not, into a dactylic rhythm." He calls this rhythm "power-mad." He also notes "a curious narcissism ... Dickey's imagination is in the poem, but somehow, he contrives to get his body in too." By doing this "he simply gets in the way and blocks off the view."

Nevertheless, Dickey's poetry seems original in contrast to that of Nemerov, Ciardi, John Frederick Nims, Whittemore, and Karl Shapiro, whom Crunk lumps together as the "'my healthy limitations' school," and a "mediocre charade." He also contrasts Dickey with "the dreary realists, like Sexton or Seidel," and their confessional poetry, for a remarkable imaginative energy flows in him. "In Mr. Dickey's work, poetry returns to its old kingdom of fantasy. He has a staggering gift for the image."

Finally, Crunk is impressed by Dickey's war poems. The authenticity comes from Dickey's experience as "a fighter pilot in both the Second World War and the Korean War ... Here again he violates the conventional idea of the poet as an incompetent boob." Bly did not know at the time, of course, that most of Dickey's vaunted war exploits were fictional.[57] Crunk concludes:

> When his imagination is interested, he carries tremendous physical energy into his poems. His courage is so great he does not fill the poem with phony Greek heroes as disguises, but instead places himself in the front of the poem, under clear glass, where you can see him for bad or good, and judge him as a fanatic, an animal killer, a lecher, a failure, or whatever you wish to. In his best poems something subterranean and preconscious is always present. He is like a big moose adapted somehow to living beneath the water in some calm island lake. The moose is constantly rising to the surface and breaking water so he can see his own huge horns in the sunlight, and giving a fixed and strange smile to the frightened bourgeoisie out fishing.

This was no small tour, with healthy portions of positive and negative.

Dickey did not come after Bly, not at first. "Some of your comments were so close to my original (secret) intentions that my jaw dropped (actually dropped). But unless you can give better reasons—or some reasons, at any rate—for your opinions it might be better to leave those sections out." Still, he says he found the essay

164

"extremely good, with that passionate personal commitment to the thing read which makes the criticism as exciting to read as poetry itself; more exciting, really than most poetry is."[58] While Dickey was actually seething, he wasn't about to blow his lid, for, as we shall see, he was anxiously awaiting publication of his Sixties Press book.

Five of the six poems in the next section had appeared in *Twenty Poems of César Vallejo*. Since many readers of the magazine did not read the press books, it makes sense, but it is surprising that there is no greater effort to tout the book. Bly translates "The Spider." Here are the first two stanzas:

It is a huge spider, which can no longer move;
a spider which is colorless, whose body,
a head and an abdomen, is bleeding.

Today I watched it with great care. With what tremendous energy
to every side
it was stretching out its many feet.
And I have been thinking of its invisible eyes,
the death-bringing pilots of the spider.

"Agape," a more personal poem, is translated by Knoepfle, and "The Eternal Dice" by Wright.[59] The one new translation in this group is "Good Sense," by H.R. Hays, whom Bly describes as "a man to whom all readers of South American poetry are indebted…his book, *Twelve South American Poets*…is still the best anthology of the South Americans." Last is "Black Stone Lying on a White Stone," translated by Bly and Knoepfle, in which Vallejo seems to predict his own death.

Parody follows, first on the "set poem," beginning with "Howard Nemerov Experiences Another Statue," by poet Henry Taylor. "America has produced three or four thousand statue poems in the last twenty years," says the introduction. Second is the Swedish artist Ivar Arosenius's illustration of a penguin in a suit. The caption reads: "A poet of the 'Twenties about to deliver another lecture on the demise of Hart Crane." Apparently, says one reader, "everyone" knew the joke was on Tate, to whom the penguin bears an uncanny resemblance.[60]

The Blue Toad returns:

>...Arthur Mizener...has sold the same article on Fitzgerald's youth to eighty-five separate magazines; he is now a fungus growing on Fitzgerald's corpse. In his career as vegetable toady for the Establishment, he has expressed his anxieties in a memorable statement: "good *New Yorker* stories are avant-garde enough."... Mizener is like people who say Stephen Vincent Benét is a greater poet than Wallace Stevens.
>
> Arthur Mizener is therefore awarded The Order of the Blue Toad. The toad is painted rising through the Seven Circles of Academic Tenure on a cloud of wingéd clichés.

This slap seems to have been in part a case of tit for tat. In a letter in the *Carleton Miscellany*, Mizener had called Bly an "infantile leftist."[61]

"Up at Uncle Jack's 1922: Martha's Vineyard," by Firman Houghton, is a parody of the "my interesting ancestors" poem. "Definitive work in this genre has been done by Robert Lowell," says the note.

> *I remember another time.*
> *Uncle Jack and Aunt Ida*
> *Were playing two-handed bridge.*
> ...
>
> *The world got to five hearts*
> *Before it stopped.*
> *Down two, vulnerable.*
> *With me over in the corner*
> *Watching everything.*
> *Shall I tell you about my cousins?*

The parodies continued to be popular, with friends like Hall and Haines openly hoping for parodies of themselves.[62] Haines clarified: "I think it was Pound who said that parody was one of the best forms of criticism."[63]

A return to seriousness comes with two poems by Vicente Huidobro (translated by Dora Pettinella), who, the note says, "has declared he does not want to communicate in poetry by manipulating the old worn out words and ideas, but instead by creating images that have never existed before, which slip between the well-known chessmen." Bly had, as Ginsberg guessed, been interested in him for quite a while. In 1958, Bly had rejected Pettinella's poems and some other translations, but he expressed interest in her Huidobro translations, saying "we…are planning a group of his poems." He offered critique and encouragement in multiple letters over the next several years. They show Bly's painstaking attention to detail, and his refusal to be satisfied until everything was just right and in line with the new poetry. This is the first part of "Adam":

Silence! Solitude! Vast silence
Of lifeless plains,
Solemn and deserted,
Luminously blanketed,
Stretching beneath the other
Endless silence of heavy skies.

Finally comes "Homage to Christina" by Logan. This six-part poem about the nineteenth century Pre-Raphaelite poet Christina Rossetti is quite formal, with fairly regular end-rhymes. The question cannot be avoided: Are there times when Bly favors his friends and lets his critical guard down?

"In Future Issues" invites parodies of "the younger poets… included in the Grove Press anthology or in Don Hall's Penguin anthology [*Contemporary American Poetry*]." Ever the cockeyed optimist, Bly declared: "There will be four issues of *The Sixties* in the next twelve months. We warn our subscribers in advance lest the shock be too much." Subscribers needn't have braced themselves; the next number did not appear for a year and a half, and the next four came between 1966 and 1972.

Hall had recently written: "I have been trying to think of a new slogan for the back of *The Sixties* on the new testing. How do you like this: "Support Nuclear Testing! / The Poor Man's / Thalidomide."[64] Bly basically approved, but felt that "The Poor Man's" was too cliché. "Use the first line as you have it, and then say 'Thalidomide for everybody!' or maybe 'Who needs Thalidomide?' The only other things I can think of are kind of long-winded, like 'So that every Mother can enjoy the benefits of Thalidomide, without a visit to her corner druggist.'"[65] But Hall and Bly's goofy, *Mad Magazine*-style brainstorming didn't get much further. Instead there was more "Wisdom of the Old," including this quotation from Tate:

> In a deliberately minor mode, Donne, Marvell, Landor, and Yeats wrote their great poems. John (Crowe Ransom) is in this formal tradition; it is this tradition which is the permanently experimental tradition. To undertake to write in iambic pentameter is a more difficult experiment than the chopped-up anapests of Mr. Pound because the risks are greater, failure being more easily perceived.
>
> I consider him now, since the death of Stevens and Frost, the dean of American poetry, whose poetry can scarcely be read by a young, coarse, and ignorant generation.

Tate, it seems, continued to be in favor of everything that the "young, coarse, and ignorant" Bly and his cronies were against, with a few exceptions.

Two or three months later, two Sixties Press books appeared simultaneously. The germ of the first is in this message from Wright to Dickey:

> if you yourself ever have any doubts about the bold stands you take..., I wish to tell you that...Bly simply went into a spasm when he read the recent "The Suspect in Poetry"; it struck him with such enthusiasms that he immediately started to shape (in his imagination, which is delightfully agile and fertile) a book of James Dickey's "Collected Reviews".[66]

After hearing from Bly, Dickey wrote in his pseudo-deferential manner:

> O Master of Worthy Enterprises,...I am delighted that you want to collect my essays, and I accept on one condition: that you yourself do the editing. I really don't know which are the "best" ones, and so you must decide...I think the book is a great idea (naturally!), and am very much looking forward to see how the whole project turns out.[67]

Much like with the Crunk article, his eagerness—traceable in more than fifteen letters—bordered on badgering. When would it

168

appear? When would he get his advance? Reviewers were inquiring! What about distribution? Royalties? Cover design?

At one point he offered to write an introduction. "All in all, I'm highly pleased; I even caught myself being interested, as though I were not reading my own work." He added: "If my introduction isn't satisfactory, and if you think you can do better (I think you can do better, though I think of mine as adequate enough), would you write an introduction—anything you want to say will be all right with me—for the book?"[68] Bly did write it, but "in the form of a blurb on the front flap of the dust jacket, thus keeping me out of the book proper...One of the few pugnacious blurbs I've ever seen!"[69]

The book finally appeared in late spring 1964. Bly's blurb covers some familiar ground (*The Sixties* platform, actually) on the dismal state of criticism:

> I admire James Dickey for spending his energy criticizing poetry...and speaking about it seriously, without fear of literary reprisal.
>
> If the distinction between first and second rate work is not made, freshly, in every generation, poetry suffers the sterility one notices in provincial countries—poetry disappears down dead-end roads without ever looking around. Young poets moreover, do not learn in their cradles how to write good poetry—nor can they learn just from reading ancient poetry. ... Criticism's greatest value remains in its usefulness to the poets themselves.

The book is divided into four sections: 1) "The Suspect in Poetry" considers "the Winters approach" of Donald Drummond and Ellen Kay, Ginsberg, Gunn, O'Gorman, Mezey, Olson, Witt, Sexton, and Booth (most of whom Bly had also criticized harshly); 2) "In the Presence of Anthologies" reviews *The New Poets of England and America* and *The New American Poetry*; 3) "The Second Birth" is on Roethke, Patchen, Nemerov, Carruth, Jarrell, Cummings, Elder Olson, Eberhart, and Brother Antoninus; and 4) "Toward a Solitary Joy" is on Snyder, Kinnell, Logan, Merwin, Stafford, and Ignatow, which looks like a list of *The Sixties'* favorites.

Benedikt was enthusiastic: "Dickey is so unhesitatingly and firmly correct—I believe that book of criticism to be one of the finest contributions to a healthy poetry which any house, firm, foundation, or shack, has made."[70] Meyers said: "I think much of what Dickey says in *Suspect* is true, and good." But, he felt "rage" at Dickey, having heard from a friend who was at a party with him that "Dickey became very drunk and began being obnoxious about Jews and Negroes."[71]

Bly reported that the book was "going to libraries & bookstores with incredible speed—I had to order 300 more this morning from Ireland. Finally we've published something librarians love—prose!"[72] Dickey was thrilled.[73]

The reviews, both laudatory and dismissive, were many. Robert Watson wrote: "These brief reviews...give the reader the impression...that Dickey's capacity for suspicion is enormous and that he likes nothing better than a quick, clean kill. On the few occasions in the book where Dickey does take the care and space to explain his positions...he can be very, very good."[74] Richard Kostelanetz was mostly positive: "Dickey emerges as unquestionably the finest critic of American poetry today." He tends to harshness, and yet, at the same time, he can be "much too nice to bad poets...Just after he finishes slaughtering a poet's work, he invariably reverses his field and turns up with something complimentary."[75] An English reviewer asked: "how long is it since our own critics displayed such splendid bad temper and enthusiasm? I am jealous for a less temperate literary climate."[76] On the other hand, Kenneth Fields said the book is "a series of literary potshots, but it is not criticism."[77] Christopher Wiseman said Dickey "pigeonholes about thirty poets. In the one hole go the 'suspect' (those he doesn't like); in the other a rather gushingly lauded 'in-group.'"[78]

Once the book appeared in print, Dickey kept after Bly, inquiring about total sales figures.[79] Bly relayed the numbers, voicing his resentment and suspicion of Dickey's intentions. Dickey was placating: "No, no, of course I don't think you're making a lot of money out of the book...But I am surely very disappointed that you didn't realize some sort of profit from *Suspect*, particularly since it seems to have sold well—or at least for that sort of book." Then he veered:

> And I surely don't have any immediate plans for bringing out the book again with another publisher. I consider you my publisher: you conceived of the book, edited it, and marketed it extremely well. I'm sorry we can't get out another edition.... Several outfits have asked for parts of it...But *The Suspect in Poetry* belongs to The Sixties Press, at least as far as the foreseeable future is concerned.[80]

By this time, the damage to their relationship was fairly well advanced, and Bly's concerns were not misplaced. Less than a year later, Farrar, Straus & Giroux had a book of Dickey's reviews listed in their catalog. Bly told Hall: "Dickey had told them he already had permission. So I wrote and told them no."[81] When pressed by Dickey, his agent, and his publisher, Bly announced his fee was $1500; they offered $150. Bly wrote to Dickey: "Ridiculous! I prefer nothing to such an offer. Why didn't you offer $4.25?...Legally, you may be able to pirate it, but it will be, literarily and morally, a pirated edition."[82] They did so. *Babel to Byzantium* included twenty of the twenty-six essays published by the Sixties Press.

The other Sixties Press book in 1964 was *Twenty Poems of Blas de Otero,* chosen and translated by Hardie St. Martin, the first collection of Otero published in English. Plans for this had begun to gel some time in 1960.[83] St. Martin's introduction says that Otero, "a man caught up in the problems of his time," writes of the "common oppression" that connects human beings. His poetry is marked by "a strange transformation in language," "a sudden twist of phrase," "the unusual logic of his imagination," and "a thread of irrationality."

Ignatow reacted with profound appreciation:

> Quieter than Vallejo, he yet projects that desperate air which is Spain, the language inside something and struggling to get out. This is quite different from American writing, which oddly enough seems to be on the outside struggling to get in, if you get what I mean...The shift is significant of a change of climate in America, more coming to the surface than ever before: the boxed in Negroes, the held down poor, the isolated artist

and writer, the lonely, lost suburbanite, the city dweller caged in his subway and claustrophobic apartment elevator. These experiences cry out for a technique that would burst the bonds and out into the open world of communication and affection.[84]

Among the reviewers, Russell Banks was congratulatory and grateful. Bemoaning the plethora of "domestic and university tragedies" so common in contemporary poetry, he lauds Bly for promoting the benefits of the poetry of Neruda, Machado, Otero, and others. He went on:

> It helps us to keep a clear head on what the poet's business really is and, thereby, what our own, as human beings, really is. For Otero, the proper business of poets and other kinds of men is self-evident: at one end of life there is birth, and at the other end there is death; in between, for most men, there is only pain.[85]

The Otero book did not cause the same kind of splash that *Suspect* had, but it was more in tune with the *Zeitgeist*.[86] For the times they were a-changin' in the U.S.A.; the Civil Rights struggle was in full swing, and the Vietnam War was intensifying. But before Bly became actively involved in protesting that war, he first took a break from the United States altogether.

10

News of the Universe

In late 1963, Bly was awarded an Amy Lowell Poetry Traveling Scholarship.[1] Wilbur had nominated him, and Hall, who was living in the village of Thaxted, Essex, on a Guggenheim Fellowship, had written a letter on Bly's behalf. Hall found Robert and Carol a house in the same village. Bly reacted to the award with enthusiasm and some sarcasm: "I am jumping up and down!… We'll have a great time. Imagine! London! (I love the English.)… I want to see J.M. Cohen, and [Colin] Falck, and [Ian] Hamilton, & Edward Thomas' widow, and Ted Hughes and J.B. Trend and Erich Fried, and Jon Silkin!"[2]

"I'm sure you'll enjoy looking at the natives in their peasant costumes," Hall wrote, "but the secret police, and the League for the Suppression of Natural Instincts, may get you down a bit. Really very nice people though, when you get to know them, the police I mean." He added that he had seen an article on The Sixties Press in *The London Magazine*. "It started out by praising a lot, and ended with its skepticism and irony. It made me a bit mad, but I am not too mad, because I realize that it is amazing at all for Ian Hamilton to be able to see anything of what you are doing."[3]

Hamilton had written: "The American Sixties Press enterprise is worth watching; it represents a deliberate reaction against academic knottiness, the Objectivist clarities and the vandalism of the Beat Generation." But he saw some "very real dangers that this movement will generate a cult of arbitrariness, of what Pound called 'any decayed cabbage cast upon any pale satin sofa.'" He declared that "the poetry which most closely follows Bly's theory of the released subconscious, which is anti-metaphoric in the sense that it seeks to sever the Image from all referential burdens, is surely doomed to either generalities or eccentricities." In addition, "there is something insidious about the speechless approval with which certain American reviewers have greeted the Sixties Press activities—it is the response that Bly's propaganda demands, and it is at the same level a guilty response, after all those years of enslavement under Brooks-and-Warren." Hamilton then quoted from Simpson's review of *Silence in the Snowy Fields*, where he compares Bly to Wordsworth, and ended with a portion of Simpson's parody of Bly, which he found "more convincing."[4]

Shortly after arrival, Bly set down his first impressions:

> I was struck on driving around the roads near Thaxted to see how prosy the landscape is! It is pure prose! Even the turnpikes, especially them, shooting from Ohio into Indiana, hold, compared to these roads, immense suggestions of poetry.
>
> Why is that? Perhaps space has something to do with poetry.
>
> And England's poetry! Incredible! Little cardboard cut-outs of people, houses painted with a door and two windows, smoke curling from a chimney shaped like a garbage can, petty quarrels of stunted quizkids with their textbooks.[5]

Thus his biases seemed still firmly ensconced.

Other close friends were abuzz. Simpson wrote: "I think, seriously, that the idea of Robert & Carol in England is one of the most classical confrontations in the history of American Literature. How can you stand it? How can they stand it? Blimey! Cor!"[6] Wright suggested to Simpson that the apparent oddity, however, was illusory, merely Bly's performance of a role, which previously had been "entertaining and even useful." He said: "I heard him tell the assembled English Departments of Carleton College and the Morris, Minn. branch of the U. of Minnesota that, compared with poetry in some other languages, 'English poetry can scarcely be said to exist.' Nonsense, yet it pleases me sometimes to think of it." And he shares the beginning of Bly's letter to him: "Well, here I am in England! I feel like a whore in a police station!"[7]

In July, Bly did a BBC radio broadcast on Dickey.[8] He was meeting English poets and translators, as planned. Work continued daily on his new book, which he was calling *Assyrian Horses*. He told Hall: "I think there's something fresh here, independent almost of me. I could call it *Getting Up Early*, the old title I had for *Snowy Fields*, but I do want something more mysterious, like *The Pre-History of the Water Horse*. (I've got to get those <u>horses out</u> of there!)"[9] He arranged for distribution of Sixties Press books in London.[10] And he was doing other *Sixties* business, spending three weeks on correspondence, "some piled up for a year," and returning submitted manuscripts. "So today a new start begins. All month I will read and write. I will commit myself to no more Sixties projects, no more books of translations!...Joy! Sunlight! Thought!"[11] We might add: "Delusion!" Thus he prepared for the official start of his fellowship year.

On October 1, the Blys moved into an apartment in Paris.[12] "Monday I'm signing up with Alliance Française. Carol gets along well already. I can talk louder, but I don't know any words!"[13] Bly was happy: "How wonderful Paris is!...We see no one, and I work and read all day. Reading Marcuse's *Eros and Civlization*, which is excellent, and Herbert Read's essays on Modern Art which I also devour."[14] Later that fall he met Paul Zweig, the start of a fruitful relationship. Bly gave a reading at Le Mistral bookstore and read Vallejo's poem "I will die, in Paris, on a rainy day." "It made the whole room come alive." Furthermore, he said, "Paris is curious. Drawing and everything visual have meant more to me since I've been in Paris than at any other time. I can read Dürer as if he were a poem. There is something mysterious here, under the ground."[15]

A letter came from Wesleyan University Press, refusing Bly's second book (which would be *The Light Around the Body*). He asked Hall for the inside scoop. "What did they have against it? Did they want a repetition of *Snowy Fields?*"[16] Hall told him about the opposition of Wilbur, Levertov, and John Malcolm Brinnin.[17] Hall then abruptly quit, joined the editorial board of Harper & Row, and wanted the new book. Bly assented gladly. "I am very much engrossed in this book, and want it to be <u>massive</u> in a certain way." Kinnell came to Paris, read the manuscript, "liked the book very much, and thought it was a big step forward from *Snowy Fields* (partly because of 'intensity')."[18]

Other projects included versions of Kabir and a translation of Knut Hamsun's *Hunger*.[19] He was editing *Forty Poems Touching on Recent American History*.[20] Bly wrote a letter to the editor of the *Times Literary Supplement*, complaining about a review, of Michael McClure's poetry, which he found "pretentious and mindless." He said: "Your reviewer goes down gurgling in his own language without ever being able to gasp out whether the poems of Mr. McClure are any good or not. If you are interested in American poetry, you might consider choosing reviewers that have developed some kind of language other than academic jargon." Bly proclaims that McClure's books are "not very good, but they deserve having even this said of them in a moderately human way. Your reviewer thrashes about like a robot fallen out of a boat into the Great Okeefenokee Swamp."[21] This is admirable, really. Bly took his message across the Atlantic in person, and stood up, in his own fashion, for American poetry and for a style of criticism of which he seemed to be the predominant advocate.

During his year abroad, Bly also got word of other awards. He received a Guggenheim Fellowship for 1965-66.[22] John Hersey informed him of a $2,500 grant from the National Institute of Arts and Letters "in recognition of your creative work in literature."[23] The citation, signed by George F. Kennan, President, calls Bly "a poet of verve and toughness, an editor who stands his ground against the encroachments of establishmentarianism, a translator who has vigorously continued his ancestral traditions of Viking exploration."[24] Odin was riding high.

Travels resumed in the spring, to Spain and Italy. Bly's Nordic predisposition was showing as he wrote Hall from Sweden in late June: "We've just arrived from the South—which we left with no regret—it is obvious Vesuvius had the right idea. Overjoyed to be here among the lichen-covered rocks." On to Norway, back to England for some hiking in Wordsworth country and in Cornwall, and then home.[25]

Meanwhile, back in the inner circle, the mutual-criticism-society of Bly and friends did not always operate smoothly, as the following few excerpts indicate. Hall wrote: "What do you mean I am 'hopeless with criticism of my own poems'? I am <u>always</u> taking your advice. Every now and then I have stuck it out and you have come around. Plenty of other times I have stuck it out, and finally decided that you were right. But even you have got to be wrong sometimes."[26] Bly said: "Don't be cross at me for what I say on poems—the harshest criticism is best. Only our friends care enough to criticize harshly."[27]

Simpson called Bly's recent treatment of his poems "butchery." He goes on at some length: "You have an infallible instinct for picking out my best lines and trying to eliminate them, on some damned principle I don't understand." His conclusion: "You make poetry into a kind of obstacle course, without joy or satisfaction."[28]

Haines, still in the process of assembling his first book with Bly's help, wrote: "Yes, I'm aware of using certain words too much—*shadows, dream, cold, frozen, dark, darkness, twilight, snow,* etc. But it's no wonder that I do. I have found that my environment sinks into me in strange ways." Then he gives it back to Bly: "A word you use too often is *tiny.* Stop using it. I always want to laugh when I see it...Well, Lorca uses words like *blood, bull, rose, green,* and some others over and over. We all do it."[29]

The exchange of criticism, as we have seen previously, sometimes strained but usually strengthened the bonds holding this group of writers together. For example, Simpson wrote Hall and Bly to share the news of his Pulitzer Prize for *At the End of the Open Road*: "I think I owe you Donald, and you Robert (what an editing job you did on the book!) one-third of the prize each."[30]

Criticism from outside the circle could, similarly, either fortify its solidarity or weaken or at least threaten it. Bly wrote to Hall: "Your old friend Thom Gunn declares in the new *Yale Review* that Jim Wright and I are dilettantes! I like that! I'll wring his neck. He did a good job on Louis' book, but hauled in every canard he could (including "absence of discursive reasoning") on Jim's book. (Gunn did a fine review of *Snowy Fields* by the way—did you see it?)"[31] And Simpson wrote:

177

> Did you see the article in the *N. Y. Review of Books*...in which Wright, Dickey, Simpson, Hall and Bly were described as "the group"? And he said that Bly was the most talented of the lot. You _____!...My own opinion is, it's a plot, to make us all start being envious of each other. Of course, you <u>may</u> be the most talented, but it's terrible when people come right out and say so.[32]

A new book had Bly, Wright, and Duffy joining with Kelly and Rothenberg to launch a new movement. Stephen Stepanchev wrote: "The emphasis that Bly, Kelly, and their associates have put on the deep image has had the salutary effect of providing a partial corrective to the projective-verse movement."[33] While it was good to raise awareness of some of these ideas, Stepanchev's false notion of this "deep image" school spawned or prolonged a misrepresentation that still persists.[34] As Bly wrote in a copy of the book he gave to Duffy: "Read the inside story of how you and I took a train one night incognito to Chicago, and met in a cellar with Robert Kelly to plan the overthrow of American poetry."

Extant reactions to *The Sixties* 7 are few. It seems that one of the consequences of the year abroad was that much of the usual correspondence was lost in the shuffle.[35] But in January 1964, Bly told Hall: "*The Sixties* 8 (German issue) [is] all done but for the Crunk article on Jim, which I'll do soon."[36] Eight months later he wrote: "Visited Michael Hamburger Thursday of last week...We worked hard on the German issue, and Michael was very generous and acute."[37] The magazine accompanied the Blys on their travels: "I put two heavy trunks full of *Sixties* MSS, and all the *Sixties* files on top of the little Austin, cranked her up, and we shot off!"[38] A year later, Hall wrote: "Some of us feel like another issue of *The Sixties*. It came over us about 18 months ago & it's still with us. If you don't bring it out I'll <u>mimeograph</u> something I'll call *The Sixties* with your name on it full of poems by T. Weiss taken from his latest volume covered with praises by James Dickey."[39] Finally, Bly wrote to Hall: "*Sixties* 8 is sent off! (It has your poem in it....) Don't be mad. Forgive the feeble minded."[40]

One positive result of the postponement is the issue's extraordinary cohesiveness. The longest issue ever, it arrived in May

1966.[41] The front cover highlighted "Twenty-Six German Poems" and two parodies, giving this latter aspect of the magazine prominent attention for the third consecutive issue.

The leading quotation, from Rilke, includes: "Try to get at the depth of things—this is one place irony never goes down to." Were the New Critics listening? The second is from Shelley, who says: "We lack the power to imagine what we know." Last is a short poem by Machado:

> *People possess four things*
> *that are no good at sea:*
> *anchor, rudder, oars*
> *and the fear of going down.*

This poem would appear again in *The Sea and the Honeycomb*, which was due to be released that same month.

The Sixties 8 opened with Bly's essay, "The Dead World and the Live World." He had, as usual, sent a draft, with the working title "Two Modernist Traditions," to two friends. Hall found it problematic on many scores.[42] Simpson had a drastically different response, calling it "one of the best things you've done" and "a fine, original piece of work."[43] This left Bly in a quandary, but he stuck to his plan.

The essay begins: "A new point of view allows the traveller to see deep into certain valleys. What we want to look into here is the landscape dominated by Robert Lowell, Arthur Miller, Saul Bellow—the American literary landscape at the moment." Some writers, like Miller, bring us "news of the human mind," but the universe is missing. Joseph Conrad's *The Heart of Darkness*, on the other hand, "like the poems of Roethke and Whitman, brings us 'news of the universe.' Conrad takes us inside a human mind, but when we get there it turns out we are deep inside a continent. We feel the immensity of nature, how much of it is beyond the ego."[44]

Bly says that the psychoanalyst Georg Groddeck sees Goethe as a supreme example of the latter kind of writer. He continues:

> The "human" poets study the three classical faculties: feeling, will, and intellect. The poets of the universe…are aware of an additional energy inside themselves. Groddeck calls this energy

179

the "Gott-natur" (The holy nature). The Gott-natur senses the interdependence of all things alive, and longs to bring them all inside a work of art...What results is calmness.

The trouble with modernist literature is our failure "to distinguish the works which were products of the dying tradition...from those that came into being precisely to break the dying tradition. *Ulysses* is part of the dead world; Trakl's poems are part of the live world. Hoddis, Rilke, Machado, Redon, and Max Ernst also belong to the live world."

He asks: "Suppose a country's literature...doesn't move on to anything new, but instead insists, like Snodgrass in *Heart's Needle*, or Lowell in *Life Studies*, on studying the exclusively human over and over? Suppose also that the human being is not studied in relation to non-human lives, or lives in other countries, but simply in relation to itself?"

Here Bly makes a breathtaking leap: "One can predict first of all that such a nation will bomb foreign populations very easily, since it has no sense of anything real beyond its own ego." Also, according to Groddeck, "the literature of such a nation will take refuge in the sensational." Sensational extremes are found in Lowell and Sexton, in Miller's later plays and those of Tennessee Williams, and in the work of Norman Mailer. "For the confessional poet anything less than an abortion or a cancer operation really doesn't justify the machinery." The sorry state of criticism is also part of the problem.

Bly insists: "I am not criticizing these writers for being interested in human beings...I am not urging a nature poetry either, but rather a poetry that goes deep into the human being, much deeper than the ego, and at the same time is aware of many other beings." This holistic view includes what might be called ecological concerns. "Certainly a sense of the 'Gott-natur' stands at the very center of Gary Snyder's work." The same is true of haiku. "The Chinese and Japanese have kept alive the kind of poetry that 'brings us news of the universe.' That is why their poetry is so much read now."

For the German section, therefore, Bly chooses poems that fit in this scheme, poems that attempt "to break the hold of the egocentric school."[45] The primary criterion is not being "modern"; poems from the nineteenth century, as well as the twentieth, can be part of the live world. One example, "'When Geometric Diagrams...,'" by Novalis:

When geometric diagrams and digits
Are no longer the keys to living things,
When people who go about singing or kissing
Know deeper things than the great scholars,
When society is returned once more
To unimprisoned life, and to the universe,
And when light and darkness mate
Once more and make something entirely transparent,
And people see in poems and fairy tales
The true history of the world,
Then our entire twisted nature will turn
And run when a single secret word is spoken.

In summary, from a total of twenty-six poems—by Goethe, Hölderlin, Novalis, Eduard Mörike, Theodor Storm, Nietzsche, Hugo Von Hofmannsthal, Hermann Hesse, Jakob Van Hoddis, Trakl, Brecht, Günter Eich, Celan, and Johannes Bobrowski ("These are his first poems published in the U.S.")—in this short but broadly representative German anthology, fifteen were translated by Bly, four of those under a pseudonym (Reynolds or Kresenky).[46]

"The Work of James Wright" is one of Crunk's most important essays. Bly had first commissioned Dickey to write it.[47] Dickey set to work: "I have a good start...I call it 'Under the Sieve,' and it's turning out well so far; at least I hope I don't dishonor my illustrious Platonic archetype of a critic, the illustrious Samuel Johnson of the fifties and sixties, Crunk." He asked when he would be paid.[48] Naturally, he also sought Bly's advice.[49] But Bly rejected the finished product. Dickey responded: "I'm sorry you can't use the article. You're right, I had little taste for it, and it didn't really satisfy me either; I had so much rather write under my own name. But it did cost me some time, and so thanks for the check; I call that fair-minded, surely."[50] Bly told Hall about the exchange, that the essay was "too vague & general, no real criticism, sharp criti-

181

cism at all, nor any praise. I said I thought it was apparent he really didn't like Jim's new work."[51]

Thus Bly once again shouldered Crunk's mantle. In Wright's first book, *The Green Wall*, "we find ourselves in the presence of a man who is climbing over a wall." But "he does not get all the way over." Crunk describes Wright's move across Ohio, "from the incredibly ugly landscape of strip-mining to a sort of pre-Industrial Revolution pastoral enclosure. Kenyon College resembled a walled castle, surrounded by Americans crying to climb over the wall, from the dishevelled South into the ordered poem." He adds that "almost all Americans at the time imagined the writing of poetry as a climb somewhat like that." Crunk continues: "Lorca's image for the act of writing a poem suggests a journey in the opposite direction...a climb from his own world into a wilder world." These two views of poetry are "absolutely irreconcilable."

He then discusses some specific poems into which Wright introduces "the scarred and the hated," and where he shows "more respect for those who break laws than those who keep them." Despite this content, "the language of the poems is conventional, literary, full of such elaborate syntax that the voices are smothered."

Wright's second book, *Saint Judas*, "expresses a fierce, almost ferocious, will to survive. The way to survival, the book says, cannot be found by changing roads, or climbing over obstacles in the road, but only by swallowing the stones in the road, gobbling down what is dark and heavy." There is "a tone of good will toward others" as well as toward himself, "one of the fundamental emotions of great art." Wright also focuses on the emotion of guilt with an intensity matched only by Ginsberg. While there are good things in the poems in this book, Crunk says, the poems are not really good.

Jumping on a favorite horse, Crunk adds: "American criticism in the 50's had been almost worthless in helping the younger poets to get a clear view of their work. Mr. Wright's work, even the weakest of it, was praised to the skies." Dickey, on the other hand, "lump[ed] Wright in with the others of the 'school of charm,' and referred contemptuously to his 'plodding sincerity.'" Wright agreed, and decided to quit.

"When he did return to poetry, the influence of Trakl brought in a new tone…[T]he poems begin to come from farther back in the brain." (Crunk, notably, fails to credit the considerable influence of Bly in this return.) With the resultant book, *The Branch Will Not Break*, Wright starts to look "back on his own life, and moves to discard without hysteria old ideas that proved wrong. At the same time a subtle and eccentric thought comes in." Crunk observes that some reviewers have been hostile to this new posture.

Of "Lying in a Hammock At William Duffy's Farm in Pine Island, Minnesota," Crunk says: "The mind here seems unnaturally, preternaturally, awake…The question the poem never asks directly is this: how is it possible for there to be so many spiritual emblems, signs, reminders of the path, everywhere, and yet for the man who sees them to have gotten nowhere, to have achieved none of the spiritual tasks that those emblems suggest?"

He goes on: "Two energies have been trying to get free in James Wright's work; the first is natural American speech, the second images." Although Wright "seems to be able to write poetry about almost anything…he often settles for easy effects; for example, he uses words with a kind of literary perfume on them." His grammar tends to be repetitive, and his images "become perfunctory at times."

Crunk's "short journey" closes with a positive summation and a simile:

James Wright is an amazingly good poet. His lines are not stiff like sticks, but flexible like a living branch. Some emotion, rising very close to the surface, always seems to keep the words alive. In thought, his words, underneath, are in touch with something infinite…Behind the subtle language…lies intellectual energy, in this case, extremely powerful intellectual energy. He goes long distances when he starts, and gives the impression of someone obeying ancient instincts, like some animal who spends all summer with his herd, and then migrates alone, travelling all night, drinking from old buffalo wallows.

Given their close relationship, Bly was acutely aware of Wright's faults and gifts (as he perceived them). Crunk's article is remarkable, as usual, for its unstinting directness. Wright read it before publication, and thought it "good."[52]

"Five American Poets" follows, with Wright's "Living by the Red River" coming first:

> *Blood flows in me, but what does it have to do*
> *With the rain that is falling?*
> *In me, scarlet-jacketed armies march into the rain*
> *Across dark fields. My blood lies still,*
> *Indifferent to cannons on the ships of imperialists*
> *Drifting offshore.*
> *Sometimes I have to sleep*
> *In dangerous places, on cliffs underground,*
> *Walls that still hold the whole prints*
> *Of ancient ferns.*

There is also the short poem "'I am a Sioux Brave,' He Said in Minneapolis."

Next is "African Violets" by Richard LaFuze. Bly liked his poetry, despite his personal eccentricity. For example, as LaFuze wrote to Bly:

> Your book of poems is the most promising of any yet in this country. There are, however, some errors which never should have been exposed to the twelve apostles of the sick rooster which squats on this country. It will be so difficult to outlive them. And some of your poems are incredibly sweet and onionlike.
>
> I have met so many strange, lovable men in the last few years and believe that I shall be a credit to your underwork in this country.[53]

Hitchcock contributes "Beneath Me the Earth Forever Thinking," which begins:

> *In the entrails of the mountain*
> *smiths labor at their forges;*
> *on its crest a wisp of steam,*
> *elsewhere: cold granite.*

Earlier, he had told Bly: "Believe me, I would rather be published in *The Sixties* than any other magazine in the country."[54] "Reclining Figure (after Henry Moore)" is by Hall. Last is Knoepfle, with "For A Child Who Lived Six Hours."

Then it's back to the issue's main theme in Bly's review of "Recent German Anthologies." He likes Patrick Bridgewater's *Twentieth Century German Verse*. *Contemporary German Poetry*, by Gertrude Clorius Schwebell, comes off less well: "New Directions, with their usual stupidity in judging translations, have this time produced a real monster." As for *Modern German Poetry: 1910-1960*, Bly declares: "[Michael] Hamburger's translations show their strength, and are many times better" than those in the other two books. However, Christopher Middleton's…are "especially turgid and colorless."[55] He concludes on a positive note, praising once again Rothenberg's *New Young German Poets*.

"On Bombastic Descriptions of Nature" is a one-page excerpt of Wordsworth's prose. Bly means to show, in part, that his own brand of sharp criticism has esteemed precedents (much as he did with "A Quotation from Tolstoy" in #4); and he also reiterates and further embellishes the view of nature he presented in the opening essay. Wordsworth notes that, with a couple of exceptions, "the poetry of the period intervening between the publication of the *Paradise Lost* and the *Seasons* does not contain a single new image of external nature." He laments the lack of a "spirit of genuine imagination" and says regarding a passage in Dryden and another in Pope's *Iliad* translation: "A blind man, in the habit of attending accurately to descriptions casually dropped from the lips of those around him, might easily depict these appearances with more truth." That sounds faintly like something Bly might say.

The Wordsworth quotation reverberates in "Madame Tussaud's Wax Museum," a feature now reappearing after a three-issue absence:

> A new species of rhetoric has recently turned up; sensational inflations of nature. The poem forces nature to confess. Butterflies are full of violence and self-hatred. Details of nature are used purely for decorative effect, as they were used by neoclassical poets in the Eighteenth Century … If tightrope walkers looked at nature no more carefully than these poets do, they would all be dead long ago.

The examples Bly presents of "phony nature description" come from poems by William Meredith, Frederick Seidel, Ned O'Gorman, and Robert Lowell, who writes in "Sailing Home From Rapallo" (from *Life Studies*):

> *The crazy yellow and azure sea-sleds*
> *blasting like jack-hammers across*
> *the spumante-bubbling wake of our liner,*
> *recalled the clashing colors of my Ford.*

Next are "Some Sentences by Jean Arp." Arp, who died shortly after this appeared, was a sculptor, painter, and poet; a Dadaist and, later, a Surrealist. The first sentence recalls some of Crunk's recent comments: "Art should move toward what is spiritual, toward reality. This reality is never the *objective* reality, the reality that is approached by naturalism, nor the *intellectual* reality, that is approached by philosophy, but rather the inner reality." The second resumes this issue's efforts to bridge the Cartesian split: "The reason developed to the point of being deformed is what has made man into a tragic and hideous figure. He is separated from nature. He thinks he has mastered nature. He believes himself the measure of all things...In my opinion, the idea of art which has supported the egotism of human beings is revolting."[56]

For just the second time, Bly reviews a single book, Lowell's *For the Union Dead*, the magazine's first and only extended criticism of an older poet. Hall had offered help: "I think the Lowell piece is gentle & that it is mostly right. I don't think it's going to raise questions in the minds of people who are not already doubtful. You yell a lot but you don't look closely at anything. I think you should look closely at one thing."[57] Bly replied: "Your poorly concealed sneers at my Lowell article were very helpful...So I changed it around, wrote more, dropped some; hope it turned out better!"[58]

Bly begins: "The older poets have all died in the last years; the publishing world feels lonesome without a great poet around. Robert Lowell is being groomed for this post. The result is evil, especially for Lowell. Mr. Lowell has written powerful poems in the past, and some good poems recently." However, "most of the poems in *For The Union Dead* are bad poems. Everyone writes bad poems at times, but advice from other poets is often a great help in keeping the worst of them from being published." Pound helped Eliot and Yeats. Lowell's problem is that he is "surrounded by flatterers."

Bly sees two intellectual traditions, "both bankrupt," coming together in Lowell's book. "One is the entire string of intellectual longings represented by the history of the *Partisan Review* ... Their insistence on the value of alienation, their academic notions of modernism, are dead." Because of these "decrepit" ideas, "Lowell has no choice but to glue the poems together with pointless excitement." The second bankrupt tradition is based on "the notion that an artist must never be calm, but must be *extreme* at all costs. This destructive notion, a bourgeois notion, flows from both right wing influences on Lowell, like Tate, and left wing influences like the *Partisan Review* writers."

Lowell has difficulty, Bly argues, with the unity of a poem. "In seven poems...the inner and outer worlds hold together...But the rest of the poems are melodrama; the inner and outer worlds have split apart."

Finally Bly says: "The question we have to ask about the book is not why there are a few good poems—there are good poems because Lowell's talent is very great—but why so many incredibly bad poems appear in the book." Not only that: "Lowell's bad poems take on the quality of lies." In sum, this is "a counterfeit book of poetry." We have seen how important Lowell was to Bly in earlier years, but as Bly's ideas developed, his esteem for Lowell diminished. He was taking this opportunity to declare his independence.[59]

Of the two parodies in #8, Henry Taylor's "Mr. James Dickey in Orbit," had been previewed in Crunk's essay.

High in my tower of steel and fuel
Which points to the stars,

Bravely phallic,
I lie strapped to my seat
In a spacesuit.

It ends:

> *I greet the face of my captain,*
> *And I smile.*
> *His perplexity does not disturb me.*
> *I climb down from my tower in triumph:*
> *Tonight I have marched through the heavens.*
> *I shout three green cheers for myself.*

Dickey's ability to laugh at himself, which was not great to begin with, had likely diminished after Crunk's treatment in the previous issue. This parody could not have helped. Their relationship continued its steady decline.

The second parody is "Protective Verse," by Keith Gunderson. Though a good deal shorter than Charles Olson's "Projective Verse," this hilarious take-off follows parts of it very closely:

PROTECTIVE VERSE

(prophylactic   (psephitic   (pseudepigraphic

vs.

The NON-Protective

In another example, Gunderson writes:

> Verse, now, 1966, if it's really going to move ahead in the sixties, if it's going to sizzle, I take it, has to wrestle with certain laws and possibilities of muscle tone, of the wrist-flexibility of the guy who breaks his sentences up. (The revolution of line-busting, 1950, the snip-snip of syntax, asks it of all you young squirts under forty.)

One final example:

> (1) the snazz of the thing. A poem is a quasi-negative-feed-back imposed upon from where it wasn't in the first place (and that might be anywhere). Get it? Yeah. The poem has to be a snazz-unredundant reification and at every point an unredundant morsel all along the line. Eh: how do you do that?

Olson's choppy Black Mountain vernacular is mimicked mercilessly.[60]

188

"Wisdom of the Old" is a quotation of Karl Shapiro: "We have many, many poets, all highly trained and expert in the skill of writing poetry. I am not trying to be witty when I say that *the* average graduate student who works a little at it can write a poem as well as Yeats. My opinion of Yeats has suffered considerably from this discovery. Was Yeats a graduate student?"[61] Preposterous!

In the same month that saw the appearance of *The Sixties* 8, the anthology, *The Sea and the Honeycomb*, was published after a long gestation period. Back in 1962, Bly had told Hall it was near completion: "I have also been choosing the last poems for [it] —the four line ones—chose the last six from Arabic-Andalusian poems—poems the Arabs wrote while they were lords of Spain. My favorite poet is Ibn Hazm."[62] Half a year later he told Hall that the book was ready to go.[63] A month after that he proclaimed it "all done."[64] Another month passed. "I have just a couple details left."[65] But the book did not appear for two more years.[66] Its title seems to come from these lines by Machado:

Near the flowering mountain
The immense ocean is seething.
In the comb of my honey bees
There are tiny grains of salt.

The cover illustration is "Oiseau" by the Symbolist painter Odilon Redon. The oversized bird is perched on an open windowsill, facing inward. Bly had quoted Redon in #5, and referred to him in "The Dead World and the Live World" as belonging to the latter.

The stated purpose of the book is "to give examples of what has been done so far in Europe and America with the poem of three or four lines" from both ancient and modern languages. This is the "sort of poem which tries, in the words of Juan Ramón Jiménez, to arrive at the greatest possible richness by the simplest possible means."[67] Bly writes in his introduction: "The strength of a new form is that it makes both poet and reader aware of feelings they'd hardly noticed before." Short poems, he says, allow for the expression of and response to rapid and swift emotions. Greek lyric poets like Alcaeus wrote such poems, but a few centuries later copyists in Alexandria could not refrain from supplementing. So it is now:

An Alexandrian scholar is lurking inside most American poets: the American poet sitting at his desk writes a fine, intense poem of seven or eight lines, then a hand silently appears from somewhere inside his shirt and hastily adds fifteen more lines, telling us what the emotion means, relating it to philosophy, and adding a few moral comments. The invisible scholar is outraged at the idea of anyone writing a brief poem, because he is hardly able to get his chalky hand out of his cloak before the poem is over!

Thus these swift, exhilarating poems do without "the scaffolding of secondary ideas." Bly cites *Paradise Lost*, where Milton's hand, like a scaffold, is always there to catch the reader if he falls. "In the brief poem, it is all different: the poet takes the reader to the edge of a cliff, as a mother eagle takes its nestling, and then drops him. Readers with a strong imagination enjoy it, and discover they can fly. The others fall down to the rocks where they are killed instantly."

Bly ends with these provocative comments: "Readers of recent poetry are used to staggering along under lines swelled with the rhetoric of philosophy courses, experiences under mind-expanding drugs, new criticism—in short, the world of prose. They find it hard at first to concentrate on a short poem, but eventually they learn to find some value in being dropped." The forty selections include poems by Whitman, D.H. Lawrence, and St. Geraud (Knott), in English. Among the other writers are Machado, Char, Quasimodo, Storm, Aspenström, Jiménez, Apollinaire, Andrade, Vladimir Nabokov, and various medieval Spanish Arabic poets.

Cuscaden called *The Sea and the Honeycomb* a "beautiful, exciting & important book...I can, literally, think of no American publisher who is doing as much for contemporary poetry as you are."[68] Charles Simic wrote to thank Bly "for a remarkable book. Everything from introduction to end line of each poem is life-giving...A short poem is like a sudden light, it comes in a kind of blessed moment when one is given to see the particular experience and all of one's life with complete clarity."[69] Margaret Randall, editor of *El Corno Emplumado* in Mexico, wrote that she had read it several times: "It's a beautiful book! In every way. The work is selected well, the translations seem good (tho' I'm no judge of most of the originals—except the Spanish) and the physical format makes us green with envy."[70] In the next issue she wrote: "Robert Bly, with infinite care and one of the loveliest physical formats seen this year, offers...an extremely useful book, both in scope and depth."[71]

Bly was again pushing poets in a new direction. But at the same time, he was focusing an increasing amount of energy on political activism. As the war raged in Southeast Asia and at home, Bly began to assume a new, more public, and more controversial role. His antiwar activities, in which his own poetry, *The Sixties*, and The Sixties Press all played their parts, now took center stage.

11

The Vietnam War and

a Rainstorm of Revulsion

While Bly was in Europe, the political climate at home was changing rapidly. In early 1965, President Johnson authorized the start of regular bombing missions in North Vietnam and the use of napalm, dispatched the first U.S. combat troops, and began offensive operations on the ground. A majority of Americans were in favor of the war, but as draft calls increased, so did antiwar demonstrations and draft-card burnings. Simpson wrote that spring: "I've been more concerned about the war in Vietnam. I even went on television, opposing the war—and within a few minutes received an anonymous phone call, threatening to kill me. The trouble with political activity is that, even if it is necessary, it is a waste of time. But you cannot avoid it entirely and be a writer."[1]

In late November, Bly went to a demonstration in Washington, D.C.[2] As he boarded the bus, this Navy veteran was conscious of crossing a line, abandoning a certain kind of "respectability" which he had always tried to maintain.[3] Simpson was eager to hear about it: "Some day I'll be seeing you in jail—or maybe we'll all be out in the hills somewhere."[4] In contrast, Haines' initial disapproval of Bly's activities was thinly veiled: "Well, did you stalk the White House? ... I feel I have more important things to do."[5]

Bly then wrote "At a March Against the Vietnam War (Washington, November 27, 1965)," which ends:

We long to abase ourselves

We have carried around this cup of darkness
We have longed to pour it over our heads

We make war
Like a man anointing himself.[6]

Bly's career had entered a new phase.

From the outset, *The Fifties* had articulated the need for poetry to reflect both the inner and outer worlds.[7] Vallejo and Neruda, who called the mixture of surrealistic imagery and political concerns "impure poetry," were crucial models. Now a new, larger, and more loose-knit community of poets began to coalesce around the opposition to America's growing involvement in the war in Southeast Asia. Some differences were set aside, while others came to light. As Bly put it years later: "The Vietnam War and the revulsion against it came down like a rainstorm and carried us away…[It] changed the way I lived: the psychic urgency dissolved calmness for most of us, and actively opposing the war meant an end to long periods of solitude."[8]

Bly's poems were thus increasingly focused on the war and its ramifications. He sent Hall a draft of "Johnson's Cabinet Watched by Ants," including this stanza:

Tonight they burn the rice supplies, tomorrow
They lecture on Thoreau; tonight they move around the trees,
Tomorrow they pick the twigs from their clothes;
Tonight they throw the fire-bombs; tomorrow
They read The Declaration of Independence, tomorrow they are
*   in church.*[9]

He was also ruffling feathers in his very conservative hometown: "I gave a talk yesterday to the local Kiwanis about Vietnam. All through it I noticed they were boiling something dark in the back. And I thought it was soup!"[10]

On February 20, a "Read-In for Peace in Vietnam," the first event of its kind, took place in New York.[11] Bly, hoping to be included, had called Kinnell just before the event, but too late.[12] He then set off on the poetry circuit in Colorado, Oregon, Washing-

Poets & Writers Against the Vietnam War (with readers Robert Peterson, George Hitchcock, Bly, John Logan, David Ray, Robert Sund, Louis Simpson, James Wright, Vern Rutsala, William Stafford, Lawrence Ferlinghetti, and others). Ferlinghetti at lectern, Reed College, March 5, 1966

ton, and Montana, and once he got to Portland, he and David Ray at Reed College decided to form the "American Writers Against the Vietnam War" and to stage Bly's readings instead as collective anti-war read-ins.[13] It took "three solid days of telephoning" to pull it all together.[14] *The New York Times* reported: "Tears and laughter mixed today when 10 of the nation's leading poets [Bly, Ferlinghetti, Hitchcock, Logan, Robert Peterson, Ray, Vern Rutsala, Stafford, Simpson, and Wright, though there were a few more] staged a two-hour 'read-in' to protest United States policy in Vietnam." More than 700 were in the audience; there had been 500 at Portland State the day before; they were heading to the University of Washington in Seattle the next day. "Mr. Ray said the organization's purpose 'is to encourage both writers and students to...take a public stand on the Vietnam war and to encourage read-ins by writers concerned at all major campuses in the United States.'... 'The artists are patriotic,' Mr. Ray said. 'To not speak up, to take no stand would be un-American.'"[15] In Montana, Bly continued to spread the word, buoyed by revived student interest in politics, "the healthiest thing I have seen happen for a long time."[16] Back home "after nearly a month in public raving," he wrote in his journal: "I feel preoccupied, and yet joyful. I have the sense we did strike a blow for fire."[17] The raving had only just begun.

Haines' remarks masked a deeper scorn: "It's one thing for someone like Mandelstam to write a poem against Stalin, but a similar thing here doesn't carry the same urgency...Settle down there in Madison and get a few issues of *The Sixties* out. Let the students do the demonstrating!"[18] Similarly, Bly recalls Berryman's refusal to participate in the read-in in Minneapolis: "No! Absolutely not! People like you are ruining American poetry. I will not be a part of this."[19]

Meanwhile, Kinnell had a role organizing read-ins in the East.[20] He and Bly began to coordinate their efforts, but were far from the only poets doing so. Adrienne Rich wrote Bly: "Everyone here is glad you'll participate in the Cambridge read-in on May 3."[21] Hall was planning an event at the University of Michigan. Bly, already the experienced ringleader, responded: "Certainly I'll M.C. My advice is no more than 10 speakers. Beyond 10 it is not a reading, but a circus, or celebrity-parade." He adds: "Avoid the clods at Iowa, and light types. I'll watch the East Read-Ins this next week, and tell you who is really effective. Meanwhile, line up Lowell."[22] Through March, April, and May, the momentum steadily increased.[23]

Typically, poets would read a poem and a quotation from a news report or other document. At Penn on May 8, Henry Braun's self-described "ironclad schedule" gave five minutes or less to all participants, including Bly, Simpson, Wright, Ginsberg, Peter Orlovsky, and Susan Sontag.[24] Before an audience of 800, Braun's schedule took a hit as Ginsberg "launched into a 40-minute long...'Witchita Vortex Sutra.'"[25] A week after Bly returned from this last run, he wrote: "For days I was tired, and could hardly write a letter! Now my energy—my soul—is back."[26]

Bly and Ray were also scrambling to edit and publish the anthology, *A Poetry Reading Against the Vietnam War*. Bly explains (in the introduction): "It was David Ray's idea to publish this booklet as a sort of memorial to the occasion. It will also help to make available material that other colleges may use at their poetry readings if they wish." On the heels of those initial read-ins in Oregon, they were looking for ways of doing the same cheaply and quickly, gathering material, thinking about format, seeking publicity. In late March, Ray wrote: "Senator [Wayne] Morse's office here in Portland called…and [he] wants to use passages from our material in his speeches."[27]

The most burdensome task was expediting the editing. Kinnell sent Bly his poem, "Vapor Trail Reflected in the Frog Pond": "It's the best I can manage at the moment. It does need time to settle. Your suggestions were very helpful…If you think this can be included as is, or with smaller changes, in the read-in pamphlet, fine."[28] For Carol Bly's poem, "On Fallout," the pressing question was whether to use the name Ann Reynolds (a pseudonymic partner for Charles Reynolds, one of Bly's aliases) or Joanna Campbell (as in *The Sixties* 8).[29]

The urgency meant that a European printer was out of the question. In early April, Bly contacted Harry Gantt in New York, who responded: "Happy to be working on this much needed & powerful sermon to the Hawks."[30] Two weeks later, Bly sent the initial corrected proofs, along with some new material added at the last minute: "We must have this booklet printed, or at least 500 copies printed, by May 3rd."[31]

Carol had written on April 10 for permission to reprint the Cummings material. The publisher's refusal came in late April, but printing had already gone ahead.[32] Bly then brought a finished copy to Cummings' widow, Marion, whom he knew from cordial encounters in the 1950s. She insisted that the books be destroyed, saying that her late husband would never want to be associated with any movement that might give comfort to the Communists. Bly at once contacted a lawyer, and then called Gantt, who, as Bly recalls, hired about fifteen women to excise and black-out the offending pages and lines. The entire edition, somewhat mutilated, was ready for distribution the next day.[33] Time was of the essence; fourteen read-ins were to take place between May 3 and 15.

Dedicated to Senators William J. Fulbright and Wayne Morse, and to foreign policy expert George Kennan, the book opens with Whitman's "To the States":

> *To the States, or any one of them, or any city of the States,*
>   Resist much, obey little,
> *Once unquestioning obedience, once fully enslaved,*

> *Once fully enslaved, no nation, state, city of this earth, ever afterward*
>
> *resumes its liberty.*

The book includes recently written poems by Bly, Ray, Creeley, Kinnell, Ferlinghetti, Stafford, Hitchcock, Wright, Robert Peterson, Simpson, Campbell, Göran Sonnevi, Herbert Burke, and John Hohn, as well as older poems by Whitman, Siegfried Sassoon, Rimbaud, Robinson Jeffers, and Winfield Townley Scott. Ray had gathered together most of the prose pieces—by Abraham Lincoln, Thucydides, Adolf Hitler, Sadao Araki, Hermann Goering, Matzuo Nagai, and Heinz Schaeffer. Recent writings by I.F. Stone, John F. Kennedy, Lyndon Johnson, and Fernand Gigon were part of the mix, and excerpts from *The Realist, Paris-Match,* the *Herald Tribune News Service,* and *The New York Times.*[34] One chilling example is from Nazi Reichsmarschall Goering at the Nuremberg trials: "Why of course the people don't want war...But...it is always a simple matter to drag the people along...All you have to do is to tell them they are being attacked, and denounce the pacifists for lack of patriotism and exposing the country to danger. It works the same in any country."

Friends reacted positively, for the most part. Rothenberg, who, with co-editor David Antin, was preparing "A Vietnam Assemblage" for *Some/thing*'s third issue, wrote his thanks, "in the hope that ours works out somewhere near as well. We're actually moving along similar lines...but the more of this that can be done, the greater the chances are that, cumulatively, it may all amount to something."[35] Knott had a point: "I thought that the Vietnam book should have been dedicated to Norman Morrison—who burned himself to death in front of the Pentagon, or to the draft-dodgers. Fulbright and Morse aren't risking their lives. Aside from that, it's a great collection."[36] Stanley Burnshaw wrote: "I have been watching some of the results of the poetry read-ins, etc., and of everything I've seen and heard, nothing equals the poem by Robert ("Ants")...It's as fine a political poem as has ever been written in the United States."[37]

The book was reviewed in several places. Lipsitz called it "the strangest book of war poetry ever written," going on to describe it as "a unique mélange…written by civilians and directed toward defusing the mine field of nationalistic assumptions we keep between spirit and reality." But he felt that quoting Hitler and Goering "to damn American foreign policy" was a dangerous tactic. He also asked the usual question: "Can 'protest poetry' work?"[38] Will Inman was more concerned about the issues than the poetry. "These American Writers Against the Vietnam War have terribly and irrevocably found the United States and President Johnson guilty of genocide against the Vietnamese and of an inhumanity of purpose and practice incredible to a sentimentally patriotic people." Then he asks, a bit hyperbolically: "But where, in America, is our Bach, our Goethe and Schiller, our Beethoven, to whom we can look for proof that we cannot, after all, be so totally lost as a people? These poets, these writers, are our such; they live among us."[39] Lastly, Rexroth chimed in: "The poetry read-ins organized by Robert Bly and his friends were exemplary examples of the poet, not as 'uncrowned Legislator' but as one of the small handful of *responsibles* without whose assumption of responsibility the human race would long since have ceased to exist."[40]

Bly's strained relationship with Haines eventually fell apart. It became impossible for either man to separate the issues of the war and opposition to it from the literary aspects of the book that would become *The Light Around the Body*. Haines said that Bly's poetry, especially the political poetry, was too imitative of Neruda, self-conscious, pretentious, and forced. He disliked most of the new poems. Distressed, Bly responded that Haines was being condescending, malicious, grudging, selfish, hostile to political poetry, rather than offering helpful criticism. "Your advice on my poetry is exactly like the advice of those people in my family who are working in Washington: namely, why don't you just give up this political stuff, and go back to writing those nice poems about the Minnesota countryside—you really know how to do that."[41]

Haines lashed out even more vigorously: "Either you are hopelessly blind to your own defects, or you seriously imagine yourself to be the great and daring poet with some marvelous truth to tell us about social and political life today." And then the question: "If a really intelligent, courageous man like Fulbright or

Morse can't get the government to change its course, how are a few well-meant poems going to do it?" He accuses Bly of "overweening self-confidence," and ends his letter with: "That's the trouble with all this, I have to feel guilty for criticizing someone who has done me so many favors."[42]

This, for Bly, was the final straw. It caused him to reflect more broadly on some of the consequences of his commitment to the antiwar effort. He noted in his journal:

> A saddening letter from John Haines yesterday, full of attack, so I finally broke off that correspondence. But I feel other attacks also, or coldness, coming from other sides, mutterings, cold burns, the Vietnam readings, the Lowell piece—angers many. I think it is good! We have learned something of affection. So now we can return to the old solitude. And try to be a brother.[43]

Meanwhile, Haines was having second thoughts about his position. A few days later he wrote Bly again:

> I've been feeling badly about all this. I went through all your letters written to me over the past six or seven years, and I realized how much I owe you in so many ways. I must seem like a very poor and ungrateful friend to have criticized you so harshly. I can't take back what I said about your poems, but I would like to apologize for any offensiveness of tone in my letters.[44]

Hitchcock, a mutual friend, wrote as peacemaker/mediator later that fall.[45] But the damage had been done; it was too late.[46]

The war continued, as did the antiwar efforts. Regarding the delayed read-in in Ann Arbor, Bly wrote to Hall: "Let's try to train some living puppets, and actors with masks. Inquire among your actor friends if any are interested. If one read a Johnson or Rusk speech, the others could do most anything."[47] Ignatow, at the University of Kansas in Lawrence, was similarly involved.[48] On September 29, Bly managed to send off the final version of *The Light Around the Body* to Harper & Row.[49]

In November, "The American Outsider," an essay by Paul Zweig, appeared in *The Nation*. It points to the importance of Bly's magazine and press and of his recent political activity. "Poetry in America has long been a dangerous enterprise, for those poets...who needed to follow their imagination into whatever hard country it would lead them." He speaks of a new temper. "A thread of continuity in this changing mood has been Robert Bly's erratic, single-handed experiment with the Sixties Press, and with the controversial magazine he has published since 1958." Despite the small-scale distribution of its books and magazines, "they have gained a large audience among poets and students, and have had an influence far beyond the numbers distributed." His work "has been as much a symptom as a cause." The bond between Bly, Simpson, Dickey, Kinnell, Wright, and Hall, "which has been catalyzed by the Sixties Press, has been less one of mutual influence than of a common resistance to the orthodoxies of American poetry since the Second World War."

Zweig went on to describe Bly's work as a two-pronged effort—on the one hand the exploration of the new imagination through a program of translation, and, on the other, literary criticism. "The whole idea defended by the Sixties Press...depends on a sense of moral engagement of which poetry is only the purest expression in language." Zweig sees it as no accident that the most recent product of Bly's press has been the antiwar anthology:

> With an almost quixotic energy...[h]is magazine has veered in the most unexpected ways, and often within a single issue, from serious and carefully argued statements, to rambunctious satire, and at times unreasonable polemics. Yet, in the end, the weaknesses of the Sixties Press are only the reverse side of its strengths. Both bear the mark of the right- and wrong-headed activist who, like Whitman in the preface and *Democratic Vistas*, has discovered that the only way he could think was to think for himself.[50]

Helen Yglesias, *The Nation*'s literary editor, had written Bly about this piece: "We are in danger of becoming 'Bly's Weekly.' In fact, you have been a very good addition to our pages, as you know."[51] *The Nation* would continue to serve as a platform for Bly's pronouncements—at least for a while.

Given the dearth of satire in *A Poetry Reading*, something for which *The Sixties* was well known, this entry from Bly's journal in December is interesting:

The American Writers Against the Vietnam War announce
Benefit Reading
...
Buy Napalm Products
Help buy some napalm from the US Government
All proceeds from this reading will go toward
Buying some napalm from the US Government
For experiments here at home.

This was followed by three statements:

– "What is good for Vietnam is good for the U.S."
– We are looking for an American family who is willing to give
one of their children to be burned by napalm.
– If you believe in what we are doing in Vietnam it is time for
you to sacrifice also.[52]

Apparently, Bly jotted these words as he planned for an upcoming
event.

Clayton Eshleman was helping coordinate the "Week of the
Angry Arts against the War in Vietnam" (January 29 – February
5, 1967).[53] Involved were actors, playwrights, dancers, musicians,
filmmakers, painters, photographers, and poets and writers.[54] Bly
was moderator of the "Napalm Poetry Reading" at NYU, "A benefit reading for children burned in Vietnam by Americans, and in
memory of the thousands of adults and children who have been
burned to death." Readers included Rukeyser, Levertov, Creeley,
Blackburn, Logan, and Joel Oppenheimer. As reported in *The
Nation*: "Interspersed with these performances, colored slides of
napalm-maimed Vietnamese children were flung upon a screen…
In the darkened auditorium Robert Bly gave a chalk talk on the
facts of weaponry, quoting from government sources, ordnance
journals and the news magazines."[55] In Bly's own notes for his
introductory remarks he says:

The United States now is like Germany in about 1934, in one
important way: it is a ghost ship drifting in an unearthly silence
toward an iceberg: the iceberg is not destruction—the United
States is not going to be destroyed militarily in the next ten
years—the iceberg is desensitization, absence of feeling, absence
of compassion, numbness… The fact that napalming is done

201

with so little public protest shows how far the desensitization has already gone.

Finally, an appeal was made for the "Writers' Fund for Helping Wounded Vietnamese Children."[56]

The next evening, a symposium on "The War, The Artist, His Work" was moderated by Paul Goodman. Panelists included Bly, Leon Golub, Maxwell Geismar, George Tabori, and Harold Rosenberg. Here Bly began to echo themes and arguments he had first voiced in *The Sixties*. He denounced "the climate of American literature during the past couple of decades, when writers under the unhealthy influence of the New Criticism subscribed to the strange doctrine that there could be a divorce of the world itself from the world of a poem. 'We have therefore only the personal poet entangled in his own psyche.'" It would be hard to overestimate the significance of this, Bly maintained. For the writers of this country, therefore, a poet like Pablo Neruda was a revelation, "for some of his most powerful poems have political content." "How can poetry touch upon things like napalm bombing?" Bly asked. "The political poet must be like a grasshopper and leap into the psyche of the nation."[57]

One result of Bly's involvement that week was a temporary *rapprochement* with Levertov, who wrote: "I want to repeat my thanks & admiration for the fine job you did...The whole thing was very impressive & in a good sense professional...We have had, & no doubt will have, our differences, you & I, but I want you to know I felt a great deal of respect & affection for the work you did that night."[58]

A second, enlarged edition of *A Poetry Reading* was in the works.[59] Some poets who had not been in the first, including Hayden Carruth, Goodman, and Lipsitz, were hoping to be in the second. Reprinting was done in March, with a few changes. The blacked-out and excised poems by e.e. cummings were replaced with: "Life at War" by Levertov, a quotation from the *Los Angeles Times* about napalm, a quotation of Mark Twain, "UP RISING Passages 25" by Duncan, and "The Discourse on Peace" by Jacques Prévert (tr. Ferlinghetti). The cover now had an illustration by Pieter Brueghel the Younger, a fantastic scene of death and destruction.

Duncan responded graciously: "You've done a great job on the 'Viet-Nam' anthology, including your preface. How rightly you pick up the thing in the war that is immediate to our own state—not what others think of us, but what we are doing to our own national psyche." He also admits: "If at first I was 'willing' for your use of UP RISING, now I rejoice in the intelligence of the context given and its intent…you make a true collage and revelation in the process."[60]

There were various projects in solidarity. Snyder, in sync with Bly, wrote: "Comrade, I often think of you & now I must send this CURSE ["A Curse on the Men in Washington, Pentagon"] to you because I'm sure it will give you a moment of pleasure."[61] Sonnevi wrote with plans for a Swedish Vietnam anthology, to contain about 85 poems, including some by Bly, Ferlinghetti, Simpson, Levertov, and Hitchcock, among the Americans.[62] Bly's work also appeared in several other antiwar collections.[63] Dissension was unavoidable here, too, as seen, for example, when Lowenfels apologized profusely—after Bly complained—for including Dickey in *Where Is Vietnam?*[64]

In April, Bly made yet another appearance in *The Nation*, with an essay, "On Political Poetry."[65] It was in part a prelude to his soon-to-be-released book. Bly writes: "Paradoxically, what is needed to write true poems about the outward world is inwardness." The central paragraph is in part a reiteration, more metaphorical:

The life of the country can be imagined as a psyche larger than the psyche of anyone living, a larger sphere, floating above everyone. In order for the poet to write a true political poem, he has to be able to have such a grasp of his own concerns that he can leave them for a while, and then leap up, like a grasshopper, into this other psyche. In that sphere he finds strange plants and curious many-eyed creatures which he brings back with him. This half-visible psychic life he entangles in his language.

Read-ins and other antiwar activities were ongoing. In 1966 and 1967, Bly appeared at colleges and universities in more than twenty states. Later that summer, he received word from

Roger L. Stevens, Chairman of the National Foundation on the Arts and the Humanities, of an unrelated award of $5,000 in recognition of "the contribution you have made in advancing the cause of the unknown, obscure or difficult writer, and in the publication of books visually and typographically distinctive, thereby helping to advance the cause of the best in American art."[66] Bly turned it down, despite the fact that he was in debt.[67] He wrote:

> Thank you…But I oppose the Vietnam War, and I cannot accept the grant. In my mind there is a link between poetry and compassion. Since the Administration is maiming an entire nation merely to advance our national interest, I think it is insensitive, even indecent, for that Administration to come forward with money for poetry.
>
> Since it is clear that a given sum of government money could go either for a poetry magazine or a napalm canister—and only chance bookkeeping decides between them—there could be no pride in such an award or in such editing.[68]

Stevens replied in predictable fashion:

> The right to free speech and thought is essential to a Democracy, so you are entitled to your opinion as to the connection between the grant and the Vietnam War. However, since the policies of this government were arrived at by representatives chosen in a free election, I am afraid that all government action cannot be stopped because of a difference of opinion in the Vietnam War, otherwise the result would be chaotic.[69]

This was followed by a letter from Carolyn Kizer, who, as the Director of Literary Programs for the National Council on the Arts and the National Endowment for the Arts, actually made the award. She, a fellow poet and friend, tried to reason with Bly, pointing out that during World War II all federal cultural programs ceased because of the war effort, and that others were trying to do the same now. "The role of the artist, as you and I both believe, has always been dedicated to an outcry against the destruction of morals and values, and to the preservation of order and beauty and human affection…But stopping one war doesn't make all right with the world. If we don't work to eliminate some of the violence and ugliness at home, it will all happen again, until nothing remains."[70]

A few days later Bly responded to them both:

Thank you for your letters, both emphasizing the value of continuing cultural programs during wartime. That's all very well if the country is on the right side. But in this war we are simply murderers, like the Germans. Stopping our cultural programs wouldn't help the Vietnamese, but it would help to alter our numb acquiescence.

A part of the German government supported culture too. All [Walter] Gieseking had to do was to play the piano while other parts of the government did ugly things. The National Foundation is not the Reich Chamber of Music, but you *are* a part of the Administration, and unless you publicly disavow them, you are part of its policies. In any case, if I accepted your grant I would be in Gieseking's position.

…How can we go on with "business as usual"—as Bruno Bettelheim put it—or "culture as usual"? You both feel a duty to your country, and keep your positions in response to that. I think a more realistic and more valuable response would be for you…to resign.[71]

Bly was thinking of how he might use this affair to benefit the antiwar movement. Once again, *The Sixties* seemed a possible vehicle. He asked Hall to look it over: "I'm enclosing my draft of the possible piece, for final pages of *Sixties* 10, the piece to be followed, I expect, by a copy of my letter. The problem is how to avoid sounding holier-than-thou."[72]

Meanwhile, 150,000 demonstrators marched on the Pentagon on October 21.[73] Bly was there with David Dellinger, Dwight Macdonald, Lowell, Benjamin Spock, Norman Mailer, Jerry Rubin, Noam Chomsky, Abbie Hoffman, Ed Sanders, and Tuli Kupferberg, among others.[74] Many protesters, including Bly, were teargassed, many were beaten by the Federal Marshals and National Guardsmen, who numbered close to twenty-five hundred; seven hundred protesters were arrested.[75] Shortly afterward, Kinnell wrote: "I had a meeting with David McReynolds & others in NY. They were planning something of the same sort as we, for the very same week, & Paul [Goodman] & I thought it better to throw in with them for that occasion. It is an attempt to close the NY induction center."[76] Early on December 5, at the protest organized by The Stop the Draft Week Committee, Bly, Kinnell, Ginsberg, Spock, Kupferberg, Jonathan Miller, and Conor Cruise O'Brien were among 264 arrested outside the Army Induction Center at 39 Whitehall St.[77]

While Bly was active on both coasts, he also remained closely connected to home, even to the church and denomination in which he was raised. He used that religious connection to push for an end to the war in an article he wrote for *SALT*, a periodical of the Lutheran Church in America. In the press release, Bly is quoted saying that he was disturbed by "the moral cowardice of the Lutheran Church, of which I am a member, and for which several of my family have been missionaries and ministers." Also, he said, "Some ministers are afraid to apply Christian teaching to the war for fear of offending their rich parishioners; others do not apply it because of their own moral laziness."[78]

Back on the question of how to make the most of his refusal of the grant money, Hall suggested the *New York Times*. "People do that all the time. It's not tooting your horn it's a political act. (You have to suffer the fact that some bastards will call it tooting your horn no matter what you do.)" If they don't print it, he said, "then send it to Bob Silvers at the *New York Review of Books*... This is a popular front matter. I want you to publish it in one of these two places because then other literary intellectuals will see it and some of them will then have the courage to turn down government money too."[79]

Bly's letter was eventually printed in the latter. Once again, he incorporates his views about the integrity of life and art. It begins: "The fact that so few Americans have resigned from the government or from responsible posts to protest the Vietnam War is remarkable to me. It is odd, particularly if you look at European history." He likens this "American failure to resign" to the fact that "the National Foundation on the Arts...distributing Administration money, has so far given over twenty-five grants to American writers, and not one has refused it. Incredible!" Bly then asks the question: "What does this show about Americans? Timidity? Materialism? Greed? I don't think so." And he answers in characteristic fashion:

> What it shows is a disastrous split between the American's inner and outer worlds. He does not aim to use his life to make himself *whole*, to join the two worlds in himself. On the contrary, he is prepared to give up one of the two worlds. The businessman gives up the inner world, and clings to the outer as *his* way. ... [W]hen a writer is opposed to the Vietnam War and still accepts a grant from the government prosecuting the war, he is doing something similar—he is letting the world split.... Instead of trying to apply what he has learned in the actions of his inner life to the actions of the world, he pulls back inside the house, closes the door, and declares he doesn't know what is going on out there, or knows but has rejected it all as outside his sphere of interest, he is "not political." But what could be more within the sphere of interest of a writer than the world? Or the prevention of a deeper split inside himself?
>
> I don't think, therefore, that refusing government money at this time is the *right* thing to do, or the *heroic* thing, etc. —it is the only sensible thing to do. It is a matter of uncommon and common sense, and it should be as natural for us to refuse as it would be to refuse if someone suggested we cut off a leg with one of the new painless saws and throw it out the window.[80]

Bly said in a related local news report that the fact that he owed his printer $2600 was not enough of an enticement to keep the money. The same article indicated that two University of Minnesota professors and poets who had accepted grants from the foundation were John Berryman ($10,000) and Allen Tate ($15,000).[81]

The *NYRB* letter brought many responses. Kay Boyle wrote: "I admire you for a number of reasons, among them your recent stand in the matter of the grant…I too have been appalled by the acceptance by American Writers of these grants."[82] Wang Hui-Ming said: "One is reminded of Sartre. In this time & this country, one often wonders why so few artists take such courageous stands…I respect you & I admire you."[83] There were others, from Brenda Ueland, Lipsitz, Nat Henthoff, and Norman Rosten.

At almost the same time, Carol, in her capacity as business

manager, sent the following letter to thirty-one (listed) private and public universities:

> We are cancelling your subscription to *THE SIXTIES* magazine and/or back-ordered Sixties Press books.
>
> We are not accepting trade from institutions we know to have money from the C.I.A. or the armed services for research on chemical and germ warfare.
>
> Of course the university library isn't the agency in question, and of course we know how tiny our flailing against such powers must appear, but I think universities should be made to know the revulsion that private citizens feel against institutions they once trusted.
>
> Even libraries shouldn't really expect to do "business as usual" when such elaborate cruelty as the proliferation of disease and torture through chemical poisoning is being worked up on the same campus.

The letter was reprinted in *The Sixties* 10 the following summer. From the assistant to the president at Harvard came two denials, one after his reception of the initial letter, and one after publication in the magazine. The next April, some students occupied University Hall, and discovered files exposing the Harvard administration's lies. Carol wrote back:

> You can imagine how your self-righteous defense of Harvard goes down—with the denials such as yours saying Harvard "found no evidence of any CIA contracts or grants at Harvard"—yet your faculty members even went to Vietnam in the pay of the CIA. How could you lie so—when you represent such a high level of society!
>
> How weak and evil to defend an organization that is manufacturing pneumonic plague—and to lie for them—when you could be protecting people from the CIA![84]

The next page has the only advertisement to ever appear in the magazine—for the War Resisters League. It begins: "Serve Your Country / Don't Go to Vietnam / If your government is waging a criminal war do you serve the country best by cooperating? / Who served Germany best under Hitler? Those who obeyed orders and helped kill the Jews? Or the handful of Germans who chose prison and even death rather than cooperate?" And then there is American history: "This nation wasn't built on 'consensus' or 'obedience' to the State. It was built by heretical Baptists, irresponsible Quakers, headstrong Puritans, freedom-loving slaves, stubborn abolitionists—by people who believed they should obey their conscience rather than the State." Finally, it declares: "The war in Vietnam is a crime. Do not cooperate."

A few weeks after the publicity associated with Bly's grant refusal, he received a note from Hall, informing him that he had won the National Book Award for poetry.[85] The official letter came from Peter S. Jennison, executive director of the National Book Committee.[86] Kizer wrote: "Congratulations on the Book Award. I'm sorry I can't be there to see and hear your reception of it next week. I am sure that you will make interesting use of this public forum."[87] In January and February, the bloody Tet Offensive initiated what later seemed a significant shift in the outlook of Americans on the Vietnam War, that is, toward increased skepticism of the government's official statements and justifications.

On March 8, New York mayor John Lindsay, National Council on the Arts chairman Roger Stevens, and the evening's honorees—Thornton Wilder, George Kennan, Jonathan Kozol, Howard and Edna Hong (Kierkegaard scholars at St. Olaf College), and Bly—appeared together on stage at Lincoln Center's Philharmonic Hall.[88] Many of the twelve hundred people who attended, mostly editors, publishers, writers, critics, and journalists, were probably anticipating some sort of disruption.[89]

Bly's acceptance speech fulfilled those expectations. It was a blistering and idiosyncratic attack. It began:

> I am uneasy at a ceremony emphasizing our current high state
> of culture. Cultural events, traditionally, put writers to sleep,
> and even the public. But we don't want to be asleep any more.
> Something has happened to me lately. Every time I have glanced
> at a bookcase in the last few weeks, the books on killing of the
> Indians leap out into my hand. Reading a speech of Andrew
> Jackson's on the Indian question the other day—his Second
> Annual Message—I realized he was the Westmoreland of 1830.
> His speech was like an Administration speech today. It was
> another speech recommending murder of a race as a prudent
> policy, requiring stamina. Perhaps this coincidence should not

have surprised me, but it did. It turns out we can put down a revolution as well as the Russians in Budapest, we can destroy a town as well as the Germans at Lidice, all with our famous unconcern.

As Americans, we have always wanted the life of feeling without the life of suffering. We long for pure light, constant victory. We have always wanted to avoid suffering and therefore we are unable to live in the present. But our hopes for a life of pure light are breaking up.

He praised William Sloane Coffin, Daniel Berrigan, and Mitch Goodman for acts of civil disobedience, and then asked:

Isn't the next step…for the institutions to take similar acts? What has the book industry done to end the war? Nothing. What have our universities done to end the war? Nothing. What have our museums, like the Metropolitan, done? Nothing. What has my own publisher, Harper & Row, done to help end the war? Nothing. In an age of gross and savage crimes by legal governments, the institutions will have to learn responsibility, learn to take their part in preserving the nation, and take their risk by committing acts of disobedience.

Then came the most electrifying moment.[90] After receiving the check, Bly called Mike Kempton, a member of The Resistance, to the foot of the stage and handed it over to him: "I hereby counsel you as a young man not to enter the United States Army now under any circumstances, and I ask you to use this money I am giving you to find and counsel other young men to defy the draft authorities and not destroy their spiritual lives by participating in this war." Bly's action was illegal, and carried a possible penalty of five years in prison and/or a $10,000 fine.[91] There was cheering and also some booing, people standing and people sitting on their hands.[92]

The Nation's description of the episode began: "Robert Bly's acceptance speech and act of civil disobedience dominated all other events of the week."[93] The passage concludes as follows:

For many years Bly has been an important influence in American poetry, as much through the work of his magazine, *The Sixties*, as through his own poetry. His critical articles, his translations of the German and Spanish poets, his extensive and impressive work in opposing the war through the formation of American Writers Against the Vietnam War, culminating in his splendid action at Lincoln Center, are exemplary for our time.

The rest of the section was devoted to a review of the award-winning book and some new poems, "the private work on which all the rest is based."[94]

Of course, copious amounts of praise for what Bly had said and done soon arrived in the mail. MacLeish declared: "I'm proud of you and happy for you (and for myself) and surer of the future of the art in America than I have been for years past."[95] Stephen Mooney, editor of *Tennessee Poetry Journal,* wrote: "There's never been anyone like you. We may have to talk the language of Zion to get you understood...You are changing many people's lives. You have certainly changed mine."[96] Kinnell said: "I was deeply moved...And in a funny way reassured, since whatever hope I have for this country rests on the few moments of public courage and honesty that sprinkle our time if very thinly. And, quite provincially, glad that it was for a poet to be the one to speak."[97] Bert Meyers wrote: "Your action has given all of us some of the dignity and hope we need."[98] Stafford spoke for many: "Hearing much witnessing from many friends of that Light of Minnesota (and points west, south, east, & north), I pen this morning...this note of admiration and friendship: – friends all over are elated at the Bly recognitions and continuing good work!"[99] Ignatow asked: "Did you notice that the *New York Times* started to carry half page ads by Harper Publishers advertising their books against the war and excerpting strong parts from it, above the editorial signature of Harper's? Directly after your accusation at the ceremony!"[100]

Philip Levine wrote: "I hope the Book Award is making it easier for you to live. Giving the money away like that you didn't even get a good drink out of it. Though come to think of it it must have been rather intoxicating to say Up Your War to the assembled dignitaries."[101] Lisel Mueller also saw a broader picture: "I am glad you won it, glad for your poetry and your politics...glad and grateful that you did what you did with the money. I become more and more aware of the influence you are having on young poets and poetry-reading students. I see it every time I meet with college students; every time I see an anthology by young poets."[102] Other positive respondents included Harriet Zinnes, Todd Gitlin, and Naomi Lazard.

But there were more equivocal letters as well. Louis Simpson wrote: "I'm not surprised at...the letters you've had saying you've 'betrayed' something. What do they think their Neruda would have done in your situation, but act exactly as you did?... You can't please everyone anyway, as you know, so to hell with it. Just write your poems."[103]

According to Ignatow, when Bly learned that he'd won the award, he at first considered "rejecting the prize outright with a written, scathing denunciation." But he then decided to accept it "on condition that he be allowed to speak as he wished." Once permission was "reluctantly" granted, Bly gathered various members of his community for support and advice. Zweig, Wright, Galin, and Ignatow set to collaborating with Bly on his speech, finishing it just hours before the ceremony.[104] Merwin, who had also been a nominee that year, was also asked his opinion, and Bly thanked him for his help.[105] Jim Harrison wrote several years later: "I remember you on the eve of your NBA in that apartment...not being overwhelmed, and then using the occasion to make a moral statement which many found 'tasteless.'"[106]

Although Bly left for Europe immediately after the ceremony, his antiwar activities did not stop. And there was another big surge of activity in the late spring of 1969, under the aegis of the organization called Resist. The plan, apparently spearheaded by Bly and Florence Howe (of Goucher College), was for a reading tour to ten cities. They sent out a letter, which began:

> Our country's mood now is of apprehensive fatigue,
> of lightning flashes on the horizon, of passion not spent.
> Especially in this atmosphere, the persistent courage of
> resisters inspires us. Hundreds of young men openly, boldly,
> continue to refuse induction. They and their supporters—
> the Boston Five, the Catonsville Nine, the Presidio 27, the
> Milwaukee 14—are not to be silenced, even by the long prison
> sentences that await them.

It's possible for poets to help raise money for resistance

Almost everyone is convinced the war is a disaster, so these readings will not center themselves on the truth about the war, but will rather be a sort of joyful testimony to the courage of resisters.[107]

Thirty-six poets signed on, many reading only locally.[108] Bly was one of those who read with five to ten others in each location. As a prelude, he spent a week as visiting poet at the University of Kansas and did a benefit reading together with R.P. Dickey, Bill Holm, and Ed Dorn. Proceeds went to the Draft Resisters League.[109] Between April 23 and May 3 there were readings in Portland, Santa Barbara, Iowa City, Minneapolis, Chicago, Boulder, Detroit, Pittsburgh, Philadelphia, and Milwaukee.[110] Most halls on the tour were filled to capacity, which ranged from a thousand to twenty-five hundred. A letter from Ted Berrigan seems to suggest that Bly was also planning another anthology. It begins: "Here is the copy of my other 'anti-war' poem, to go with the poem 'Resolution' in *Many Happy Returns*, for the RESIST book."[111]

Eventually, Howe sent Bly an accounting of the dollars raised and other details. She ended the letter: "Of course your own contribution of energy and poetry cannot be calculated or measured bureaucratically. People we met or correspond with are still talking about the reading they attended, as I am about the one in Philadelphia. Obviously, wherever you go you raise more than money."[112]

The truth was that, by this time, Bly had achieved something akin to rock star celebrity, as this letter from Hall to Carol that fall indicates:

I'm sorry about Bob getting tear-gassed...On Thursday, just before the march, I read Bob's poems to my big class in the introduction to poetry. In Washington, I saw a great many kids from that class...He called up from Minneapolis while I was just sitting around here waiting to go down to Canterbury House for an Artists and Writers rally against the war, where I was going to read his poems...I didn't know if he would make it before the rally broke up. I read his poems, and then there was some folk singing going on and then Bob showed up...I went up to the front of the room to tell Ted Berrigan to announce Bob after he had finished reading his (Ted's) poems. The word seeped out, among the people standing around the platform, and spread through the whole place: "Bob is here!" and they cheered. They really cheered...Can you imagine a scene like that about twenty years ago with any poet? Amazing. Wonderful.[113]

Of all Bly's antiwar poetry, *The Teeth Mother Naked at Last* probably made the greatest impact. It was first published in 1970, the product of a few years' work. Three years earlier Bly had written a play, *The Satisfaction of Vietnam*, which anticipates it. In Scene 6, the chorus of shadows says:

Now the president lies about the date the Appalachian Mountains
   rose,
He lies about the population of Chicago,
About the weight of the adult eagle,
About the acreage of the Everglades,
He lies about the composition of the amniotic fluid,
About which city is the capital of Wyoming,
He lies about the birthplace of Attila the Hun,
About the number of fish taken every year in the Arctic.
He declares that Luther was not a German,
And that only the Protestants sold indulgences.
He says that Leo X wanted to reform the church,
But the liberal elements prevented him,
That the Peasants' War was fomented by Italians from the North:
Then he lies about the time the sun sets ------

This is only the deep longing for death.

It is a desire to eat death,
   to gobble it down
     to rush on it like a cobra with mouth open
And take death inside
   to feel it burning inside, pushing
   out velvety hairs,
   like a clothes brush in the intestines.[114]

These lines next appeared in the *Nation*, slightly changed and in different order, in the poem "Lies."[115] Bly kept tinkering, finally incorporating them in *Teeth Mother*. He recalls Ferlinghetti's involvement: "He and I gave readings around California when I was

214

developing that poem, and sometimes I would do the lines right on stage, and write them down when I got off. We were driving up to San Francisco when I did the final lines," as follows:

> ...*the mad beast covered with European hair rushes through the mesa*
>   *bushes in Mendocino County,*
> *pigs rush toward the cliff,*
> *the waters underneath part: in one ocean luminous globes float up (in*
>   *them hairy and ecstatic men) –*
> *in the other, the teeth-mother, naked at last.*

> *Let us drive cars*
> *up*
> *the light beams*
> *to the stars ....*

> *And return to earth crouched inside the drop of sweat*
> *that falls again day after day*
> *from the chin of the Protestant tied in the fire.*

Bly continues: "Ferlinghetti said, 'Robert, do you know that you are insane?' It was sort of nice. The poem had gone beyond French surrealism, and he couldn't quite follow it."[116] He wanted it for City Lights Press. Bly agreed, and Ferlinghetti responded: "Great. Would you like it in the Pocket Poets Series format (as enclosed) or just as a (also enclosed) [folded] broadside?"[117] Tentative titles found among Bly's papers include: "The Fathers Are Dying," "The Eagle Falling," "Do Not Be Angry at the President," "As We Like It," "One Law for the Lion," and "The Ice Begins to Show its Teeth." Bly then contacted Gantt, once again, to do the folder.

Just as the read-ins and the Resist tour had been benefits for draft resisters, Bly and Ferlinghetti put out the first version of *The Teeth Mother* as "a gift to the Resistance." The American Writers Against the Vietnam War, by now a virtual branch of the Sixties Press, is again listed as the publisher. The foldout version went through three printings, and then the City Lights edition was ready.[118] Finally, Joan Baez asked for permission to include the entire poem in a flyer inserted in the album "Celebration" (recorded live at the Big Sur Folk Festival in 1970).[119]

Kinnell had some suggestions: "It is a great poem.... One starts it & is swept all the way to the end. It stands with *Howl* & no other modern poem of its length in that regard—in its wholeness, therefore that it be perfect or nearly perfect matters everything."[120] Later that year, Logan wrote from SUNY Buffalo: "I never heard you read so well as you did when you were here. The Teeth poem is the best anti-war poem (among other things) to have appeared."[121] Bly's old but friendly antagonist, John Hall Wheelock, wrote that it was "surely one of the most horribly, heartbreakingly bitter and powerful poems ever written. It is good to feel so powerful, so authentic a hatred levelled against so hateful a thing. I hope the poem may find many readers."[122] Ignatow wrote: "It has tremendous epical power. I am very proud of this poem being written in my time. It means to me that we are at the very height of our poetic, visionary powers as a people, staring Maya in the face. The poets remain prophets, from ancient days, and you are in the tradition."[123]

In this context of prophetic tradition *The Teeth Mother* is apt to invoke the persistent Odinic characteristics of provocation, of journeys between worlds, and of poetry itself. In retrospect, Bly says that for *Teeth Mother* he decided on "a line that embodies power in a direct way...adapted from earlier poets that throws or catapults itself into the outer world." He calls it "the Smart-Blake-Whitman line." Each of those poets "adapted it, independently, from the King James translation of the psalms and the books of the prophets." Finally, Bly says, the line "belongs in general to declaration rather than inquiry, to prophecy rather than meditation, to public speech rather than inner debate, and to rhetoric rather than exchange of feelings."[124] In fairness, we might also append the name Ginsberg, reaching back to *Howl*.

Among the critics, one reviewer called this "no doubt *the* long-awaited poem concerning the Vietnam war-horror," saying that it is "dense, not rambling; penetrating, never superficial," and that Bly "deals intellectually with the psychological warmongerish causes, rationales, and deceits that make us all parents to the black death we wage in Vietnam."[125] Richard Sugg called it "perhaps the best postmodern war poem in American literature." And he says that Bly had developed a "poetics of apocalypse" with two distinct elements. "The first is the expression in both theme and style of Bly's increasing belief that in times of extreme partisan politics the poet's first duty is to serve as the defender of the integrity of the language itself by exposing its politicization and subversion." Language had been co-opted and corrupted through years of policy statements and news reports about the war. Bly wanted to reclaim it. "The second new element...is his overt use...of the Jungian model of the psyche, especially Jung's concept of a collective unconscious that expresses itself through such archetypal symbols as the Teeth Mother."[126]

A few months after the poem's initial publication, Bly wrote to Hall about President Nixon's latest move:

> I was in NY during the Cambodia invasion—everyone was absolutely wild. The taxi drivers were talking of impeachment. Nothing could better bear out the theories of *The Crazy Ape* (the book by the seventy-five-year-old Nobel scientist) that the world is being run by fifty- and sixty-year-old "moral idiots." He says there is nothing to do but to wait for this (pre-Hiroshima) generation to die—"but there may not be time enough for that." I was stunned by the invasion. Suicide—suicide![127]

The war and madness had yet to subside.

12

Aggression and Un-Aggression

Despite the intensity of Bly's antiwar efforts, he also found time for almost as much constructive literary work as usual. Meanwhile, skirmishes, attacks, and counterattacks continued to flare up between poets of various factions, in spite of the new alliances they had formed in opposition to the war. And Bly, argumentative as ever, was often in the center of the commotion.

Many responses to *The Sixties* 8 focused on the treatment of Lowell. Before its publication, Dickey had predicted an onslaught, but Bly persisted: "I don't mind being vulnerable...: 'all the vanity is in the not-doing.'"[1] After, he told Hall that the piece was "causing some howls." Hecht, furious, telephoned Wright, wanting him "to break his association" with Bly.[2] Simpson, although he was usually in favor of the "new critical spirit" of which Bly was the central exponent, in this instance disagreed publicly.[3]

Others approved, however. Sexton, having not yet seen the issue, wrote that she had heard that Bly "knocked Lowell" and was curious to "see why and how." The reason being, she continued: "I do not connect my poetry with his, despite the fact that critics like to do so (even you, if I recall correctly)."[4]

Conrad Hilberry thought the essay "absolutely marvelous. It ought to be distributed to every reader of the *New York Review of Books*. It's time somebody said those things out loud—and you've done it."[5]

Among the more sweeping reactions, Eshleman (soon to start *Caterpillar*) was feeling his oats and seeking common ground. He called the attack on Lowell "OK, a beginning at least." Further, he suggested that "*The Sixties* can widen a great deal." Eshleman, like some others, could not comprehend Bly's distaste for Olson. He also thought the magazine's poetry was in a rut, and had words for Bly's. "I have a feeling that only a small portion of your very considerable energy is being turned loose in your <u>poetry</u>." He sought to clarify that he was doing as Bly himself taught: "Please don't misunderstand me: everything in this letter is meant to be encouraging."[6]

Haines, attempting to maintain some semblance of their customary give-and-take, offered a detailed but incisive critique—with a tone of condescension. He liked the opening essay, and also the essay on Wright, but felt that Bly had begun to parody himself. He also liked the Lowell review. "But! if only you had the sense to realize that much of what you say about people like Lowell could also apply to you as a poet: 'has always had a poor grasp of the inner unity of a poem.' This is even truer of you than it is of Lowell." Otherwise, he enjoyed the issue. "I never fail to learn one or two new things from each issue, which is more than I can say for most other magazines."[7]

About Bly's growing influence in general, Paul Carroll, now teaching at the Iowa Writers' Workshop, wrote: "The students know your work, and <u>many</u> of them are ardent champions of it, including your CRUNK articles! which I have always admired."[8] George Hitchcock wanted Bly to be more prevalent: "Look, if you ever get tired of bringing out *The Sixties* I'd be glad to give you complete charge of criticism & reviews for as many pages as you like in *kayak*." His reasoning: "*The Sixties* hardly ever comes out & we are all missing your critical articles. At the present rate, you will have done perhaps <u>five</u> articles in a decade & that's hardly giving leadership to the Epoch."[9]

After the busy spring of 1966, in early July, Bly and four other translators, Wright, Hays, Ben Belitt, and Eshleman, participated in a reading with Neruda at which MacLeish presided. Galen Williams, secretary of The Poetry Center, wrote: "Did you know MacLeish had been trying for years to get Neruda to this country?"[10] Bly may have gotten through to his former, mostly Anglo-centric teacher.

Later that year he visited the American Southwest, starting with the National Council of Teachers of English conference in Houston. "I went to the airport in Chicago on Thanksgiving Day, into a bar and there was Creeley. We went over to another bar and found Don Hall, Gary Snyder, & W.S. Merwin there. So we all five [i.e., Crunk and four of his subjects] got on this plane & went down to Houston, having a great time. Snyder I had not met, and liked tremendously."[11]

A published account of that conference, with six thousand attendees, begins:

> Robert Bly, it was, who lunged from his place in the front row among the dozen gathered poets, turned to the NCTE audience at the 1966 Convention, and—quite expectedly—blew the top off....
>
> Richard Eberhart as main convener and speaker for current American poets had just finished his opening lecture.... The general drift had been that poetry draws on the wellsprings of life and that we should all accommodate to various kinds of poetry, and be happy to bring students into such a rich heritage.
>
> "Not at all!"—from the front row. And—alive and kicking—the assembled ingredients went critical. Robert Bly did not accept easily some kinds of poetry. Further, he contended that poets and all others present should never blur immediate first issues that their society faced—namely, for the American people, the war in Viet Nam.

It was not the usual Convention that followed.[12]

After the meeting was over and he had returned to Minnesota, Bly told Hall: "What a wonderful, salty, funny trip I had! I am like a young animal learning brotherhood, love, affection. How strange they are. I see myself perfectly in Konrad Lorenz's book *On Aggression* as a young animal learning un-aggression, or how to shunt aside aggression, in himself and in others." He continued: "I...drove to San Miguel, where some friends of Gary's were. Gary had agreed to do a benefit reading that night, and asked me to read with him. It was a wild reading!...He would read two poems and then I would try to find something in a poem or two of mine to answer him, and then he would answer mine, etc." After a few days in Tucson, they went to Albuquerque, "to stay in Creeley's house (now rented to a Black Mountaineer) and visit Indian pueblos." George Starbuck was giving a reading, and "the silence reminded me of the…academic poetry readings in the 50's…so I decided to break the silence, and I attacked him from the audience about half way through." He wasn't sure if the reading was good or bad, but he just had to do something. "There was this feeling of a stomach having popped open, and intestines flew all over the place. Neruda's lines, 'there are hideous intestines / hanging over the doors of houses that I hate / there are false teeth forgotten in a flowerpot.'"[13] So much for shunting aside aggression.

More importantly, Bly and Snyder had hit it off. Snyder wrote: "It was a good meeting. Now back to work in the stream of plans & politics here—before returning to Japan in February…I am working to see if there's a way to get you out here in January."[14] As Snyder indicates, Bly had also found in the Southwest a piece of clothing that became his signature: "I see you flapping and striding in your Juarez sarape."[15] At this point Bly really started *looking* like a poet. His suit and tie days were over, as was surely evident in March, when he was poet-in residence at the University of Kansas, and later that year when he read at the Academy of American Poets in New York.[16]

Pleased with the successful rush-job on *A Poetry Reading Against the Vietnam War*, Bly looked to Gantt, who readily agreed to oversee the printing of the next issue of the magazine.[17] Continuity in physical appearance, including the typography, was important, and Gantt did the best he could.[18] The issue appeared mid-summer 1967.[19]

The cover proclaimed "The Collapse of James Dickey" and the long-awaited "Many Pages in Honor of Miguel Hernández." Of the two opening quotations, the first, from Andrei Voznesensky, further confirms the magazine's position on form: "In poetry, as in architecture, technique is changing and becoming astonishing. You can balance a building on a needle's point. Rhyme has become boring. In our poetry, the future lies with the ability to associate. Form must be transparent, infinitely disturbing, and have its own subtle meaning, like a sky in which only radar can sense the presence of an airplane." The second is from Hernández: "The lemon tree in my garden is a bigger influence on my work than all the poets together."

The Sixties had been inviting poets to send translations of Hernández, whom Bly had been interested in for years. Hardie St. Martin was working on him in 1960.[20] So was Wright, who told Bly: "This morning and afternoon I went through all the poems of Hernández that I brought back [from New York]. My head swam. They are fantastic, he is like no one else."[21]

The section begins with "Letter from Lorca to Hernández," in which Lorca tells the younger poet (in St. Martin's translation): "I think about you often because I know you're suffering in that circle of literary pigs...You'll learn to keep a grip on yourself in that fierce training life is putting you through...Write, read, study, FIGHT!"

Second is "A Conversation about Hernández," from Bly's recent interview with Neruda, who, referring to his own magazine, *Caballo Verde*, says: "I printed his poems—not his very first—but the ones that made the revolution in himself. I must note that he had been doing a lot of reading in my *Residencia En La Tierra*... And that reading changed his stiff composition, his classical composition, and gave him much more freedom."

Rafael Alberti's "First Impression of Miguel Hernández" is also translated by St. Martin: "Neruda...used to say: 'Miguel, with that face of his like a potato just lifted from the earth.'...If I have ever known a boy with his roots showing, the pain of being pulled up still on them, pulled up at daybreak, it was he." Hernández had a "fluttering preoccupation with death, where matter is always remembered as perishable at any moment." He fought in the Spanish Civil War, and died in Franco's prison at age thirty-one.

After this three-part introduction come seven poems. Bly translates three. "I have plenty of heart" begins:

Today I am, I don't know how,
today all I am ready for is suffering,
Today I have no friends,
today the only thing I have is desire
to rip out my heart by the roots
and stick it underneath a shoe.

Wright also translates three. "The Wounded Man" reads, in part:

> The wounded stretched out across the battlefields.
> And from that stretched field of bodies that fight
> a wheat-field of warm fountains springs up and spreads out
> into streams with husky voices.
>
> Blood always rains upwards towards the sky.
> And the wounds lie there making sounds like seashells,
> if inside the wounds there is the swiftness of flight,
> essence of waves.

Gabriel Celaya says that Hernández "stands as a bridge between the Spanish poets of 1925—Lorca, Alberti, Aleixandre, etc. —and the post-war Spanish poets." He was steeped in the poetry of the earlier generation, and in the classics. "Because he had travelled all the old roads, he was able to make new ones, and, in spite of his premature death, he came up with solutions that are still valid and almost unsurpassed." Hernández wrote: "I believe all theatre, all poetry, all art should be today more than ever, a weapon for war. For war against all the enemies that persecute our body and spirit." His place in Odin House is thus assured, and it is clear why he was a model for Bly and company.

Four poems by American poets are next. "In Memory of Leopardi" is by Wright. "All over the dry grasses," by Snyder, is a sort of lament for California in its pre-civilized state. "On the Eve," by Simpson, ends:

> The businessmen of San Francisco
> Are mildly exhilarated.
> Lifting their heavy arms and feet
>
> They stamp on the ocean floor.
> They rise from the ooze of the ocean floor
> To the lights that float on the surface.
>
> It is like night in St. Petersburg.
> From the Bay a foghorn sounds,

And ships, wrapped in a mist,
Creep out with their heavy secrets
To the war "that no one wants."

Finally, a poet from Wisconsin, James Hazard, contributes "One White Moth."

Crunk takes on "The Work of Denise Levertov." Bly had known her since the late 1950s, and their friendship waxed and waned.[22] With seven books published, she was notably more established than Crunk's other subjects, and the only woman. "Reading Denise Levertov's best poems we sense water passing over some submerged stone threshold from one sea to another. Finally we are pulled down into deep water, and we begin to see a kind of phosphorescence in the deep sea holes."

He then proceeds, book by book. Although it's clear from her first, *Double Image*, that she is "a born poet," most of the poems are "poetic in the bad sense of the word" and "completely tangled up in language." *Here and Now* "is small, but strong." *Overland to the Islands* shows "that the ideas of Williams and Creeley are precisely what she needed to pull herself out of the soporific language of post war English poetry." However, a persistent weakness in her poems is that "there are no real *ideas* in them," rather "there are liberal *attitudes*." As for *With Eyes at the Back of Our Heads*, Crunk says: "The poems in this book gleam with one of her greatest qualities: the marvelously crisp sound." He quotes the closing lines of the title poem and says: "To me the sound of these lines cannot be overpraised. They outdo any six lines of Williams in their decisiveness, and far outdo anything of Marianne Moore's."

In *Jacob's Ladder* her "characteristic strength comes through… At the same time, two weaknesses begin to appear—sentimentality and talkiness." Bly identifies *O Taste and See* as Levertov's "weakest" book. In her new one, *The Sorrow Dance*, he deems her language "increasingly Victorian…often prosaic…Her energy however breaks through in several marvelous poems…In the war poems she is not a poetess among her subjects, winning easy victories over words; she is rather a human being facing her enemy, the Pentagon, who is stronger than she is. The result of this confrontation is not propaganda, but private poems whose movement is at times magnificent."

Because Crunk sees Levertov as "somehow caught inside the Black Mountain net of ideas," he uses this as an opportunity to digress and criticize that group of poets for their "artistic smugness," their "herd instinct." He turns to mockery: "At the slightest sound of danger, they lower their heads, paw the ground, and repeat louder: Break the line at the right point! Watch your breath!"

Crunk approaches the end of the tour with the usual metaphorical spin:

> Despite the criticisms I have made, Denise Levertov is an absolutely genuine artist, in whose best poems words come alive by mysterious, almost occult, means. She does not think her way through the darkness of a difficult subject, she feels her way through the tunnel with her hair and the tips of her fingers that seem to give off light. When she comes back up into the daylight with the water she has found, it burns on the plate like pure alcohol, leaping up into the cold places.

Levertov reacted: "There are things in it...I think are wrongheaded & wd think the same whoever they were supposed to be about—but also some kind things—& in any case it made some of my friends much madder than it did me. There are bigger issues—war & peace—on which we are in profound agreement. Pax."[23]

One of those angry friends was Duncan, who bemoaned "Bly's crippled, critically crippled, sight of the poetry" and sees his "contempt for all ideas of the universe as revelation." This is followed by a more general (and, let it be said, erroneous) statement: "I take it the whole school of the deep image views revelation as being from the subconscious alone; and atheistic and mechanistic, refuses any hint that spiritual reality is shown forth all about us."[24] Levertov responded: "I'm so glad Robert Bly wrote as he did, for it brought me your letter which made me feel like a million dollars. ... He is so sophomoric & *ignorant*, gets so many simple *facts* wrong...that one can't take him seriously."[25]

Three parodies follow. "A. R. Ammons Discusses the Laccaria Trullisata," is a found poem, consisting of prose taken from *The Mushroom Hunter's Field Guide*, but given line breaks and set in stanzas. Although otherwise unattributed, it had come from

David Ray, formerly Ammons' colleague at Cornell, who angrily wrote after publication: "You were a prick to print that mushroom thing with Ammons label. You know he's a good friend, and his work's not that way…Forgive these words harsher than I mean, as Archie will forgive the satire I'm sure."[26] Ammons then wrote to Bly: "Dave told me he wrote the parody of me. It's one of his better poems, so I'm happy for him, at least."[27]

"Life is a Handkerchief Full of Snot by Quarrels Bubullski" is by Phyllis Onstott Arone. The note says: "Charles Bukowski has met his match." It begins:

every day I sit around in the maggot-ridden room
drunk again or maybe still on buckagallon wine
just setting fire to the hairs on my chest
with my 267th cigarette of the day
and putting them out again with my dirty bare hand
because life is a sad handkerchief full of snot…

Last, but not least, is "And Robert Bly Says Something, Too" by Henry Taylor:

I
I wake to find myself lying in an open field.
About my head the ends of grasses
Wave softly in the wind.

II
I raise my head and turn on my side
And see a horse's tail swishing at flies.
It is attached to the end of a horse.

III
In my way I love to consider things I love –
Oh, often even in summer in this kind of field
I think I should be covered up with snow!

This is the second parody of Bly in his own magazine.

Then comes the piece on Dickey's "collapse." As we have seen, while Bly had been shepherding *The Suspect in Poetry* to publication and writing the Crunk article on Dickey, his opinion of his friend took a nosedive. Vietnam only made matters worse.

226

Among Bly's papers is this contemporary (but unpublished) Blue Toad award:

> THE BLUE TOAD is awarded to James Dickey not for his poems but for his courageous defense of the political and military establishment.
>
> As a patriotic American, he feels it incumbent on him to support the Administration, and give lectures on the college campuses urging Gung Ho to the Orient, to the land of spices and rain! Even his ideas are sad and frayed—pitiful remnants of middle class Southern prejudice. As a political thinker, he is a Southern cracker Kipling.
>
> The poet in him, who wrote the fine poems in his first three books, is increasingly being pushed out by the patriotic American, the jet-fighter pilot, the New Yorker operator, the advertising man who is going to make poetry <u>pay</u> ...
>
> The Toad is pictured driving a huge Dactylic Cadillac. In one hand he holds the New Yorker, in the other a gift certificate for war-toys at Hammacher-Schlemmer. On the fenders of the car are pickaninnies and retired generals. The hubcaps read: Lord Kitchener is alive!

Bly apparently decided that, for the abomination he saw in Dickey's new book and behavior, mere satire was inadequate.[28] It required the force of full-blown invective.

Bly told Hall that he had written Dickey about *Buckdancer's Choice*, saying "that though I liked two or three poems ... I thought it was his weakest so far, and I especially disliked 'The Fiend.'"[29] Dickey responded: "when I want your advice, as they say, I'll ask for it. You know I've never been able to buy that assorted childish buncombe which you dispense to the hopeful Knott-heads of the world."[30] The book went on to win the National Book Award in 1966.[31] Then Dickey was appointed Poetry Consultant at the Library of Congress (roughly equivalent to the current position of U.S. Poet Laureate).

Carroll wrote: "From rumors I hear Jim has been giving fierce and it sounds hysterical lectures at various universities in which he puts down <u>all</u> of us, each and every one."[32] Bly told Dickey a couple of months later, "I was at Knox College recently after you were there, and found that you had a pet phrase for me, 'a stupid farmer from Minnesota'—that was worthy of Anthony Hecht."[33] Dickey stood by the phrase, but claimed it was taken out of context, and was immediately followed by: "He is what someone called Ezra Pound, a 'village explainer,' and he has a good many of the characteristics of the young Pound: enthusiasm and drive, and the excitement about poetry that only those have who come upon it as the great discovery of their lives. In the current scene he is one of the most interesting figures."[34]

Ignatow had reviewed Dickey's new book positively, for which Bly took him to task. Ignatow responded: "I just don't see it as a fascist work. To me, it's a poem of guilt. Maybe I'm wrong."[35] Later that summer, he saw the light: "I have just read the *Life* Magazine article on Dickey, a more repulsive self portrayal I've never read. I am sick at this man being in our midst a poet. He has revealed all the evidence of his own future self destruction—tumorous growths everywhere."[36]

Months later, Hall wrote: "Had a nice day with Jim Dickey in Washington. Sweet, lovable guy. Wants to break your jaw."[37] And a few months after that: "Jim Dickey wanted to kill me because someone said I said he was a fascist who wanted to napalm bomb all Orientals. When you publish that essay, arm yourself."[38] Wright urged Bly not to publish it.[39] There can be no doubt that Bly knew the potential consequences. The review became the most notorious piece of criticism ever published in *The Sixties*.

Bly gets straight to the point: "I thought the content of the book repulsive. The subject of the poems is power, and the tone of the book is gloating—a gloating about power over others." He cites "Slave Quarters" as "a perfect example. A true work of art is sometimes able to be a kind of atonement." However, this poem "brings with it no grief: it gives the old romantic lying picture of the slaves, and of the slave owner. It is pure kitsch...Being sentimental, it does not help cure illness, but instead increases the illness...It is...bad tasteless slurping verse." "Firebombing" has the same tone: "As objects of sadism, the Negro women have been replaced by the civilian population of Asia...In these matters, Dickey balances on his shoulders an absolutely middle class head. He embraces the psychoses of the country." "The Fiend" is yet another "ugly" poem, "a foggy, overwritten fantasy about another sort of power...symbolized this time by a window-peeper... and the curious malignance he feels toward defenseless people, toward stenographers and working girls."

Bly then summarizes: "The language is inflated, the rhythms manufactured...The humanistic mumblings at beginning or end hide the naked longing for power about as well as a Johnson white paper on foreign policy hides its own realities." Then Bly asks the question: Why did none of the reviewers notice all this? "We can only lay this blindness to one thing: a brainwashing of readers by the New Critics. Their academic jabber about 'personae' has taken root."

The review is not total devastation. "Not all the poems in the book are as bad as these three, though all are touched by the same inflation." Reading a couple of them, "some of the old affection I have always felt from Dickey's good poems returns." A typical Crunkish metaphor appears: "James Dickey reminds you of some 19th century flying enthusiast, whose deflated balloon is on the ground, and he is trying with tremendous wild power and large lungs to blow it up himself." Bly ends with a venomous, *ad hominem* crescendo:

> When Mr. Dickey visits college campuses for readings, he makes clear his wholehearted support of the Vietnam war. This is his business, but we must note again the unity of the man and his work...As a poet and as a man, Mr. Dickey's attitudes are indistinguishable from standard middle-class attitudes. In an article about him recently, Mr. Dickey boasted that he had made $25,000 on poetry last year. Obviously his decision to make poetry a "career" like football or advertising is associated somehow with the abrupt decline in the quality of his work. ... One cannot help but feel that his depressing collapse represents some obscure defeat for the United States also. He began writing about 1950, writing honest criticism and sensitive poetry, and suddenly at the age of forty-three, we have a huge blubbery poet, pulling out Southern language in long strings, like taffy, a toady to the government, supporting all movements toward Empire, a sort of Georgia cracker Kipling.

Dickey's position in Washington did not entail diplomatic immunity. Although he knew that the review was coming, given the fact that Bly's previous evaluations of his poetry had been mostly complimentary, he was "unprepared for the severity" of it.[40]

The back cover is a full-page "advertisement" that begins where Crunk, in his excursus on the Black Mountain School, left off:

READ THE MAXIMUS POEMS!

Within three to five days after reading *The Maximus Poems*, a small red bump will appear.

This shows that your reading of *The Maximus Poems* has been successful.

During this time you may wear a loose fitting garment. You should have no association with anyone who has not read *The Maximus Poems*. Immediately after finishing the book you will notice a general improvement in your body-tone; you will stand taller, and breathe more deeply.

"Before I read *The Maximus Poems*, I couldn't hardly write at all. Then I read them in the semester break. I banged out three epics just this month."

—JOE JUMPS
East Allendale, Pa.

"*The Maximus Poems* cured my hemorrhoids without surgery."

—CHARLES TIMLONSON
London, England

"Youngsters" are invited to send in the coupon "together with four poems using slashes," for which they will receive their own "*personal* Charles Olson ring, with its scientific BREATHER-ATOR for measuring variable feet."

Turning to other matters, Bly took up Hitchcock's standing invitation for a critical article, and "The First Ten Issues of *Kayak*" appeared in the fall.[41] This essay is integral to our story for various reasons: it shows Bly the critic at work; it fits neatly with his mission to help young poets; and it gave rise to a significant hullabaloo. Hitchcock has acknowledged his debt to Bly and to *The Sixties*, a model of "what could be accomplished by energy and cantankerous individual taste."[42]

Bly's essay begins: "George Hitchcock asked me for some prose for *kayak*, and I asked if I might do an attack on his first ten issues. He thought that was a good idea." Bly characterizes the critical writings of the poets of the Lowell-Shapiro generation as "either sheer gush (out of ignorance or guilt) or a transparent attempt to weaken competitors." The Black Mountain poets (as Bly takes aim yet again), for example, "still refuse to make judgments of anyone if he has professed loyalty to the Olson creed." Bly notes another possibility: "those who are interested in the same sort of poetry attack each other sharply, and still have respect and affection for each other." We know whose credo that is.

He declares that the first ten issues have been "on the whole clogged and bad. As an editor...Hitchcock is too permissive." Bly characterizes a typical *kayak* poem: "usually someone is stepping into a tunnel of dark wind and disappearing into a whistle; the darkness is always pausing to wait for someone. One gets the feeling that as long as there are a few skeletons of fossil plants in the poem, or some horses floating in the mind, or a flea whispering in Norwegian, in it goes!" He does the same for the images, giving examples. Adjectives like "tiny," "dark," and "great" are overused. There are too many passive verbs. Often, he says, "an image with literary resonance will be followed instantly with an off-hand remark from the world of truck-drivers." In addition, "all *kayak* poems seem to take place in the eternal present: the poet uses the present progressive tense...As a result, those hands are still choking that poor cat in the liquor store, and the horse is forever galloping up and down in that pasture."

Then Bly notes what is valuable, and says that, while no one would mourn the disappearance of the *Kenyon Review*, if *kayak* "developed a leak and sank" it would be missed. The magazine offers much nourishment. Furthermore, it is like a fist "raised against stuff like this, crystallized flower formations from the jolly intellectual dandies" (here he quotes four lines of Wilbur) and "also against the high-pitched bat-like cry of the anal Puritan mandarin" (he quotes four lines of Sorrentino).

Still, in too many *kayak* poems, the images remain rational, lacking something genuine. "Poems of that sort are like movies of mountain scenery shown on the inside of a stationary train window." Hitchcock publishes the best poems he can get, and "about fifty at least" have been marvelous. "The truth is we don't write enough good poems to fill a large magazine like *kayak*" that comes out four times a year.

In part two, Bly asks: "if a poet has written a conventional *kayak* poem, what mistake has he made? First of all, I think he has mistaken a way of living for a style." One can't write successfully about nature while sitting at a desk. One can't achieve great simplicity in style while maintaining an over-socialized life, such as teaching at a university requires. Solitude and pain are necessary if a poet is to express, as Bashō says, "the flavor of the inner mind." Bly ends: "The Japanese say, go to the pine if you want to learn about the pine. If an American poet wants to write of a chill and foggy field, he has to stay out there, and get cold and wet himself. Two hours of solitude seem about right for every line of poetry."

Bly's critique inspired "an unprecedented amount of comment," and Hitchcock included excerpts from ten of the many letters he received in the next issue of *kayak*.[43] Most found something positive to say. Bert Meyers wrote: "I think Bly's the best critic of American poetry writing now...But he's narrow minded, like most good critics who are also poets...Bly often seems in a hurry to get to a heaven where only one style of robe's allowed." Wilbur and Louis Hammer answered in poetic form. Several respondents felt that some of the faults Bly highlighted were, in fact, his own faults. Haines seemed to speak for them when he said: "Good we need this. But also, 'Physician, heal thyself.'" Hays wrote: "The crack about 'four issues a year' should not be permitted to pass, since he lives in his own glass house." Bly, he said, has never shed "the taint of dilettantism...It obscures the real value of some of his criticism. Something has to be kept going."

Meyers wrote to Bly later: "I read all the criticism of you in *Kayak*. I'm sorry, now, that I also criticized you without being more understanding and compassionate. I'm going to answer some of the letters...they seem so happy for the chance to attack you, and they're so blind to what I think is the political basis of

232

your remarks on violence and solitude."[44] Haines wrote: "Well, old warrior…you sure stirred up a nest of yellow-jackets, didn't you?…You see what nasty feelings against you have been lurking just below the surface, and now you've given them an excuse to show themselves."[45]

Hitchcock, in Blyish fashion, had a positive outlook on the brouhaha: "The steady flow of letters alternately lauding and damning you has by no means abated—outlying precincts are now being heard from…At any event, you certainly kicked the old somnolent wasps' nest dead center. It has been highly entertaining."[46] Finally, Bob Peters wrote to Hitchcock, reacting to the published reactions:

> After reading the various blasts, eructations, squeals, blubberings, stammers, shouts, and shit squirtings re Robert Bly in *kayak* 13 I am reminded of those cute gnomes and weirdos in a Breughel painting with funnels for assholes, scissors for noses, forked tails for cocks, etc., scrambling around for a thorn-subject in the midst of a flaming universe. About six poets cut themselves down to size for me, & may their squealing disappear in the smoke! I know of no contemporary poet-editor more generous with his encouragements, criticisms than Bly—I have a file here to prove it. So: may he continue tramping through the landscape publishing his magazine whenever he feels like it, delivering his bunyanesque judgments at every opportunity, and continuing to write some of the best poetry going. Creatures nibbling at his ankles and toes will drop off into the muck as soon as he is well into the next swamp, their suffocations sounding like so much fart music.[47]

It is fitting, remembering Odin, that Bly's combative stance is seen as essentially benign and fatherly.

The Sixties Press published *Twenty Poems of Pablo Neruda* in 1968. Poems by Neruda had appeared in three issues, and Bly had been planning this book since 1960. A year later, Wright sent his translation of "Friends on the Road," clearly foreseeing the effect it would have on their own poems:

> I felt so happy yesterday afternoon, reading Neruda's poem, gaining for the first time some really clearer and deeper understanding of the man's nobility; and remembering how

much strength we all felt when the Trakl book arrived, and how we did exactly the right thing with that strength (we ploughed it back into the imagination).[48]

Soon Bly sought the indispensable services of St. Martin, who sent notes and corrections.[49]

Once the translations and commentary were done, Bly wrote Neruda for permission, offering payment. "I mentioned to him that we didn't have much money, but we could promise that many of the young poets in the U.S. would read the book."[50] Neruda responded: "I knew, liked and admired since long ago the "Sixties Press."[51] He granted permission with one request: that the $150 be sent to a bookseller he owed money to in Barcelona.[52]

The next spring (in England), Bly had a surprise visitor. "Neruda walked in the other day. I was astonished; he was on his way to Moscow, but will come back to England in July, and I hope to see him there again." Bly offered to do an interview for the *Paris Review*, "but [Larry] Bensky didn't accept, and implied I wasn't good enough to do it, so the devil with it, I'll do it for *The Sixties*. That is better anyway."[53] After the interview, Bly wrote: "Neruda was great! Unbelievable!...You can feel the love and affection there so deep inside him. He makes Whitman much clearer."[54]

The introduction, "Refusing to Be Theocritus," says: "Neruda has a gift...for living briefly in what we might call the unconscious present." He, "like a deep-sea crab, all claws and shell, is able to breathe in the heavy substances that lie beneath the daylight consciousness. He stays on the bottom for hours, and moves around calmly and without hysteria." After a biographical section, with more discussion of the poetry, Bly writes: "What is most startling about Neruda, I think, when we compare him to Eliot or Dylan Thomas or Pound, is the great affection that accompanies his imagination." The body of the book consists of eight poems from *Residencia En La Tierra*, ten from *Canto General*, and two from *Odas Elementales*. "The Lamb and the Pine Cone," Bly's interview with Neruda, brings matters to a close.

Benedikt responded: "The book is really magnificent, Robert—just a glorious creation. Your translations are among your most beautiful...I think that this Neruda book is so essential to all of us on so many levels that I find it hard not just to fall down in delight, without analysis."[55] Levine said: "I thought it was marvelous. For me there wasn't a bad translation in it."[56] A new respondent, Barbara Guest (with ties to the New York School) wrote to Bly and Wright: "Thank you for this splendid translation...How good it is at last to see this poet surrounded by his proper nouns and verbs and the adjectives as he selected them. I really, given my limited knowledge of languages, am most grateful to you for this book—as well as for the César Vallejo."[57] English poet and critic Donald Davie wrote: "It's the first thing I've read that convinces me Neruda is indeed a great poet...A book you gave me those years ago in Thaxted alerted me to Vallejo...Very plainly I'm one of those whom the Sixties Press exists to serve, so now that I'm permanently resident in this country I want to subscribe to *The Sixties*."[58] Dennis Schmitz called it "absolutely the best translation of anything I have read in years & years. It is also the best book in The Sixties series. Do another twenty poems. There is much to undo that Belitt, for instance, has done."[59]

The reviews were also positive. In *The Times Literary Supplement*: "The quality of the translation is usually accurate, capturing without strain the spontaneous proliferation of images characteristic of Neruda.... The drawback of the selection is that it is too brief."[60] Richard Howard, in *Poetry*, said much about Bly and his enterprise:

> Vallejo, Blas de Otero, now Neruda—The Sixties Press, which is to say Robert Bly, the most entrepreneurial of our poets, is doing our poetry as well as the poetry of the Spanish-speaking worlds a considerable if not a disinterested service by sharpening the focus (though scarcely enlarging the scope—twenty poems of Neruda is a drop in the Orinoco) of our exposure to these remarkable writers, all of whom are concerned, as Mr. Bly has declared himself to be concerned, to bring forward from "inward experience" another reality *by the use of images*.
>
> It is but a part of Neruda, then, that these beautiful versions...afford us,...and because it is a part coincident with or catalytic to Bly's own central inspiration, these are the best translations of Neruda we have, the closest to something that is not translation at all, simply (simply!) magnificent poetry.[61]

Finally, affirmation came from Margaret Randall's little magazine out of Latin America, *El Corno Emplumado*:

the book has been very carefully made, very thoughtfully constructed and gives, as a result, a penetrating arrival at Neruda...the translation is generally very fine. The introductory essay and the interview which ends the book complete a precise picture of both work and man. The Sixties continues making Spanish language poetry really *available* to readers of English.[62]

Thus this chapter ends on an un-aggressive note. But it had been a lively and eventful span. The visibility of Bly and *The Sixties* had never been higher. As a result, he now had that "beautiful crop of corn down the middle of main street" that had been predicted for him twenty-five years earlier in his high school yearbook. While he maintained his aggressive ways when called for, he also continued quite willingly to make himself a target for others, at the same time focusing his efforts on the creative task of revivifying the poetic landscape.

13

Completing the First Turn

on the Merry-Go-Round

A respite from the general turmoil came with another stay in England, courtesy of a Rockefeller Grant for 1968. The Blys had planned to winter in New York, board a ship for the U.K. in early February, and stay there until August or September.[1] However (as seen above), the National Book Award necessitated deferring their departure until after March 6. The next month, they were once again in the English village of Thaxted. Bly was glad for the sudden lower visibility, although it was not a perfectly clean getaway:

> It feels so good to be over here, with no obligations! No places to speak! I brood on the salt marshes over by Bradwell-on-Sea, or read occult books for days on end. Once a week or so I go into London, and poke about. Old Jim Dickey was there this past week…and let it be known he didn't consider this little ole town big enough for both of us. He said to someone, "Do I look like the kind of man who burns babies?" It's like the wolf saying, "Do I look like the kind of man who'd blow down houses?"[2]

Bly also had many letters to answer regarding the NBA acceptance speech.

But he did take a break from magazine editing. In addition to his principal occupation—working on his own poems and translations—Bly kept busy in other ways. He went to Dumfriesshire,

Scotland, to study Tibetan Buddhist meditation with Chögyam Trungpa, who was working on his book, *Meditation and Action*. Bly helped him "by rewriting bits of it here and there."[3] That would prove to be an important association.[4] He was reading Gurdjieff.[5] He also met other poets. Tom Pickard wrote: "I had such a good journey up to Newcastle with you and an extremely inspiring night at the [Morden] tower...hearing you read certainly helped me find my feet again as a poet."[6] Bly told Hall about that trip, adding: "I met Basil Bunting in the dining car! He was eccentric and sensible." In late May the Blys traveled to Sweden and stayed for a couple of months, visiting Tomas Tranströmer and others, and then went on to Norway.[7] They returned to Minnesota in late August.

It was too late for Bly to speak at Harvard's International Seminar, even had he wished to accept the invitation from his college classmate, Henry Kissinger.[8] While he was gone, Martin Luther King, Jr. and Robert Kennedy had been assassinated, and cities across America were burning. Just after his arrival home, there was fighting in the streets of Chicago during the Democratic National Convention. Bly quickly resumed his antiwar activities and his customary schedule of readings. He also continued working on *Teeth Mother*, prose poems (for *The Morning Glory*), some haikus of Issa, and other material.

After a decade of *The Fifties/Sixties*, several of Bly's poet friends thought it a good time for taking stock. Merwin remarked: "Whatever criticisms you must be assailed with, it's a real contribution to other poets, Bob, what you've been doing—it's nearly ten years now, isn't it (the magazine, I mean)?"[9] Carroll, on behalf of Follet Publishing Company, wrote: "What would you say to a paperback selection of the best from the *Fifties* and *Sixties*?...I think such a book would have needed influence on young poets, etc. who may not have seen all of your issues, etc."[10] He had long been pestering Bly with another, related idea, as he wrote somewhat later: "Robert, old *il miglior fabbro* of the critical act...I continue in my hope that you might let Big Table Books bring out a volume of your criticism...I think you are the most interesting critic in USA poetry today."[11] Stephen Mooney, editor of

Tennessee Poetry Journal, was starting to prepare an issue devoted to Bly. And Ignatow, now editor of *Chelsea,* made an offer: "The idea occurred to Jim Wright that you might be interested in merging with *Chelsea*...we need help."[12]

Bly's influence and notoriety had reached new heights. The numerous reactions to #9 were, given the attack on Dickey, even more pointed than before, and thus I give them more attention here. While many of the positive responses came from the usual suspects, Bly received a few favorable replies from elsewhere along the poetical spectrum. Margaret Randall wrote from Mexico City:

> what an incredibly fine issue...the great homage to miguel hernández (well-translated, well-documented, well done, beautifully embraced both by selection and additional material), and the funny funny put down of bukowski, the serious and courageous put down of dickey, the sane balancing of denise's work. it's the best issue, by far, i've seen of yours and one of the best issues of any mag i've seen in a long time....[13]

Other editors also offered kudos. James Liddy wrote from Ireland: "Please let me thank you for NINE. I am reluctantly forced from time to time to consider *The Sixties* the best mag I have read, 'reluctantly' because I used to publish one [*Arena*] myself."[14] Robert Bonazzi, of *Latitudes,* wrote: "I was overwhelmed by your tremendous #9 of *The Sixties.* It is a marvelous homage to Miguel Hernández and I want to congratulate you...I think you're doing such beautiful things there. I must say too that I enjoyed immensely your pieces on Levertov and Dickey."[15] Jules Chametzky, of *The Massachusetts Review,* said: "Glad to see your piece on Dickey, richly deserved, and the good appraisal of Levertov. You've got the most consistently interesting and readable magazine in the country. I envy, admire and am grateful. Keep it up, for all of us."[16] David Curry, of *Apple,* wrote: "I like you, & poetry needs you, but what you have sd. of Denise Levertov in yr. #9 is a violation of one of the best persons around...Your words on Dickey, on the other hand, are really worth having."[17]

Jonathan Williams, poet, Jargon Society publisher, and Black Mountain College alumnus, was struck by the satirical advertisement for *The Maximus Poems:*

If you'd had to deal with the Stuffed-Cyclops of American Literary Pomposity, alias Charles John Olson, Jr., for as many years as I, you'd have much worse wrong with you than hemorrhoids!!! Still, I thought your *Maximus* adv. was great. I have added that Great Man to membership in the Niggards Club, where he may thrive on goosedung forever, along with Mr. Creeley and Mr. Zukofsky, who would starve us all to death with their adventitiousness and icy self-seeking.[18]

Snyder limited his comments to the translation: "The Hernández *Sixties* is nice. Hernández <u>beautifully</u> presented…We are removing to the US in the Fall, maybe tour the west a few months, stop by your chickencoop someday."[19] Ammons wrote: "I guess you're pretty near right about Denise. Sometimes it's soft and sometimes incredibly good."[20] Another take on the Levertov essay is Rexroth's, written to James Laughlin of *New Directions*, who had published both of them: "Did you see the piece in *The Sixties*—just out? It is true she is slowly reverting to the type of British writress encottaged in a nook of the Sussex downs—even personally—even physically. Oh well—better than becoming a female Gregory Corso."[21]

Keith Botsford, director of the National Translation Center in Austin, Texas, wrote: "Your issue on Miguel Hernández has some first-rate stuff in it: I like your versions better than Wright's though. Also your knuckle-dusting on Dickey and an intelligent review of Levertov's work. Nothing to say except appreciation."[22] Levine found it generally invigorating: "I enjoyed it very much and don't quite understand why the magazine manages to seem fresh & important. Most poetry publications crap out in a year. Thanks too for fighting against the war & the wars ahead."[23]

In one letter, Hall said: "That was a great piece on Prickey."[24] Later he was more expansive:

Seriously I think you ought to have a gun in the house in case he comes out to break you. He'll want to hurt you a lot, & you're not much more of a fighter than I am. Shoot him if he tries to hurt you, that's all there is to do…That ending is the best vituperation since Mencken. You may not like that comparison, but by God, "Georgia cracker Kipling" is something like that—& also like Shakespeare. Wow.[25]

240

Bly was pleased with Hall's comments: "The letters on Dickey have only two forks—half of them say, Great, Socko, It's true. The other half, a little more forward looking, wonder aloud when the other shoe will fall. Thank you so much for your last letter, so pungent and woody and marvelous. It's my favorite letter from anybody for three years."[26]

William Witherup said: "Enjoyed the latest *Sixties*, the fine section on Hernández, the satire on Olson, the brilliant parody of Bukowski—one of the funniest you've had in your mag...Good luck in your title bout with James Dickey."[27] Ray reacted from abroad:

> You know I don't agree with you about Dickey. He can hide behind personae forever. There's something wrong there, but... you attack around the periphery...that essay on Levertov...is magnificent, one of the most brilliant pieces of prose I've ever read. It exposes her completely and organically, in a way that she can use if she wishes (the ultimate test of decent criticism). But it is full of wisely considered statements.[28]

Arone wrote: "if Bukowski is representative of what you once called 'a deep ickiness in the American soul,' Dickey is the prime representative of an even deeper and more dangerous ickiness. Your essay was a telling one, and I hope it gets a wide reading."[29] Naomi Lazard said: "I've seen the new issue of *The Sixties*, read your essay on the poems of James Dickey, and want to tell you how much I agree with you. It seems to me that what you said was necessary, absolutely necessary to say, and perfectly true."[30] Milton Kessler called the review "absolutely perfect and right."[31] Judson Jerome said: "I thought your discussion of James Dickey...was excellent—relentlessly humane."[32] Peter Schjeldahl, a young poet who had gone to Carleton College in Minnesota (later the art critic for *The New Yorker*), submitted a poem, mentioned his association with the poets of the Lower East Side, and added about the Dickey essay: "I...admire it a lot, more for what it <u>is</u> than for what it <u>does</u>, though what it does certainly needed doing. What it is is brave, passionate, and clear-headed. To broach my favorite subject, it reminds me a little (its tone) of Pope on Addison, though Dickey's no Addison, of course. The trick is in saying hateful things with love. You turned it, I think."[33]

A brief aside: Poet Richard Tillinghast remembers a drunken lunch he shared with Lowell and Dickey shortly after both had been attacked in *The Sixties*. Dickey showed them a large bandage on his back as he told about a recent hunting trip. He had been attacked by a bear, which he then killed with his bow and arrow. Lowell interrupted, "But the bear wasn't dead, Jim. When you got back to your office, the bear was sitting on your desk. It was Robert Bly."[34]

Told of the many negative reactions, Merwin was forthright and reassuring:

> Well of course you will get howls. You can't expect much general agreement (I differ with you regularly on matters of detail, emphasis, means, etc.) and your procedure is scarcely civility itself, much less gentle. Further, both tone and the bases of judgment are undisguisedly personal, which makes it all harder. But even though I, for one, am not always with you in particulars I profoundly sympathize with what you're after, and with the passion you display in trying to print it and defend it...I thought the essay on Denise excellent, and typical of your critical writing at its best. The balance must have been hard to strike and you said some just and very penetrating things...Of course your plugging of foreign writers is a real contribution. I will probably be bursting with spleen and eating my words ever so in short order: you should have the new book by now.[35]

The Objectivist poet Carl Rakosi wrote:

> Your packet came yesterday. I have been spinning with excitement since...All the things you do and select have the clean, hard substance which alone satisfy me...With re to Dickey, the conclusion I had come to about him is similar to yours. I concluded that I had mistaken energy for passion and that in all that excitement and agitation there was no heart. In that sense he is like a revved-up copywriter...I hope you keep going for a hundred and fifty years.[36]

Roland Flint's gratitude was qualified:

I read the mag. cover to cover. I was never bored. I admire the Hernández poems enormously, even to imitation...I liked both parodies, of you and Bukowski, and the little poem by Hazard knocked me out...I enjoyed the Levertov piece, but I thought you were too tough on Dickey, even irresponsible. I deplore his Vietnam hangup and his fake liberalism, but the name calling, though often witty and always spirited, really gets out of hand.[37]

Similarly, Carroll felt that Bly had gone too far:

Congratulations on the current *The Sixties*. One of your very best, most swinging. I couldn't help howling when I read your homage to Olson on back cover: it was brilliant, and so true.

One bone to pick...: Your essay on Collapse of Dickey was brilliant and had lots of balls, but in your zeal to lambast Jim for his poems praising power over others and violence, you slip into the kind of error which, I think (in fact, I know) you'd be first to condemn in a piece by another: You keep saying that Jim is a moral leper because he writes in praise of lust for power and that therefore his poems containing such praise are bad poems. That don't follow, and you know it.[38]

A lengthy comment from Barent Gjelsness (later editor of *Changes*) sees the attack on Dickey in both positive and negative terms. "Your essay on his 'collapse' is still the best thing that has been done on his negative aspects. And no doubt he deserved it... No one else in this country had either the courage or the insight to do it but you. Yet <u>at its worst</u>, it was needlessly cruel." Then, ranging over the entire life of the magazine, he puts it into a larger context with remarkable perceptiveness:

Your own stance as the *enfant terrible* of American literature has had an incredible effect, like blowing an enormous hole in a lugubrious, pompous and self-conscious, even silly, wall. Now we can see through it to the universe beyond; and we can see detail out there as well as span. But harsh criticism is like acid too; a little goes a very long way, and now many people fear and hate you who should not. Yet so many other people fear and hate you who should, who deserved your rejections because of their unbelievable phoniness...It doesn't seem to me that you should abandon entirely your harsh, uncompromising positions and stances. They have a kind of

magnificence, like any predatory bird's: hawk, eagle, etc. They
have great beauty.

Then Gjelsness's assessment proves that more than one aspect of
the Odin connection still has force:

> It seems to me that your critical positions have been the most
> sobering and salutary, and effective, on the very youngest of
> the poets in this country. The youngest and most gifted. They
> identify with you as they do with Ho Chi Minh, say; a strong
> Father-image. This generation needs that image, and I think you
> have helped to give it a conscience too…You're an essentially
> modest man who has chosen an immodest, often arrogant
> position; a most interesting paradox.[39]

To end this spate of comments, David Dwyer's are unusual,
au courant, and irresistible:

> jazus g*d what a smoothly-rounded golden-assed magazine you
> guys make; it is nutritious, daedal, delicious & stays crispy under
> cream & sugar, crackles in the bowl like drano & *mirabile dictu*
> can be read thru from cover to cover without gastro-intestinal
> discomfiture / chr*st, i'm in love / you are under sentence,
> i put a spell on you, the runes are cast / you are the only
> magazine i ever saw i really want to grapple under the winding
> sheets / i'm gonna keep sending you stuff 'til you puke blood
> & stars at the very mention of my holy & unhallowed name / o
> beautiful motherlover of a magazine, tower of ivory, *stella maris*,
> *de profundis clamavi ad te*, etc.[40]

The next issue had been promised for the previous September,
and, naturally, some subscribers were becoming impatient. The
contents were mostly ready before Bly left for England. While he
was abroad, he enlisted his cousin Orrin (among others) to help
with the details.[41] Gantt arranged to have 5000 copies printed, an
all-time high, and the issue appeared in August, just as Bly was
returning home.[42]

The first epigraph is from Tolstoy:

> Our whole life actually stands in a flat contradiction to everything
> we consider right and know inside. This contradiction exists in
> all spheres of life—economic, political, and in our relations with
> foreign governments. Forgetting what we know deep inside

and putting aside [what] we believe (we have no choice but to
believe, because human life rests on belief) we manage to act
in everything contrary both to what our conscience and our
common sense demand.

This observation is augmented by Yeats, who makes the connection to art: "The power that awakens the mind of the reformer to
contend against the tyrannies of the world is first seen as the star
of love or beauty." These are magnificent thoughts. But the issue
itself, while rich in substance, lacks the coherence of most of its
predecessors.

It opens with six short poems. The first, by Dōgen, a Zen
priest who died in 1253, is translated by Lucien Stryk and Takashi
Ikemoto:

This slowly drifting cloud is pitiful;
What dreamwalkers men become.
Awakened, I hear the one true thing—
Black rain on the roof of Fukakusa Temple.

Ignatow's epigrammatic poem is "The Question":

I wish I understood the beauty
in leaves falling. To whom
are we beautiful
as we go?

"To Tlacachuepan" is a Nahuatl hero-poem.[43] Others are "My Father," by Don Olsen, a Minnesota poet who was also a letterpress
printer. Bly's translations of Rilke and, from Arabic, via a Spanish
translation, "The Dawn," by Sahl Ben Malik.[44]

Next, in a dramatic change of pace, comes "The Bear," by Kinnell. Fantastic, elemental, and earthy, this narrative "body" poem
is ultimately about the poet, poetry, and poetics. It summons all
five senses, involves excrement, blood, hunger, life, death, and
metamorphosis, and ends as follows:

the rest of my days I spend
wandering, wondering
what, anyway,

was that sticky infusion, that rank flavor of blood, that poetry,
by which I lived?

This is surely a high point among the poems printed in the magazine.

Crunk criticizes David Ignatow who, a couple of years earlier,
had asked Bly for comments on his new book manuscript. "You
were very helpful with *Say Pardon* and *Figures of the Human* for
which I have been grateful ever since. You're absolutely one of the
best judges of what I'm trying to do."[45] It is easy to imagine that
Ignatow looked forward to getting Bly's Crunk treatment, but
the piece was in fact written (anonymously) by Paul Zweig, then
teaching at Columbia.

Crunk begins: "We expect a poet to take pleasure with his
words... David Ignatow takes few pleasures with himself. His poems describe a world of unresponsive faces and emotions." Ignatow's poetry had gone largely unappreciated in the 1950s. "Those
who knew the poems were repelled by their flat rhythms, and by
a language of personal suffering which had none of the literary
pleasures of 'style' to relieve it." The poems in his first volume, *Poems*, are weighed down by "literary striving." Those in *The Gentle
Weight Lifter* "descend more deeply now into a kind of psychic
poverty; an imprisoned, endlessly deprived humanity which he describes in himself... The flatness of the language is prose-like. And
yet it is this very quality of flatness which becomes poetic."

In *Say Pardon*, the subject matter includes "the city, the
grating struggle with his father; the impoverishing concern with
money." The book "contains some of Ignatow's best poems," but
others "lack energy." Some are marred by "a kind of religious sentimentality" and are "too literary." In *Figures of the Human*, the
poet writes: "The song is to emptiness." Crunk says: "By drawing
close to this emptiness, Ignatow, at his best, will avoid complaint
and self-pity. He will be hard with himself, not only to gain our
sympathy—the pitfall of confessional poets like Lowell and Anne
Sexton—but because the hardness is a revelation." Improvements
abound, and the poems are freer.

About the new book, *Rescue the Dead*, Crunk says: "Its best poems…give one a sense of growing power. In addition to a number of short parables, which are among the most moving Ignatow has done, there are poems which create an almost lyrical mood of terror mingled with humor." Terror has its own complexity. "Between the inner and outer terror, a link has been made: the two worlds are one. We drop bombs into the jungle, and drive our family off a cliff, with the same self-hateful smile. Because he knows this, Ignatow's political poems…are effective." Crunk concludes:

> David Ignatow speaks to us from a comfortless underground. His isolation is not simple, nor is it the gilded, half-public isolation of the Beats. His poems are like letters from a prison, where he has always lived, and which he himself has partly built. They are profoundly simple, expressing, at their best, the authority and the spiritual grace of a man who has had much time to think, in his prison, and more to feel. Whenever the smells and shapes of the world flood, momentarily, through the angular window of his cell, they reverberate in the emptiness, taking on a terrifying presence.

Ignatow vigorously protested Zweig's critique. He was especially dismayed at the "gross inaccuracy" of the suggestion that he had been "ignored or quickly forgotten" in the 1950s. He continued: "He's perceptive in finding the suicide urge and the sense of absolute emptiness but terribly wrong in putting down the early city poems, and the religious, in quote, poems, as both formed the basis for any appreciation of what I was doing then."[46]

A section of American poems, linked by an emphasis on the physical body, follows. The first is "Voi(poem)ces" by Saint Geraud (Bill Knott's pseudonym). Knott's first book, *The Naomi Poems: Corpse and Beans* (referencing Robert Desnos' *Corps et Biens*), was soon to be published. Not so incidentally, Bly was one of the dedicatees. Knott said: "Robert was a very great help to me…He showed me how to edit my poems—where the real poem began and where it ended."[47] The poem includes this stanza:

> *I blink away the stinging gleam*
> *as my country sows desert upon Vietnam.*
> *We, imperious, die of human thirst*
> *—having forgotten tears are an oasis.*

Next is "Self Portrait," by Zweig:

The roads of the body
Lead me past chilled houses.

A black shape hovers over the street lamp,
With fingers that open and come together.
Handfuls of yellow grain are scattered
On the sidewalk.

A trembling in my body;
I am long and think,
Floating out over the dark air.

He also has a second poem, "The Road Back."

"Going Home by Last Light" is Kinnell's second appearance in this issue. It tells of two mosquitos making love on top of this poem. All bodies, not just of insects, are ephemeral. Finally, "Divine Love" is by Michael Benedikt.

Aside from the standard responses to rejections, the "Letters to the Editor" features one from a writer who's angry because he paid for the Neruda book in 1962, and still has not seen it: "I am sick and tired of self-styled egotists like yourself who mask under a cloak of idealism. You are ready to attack the U.S., and the business community, for its commercialism, and etc. Yet when it comes to your own business dealings you are the crassest hoodwinkers of the public." Bly responds: "Mr. Springer has a point. The Neruda book was first announced in 1960. It was more work than we thought." This is, in effect, a public answer to the avalanche of private complaints that the magazine and press received because of perpetual tardiness—complaints that Carol, for the most part, had to deal with.

A caustic letter from Knott suggests that the failure of most U.S. translators is tied to racism and a sense of superiority over all foreigners. "Belitt doesn't have to translate Neruda truly because Neruda is only a spic...and never mind what Vallejo wrote, if he had been one of us WASPS this is what he would have written, says Eshleman." Knott speaks directly to Bly: "I know you've been attacking U.S. translations, but not sure you got down to the root—.'"

Creeley's amicable letter points out Crunk's erroneous statement in #9 that he and Mitch Goodman (Levertov's husband) had been college roommates. Bly occasionally got the details wrong, as he would readily admit. Creeley adds, implicitly defending the Black Mountain poets: "Denise was, as she continues, a singularly gifted and perceptive woman—with extraordinary poetic intelligence…In discussing her work, I felt Crunk tended to cite 'influence' a little simply, i.e., we were all looking for water as is usually the case."

The next section, all Bly's, serves as a tacit acknowledgement that Norway remained *terra incognita* for most American poets. Taking into account his year there a decade earlier, as well as his proud heritage, it is surprising that the poems by Brekke in #6 was as far as he had yet gone. There remained much introducing to do. "Olaf Bull," Bly writes, "is a poet of suffering, like Miguel Hernández." He "allows his suffering to stand simply in a clear light. He remains inside the light without grimacing." Bull, who died in the 1930s, is represented by six poems. "The Circle of Stars" shows the aptness of Bly's description. It begins:

> *My heart is tired and sad—how much it hates*
> *the sky's ring of stars*
> *that swims every night so self-*
> *content in its own light!*
> …
> *Now you fence of stars that circles the mind,*
> *help me in my need!*
> *Open up and let my soul out*
> *into endless death!*

Bly continues: "Of all the Norwegian poets of the last hundred years, I like Olaf Bull and Rolf Jacobsen best, so the largest number of poems here are theirs." The rest is a "tiny sampling" of five other poets. Of Henrik Ibsen, Bly says: "The shame he felt in Norway is like the shame many American writers now feel over the U.S. The shame bit into him, and changed the whole course of his work from the lyric praise of Norway to the attack." The others are Gunnar Reiss-Anderson, Emil Boyson, Claes Gill, and Peter Holm.

The counterweight to Bull is Rolf Jacobsen, "the most 'modern' Norwegian poet, and one of the freshest and most original poets in Europe. None of his poems have been put into English yet." (Ten years later, Bly would publish a *Twenty Poems* volume.) "In Jacobsen's poems, lines lose the 19th century stiffness, and the poems wave lazily about like a cat's tail, or a snake's head." There is a kind of self-acceptance in Jacobsen "which relaxes the line, and at the same time fills the poem with *space*... We see that same space in Antonio Machado's poems, in Lorca's, in Tomas Tranströmer's poems, and in the final poems of Roethke, in so many poems in which we feel something deeply twentieth-century." He's in good company.

"Rubber" describes the expansiveness of an ant's world in a tire track. "Heredity and Environment," was written in 1934:

> *Now with innocent eyes*
> *And twisted eyebrows*
> *The gasmask stares out over the world*
> *With its snout curiously pursed*
> *Like a child.*
> *So we go to start dancing*
> *Under cold floodlights, white floodlights.*
> *Tango and*
> *Cucaracha*
> *To machine-guns, so:*
> *Arms raised. Two steps to the side.*
> *Bend clumsily in the knees.*

This captures, chillingly, the sense of impending doom in Europe. And it serves as an effective transition to the three pieces that follow: the notice that *The Sixties* was cancelling the subscriptions of universities engaged in military research (see Chap. Eleven); the advertisement for the War Resisters' League (ditto); and "Excerpts from LeRoi Jones' Statement," in which Jones tells of being beaten and wrongfully jailed by the New Jersey Police in 1967.[48] Police brutality and racism run amok, a government continuing to draft young men for a misbegotten war, and universities in collusion with that government—all these were tyrannies (recalling the Yeats epigraph) that could not be ignored by poets.

Looking ahead, Bly writes: "With this issue, Issue #10, *The Sixties* completes its first turn on the merry go round. With the next issue, 11, it takes a second breath, and starts out for the run from issues 11 to 20. We expect the magazine to fall over the finish line of #20, and promptly expire, like a three-hundred-year-old tortoise."[49]

One reader, Bill Harmon, sent a poem, and indulged in some speculation: "It's been years since I've sent anything to *The Sixties*. Soon *The Seventies*, I guess…. I see you as an old old man throat-deep in Minnesota snow still running them off, *The Eighties*, *The Nineties*, on & on."[50] It's easy to get wistful about what might have been, but the next issue would be unique, and the last.

Finally comes this ridiculous exchange under "Wisdom of the Old," from an interview in *Shenandoah*:

Dickey: Even the sense of evil, which is very strong with me, would not exist if I had no sense of what evil was.

Kizer: I remember Mr. Ransom saying once that a sense of evil was absolutely essential to poetry.

Dickey: I agree with that.

Kizer: And he said the trouble with somebody like Wordsworth was that he didn't have it. And that you've got to be wrestling with this all the time in poetry.

Dickey: And somebody like Baudelaire capitulated to evil so much that it became a kind of Puritanism in itself.

Kizer: But in another sense he lost the other end of the dialectic.

Dickey: That's right.

Kizer: You have to keep the tension between the two, as Stanley Kunitz says.

Dickey: This is more or less, I think, the case.

How Kizer and Dickey reacted to this excerpt is unrecorded. But Kunitz wrote: "I…forgive you for being made to sound so damn foolish on the back cover of the *Sixties* (current issue). After all, you were only quoting, with your usual sharp eye for the higher nonsense."[51]

Although the Jiménez book had by now been announced, it would not appear for almost another year. The Sixties Press took a chance in having the book printed in Spain, and the result was a slow-motion misadventure.[52] *The Fifties* 2 had included Zea's translations of Jiménez in 1959. In 1964, Bly wrote in his journal: "Worked on the Jiménez this morning: decided the best thing would be a selection over his whole work, some of Zea, some of Wright, some of mine."[53] St. Martin helped with the literal translation.

Tim Bilodeau, a recent college graduate, was spending the year (1966-67) in Spain, and Bly assigned him the task of finding a Spanish printer: "choose someone who agrees to a two month job at the outside—then you'll have a couple of months leeway when he lies and puts off work on it."[54] Even allowing for double the promised time would prove to be wildly optimistic.

Bilodeau finally settled on a printer whose estimate was the most affordable.[55] In April, he wrote: "I think the galleys will be ready first of week—only thing—I think they'll want a down payment before they give them to me!"[56] However, the date for the young man's return home was looming. Shortly before his departure, he wrote: "We owe the printer $650…They said they had 'trouble' with the last check—they had to send it back to the States, or something, —it wasn't our fault, but the bloody Spanish red tape! … I would guess they'll be done by the end of the month."[57] Bly asked Bilodeau to have the printer send him a copy airmail, and then he'd send a check.[58] A single copy arrived some time thereafter, but delivery of the rest was delayed.

Bly wrote to Hall that fall: "We found out today what has held up the Jiménez book for 3 months—Franco's censors! Seems they found some indelicacy. I referred to Franco's crewcut, I guess."[59] He had to delete all mention of Franco from the introduction. The new contact in Madrid, Gordon J. Fraser III, wrote to Bly in November 1967: "Your received text was given to the printer who is going ahead incorporating it in the book."[60] Both sides of one sheet needed to be reprinted and glued to the stub of the excised sheet in each copy. More silence followed, and delay after delay. At long last, in the spring of 1969, Bly received a shipment of two cases of paperback books from Madison. The 2000 hardcover copies he had paid for never came.[61] The saga was over.

In the book's introduction, "Juan Ramón Jiménez Under the Water" (an expanded version of a brief essay in *The Fifties* 2), Bly writes:

> Jiménez's poems ask the question: what sort of life shall we live so as to feel poetry, ecstasy? His emphasis on how the poet *lived*, rather than on his rhythm or technique, is precisely why so much poetry flowed from him into the young poets. In his life he embodied as Yeats did some truth about poetry that everyone, but especially poetry professors, try to ignore and do ignore.

Again, it is plain how these ideas aligned with Bly's own. Jiménez writes "only of solitude, and the strange experiences and the strange joy that come to a man in solitude." Bly continues: "He... spent years editing poetry magazines and starting publishing ventures to get poets in print, endless afternoons poring over young poets' manuscripts." The forty poems (double the usual number, given their brevity) range over Jiménez's career. One of the short later poems, "Yo No Soy Yo," is especially memorable:

> *I am not I.*
>   *I am this one*
> *walking beside me whom I do not see,*
> *whom at times I manage to visit,*
> *and whom at other times I forget;*
> *who remains calm and silent while I talk,*
> *and forgives, gently, when I hate,*
> *who walks where I am not,*
> *who will remain standing when I die.*[62]

Another, "At First She Came to Me Pure," tells both the history of Jiménez's love for poetry and one version of the history of poetry itself:

> At first she came to me pure,
> dressed only in her innocence;
> and I loved her as we love a child.
>
> Then she began putting on
> clothes she picked up somewhere;
> and I hated her, without knowing it.

After a few more stanzas, the poem ends:

> Then she took off the cloth
> and was entirely naked...
> Naked poetry, always mine,
> that I have loved my whole life!

Jiménez's "naked poetry," that is, "poetry near the emotion," as Bly put it, became an ideal for many poets.[63] In these terms, Bly's chief criticism of much otherwise good poetry was that it was not only dressed, but overdressed, and needed to be stripped.

Levine wrote: "I thought you did awfully well. I tried translating him 3 years ago & got the most boring, ordinary poems for my troubles."[64] But there were very few published reviews, doubtless because of the book's delayed appearance and its drastically reduced print run.[65]

Just then, in the wake of this *contretemps*, came a timely offer from Jeremy Cott, editor of Beacon Press in Boston:

> I am writing...to ask whether you might be at all interested in working with Beacon Press—if just casually, not as a full-time commitment—as an editor and translator of the kind of poetry which you have been involved with and which clearly deserves much broader distribution...One specific idea: that old genre, the "primer" or "appreciation" of poetry, continues to be written—always dull and outworn—but the way you and some of your friends go about describing poetry in those brief prose essays suggests a "poetry primer" which could be absolutely unlike others.[66]

This offer would eventually mean new life for the Jiménez book (among others), a larger audience, and welcome relief from some burdensome business details. Cott's talk of a "poetry primer" was also felicitous; the term would serve as an apt description of the next and final issue of the magazine, which later became a Beacon book.

14

Feeding the New Brain

From the beginning, Bly the Midwesterner had been spending extended periods in New York and in Europe, especially England, Norway, and France. Yet as this story nears its end, a notable re-orientation takes place. He had been interested in ancient Chinese poetry for many years. But now, with his deepening involvement in Tibetan Buddhism and meditation, not to mention his work on Kabir, he began to turn more often toward the Far East. Soon he went to California, as though setting his sights more clearly on Asia.

But first things first. For the "Robert Bly issue" of *Tennessee Poetry Journal,* in addition to Bly's poems, his NBA acceptance speech, and a 1966 interview, editor Stephen Mooney asked some Southern writers and editors for comments on "his ear, his poetic vision, and his political sophistication or naïvete."[1] Two negative responses are entirely predictable. Dickey wrote: "I authorize only a one-word statement, and that is—Pitiful." Tate's reply was longer: "He has some merit, but not enough, in my opinion, to justify his uninformed attacks on other poets, his self-advertising through his own journal *The Sixties,* his publicity-seeking at sit-ins on the Vietnam War, his general insensitivity and boorish public manners."

Several of the more extended comments are favorable. William Matthews writes: "For all his talk of solitude Bly has come to dominate American poetry. Young poets refer to him either with rancor or like Sunday golfers talking about Arnold Palmer. Some magazines are obsessed by him." Furthermore, "Bly's incendiary criticism and crusade for the poetry he admires have annoyed many and threatened not a few." Matthews proclaims it "nearly impossible to over-emphasize the importance of Bly's criticism," calling Bly both a "solitary saint" and a "fiery preacher," and comparing him to D.H. Lawrence. About his Lawrentian preachiness, Matthews continues:

> Some consider this an unbearable breach of decorum, like burping at table; I do not. I am tired of the ironists who sit around protecting themselves with cynicism while men like Bly, Dr. Spock and Rev. Coffin go out on a limb…Furthermore, preaching gives expression to a side of Bly's personality which he has suppressed in his poetry. He obviously enjoys his roles of editor and critic; he enjoys literary correspondence; he enjoys his anti-war activity though he detests that it is appropriate.

Meanwhile, responses from Bly's listeners and readers were piling up. X.J. Kennedy acknowledged that his friend Bly would have no use for his new publication *Counter/Measure*'s emphasis on formalism. "Oddly enough," he wrote, "I expect the magazine will be influenced by *The Fifties*, *Sixties*, and *Seventies*. I will be happy if it does one tenth as good a job of advancing its fixed ideas with humor and with some recognizable personality."[2]

Carl Rakosi wrote after a reading: "Last night I would have been willing to cut open a bird and examine its entrails if you had so directed me, that's how powerful you were, dear shaman, in your long flowing sarape from another age."[3] Another poet, Barbara Gibson, wrote: "I think I need you for a guru. I'm not kidding…Your <u>mind</u>, your whole <u>self</u> is large, <u>huge</u>—I want you to lead a movement or something. Start a commune and be the guru. Start a school and be the president. Make a movie and put all of us in it."[4] Gene Fowler wrote: "Except for some very aged gents who would assume on sight that I was totally illiterate, the two major career makers…around are you and Charlie Olson."[5]

Matthews, co-editor of *Lillabulero*, wrote after hearing Bly in Ithaca: "Remember how I wrote in *TPJ* that friends should be people you love no matter what? We talked when you were here about people's needs to kill off their literary fathers. Well, you are probably mine, but to hell with killing off people you love."[6] An admiring couple wrote after a reading in Hawaii: "We met Bob Mezey…He thinks highly of you; digs you as a person and feels you're the most important person around in poetry since 5-10 years back. Echoing what Peter Nelson said in introducing you at the UH reading, you're 'revolutionizing' poetry."[7]

Some of the roles being assigned—preacher, shaman, guru, career maker, literary father, revolutionary—are plausibly Odinesque, and together they signal Bly's growing influence. It was threatening to get out of hand, as his wife and Sixties business manager Carol indicated: "Here is all of immediate interest in the mail, 22 business letters, 5 grasping USA women, 10 fawning admirers, etc. How can life go on? Where are the Chicago police? Why don't they put these people away?"[8]

Diane Wakoski, a fellow participant at a recent poetry festival in Michigan, had concerns about excessive influence and the cult of personality:

> I think part of my frustration about you at the conference
> comes from my deep conviction that poetry, each man's poetry,
> must be the story of his spiritual journey. Good poetry leaps off
> the page with that story. And yours certainly does this, always
> has. But I felt you presented it in such a way as to be messiah-
> like (and all prophets are false prophets, I think), therefore
> obscuring that basic message of poetry that each man's journey
> is beautiful because it is his own, and should not be embraced
> by anybody else.[9]

Back in Minnesota, Bly formally adapted the one-room schoolhouse that he had earlier moved to his property as his study. He called it "my intellectual home."[10] It also served as a more capacious base of operations for the magazine and press. Several notable visitors came to the farm in these years. Ginsberg and Peter Orlovsky, Ignatow, and Merwin, who wrote after the fact: "I'll think of you both…now that I can imagine the spot, the red house, the barn, the new poultry, the gray schoolhouse."[11]

Bly wrote to Hall: "For some reason, only recently have I realized how much responsibility we have to our work—I mean, not to the country, or to wife, or children, or even decency (whatever that is), but to the strings of words unborn inside us, secretly holding some sort of marvelous spiritual genes."[12] And Simpson reflected, in a similar vein: "What strange years these have been for poets, especially poets 40 years old or about! Instead of the usual thing—one book after another, each less necessary than the last— we haven't been writing 'poems' any more, but each one trying to work out his own salvation."[13]

Bly was trying to do five hours of mental work each morning. "Then after—sometimes—a nap, or meditation (what the old hermits called 'rest'—'fuge, tace, quiesce')—then physical life—I take the children swimming and diving…that is good! Marvelous to feel the body balanced and conscious of itself."[14] Benedikt touched on this ascetic character: "One of the things I keep thinking about…is the extraordinary 4 (or so) page poem you read… in which you end with your head in yr. hands. It reminds me very much of the struggles of certain (or maybe I mean all) Christian mystics."[15]

In early September 1970, Bly and his family decamped to Inverness, in Northern California, for a nine-month stay.[16] He needed privacy and solitude, time to think new thoughts, and some kind of revitalization. Bly had been reading Erich Neumann's *The Great Mother* and, more importantly, *The Origins and History of Consciousness*. He was working out the poems for *Sleepers Joining Hands*, and the prose sequence, *Point Reyes Poems*. He nevertheless did a lot of readings that year, and made many new West Coast connections, as reflected in his subsequent publishing history.

Near the end of that furlough, Bly was interviewed in *The San Francisco Book Review*, another magazine number devoted solely to him.[17] During the interview we hear a wide range of cerebrations that would later be manifest in *The Seventies*. He speaks of "the interior animal life" as opposed to "the interior intellectual life," and of using animal imagery, as Lorca does, "to penetrate down into an evolutionary part of the mind." This leads to thoughts on surrealism, meditation, the Tibetans, and his study with Chögyam Trungpa. Finally, Bly says that "poetry readings have been important for the growth of American poetry…The problem, actually, is to try to help the people listening to respond to the poetry, not to your personality." When asked if he sees himself "as part of a movement toward a new consciousness," he responds: "I hope so. I hope so." Donald Junkins reacted to the interview: "Wow! I like the way you thrust your ideas down everybody's throat, dazzling pot gooks and academics (the ones with heart) alike...Robert, you are a good person, and you preach the gospel."[18]

Bly was learning about the perquisites of fame and the hazards of celebrity.[19] For example, a diatribe titled *The FameGreed Father Bare-Assed at Last* excoriated him for selling out. He wrote in his defense, concluding: "surely the older and younger generations should love each other, especially the generations of those who already love poetry."[20] Those responsible for the diatribe shot back:

> we attacked you from the vantage of your recent acts, which
> seem to be a series of corporate mergers: the move to Beacon,
> well-paid readings at universities, the appearance of poems...that
> look as if they were culled from old notebooks, or else crawled
> through layers of cerebral fat to lie gasping on the page. Your
> fine long poem *Teeth Mother* shows a good understanding of
> corporate-monopoly capitalism and the commodity spectacle—
> why then do you submit yourself to it?...We loved & admired
> you...You were a model for struggle...Now, in light of your
> recent actions, we feel slightly betrayed, and, as it is with all
> betrayals, foolish and angry.[21]

In this classic example of psychological projection, Bly was being made to bear the burden of all sorts of expectations. At the same time, Bly himself—who, by means of his magazine, primarily, had led the charge against old-fashioned poets of the previous generation—had become representative of a new status quo. Thus he deserved and should expect similar treatment from the rising generation, now flaunting its radicalism and flexing its muscles.

Along similar lines, Bly received a letter from Franklin Rosemont and the other eight members of the Chicago Surrealist Group:

> For some time we have been perfectly aware that you are among
> the most contemptible of swine; an enemy of everything that is
> important to us in the world—love and freedom, for example; a
> particularly loathsome reactionary cretin who deserves only to

be pushed into the grave, along with those unforgivably shitty exercises in stupidity which your sickening vanity has led you to confuse with the practice of poetry. However, your scurrilous review of the poetry of Octavio Paz, published in the *New York Times Book Review* (18 April 1971) exceeds the limits of our endurance.

They ended with a threat: "If we ever run into you in person, we intend to correct this reprehensible outrage which is the measure of your vileness. Vengeance will be ours, no matter what."[22] Five years later, one of the Chicago Surrealists threw a pie in Bly's face at a reading in Chicago, while others threw fists full of flour and macaroni.[23] Bly said it was not only the review but also his support of Neruda that angered them.[24]

The first book of the Seventies Press, *Twenty Poems: Tomas Tranströmer*, appeared before the first issue of *The Seventies*. Bly and Tranströmer had begun translating each other's poems and corresponding in 1964.[25] They first met face-to-face in Sweden in June 1965.[26] When Bly sent his translation of "After Someone's Death," Tranströmer noted a few problems. "But," he added, "otherwise the grasp of the whole and the concentration seem perfect—damn, that poem has to be published for the American people sometime, it seems more persuasive somehow in American than it does in Swedish."[27] In another letter he says the translation of "Open and Closed Space" is written "in very good Blyish indeed." And, he imagines, "Maybe the poems will actually be as alive in English as in Swedish."[28] A few months later he wrote: "'From an African Diary' sounds so good in your English version that I wonder if it wasn't conceived in English from the outset and the Swedish text isn't a kind of translation."[29]

Bly intended to publish five of the poems in the ninth issue, to which Tranströmer replied: "to be published in *The Sixties* now seems to me to be a significantly greater honor, fully comparable to arriving at Valhalla and drinking beer with the great heroes."[30] He likely imagined Odin there too, saying: "Welcome to Odin House!" Although he didn't fit into #9, the translations started appearing in other little magazines. And Bly had a small anthology in mind: "I'm getting ready to publish soon *Three Swedish Poets* also—it will be 7-10 poems apiece of Martinson, Ekelöf, and Herr Across-the-River [i.e., Tranströmer]."[31]

The selection of a printer seems haphazard. Bly described Edwin Burton II, of Morgan Press, in Milwaukee, as "an amateur printer whom I met at a be-in."[32] Enamored with Bly's work, he offered to do the job for free, charging only for the cost of materials. In 1969, Bly told Tranströmer that the book was "about to go to press, at last! (We've had no money.) I predict for it a sale just under that of the King James Bible!"[33] There were the usual concerns: finding the right paper, the right typeface (with Swedish accents), and a bindery with a cheap enough price.[34] Bly had a friend, Franz Allbert Richter, from nearby Clarkfield, do the jacket illustration. At the same time, he took on Tranströmer's new book, *Mörkerseende*. "Then, when you come over here next, on a triumphal reading tour, like Charles Dickens, you'll have two books on the market!"[35]

A year later, the Seventies Press book still was not done. A new deadline of October 15 was extended for another month.[36] November 15 came and went, as the printer discovered an English stanza was missing. Bly, in California, retranslated the lines and sought Tranströmer's approval. And he said: "With all the problems, you'd think we were printing *The Decline and Fall of the Roman Empire*! I'm sorry we're so slow and hopeless (the printer is worse than I am, honest)."[37]

At last, in April, Burton told Bly it would be done in two weeks.[38] Bly sent the unbound pages to the author, who noted a problem: "the printer was probably drunk when he typed "Out in the Open" (or perhaps he is a hawk and did not like My Message) so he transformed a building into a wood-stack... Such accidents also happened to Shakespeare, so I don't want to be finicky."[39] The finished product arrived in early September. Among other comments, Tranströmer said: "too much praise on the cover! My wife thought it to be accurate but personally I think I am not nr. 7 or 11 on the ranking list of 20th century Swedish poets. Most literary officials in Sweden would think I am nr. 24 or 29. Your own reputation is in danger!"[40] Bly's retort: "Every word I say on the jacket of *20 Poems* is the exact and literal truth—Monica knows that."[41]

Bly and Tomas Tranströmer in Madison, 1971.

In an unprecedented move for the Sixties/Seventies Press, Bly organized a brief reading tour. He wrote: "In a couple of them, I hope I can be with you—you read the poems in Swedish, and I'll read them in English—or the other way around! Swedish with a heavy Sioux accent."[42] The readings included solo performances at Cornell and the Academy of American Poets in New York; joint appearances at Oberlin and in Minnesota at St. John's and Gustavus Adolphus (with a stopover in Madison for the baptism of the Blys' son Micah, born in May, with Tranströmer as godfather); then out to Boulder, Pocatello, San Francisco, and Los Angeles.[43] Tranströmer's earlier remark is apropos: "I definitely have a better reputation abroad than in Sweden. I am inclined to suspect your translations are better than the original poems. That does not disturb me. What matters is that the texts give people something, if you or I am responsible for their experience is irrelevant."[44]

In the introduction, Bly says: "He has a strange genius for the image—images come up almost effortlessly...like water rising in some lonely place, in the swamps, or deep fir woods."[45] While most Swedish poetry tends to be "very rational," Tranströmer's is "a poetry of silence and depths." He adds: "His poems are a sort of railway station where trains that have come enormous distances stand briefly in the same building. ... The poems are mysterious because of the distance the images have come to get there." To this last remark, Tranströmer reacted: "Nothing written about my poems has made me so glad as your railway station metaphor—it is so beautiful in itself, a poem, and I can only hope that it is true too."[46]

This is the published version of "After a Death," written following the demise of Tranströmer's uncle and of President Kennedy:

> *Once there was a shock*
> *that left behind a long, shimmering comet tail.*
> *It keeps us inside. It makes the TV pictures snowy.*
> *It settles in cold drops on the telephone wires.*
>
> *One can still go slowly on skis in the winter sun*
> *through brush where a few leaves hang on.*
> *They resemble pages torn from old telephone directories.*
> *Names swallowed by the cold.*
>
> *It is still beautiful to feel the heart beat*
> *but often the shadow seems more real than the body.*
> *The samurai looks insignificant*
> *beside his armour of black dragon scales.*

Philip Dacey wrote in his review: "This is Tranströmer's first book in English...and, reading it, one wonders how one managed not to hear of him before now...Other translators have been napping, while Robert Bly continues to serve well the American poetry audience."[47] Ferlinghetti wrote: "Really remarkable! The strongest poetry I've read in a long time. The translations read as if they must be very accurate, like branches exactly mirroring the roots."[48]

The back of the book's dust jacket announced *The Seventies.* "The entire issue is devoted to the relationship between surrealism and some modern brain research." In June, Bly wrote that it was "almost ready to go."[49] Then, in early July, Bly's older brother Jim, who had taken over the family farm, was killed in an automobile accident. This was a blow, as Bly wrote to Tranströmer: "I have lost most of my energy, and can't seem to get anything done. All I want to do is to be with my children, and I waste day after day."[50]

Thus more delay. An irate subscriber wrote that friends had told him *The Seventies* was finally available, but he hadn't received his copy. Carol responded:

> I don't know whether you'd be better off breaking up with your friends who have lied to you like that, or breaking off with us who are so late bringing out *The Seventies* #1. It is, however, at our printer's...and it could have been expected by you this summer but for one thing. My husband read your amusing letter and said this is tremendous—tremendous! We will stop the presses and see if we can get [him] to write any more funny letters. (You might send him a postcard, refusing.)
>
> We both love funny infuriated (justified) letters—we thank you for yours. We beg your patience some more. If you are really very goddamned mad, though, let me know and we will refund your money.[51]

Half a year later, Bly got a letter from John Melcher, U.S. Congressman of Montana, on behalf of a constituent still waiting for his issue.[52]

During his sojourn in California, Bly had made the printing arrangements, with various measures taken to keep costs low.[53] Holbrook Teter did the typesetting for Clifford Burke's Cranium Press. The issue finally appeared in March 1972, almost four years after its predecessor.[54] In appearance it was pretty much the same as previous issues, but the relatively enigmatic declaration of subject matter on the front—"The Three Brains," "Leaping Poetry and Dragon Smoke," and "Assyrian Dogs & Rundown Churches"—suggested that this was, in fact, a horse of a different color.

José Ortega y Gasset (from *The Revolt of the Masses*) is quoted first: "So many things fail to interest us, simply because they don't find in us enough surfaces on which to live, and what we have to do then is to increase the number of planes in our mind, so that a much larger number of themes can find a place in it at the same time." The second epigraph is from Lorca:

> I am thirsty for odors and laughs,
> I am thirsty for new poems,
> poems with no lilies or moons,
> and no love affairs about to fail.

The table of contents reveals the absence of the usual "departments": no Blue Toad, no Wax Museum, no Wisdom of the Old, no Letters to the Editor (i.e., no parody or humor of any kind), and, maybe most surprising, no Crunk. The masks have all been dropped.

"Looking for Dragon Smoke" is the first of eight essays by Bly.[55] One of his most memorable, it begins: "In ancient times, in the 'time of inspiration,' the poet flew from one world to another, 'riding on dragons,' as the Chinese said. Isaiah rode on those dragons, so did Li Po and Pindar. They dragged behind them long tails of dragon smoke." He continues, getting to the heart of the matter: "This dragon smoke means that a leap has taken place in the poem. In many ancient works of art we notice a long floating leap at the center of the work. That leap can be described as a leap from the conscious to the unconscious and back again, a leap from the known part of the mind to the unknown part and back to the known." Odin, we remember, can journey between worlds. Bly notes leaps in the *Epic of Gilgamesh* and in the *Odyssey*. But then came an interruption: "As Christian civilization took hold, and the power of the spiritual patriarchies deepened, this leap occurred less and less often in Western literature ... Christianity taught its poets—we are among them—to leap *away* from the unconscious, not *toward* it."

Bly goes on: "If a European avoided the animal instincts and consistently leaped away from the unconscious, he was said to be living in a state of 'innocence.' ... To Christian Europeans, impulses open to the sexual instincts or animal instincts indicated a fallen state, a state of 'experience.'" Obviously, "Blake thought the whole nomenclature insane, the precise reverse of the truth." Bly's discussion gathers strength and momentum from the historical and literary contexts he provides.

That "long floating leap" is important, but "the work can have many leaps, perhaps shorter." Modern poetry is showing more evidence of leaping. In terms of language, "leaping is the ability to associate fast. In a great ancient or modern poem, the considerable distance between the associations, the distance the spark has to leap, gives the lines their bottomless feeling, their space, and the speed of the association increases the excitement of the poetry."

This exhilarating programmatic introduction limns Bly's past, present, and future intellectual explorations. The leap had been an aspect of Bly's image-centered poems from the beginning.[56] But now this fully developed notion turns our attention to energy, to the energetic nature of the associative poetry that Bly sees as essential.

Examples follow. The first poem, Lorca's "Landscape with Two Graves and an Assyrian Dog," is translated by Bly. It begins:

Friend,
get up so you can hear the Assyrian
hound howling.
The three nymphs of cancer are up and dancing,
my son.
They brought some mountains along painted with red enamel
and some rough sheets that cancer slept on last night.
The neck of the horse had an eye
and the moon was up in a sky so cold
she had to rip up her own mound of Venus
and drown the ancient cemeteries in blood and ashes.

"The Holy One of the River" is by Chu Yuan, an ancient Chinese poet (translated by Ho Yen Chi). Here at the start, the dragon smoke is almost visible:

We two are exploring the Nine Rivers together.
Storm winds fall, sweeping up the water.
I ride in the water-car, its roof is all lily pads,
a naked-headed snake and two dragons are pulling it.

Shinkichi Takahashi, a modern Japanese poet, follows with "Fish" (translated by Lucien Stryk).

In the short essay, "Spanish Leaping," Bly notes "how seldom American poets or critics mention association when they talk of poetry." The prevailing view is that a poem's content is all-important, and that something like association is merely a device or a technique. However, Bly suggests, "rapid association is a form of content." French poets "were the first, as a group, to adopt underground passages of association as the major interest. We hide all that by calling them symbolists...." Stevens and Eliot learned to associate from them.

"But," says Bly, getting to his main point, "the Spanish poets of this century—much greater than the French in my opinion—loved the new paths of association even more than the French. They considered them *roads*." Machado and Jiménez exemplify this. He continues: "So much of the experience of the ecstatic widening of association has been denied to us, because poetry in Spanish is still underrated and underread." Since most American poets of the 40s and 50s did not read Spanish poets, neither did they translate them. The result was that professors and scholars did the translation. Although well-intentioned, "they changed the great Spanish leaps back into the short plodding steps we were used to, they translated wild association into dull association."

Bly also notes "the grudge American critics and university teachers have always had against surrealism," and the lack of "a single important surrealist magazine in the United States" in the 50s and 60s. And he makes a tried-and-true generalization: "if the Americans do not have European poets to refresh their sense of what association is, their work soon falls back to the boring associative tracks that so many followed through the *Kenyon Review* times and the dull political landscapes of the *Partisan Review*."

Vallejo's "Poem to be Read and Sung" is translated by Wright and Bly. Here is the first stanza:

I know there is someone
looking for me day and night inside her hand,
and coming upon me, each moment, in her shoes.
Doesn't she know the night is buried
with spurs behind the kitchen?

Bly remarked that "Neruda doesn't move as fast" as Vallejo, "but he puts his feet down with great firmness." "The Ruined Street," translated by Bly, begins:

A tongue from different eras of time is moving
over the injured iron, over the eyes
of plaster. It's a tail of harsh
horsehair, stone hands stuffed with rage,
and the house colors fall silent, and the decisions
of the architecture explode,
a ghastly foot makes the balconies filthy,
so slowly, with saved-up shadow,
with face masks bitten by winter and leisure,
the days with their high foreheads drift between
the houses with no moon.

In an even shorter essay, "Wild Association," Bly attempts to differentiate further between Spanish and French surrealism. First, he says, "the Spanish 'surrealist' or 'leaping' poet often enters into the poem with a heavy body of feeling piled up behind him as if behind a dam. As you begin the Spanish poem, a heavy river rolls over you." Both types "contain wonderful leaps, but whereas French surrealism often longs for the leaps *without* any specific emotion—many believe that the unconscious does not *have* emotions—the Spanish poets believe that it does." Furthermore, "Powerful feeling makes the mind associate faster, and evidently the presence of swift association makes the emotions still more alive...." When intense emotions are successfully united "with the associative powers of the unconscious, we have...a new kind of poem...which we could call the poem of 'passionate association,' or 'poetry of flying.'"

Relying on Lorca's essay, "Theory and Function of the Duende," Bly says: "Duende involves a kind of elation when death is present in the room, it is associated with 'dark' sounds, and when a poet has duende inside him, he brushes past death with each step, and in that presence associates fast." It is wild association then that is necessary, not the "tame," "approved," "sluggish," "plodding" association that, regrettably, is so common and extinguishes poetry's excitement for so many students. Two poems of Otero (one translated by St. Martin), two of Lorca, and one of Vallejo (all translated by Bly) follow.

This excerpt from Lorca's "Rundown Church (Ballad of the First World War)" exemplifies the essay's main points:

I drew out a chicken foot from behind the moon and then
I understood that my daughter was a fish
down which the carts vanish.
I had a daughter.
I had a fish dead under the ashes of the incense burner.
I had an ocean. Of what? Good Lord! An ocean!
I went up to ring the bells but the fruit was all wormy
and the blackened match-ends
were eating the spring wheat.
I saw the stork of alcohol you could see through
shaving the black heads of the dying soldiers
and I saw the rubber booths
where the goblets full of tears were whirling.
In the anemones of the offertory I will find you, my love!
when the priest with his strong arms raises up the mule and the ox
to scare the nighttime toads that roam in the icy landscapes of the
chalice.

In "Poetry of Steady Light," Bly considers poems that "do not leap about inside the psyche," like those sluggish ones mentioned earlier. "Another sort of poetry is written by a poet who remains by choice for the time of the poem roughly in one part of the psyche. His poems give off a steady light... (The leaping poem by contrast gives off a constantly flashing light as it shifts from light psyche to dark psyche, resembling the flashing lights of flying saucers.)" Despite this issue's focus, Bly says: "I like the poetry of steady light very much. Shakespeare's sonnets are often poetry of steady light, as are some Wordsworth poems, and the poems of Robert Francis. It's clear too that one poet can write both kinds if he wants to." He closes with the example of "Track," by Tranströmer (also in *Twenty Poems*).

We return to leaping poetry with Lorca's "The Quarrel," followed in turn by the essay "Hopping." The image conjured up, of failed and silly attempts to leap, is a criticism of the New York School's successors, the St. Mark's and Bolinas poets. It begins: "European poets led and still remain the leaders in poetry of association." He points out that some European painters, like Max Ernst and Salvador Dali, leap, too. "In America, the painters and poets have had little in common, and that has contributed to the American poets' unawareness of leaping as a principle in art." Then Bly mentions two of his Harvard classmates. "Frank O'Hara had a deep interest in painting in general, especially in French painting, and so does John Ashbery. So we have a link of sorts there. Ashbery has real leaping in his work."

The descendants of Ashbery, Bly says "leap, but without that 'head of emotion' that gives such power to many Spanish works of art." He calls O'Hara and Ted Berrigan "extremely talented poets," but both, he thinks, are "for the most part poets of pleasure, a very different thing from being a poet of emotion." Bly grants that poetry of pleasure, "in a brutal, job-ridden, Puritanical, Billy Grahamized America…is a victory of sorts." But the pleasures of Berrigan, for instance, are entirely conscious, and, as for the rest, their pleasures mostly "are of an even more rational sort." Again he praises Ashbery, but sees the next generation of New York poets suffering "from a lack of growth so far." He says this poetry, "though it appears to leap, actually leaps about inside one room of the psyche only… [I]n other words, it is not leaping so much as hopping. It's fun to hop."

Creeley again eludes the sweeping disparagement: "The St. Mark's poets learned from Creeley to stay in one cave of the mind; but they are not far enough back in that room. There is agony in Creeley's work, which means he is living far back in the archaic part of his cave. The intensity comes from that, and it is the intensity that makes his best poems give off light." Bly sees "a leisure class mood" in these other poets, "who see nothing to fight for." He disapproves of their hedonism, apathy, and lack of intensity, and he wraps up: "This is not to say I hate their poetry; on the contrary, I enjoy it, but they long too much to stay in one part of the psyche, a fairly well-lit part, as Hemingway called it, and the result eventually has to be boring."

Before Bly introduces two Swedish poems, he says: "You'll notice they do not start with the great head of emotion the Spaniards have—but they manage to leap all right." First is "Monologue with Its Wife," by Ekelöf. Then Tranströmer's "Out in the Open," the poem which, as Bly said earlier, "inhabits three different sections of the brain in turn."[57] It thus prepares the way for the following essay, "The Three Brains," the longest and most unusual one here.

Bly believes the neurologist Paul MacLean's recent research has much to say about association in poetry. "MacLean's map of the head isn't psychological, as Freud's Ego, Id and Superego, but geographical—the three brains are actually in the head." MacLean suggests "that each of these brains is to some extent independent." First, the limbic node, at the base of the skull, Bly calls the reptile brain, whose job "appears to be the physical survival of the organism...Should danger or enemies come near... the reptile brain takes over...The increasing fear in this century means that more and more energy, as a result, is going to the reptile brain: that is the same thing as saying that the military budgets in all nations are increasing." The connection to politics is, at this point, plainer than that to poetry. "In a settled society, if there are no true enemies, the reptile brain will imagine enemies in order to preserve and use its share of the incoming energy."

As evolution progressed, mammals developed a cortex, "a second brain...simply folded around the limbic node." As a consequence of this "mammal brain," as Bly calls it, came "a sense of community: love of women, of children, of the neighbor, the idea of brotherhood, care for the community, or for the country." Again we find ourselves in the socio-political world of the 1960s: "Evidently in the mammal brain there are two nodes of energy: sexual love and ferocity...'Make love, not war' means 'move from the reptile brain to the mammal brain.' Rock music is mammal music for the most part; long hair is mammal hair." Just what this has to do with leaping is not yet clear.

"In late mammal times," Bly then says, still following MacLean's thesis, "the body evidently added a third brain." Called the neo-cortex, it is "incredibly complicated, more so than the other brains." Furthermore, its potential has barely been tapped. He cites Charles Fair, who, in *The Dying Self* (1969), "suggests that what Freud meant by the 'Id' was the reptile and mammal brain, and what the ancient Indian philosophers meant by the 'self' was the new brain." Now we seem to be getting closer. "He thinks that the new brain can grow and that its food is wild spiritual ideas... The Greek mystery religions, and the Essene cult that Christ was a member of, were clear attempts to feed the new brain."[58] In Europe, the use of the third brain peaked around 1500. Bly continues:

> Since then, "secularization" means that the other two brains
> have increased their power. Nevertheless a man may still live if
> he wishes to more in his new brain than his neighbors do... A
> "saint" is someone who has managed to move away from the
> reptile and the mammal brains and is living primarily in the new
> brain. As the reptile brain power is symbolized by cold, and the
> mammal brain by warmth, the mark of the new brain is light.

The three brains are in continual competition for their share of energy. How is this manifested in the present time? Bly says: "The United States, given the amount of fear it generates every day in its own citizens, as well as in the citizens of other nations, is a vast machine for throwing people into the reptile brain." But there is good news. "The ecology workers, the poets, singers, meditators, rock musicians and many people in the younger generation in general, are trying desperately to reverse the contemporary energy-flow in the brain." Can we get stuck? "We do not spend the whole day 'inside' one brain, but we flip perhaps a thousand times a day from one brain to the other." One can learn to control, to some extent, the movement from one brain to another and achieve spiritual growth. Bly says: "Energy that goes normally to the reptile brain can be transferred to the mammal brain, some of it at least; energy intended for the mammal brain can be transferred to the new brain."

The movement between brains is now called a "leap." "'Meditation' is a practical method for transferring energy from the reptile to the mammal brain, and then from the mammal to the new brain. It is slow, but a 'wide' road, a road many can take, and many religious disciplines have adopted it." Since Christianity lacks a formal practice of meditation, "the ecstasy of the new brain" has been experienced by fewer in the West. However, "Thoreau managed to transfer a great deal of energy to the new brain without meditation, merely with the help of solitude. Solitude evidently helps the new brain."

In the final section, Bly explicitly relates all of this to poetry, indicating that poets, like all persons, are often dominated by one brain. "Chaucer is a great poet of the mammal brain; clearly St. John of the Cross and Kabir are great poets of the new brain. The reptile brain seems to have no poet of its own... Robinson Jeffers is a man with an extremely powerful mammal brain, in whom, nevertheless, the reptile brain had a slight edge." As for musicians, Bly says, "Bach makes music of new brain emotions; Beethoven primarily out of mammal brain emotions."

Then it's back to Blake, who figured in the introductory essay: "Blake is such an amazing poet because he talks of moving from one brain to another. His people in 'the state of experience,' after all, have been pulled back into the reptile brain... When we are in a state of 'innocence,' Blake says we are feeling some of the spiritual ecstasy of the new brain." Therefore, Bly continues: "I think poetry ought to take account of these ideas. Some biological and neurological speculations are marvelous, and surely that speculation belongs in literary criticism as much as speculation about breath or images or meter. A man should try to feel what it is like to live in each of the three brains, and a poet could try to bring all three brains inside his poems."

Another Lorca poem follows, and then another essay, "Surrealism, Rilke, and Listening," that ties together some loose ends. "If we go back and read some of the surrealist poems of Lorca printed earlier in this issue, it's clear that Lorca is often leaping from one brain to the other." But, Bly continues:

Mere mechanical pulling of images out of memory stores will not produce leaping poetry; and that is possibly why so much mechanical surrealist poetry fails. Lorca's energy input to his new brain was immense, and he increased it by living and writing in a certain way. When the new brain is receiving energy from the other brains, then leaping poetry is possible. In other words, leaping poetry probably cannot be written without great spiritual energy.

Furthermore:

> Lorca's surrealist poems, the good ones, are models of the human brain…The reason surrealism is weak in the United States is because the North Americans are obsessed with unity and identity. The critical point of view represented by the *New York Review of Books* in America and *The Spectator* in England is hostile to surrealism, and longs for the old non-existent unity, which seems to them civilized and terribly elegant.

Then, like Euripides relying on a *deus ex machina*, Bly summons Rilke, "the greatest spiritual poet of the twentieth century, and the greatest poet of the new brain…His poetry is always about change, paths, doors, roads opening. The story of Orpheus became important to him, because Orpheus was a man who kept his paths of association open." Mircea Eliade saw Orpheus as "an early shaman figure, who flies 'from one world to the next.'" Orpheus followed Eurydice down into the darkness, and returned to the light. "This leap between two worlds became another theme of the *Sonnets to Orpheus*."[59]

Of the four sonnets that follow, this is the ninth:

> *Only the man who has raised his strings*
> *among the dark ghosts also*
> *can sense it and give*
> *the everlasting praise.*
>
> *Only he who has eaten poppy*
> *with the dead, from their poppy,*
> *will never lose even*
> *his most delicate sound.*
>
> *Even though images in the pool*
> *seem so blurry:*
> *grasp the main thing.*

Only in the double kingdom, there
alone, do voices become
undying and tender.

A half-page statement, "Home Grown Poems," serves to introduce thirteen poems by eleven poets. It begins:"Voznesensky said a few years ago, 'Rhyme has become boring. In poetry the future lies with the ability to associate.'"[60] Bly continues: "And Russian poetry has a lot of leaping. So has South American poetry, and 'primitive' poetry." He grumbles: "In leaping, we are the dolts." Nevertheless, "we do have leapers. And here is a sampling, including old hands and new hands. There are many more poets, both English and American, who belong here, but even these few suggest the varieties of mood possible." For Bly's magazine, this is an unprecedentedly eclectic gathering.

The new hands are three poets in their early twenties, Gregory Orr, Raymond Zdonek, and Tom Pickard. This is "Silence" by Orr:

The way the word sinks into the deep snow of the page.

The dead deer lying in the clearing,
its head and antlers transparent.
The black seed in its brain
parachuting toward earth.

Repeat contributors include Knott, Rothenberg, Snyder, Edson, and Bly himself. Here is Rothenberg's "Crazy Dog Events":

1. Act like a crazy dog. Wear sashes & other fine clothes, carry
a rattle, & dance along the roads singing crazy dog songs after
everybody else has gone to bed.

2. Talk crosswise: say the opposite of what you mean & make others
say the opposite of what they mean in return.

3. Fight like a fool by rushing up to an enemy & offering to be
killed. Dig a hole near an enemy, & when the enemy surrounds it,
leap out at them & drive them back.

4. Paint yourself white, mount a white horse, cover its eyes & make
it jump down a steep & rocky bank, until both of you are crushed.

This is an example of the "primitive" poetry to which Bly just referred. It comes from the Crow Indians, and was merely "arranged" by Rothenberg.

In "The Way West   Underground," Snyder marvelously encompasses the whole world, moving from place to place—Oregon, Japan, China, Tibet, Finland, France, Spain—following the bear by way of appearance, practice, language, and cave-paintings.[61]

Bly's "from Sleepers Joining Hands," a poem in process, includes these lines:

> *There are fears coming up from underneath,*
> *pulling us down,*
> *the ecstatic orifices closed to the blue stormlight,*
> *Antares and the Orphic nests swirled in the surd rivers,*
> *the outer eighth-inch of the brain giving off smoke, like mist*
> *   boiling off hailclouds,*
> *I am afraid.*
> *The insubstantial bodies stretched out ten miles long in the*
> *   sixth dimension,*
> *the death birds flying along the corridors we make for them with*
> *   our own*
> *bodies after death,*
> *ships rising and falling, no way out.*

This poem seems to be an *exemplum* of the three brains essay.

One old hand is the "curious genius" Russell Edson, whose "Conjugal" is an erotic prose poem. The other old hands are new to the magazine. Ginsberg's contribution is from "The Car Crash Poem." Part three begins:

> *Raw pine walls, ice-white windows*
> *three weeks now, snowy flatness*
> *foot-thick down valley meadows,*
> *wind roar in bare ash arms, oak branch*
> *tendrils icy gleaming, yellow*
> *stain of morning water in front*
> *door's snow—I walk out on crutches*
> *to see white moonglow make snow blue*
> *—three men just rode a space ship*

round the moon last week—gnashing
their teeth in Biafra & Palestine,
Assassins & Astronauts travelling from
Athens to the sea of Venus Creatrix—
Lover's quarrels magnified decades to mad
violence, half naked farm boys stand
with axes at the kitchen table,
trembling guilty, slicing egg
grapefruit breasts on breakfast oilcloth.

The familiar territory of snowy fields quickly assumes the appearance of a more Ginsbergian tableau.

"Fantast" and "The Hand Moves The Word Flies" are by Philip Lamantia, already mentioned as a Breton-influenced surrealist. And "Two Years Later," by John Wieners, is from *Ace of Pentacles*:

The hollow eyes of shock remain
Electric sockets burnt out in the
    skull.

The beauty of men never disappears
But drives a blue car through the
                stars.

This issue comes to a close with the words of Chögyam Trungpa on the back cover:

The Zen teacher hates the horse
but the horse carries him.
At the river both have to get into a boat.
For crossing the mountains
it's best just to carry an old stick

When the first issue of *The Seventies* appeared, no one, not even Bly himself, knew that it would be the last. Yet Odin and his horse might have sensed that something was up. Sleipnir, like Pegasus before him, was finally abandoned. But this wasn't the bitter end, the final destruction, *Ragnarök* (or *Götterdämmerung*). For the rider, now off his horse, there were new journeys ahead, across rivers and over mountains.

With his wide-ranging and omnivorous intelligence, Bly continued to change and grow. His attentive and patient readers were quite prepared to follow along. As we shall see, never had the reactions been so passionate and so effusive. The magazine was going out with a bang.

15

Letting the Tortoise Expire,

Prematurely

Sadness over the end of the run may be tempered somewhat by the sustained and fervent applause which greeted the final issue, coming from several quarters. First, from among the contributors, Tranströmer said: "I think, being published there, I have reached the absolute summit of my public life."[1] Orr called it "very spectacular, but everyone says that & so, just add my compliments to the list."[2] Lawder said it would be a shame if Bly stopped editing. "Teaching 'poetry writing'...I don't know what I'd do w/out copies of the *Fifties, Sixties*—a lending library that's ragged, dog-eared, chewed up."[3] Edson, too, was grateful for being included. "You're such a pill in choosing stuff, but how well it pays off, everything seems right and highly charged."[4] A month later his appreciation had grown: "Everyone seems to love [it]... The expression in your essays seems to have signaled to poets that they can and should trust their interiors." He closed with a credo: "I believe in you, Robert, as one of the most insidely lit poets writing today."[5]

Second, from among old friends, Stafford wrote: "I want to be a leaper!"[6] MacLeish, Bly's teacher at Harvard, said:

> I like the feel and sense of your metaphor of the leap. "Leaping is the ability to associate fast." Which becomes "the speed of the association increases the excitement of the poetry." This adds

to Baudelaire's "analogie universelle" which I would have said cannot be added to, being the last footstep on the path before the path drops out from under. Thus you are now the teacher and I the learner.[7]

Hall's reaction was really heartfelt: "I had wanted to write to you for a long time, to say that the new issue is the best one ever, and that it is a book, and that it should be published by itself. Beautiful. It has its own leaping."[8] Others also would remark on its self-contained structure. A couple of years later, Beacon Press repackaged it as *Leaping Poetry: An Idea with Poems and Translations.*

Third, some up-and-coming poets were profoundly affected. Etheridge Knight wrote: "The paper you did about 'The Leap' in the latest issue of *The Seventies* is outta sight."[9] Stanley Plumly, poetry editor of the *Ohio Review,* called the issue "incredible. It seems to me that it's as much a synthesis of our best poet-past as it is a definition of the shape of the future. I think your taste in poetry is sometimes quirky but I think you have the best instincts of anyone since Pound. And pardon my young opinions."[10] Carolyn Forché, still a student at Michigan State University, wrote: "I have just finished going without bridges in your last issue of *The Seventies,* through the dragon smoke with exuberance. Your collection is more on fire than any other I've seen in recent years (my years have only been recent). A joyous defiance, the woods are strung with proofs that the potions live."[11] Gregory Hall responded: "you of course amaze me—your magazine." And also with this, taking the long view:

> ...by the time the
> *Eighties* flies from the worm
> in the howling alkali vaults of crumbling, lovely,
> strangely america, I will have perfected my
> *translations of the selected writings of the moon...*
> bless you, robert bly, bless your vision—[12]

There were many other responses from various sources, known and unknown. Bob Grady wrote: "Better than ever...I don't know why I was so surprised—your mag. has always been premium, rather than precious. Tho, paradoxically 'precious' in the rare sense.

When I look back at the literary mags I still have from the 1950s... your *Fifties* stands like a rock, unsinkable."[13] Roger Sauls said: "It is the best document I have seen on modern poetry. It should serve as a textbook for young poets, as both theory & practice. The *Seventies* ought to come out more often. It's such a valuable publication."[14] Barbara Riddle also saw the educational value: "Should be read by every aspiring or practicing American poet, should be distributed to every elementary and high school, should replace all textbooks in all university seminars. I mean it. It's important because it not only clarifies why so much existing poetry is boring, but because the insights can really be used to <u>generate</u> new poems."[15] Thomas McKenna, a publisher in Newcastle and friend of Pickard, said: "Your *Seventies* comes across like a packed fist. A very solid punch. I'm sure you don't go much for the pugilist terminology, but I'll bet that's how it hits a lot of people."[16]

John Carpenter thought it "a marvelous issue, throwing off sparks in all directions; your essays, or commentary, and the translations were integrated very tightly and effectively—quite a *tour de force*."[17] Bob Callahan, a Bay area writer, wrote: "I think I already told you that in my judgment *Seventies* is the best poetry (new word needed) magazine of the decade."[18] Andrew Glaze, a young New York poet, offered his opinions:

> I think you are absolutely on the right track. Whether or not you have come up with the correct theoretical explanation in the "three brains" I am not competent to judge, but I suspect it is not that simple. But in my bones I know you could not be more right...
>
> It is the first theoretical effort to explain what is going on in poetry nowadays which seemed to me at all adequate.[19]

Gary Pacernick of Wright State University was stirred up:

> The translations, criticism, poems comprise the most stimulating poetry experience I can remember in a long time—comparable in intensity and joy to reading Roethke's madhouse & love poems, Hart Crane's *The Bridge*, Ginsberg's *Kaddish*, etc. Your translations of Lorca affect me most strongly...Lorca (in your versions) is a great artist—pictorial, musical, lucid, brilliant. The brain waves seethe in every line.

282

He concluded: "Your inspiration can give us all a shot in the arm."[20] There was another unexpected respondent, as Bly told Hall: "Joyce Carol Oates just sent me a long five page letter … She was enthusiastic about *Seventies* 1."[21]

Of course, not everyone was happy, grateful, or positively impressed. Michael Brownstein responded in particular to "the, to me, extremely mysterious article titled 'Hopping.' Mysterious—or peculiar—not only because of the distinctions drawn between pleasure and emotion, but also because of the highly uncomprehensive view of some poets whose work I know fairly well … I certainly didn't swing with that article!"[22] Brownstein was associated with those New York poets who were being lampooned.

Another jolt of negativity came from Haines: "My first reaction was, 'My God, there's a lot of shit in this issue!' A large rehash of everything you've been saying for years, and the American poems are mostly bad. It begins to sound stale." Yet on top of several negative reactions, he wrote, "there are some strangely positive ones too. As always, you do manage to say some things that lead a man off into some new area of thought. I guess the most important thing I have found in it is a new sense of what 'associations' can mean … something of possible importance to myself … and for that I am grateful."[23]

To finish this look at responses, several are focused on "The Three Brains." First, McGrath's:

> your three-brain theory has certain parallels to the Aristotelian
> idea that man is composed of three natures—vegetable,
> animal, and rational. The vegetable man has, as his highest
> good, security. This leads Dante in his explanatory note on the
> *Comedy*…where he offers a simplified picture of the three natures
> to argue that the kind of poetry proper to this side of man's
> nature concerns the arts of war. For the animal man, love poetry;
> for rational man, philosophic religious poetry—the highest
> good for the rational man is the good of the intellect, which is
> knowledge of God.[24]

James B. Allen of Ann Arbor observed: "The essay on the 3 brains strikes me as close to Boehme's three worlds of darkness, fire, and light, from self-directed energy to love-directed energy, for him found in Christ. Anyway, an excellent essay. I am continuously struck by how 'science' corroborates the intuitions of mystical / creative minds."[25]

Nick Teele saw a connection with the Japanese poetic tradition:

Your final idea—that a poet should try to bring all three brains inside his poems—seems to me to have been a central consideration of the old *waka* masters of Japan. Their method of doing it was to take a given instant and throw it upon the wind so they might catch & put into a poem (or painting) some of its reflections from constructions of mirrors both inside and outside their brains.[26]

Eleanor Reskès was looking in a different direction:

When I read "The Three Brains," I had the curious feeling that a new force was being unleashed and also explained. I recalled a statement made by Freud in his *Civilization and Its Discontents,* in reference to his study of Goethe—"And one may heave a sigh at the thought that it is vouchsafed to the few, with hardly any effort, to salve from the whirlpool of their own emotions, the deepest truths, to which we others have to force our way, ceaselessly groping amid torturing uncertainties." Also in another of his works which I have not been able to locate, he restates this by saying that it is a constant source of amazement to him that a poet can, by a single leap, arrive at a conclusion which he, himself, arrived at only after many years of study and deliberation, constantly beset by grave misgivings.[27]

Aristotle, Dante, Boehme, Japanese *Waka* masters, Goethe, Freud—Bly's theorizing and speculation was putting him in some hallowed company.

Finally, Bly heard from the author of the whole idea, Paul MacLean (an MD at the National Institute for Mental Health), whose response was friendly:

I envy the engaging way in which you express yourself, and I must say that I wish that a number of us in our field could be as perceptive in our writing.

There is a saying that something does not exist until you give it a name. It also seems that the pollen of ideas never gets spread to the heart and guts of a society unless it attracts the attention of literary people and philosophers. The last paragraph of your article on the three brains left me with as satisfying a feeling as I have experienced in a long while!

I have a brother (an English professor at the University of Toronto), two nephews, and a son, all of whom aspire to writing poetry, and I would like to order four copies of this issue of *The Seventies* to send to them.[28]

Even with all this approbation, the magazine's discontinuation was a bitter pill. *The Seventies* 1 was not going to be the first of another ten issues, as Bly had declared. Laughlin of *New Directions* wrote: "I was disappointed to learn…that you are planning to give up the magazine after four more numbers. I can well understand that it is a terrible drain on your time and strength and resources, but it has been so distinctive, and so good. I…hope that you will change your mind later on and do another series."[29]

Haines had a shaky premonition: "I was going to say—Stop! You've done enough, and from here it's all downhill. But maybe you shouldn't."[30] To use Bly's own metaphors, the second turn on the merry-go-round ended prematurely; the tortoise never made it to the finish line.

The times were partly to blame. In 1973, when United States armed forces withdrew from Vietnam, the tumultuous decade of "the sixties" may be said to have ended. Many of those who, like Bly, had invested so much time and energy pressing for change were emotionally exhausted. The Watergate hearings also began, which added to a general sense of weariness and malaise.

And yet, measured by his output of poems, translations, and editions, the early 70s was a very productive period.[31] He started writing a column for *American Poetry Review* (seven essays between 1973 and 1977). Under his leadership, the first annual Great Mother Conference was held in 1975.[32] He was the prime mover behind the Minnesota Writers' Publishing House, a collective modeled after a Swedish organization designed to "give the writers influence over publishing conditions of their work, oppose the centralization of power in the publishing world, and attack radically the habit of charging high prices for new work."[33] Thus, while his drive showed no signs of letting up, it seems the magazine had become a burden that he was no longer willing to bear.

In addition, he was still striving after an ascetic ideal, as this letter from Edson indicates: "Reading the interview in *Stone Drum* I am enchanted by the various stations of your isolation, from the first, more worldly level of your chicken house study, to a place some miles from your farm, to an even more remote place in northern Minnesota. I am reminded of how oriental monks go into the mountains, and are seen sometimes to float."[34] Related is a comment Bly made when asked if he ever gets "tired of words," that is, of talking: "that's why I stay on the farm about nine, ten months a year where I have no literary friends."[35]

Meanwhile, the amount of correspondence did not noticeably diminish. R.P. Dickey (in a letter criticizing Bly's poetry and politics) wrote:

> You are one of the most generous spirits in contemporary poetry; you're a miniature latter day Pound in that, and many of us know it and talk about it and build the good legend of your true generosity. ... Another thing I love you for....you are, in fact, as I said in my poem on you, probably the number one best reader since Dylan Thomas. You are the boss man, Robert, when it comes to reading.[36]

Helen Vendler, not yet the renowned critic, wrote with a Yeatsian flourish: "I hope you will let me know if you are reading in the vicinity of Boston. I heard you, if memory serves, once 10 or 11 years ago at Cornell. Like all scholars I am always somewhat appalled when my Catullus walks my way, but I would like to hear you read again."[37] The next year she sent a belated note: "I...feel bound by our mutual attachment to poetry to thank you for your magical translations of Rilke's *Sonnets to Orpheus* in *The Seventies #1*."[38] After another year, she added:

> I do think you are a super translator, & the cause of super translating in others, to judge from the Miguel Hernández book, which for me was unforgettable. I really am deeply grateful for the poems, & for the fact that the bilingual format encourages entry into the original; I don't know how you get translations literal enough to be useful as a "trot" and at the same time so beautiful in themselves—it's a marvel...I look

forward to knowing new poets through you in the future: thank you in advance.[39]

Friends continued with their encouragement and praise. Hall wrote: "I repeat what I said a couple of years ago, that I think that you will receive the Nobel Prize. With any luck, they'll wait until you are 82 before they give it to you, so it won't do any harm."[40] Stafford, about to embark on a poetry circuit, said: "This letter is mostly just to affirm loyalty from your sidekick…I expect to stumble onto your big tracks at many of these places. I'll kneel to worship every time."[41] Knott wrote:

> I revere your opinion above anyone's—you are not only a great poet (I think so, anyway) but your critical ideas are the best and most intelligent, insightful, etc.—you know I feel this way—and have always—even if I haven't said it straight out to you—even my "surrealist" period was from your saying in a *Fifties* issue that USA poets should go thru surrealism.[42]

Simpson saw *Friends, You Drank Some Darkness* in a long line of successes: "These translations you have done: Vallejo, Neruda, et al., and now these three [Ekelöf, Martinson, & Tranströmer], are making a great difference to people's idea of poetry."[43]

At the same time, friends could criticize. Hall wrote: "In fact, you are easily the most generous, the most kind, most giving person whom I know. You are also the most brilliant, and the best poet. And I love you dearly. But as you acknowledged over the telephone the other day, you too can have faults."[44] Others took a shot at naming some of those faults. Orr wrote:

> You treat younger poets differently in your "attacks" than you do your peers or elders, but you are quite well known for seeing everyone as a rival, although you always cloak it in terms of their various failings as poets…There is a rather large group of younger poets (age range approximately 25-40) who are grateful to you for having helped them when they were just starting, but who are now deeply alienated from you in large part because you seem to have turned on them.[45]

Bly may have shared these comments with Hall, who identified the desire for dominance as Bly's "particular devil":

Your *libido dominandi* doesn't do you any harm around
me, or around your family, because although I admire you
tremendously, and Carol does, and others who are close to
you, we still are critical of you. But it does bother you a great
deal when you are on the road, or when under any other
circumstances you are surrounded by acolytes. This is where
your devil can destroy you. I think you should restrict yourself
to friends, and cut your followers off.[46]

This was a warning from a benevolent friend and peer. Bly had
been alienating people since the magazine first began, of course.
But as his influence peaked, and he attracted more and more followers and disciples, it was probably good to be reminded of some
of the inherent dangers of his position.

A new wrinkle became evident as Bly was beginning to focus
on both masculine and feminine consciousness.[47] He wrote to Michael True:

Please do write me a bit more of your sense that the reading...
was too masculine and pushy...I finished the series at
Hampshire College and there I felt more strongly than
anywhere I had been this longing...The "male pole" planted
"in the world" has dissolved, or has not been planted—a
situation apparently the reverse of ten years ago, when the
pole was firmly planted "in the world," in protest, or help, but
whether anything inward could take place then was uncertain.[48]

In a similar context, another well-meaning friend, Miriam
Palmer, warned Bly of his masculine power and its inherent dangers:

Robert, I worry about you sometimes. Everywhere I go women
are angry (and rightly) at male poets—the groupies of the
poetry circuit are fighting back! And sometimes I hear the same
anger directed at you too—women who feel they were taken too
lightly, women who feel you were trying to make them, women
who were too angry to start with, to even begin to listen to
what you might say...The guru role is rapidly becoming a
despicable one for men to play to women...Perhaps the time
has already come when you will have to keep a respectful
distance from women who don't know you—you must have
learned something about women and anger by now; that is, if
you have been serious all this time about mother consciousness

and father consciousness, etc. and I believe you have been. Well, a word to the wise…Preach to your own kind, all the eager young men out there who <u>will</u> listen to you…and be careful what you say to women.[49]

Bly weathered these storms, and continued, as always, to foster the growth of younger (albeit primarily male) poets, including Edson, Gerald Stern, Benedikt, Orr, Knott, and Simic. He also maintained his connection to friends like Ginsberg and Anne Waldman, stopping in Boulder for a visit. Ginsberg invited him to be formally involved in the nascent Jack Kerouac School of Disembodied Poetics at Trungpa's Naropa Institute. Bly signaled his interest, but then distanced himself after an uproar that fall involving Trungpa's mistreatment of Merwin.[50]

There were two final book publications. In 1977, the long dormant Seventies Press revived with *Twenty Poems of Vicente Aleixandre*, edited by Lewis Hyde. As a student at the University of Minnesota in the mid-1960s, he wrote for the school's literary magazine, *Ivory Tower*. Hyde first became aware of Bly when the editor, Garrison Keillor, invited him to do a reading. Later, in November 1965, they rode the same bus from Minneapolis to an antiwar demonstration in Washington, D.C.[51]

In *The Sixties* 9, Bly included an implicit summons regarding Aleixandre: "Very little of his thorny and difficult poetry has been translated into English." It was just about this time, says Hyde, that Bly "suggested that I look at Aleixandre, and…handed off Unamuno to me." In late summer 1971, Hyde was at the farm for two weeks, helping Bly with two Beacon Press books.[52] Plans for doing Unamuno and Aleixandre, in one volume, also for Beacon Press, started coming together.

Hyde, while in a graduate program in Comparative Literature at the University of Iowa, told the Blys about getting a response from Aleixandre: "It is very nice…He 'concedes' the authorization to do the book. He is happy I translated *Mundo a Solas* and would be glad to see it published complete. He remembers Robert visiting him. And he will help me choose the poems."[53]

St. Martin, Hyde said, "was tireless in his attention to translations in progress. He responded regularly and fully to everything

I ever sent him." Another year passed, and Hyde had finished his portion. He wrote: "Aleixandre … thinks the book is wonderful."[54] Meanwhile, he bridled at Bly's initial idea of the pairing with Unamuno. In 1975 he wrote: "I would like to submit the Aleixandre book to the Seventies Press for an edition like the one you did of Tranströmer's 20 poems."[55] Bly assented, and they set to work.

Bly always intended to incorporate some of his own translations, which, as Hyde recalls, he had on hand before the project began. Although in the final version four translations are Bly's, and sixteen Hyde's, the text was very much a collaborative effort: "we worked on each poem together before they were finished," Hyde later recalled. Bly also sought help from St. Martin, who wrote: "Is there to be a revival of the Sixties series of poetry books? That would really be good news! But I'm sure you're saddled with too much other work to resume the series."[56] Hyde, now working in a hospital in Cambridge, Massachusetts, was given the task of finding a place to print and bind the book.[57]

In his introduction, "When Fish Dissolve in Light," Hyde points out how Aleixandre's early poems are marked by sadness, loneliness, emptiness, death, distrust of the social world, and that they were always "longing for the light." Though he didn't consider himself a surrealist, Aleixandre "described the poet the same way that the surrealists did, as someone who speaks for the earth with forces that rise through the soles of his feet." Then, in a dramatic shift mid-career, his poems began to affirm "human fellowship, a spiritual unity, friendliness."

The book is divided into two parts, "Poetry of Red Light" and "Poetry of White Light," for the two stages. From "The Body and the Soul" (translated by Bly) in Part I, the first stanza:

But it is sadder than that, much, much sadder.
Sad as a branch letting its fruit fall for no one.
Sadder, much sadder. Like the mist
the dead fruit breathes out from the ground.
Like this hand that rises from the corpse lying in state
and merely wants to touch the lamps,
the grieving smile, the night speechless and velvet.
Luminous night above the corpse stretched out without its soul.

The soul outside, soul outside the body, swooping
with such delicacy over the shape sad and abandoned.

From Part II, "The Old Man and the Sun" (translated by Hyde) begins:

He had lived a long time,
the old man. In the evenings at sunset he used to rest there on the large,
*   solid trunk of a fallen tree.*
At the end of the day I'd pass that place and stop to look at him.
He was an old man with his face full of lines and his eyes dim, but
*   not sad.*

The poem ends:

I used to go by there and see him. But sometimes I could see nothing
*   but a face made of air, just the lightest lacework of a person.*
All that was left after the loving man, the kind old man had
*   passed over into light*
and was slowly, slowly pulled off in the last rays of the sun
like so many other things we cannot see in this world.

The book arrived in April, but Bly sat on it. Review copies were sent in the fall, giving November 1 as the publication date. A few weeks before then, a serendipitous event: "What an exciting day! Carol came skipping out as I was sawing down a maple, saying Aleixandre had won the Nobel Prize! Astounding! Calls all day from *Times* and other papers. Busy all day. Euphoria of praising, wrote essay for [*The New York Times Book Review*]."[58] Some excerpts from that:

How fitting it is that Vicente Aleixandre has won the Nobel
Prize! He is one of the greatest poets alive and his work stands
for endurance, the roots under the tree of consciousness,
the slowly growing trunk…[He] was and is a kind of river,
carrying trees torn up by the roots, everything turbid and
wheeling, things turned up frightening in the sunlight…[His]
generation…jumped feet first into surrealism, which they felt
not as a clique but as an ocean, encouraged each other, tried to
pull poetry simultaneously into surrealism and into song, and

worked to help Spain feel in herself the new energy rising, both
rebellious and sexual.

… Spain is waking up after years of sleep, and Aleixandre's
poetry and stubborn presence have a strong part in that
awakening.[59]

In the happy circumstances, this constituted free publicity for the
book, and the first edition almost immediately sold out. A second
soon followed.[60]

Almost simultaneously came *Twenty Poems of Rolf Jacobsen*.
The first reference to the project is found in a letter from Bly to
Tim Baland in 1972: "I think I may print in the Seventies Press…
three more books of Scandinavian poets. I'll gladly pay you $100
if you'll see the next one through the press—Rolf Jacobsen. I'll
read proofs of the Norwegian, and make sure the right poems are
facing each other, and the rest you would do."[61] Bly got help from
Harald Næss in the Department of Scandinavian Studies at the
University of Wisconsin, Madison, who wrote:

I think your translations are very good, many of them have
given me new insights. I would like to write a pre-publication
article in *The American-Scandinavian Review* (which
might help the sale of your book)…I also think it would be
wonderful—when the poems are out—if we could get Rolf
Jacobsen to visit this country (he told me he wanted to very
much) and read his verse to American-Scandinavian Foundation
chapters (and universities) from New York to San Francisco.[62]

A Norwegian friend in Berkeley, Gregory Nybo, also vetted Bly's
work: "A few minor corrections here and there and a couple of
lame suggestions…I think you've done an excellent job of it."[63]

Baland, however, did not take up Bly's offer. Instead, a few
years later, two young poets in Duluth, Louis Jenkins and Phil
Dentinger, oversaw the production of the book via their Knife
River Press. Jenkins says: "We printed, among other things, a little
booklet of Robert's 'Hockey Poem' and we were always trying
to make a buck." He admits: "I was never really happy with the
outcome; the jacket never fit the book correctly. Also, my skills as a
printer were limited so the whole thing, I felt, was not first class."[64]
The edition was ready in May 1977, and at least some copies were

distributed then, but Bly again delayed the official publication until November 1.[65]

Bly's introduction, "White Shadow," begins: "Rolf Jacobsen is not an underneath poet as Li Ho or Trakl, letting us feel the past of the human race, nor an underwater poet like Neruda. He somehow takes the seed that is buried under the water, in the dark, and carries it up through his body, into the light." Bly sees Jacobsen's modernity in his relaxed language and self-acceptance.[66] Here is "Guardian Angel":

I am the bird that flutters against your window in the morning,
and your closest friend, whom you can never know,
blossoms that light up for the blind.

I am the glacier shining over the woods, so pale,
and heavy voices from the cathedral tower.
The thought that suddenly hits you in the middle of the day
and makes you feel so fantastically happy.

I am the one you have loved for many years.
I walk beside you all day and look intently at you
and put my mouth against your heart
though you're not aware of it.

I am your third arm, and your second
shadow, the white one,
whom you cannot accept,
and who can never forget you.

Leif Sjöberg, in his review, says: "for years I have not had such a satisfactory reading experience in poetry.... We have to be deeply grateful to translators who, in spite of unfavorable circumstances, cynicism, neglect or ignorance on the part of publishers, manage to introduce us to new artists from the 'small' languages." He praises Bly as "one of the chief American ambassadors of international poetry."[67]

Patricia Goedicke, calling Bly "the sovereign poet of darkness," understands his attraction to Jacobsen's luminosity, "for in both...I feel the presence of much the same largeness of spirit, the same inner radiance, a radiance shared by light and dark alike...No wonder the darkness is attracted to the light! One without the other is unthinkable, and Bly's recognition of that fact, in translating and publishing this great Norwegian poet, is enormously to his credit."[68]

THE REMAINDER OF THIS chapter will take up some of Bly's unused ideas and unfulfilled plans, first for the magazine, and second for the press.[69] The point is not merely to wonder at what might have been, but to get an additional sense of some of the acknowledged thoughts from Bly's ever-teeming mind.

In *The Sixties*, Bly thought of including:

– Notes on Translation: for instance, examples of really bad translation—take "Hunger in the South," from *Canto General*, Belitt's translation, page 162, with literal alongside and Spanish version
– Notes or reviews commissioned from Louis Simpson, Keith Gunderson, Richard Kostelanetz
– Notes on Yvor Winters, John Crowe Ransom, and Richard Wilbur
– "The Bankruptcy of Criticism," with quotations from various reviews
– "Hemingway and Herbert Gold"
– Meredith, Blake, and Winters on "Unworthy men"
– A selection of haikus or brief poems in each issue

He also had ideas for more Blue Toad awards:

– First Blue Toad to Belitt—as worst translator in the U.S.
– Next month we will award a Blue Toad to the worst prose writer in the U.S.—Edward Dahlberg.
– The worst poet—Louis Zukofsky?

Apparently the following was an unused portion of the satirical ad for the *Maximus Poems* (in *The Sixties* 9):

I have read through the entire *Maximus Poems* and have not found a single attack, as I have come to expect from the Press, on Richard Nixon.

—Richard Nixon

Hall relayed to Bly a request he had received from Boston University for starting the acquisition of his papers; it mistakenly addresses him as "David Hall." Bly wrote back, with further plans for the magazine:

> Lovely thing from Boston U! Gorgeous! Peacock-like in its multi-eyed brilliance! May I keep it for a dossier I'm putting together called "The Writer in the University"? This small collection of documents will have the instructions from Purdue, ordering instructions to <u>plant</u> good questions with students so William Saroyan will have a good (time) (impression of Purdue); Louis' parody of Tate's letter to Jim (the one act play) [this regarding Wright's being fired from the University of Minnesota] etc. Then there will be the wonderful drawing of Bosch's called "The Ass at School," showing a male ass teaching a wild schoolroom of Bosch schoolchildren. It will be called "The Poetry Workshop at Iowa."

A folder labeled "Things recently accepted" includes these:

– Selden Rodman translation of O. Paz's "Sunday in Elephant Island"
– Quotation of William James from *Psychology*
– Indian translations
– Pashtoon Afghanistan translations
– Bram Dijkstra essay, "A Dissenting Opinion on Walt Whitman"
– Translations of 30 Hausa proverbs of West Africa
– Robert Francis

There were many ideas for future issues.[70] *The Seventies* 2 was to be a "young poets issue," to include those left out of Carroll's anthology, *The Young American Poets* (1969). Among the thirty-seven poets are the usual suspects as well as Floyce Alexander, John Wieners, Richard Deutsch, David Young, Marvin Bell, Kathleen Marshall, Tom Hennen, Rosellen Brown, William Witherup, Audre Lorde (Rollins), Michael Kincaid, Warren Woessner, Charles Wright, Robert Sund, Bill Holm, Jane Kenyon, Sanford Lyne, Carol Morris, Dave Kelly, Sonia Sanchez, Jeanne Hill, and Duane Niatum. A note on the same page says: "Jim Carroll's poems are not bad in *The World* 19."

He mapped out the *The Seventies* 13 as entirely given over to an "Homage to Antonio Machado." A notebook labeled *The Sixties* 15, also called "The Blue Trout of Kijan," has one poem by Wang Wei and one by Liu Chang Ch'ing, both translated by D. Gordon from Wiscasset, Maine. Another folder identified as "Wang Wei and P'ei Ti" may point to this as well.

There were many ideas for reviews: a Blyth book, Yeats' last book, Lou Lipsitz book, Alan Watts, Bosch book, *White Pony* (an anthology of Chinese poetry), *Poems of Solitude*—Michael Bullock (another Chinese anthology), Robert Creeley—*Words*, Rothenberg's anthology, and Neruda's *Odes*. Bly also was considering books by Hecht, Merwin, and Peter Schjeldahl's *White Country*.

A list of quotations identified for possible use:

– Barlach: "Every art needs two—one who makes it and one who needs it."
– Blake: "I must create a system, or be enslaved by another man's."
– Cezanne: "I am the primitive of a new art."
– Wallace Stevens: "A poem should stimulate some sense of living and of being alive."
– Blake: "Jesus and his Apostles and Disciples were all Artists.... The Old and New Testaments are the Great Code of Art.... The whole business of Man is the Arts.... The unproductive man is not a Christian, much less the Destroyer. Christianity is Art and not Money. Money is its curse."
– Blake: "A Poet, a Painter, a Musician, an Architect: the Man or Woman who is not one of these is not a Christian."
– Blake: "Great things are done when men and mountains meet; / This is not done by jostling on the street."
– Mallarmé: "To name is to destroy; to suggest is to create."
– Alfred Fabre-Luce: "It is in the shadows that momentous encounters take place."

Some quotations seem intended for "Wisdom of the Old," such as William F. Albright's: "We can be reasonably sure of the approximate absolute chronology...." Under the same rubric slightly altered, "Wisdom of the Prematurely Senile," was this quotation of Kenneth Koch: "Something about Frank [O'Hara] that impressed me…was his feeling that the silliest idea actually in his head was better than the most profound ideas actually in somebody else's head."

As for books, a few of the projected ideas for the Sixties or Seventies Press eventually appeared in other forms with other publishers. One early list includes:

- *Thirty Poems of Rainer Maria Rilke*, translated by Robert Bly
- *Twenty Poems of F. Garcia Lorca*, translated by James Wright, Robert Bly, Robert O'Brian, etc.
- *Twenty Poems of René Char*, translated by Robert Bly
- *Twenty Poems of Yves Bonnefoy*, translated by various poets
- *Twenty Poems of Miguel Hernández*, translated by various poets
- *Ten Poems of Pindar*, translated by Robert Bly
- *Twenty Poems of Antonio Machado*, translated by Robert Bly

The same list also has: Paz, Guillén, Jorge Carrera Andrade, Pavese, Alberti, Ungaretti, and Unamuno. Maybe most surprising is a small folder labeled "Biafran writers," with about ten names.

We have already seen that in 1961 Bly was planning *"The Horse is Loose*—twenty Minnesota poems, Robert Bly and William Duffy," but also others, like *"Thirty Political Poems*, edited by Robert Bly and David Ignatow," *Twenty Poems of Rimbaud*, and *The Letters of Antonio Machado to Juan Ramón Jiménez*. His note on the front flap of *The Suspect in Poetry* says it is "the first in a series the Sixties Press intends to publish, carrying criticism of poetry at the present moment." The series went nowhere. In 1965, St. Martin was well into *Twenty Poems of Rafael Alberti*, a good number of which Bly had already accepted.[71] The project languished for unknown reasons.

There was, not surprisingly, a plan for a book of parodies. Bly sent Hall some versions in 1962:

I have a parody of Eliot but everyone has done that—I actually have 10 parodies in the book so far (the rest are Blue Toads, Wax Museums, etc.) —parodies of Robert Lowell (by Firman Houghton, very funny), Diana Trilling, Leslie Fiedler, Ray West, "I Love Italy" poem, Zeus in the Suburbs (a new one of the "Will" poem), "Squeal" (on Ginsberg), *Paris Review* interviews, Louis' parody of *Sixties* "Homage to Pablo Neruda," Syllabics article, possibly "An Essay on John Dryedupden, by T.S. Eliot." Forty pieces altogether.[72]

Hall wrote: "I Love Italy isn't enough. I love Zeus is better. Playing fast & Zeus. Clare Boothe Zeus. Au Claire de la Zeus. Zeus in the Suburbs. Greek Myths in Glendale Manor. I don't know. The Fulbright Poets. The Influence of Senator Fulbright on Contemporary American Poets."[73] Elsewhere Bly indicates he has collected parodies of contemporary poets: Nemerov, Dickey, Bukowski, Wright, Merwin, Simpson, Creeley, Olson, Hall, and Whalen. Needed are: Stafford, Duncan, Justice, Logan, Kinnell, Snyder, Hugo, Wieners, and Knott. Crossed out are: Whittemore, Wilbur, Hecht, Merrill, Bowers, Snodgrass, Corso, and Ashbery.

In another folder is a book idea in a similar vein, with the title *Take Me to Your Leader!*, and the subtitles *A Book about Finkdom in the USA*, or *A Book of Finky Quotations from the USA*. An alternative title was *The Duck-Billed Platypus Anthology of Contemporary American Poetry*. Bly's notes also mention gathering "finky statements," including: Establishing the <u>essence</u> of finkdom; The herd instinct, in literature and in politics, and; Typical statements by our wonderful leaders, who get away with murder and are then revered as fine old men.

Bly finally terminated the project referred to several times in the course of this book, *The Continent Rising from the Sea*. It had been conceived in 1960, as Bly told Hall: "I'm thinking of calling it *The Black Lion: An Anthology of the Younger Generation of American Poets*. How do you like that? There will be only three poems apiece of 15 poets."[74] Progress continued: "I am typing up the anthology now, and it really looks wonderful, to tell the truth. I am arranging it partially with an eye to contrast, with Creeley after Merwin, etc., and the amount of strength displayed is very impressive. ... We have many advance orders already."[75]

The list of poets included Snyder, McGrath, Creeley, Kinnell, Ignatow, Levertov, Wright, Logan, Duffy, Ginsberg, Stafford, Hall, Merwin, Dickey, Simpson, and Haines. At other times, Corso, Robert Hazel, Snodgrass, John Woods, Knott, and Wieners were there. Although imminent publication was announced time and time again between 1960 and 1967, and although friends kept prodding, it never happened. Whether Bly felt it was superseded by another anthology or whether he just lost interest is unclear.

Also, as previously noted, Brekke's anthology, *Modernistisk lyrikk fra 8 land*, had a profound effect on Bly. After he returned from Norway, Brekke gave his permission for an expanded English edition.[76] A small binder from that time, labeled "The New Imagination," includes the names of poets and various titles for the book:

– *Poetry of the New Imagination from Twelve Countries*
– *The Black Horse: An Introduction to About One Hundred Poets of This Century from Eight Languages*
– *The Poem That Is Alive*
– *Poems of the New Imagination*
– *Modern Poets from Eight Languages*
– *Good Poets from Ten Countries*

All are chosen by Bly and Brekke, and translated by Bly. There are to be ten sections of twenty pages each: Spanish, Spanish-American, French, American, Norwegian, Danish, Swedish, German, English, and Italian Poems. Some sections are noted as done, others at various stages. There are suggestions to add other poets. In 1964, Bly told Hall: "I have finished a book of translations of which I'm very proud—it is the old anthology Brekke began... all translated by me...So there are 100 poets represented—a sampler!"[77] Again, after a great deal of work, the plans were dropped without explanation.

One similar story has a happy ending—the epic journey of *Forty Poems Touching on Recent American History*. It was first announced in 1961. In 1964, Bly sent the manuscript to his printer. When the galleys were done, Bly sent a copy to Hall who quibbled, wondering why Bly had left out Sorrentino, Berryman, Lowell, and Ginsberg.[78] Bly followed his advice by adding Ginsberg and, in a fateful decision, Lowell. Efforts to get the permissions were time-consuming. In 1967, Bly sent Kerryman the corrected proofs and ordered 5000 copies.[79] Nolan apologized several months later, explaining that the main printing press had broken down and they would not be able to get to the book until the new year.[80]

Such delays seemed routine, but then real trouble arrived, as Farrar, Straus & Giroux denied permission for Lowell's "At the Mouth of the Hudson." The main problem was printing the book in Ireland and importing it to the U.S, as it involved U.K. rights.[81]

Eventually, and quite unexpectedly, a door opened. Bly received the invitation to the Boston-based Beacon Press.[82] *Forty Poems* became, in 1970, the first of several Beacon publications identified as "A Seventies Press Book." Lowell's "At the Mouth of the Hudson" was now included. And thus the tie with Kerryman, long withering, finally dried up.

In the early 1970s, Bly gave an appraisal of his venture as an editor and publisher: "All that it amounted to is that I drove a forties car during the fifties and a fifties car during the sixties. That's all it amounted to."[83] He was being glib (maybe he wanted the interview to be over) and unduly modest.

The influence of the magazine and press, while certainly immense, is not easy to gauge. Bly's various publishing ventures became a powerful incubator of a "new poetry" and a "new imagination." Through it, Bly gained the position of a cultural authority and a public figure. He cut a wide swath, he set an example, he created a climate of opinion—it was as though his ideas were in the air and the water—and thus he was virtually unavoidable. The result was the diffusion of his notions, extending far beyond the bounds of mere tribal loyalty, through various poets, critics, editors, and teachers, and then from one generation to the next (aided, ironically, by the vast proliferation of creative writing programs, which Bly vociferously opposed). His program was comprehensive, and it had a profound and catalytic effect on its readers and practitioners. Even those who never subscribed to Bly's poetics or general outlook, but who engaged and grappled with it, were affected to some degree.

Thus also comes the end of an era. The magazine was the lifeblood of the press; the press books grew out of the magazine and flourished in its shadow. Therefore the decision to quit the magazine was the definitive one. Bly's days of being a publisher and editor were hardly over, but the close of the decade in which *The Fifties/Sixties/Seventies* magazine expired is an appropriate time for this account to terminate.[84]

Odin, take a bow.

Bly (as Odin?) with summertime 1966 assistant Tim Bilodeau; Odin House in background.

Endnotes

When citing letters, journals, and interviews in these endnotes, initials are used instead of full names. A short list of the most commonly appearing initials—in alphabetical order by last name—is given here. Of course, the full names of these and the numerous others whose initials are *not* part of this list are found in the text where the note's number originally appears.

RB   Robert Bly

CB   Carol Bly

JD   James Dickey

WD   William Duffy

MG   Mark Gustafson (interviewer)

JH   John Haines

DH   Donald Hall

DI   David Ignatow

GK   Galway Kinnell

DL   Denise Levertov

PL   Philip Levine

JL   John Logan

WSM   W.S. Merwin

DR   David Ray

LS   Louis Simpson

WS   William Stafford

TT   Tomas Tranströmer

JW   James Wright

Introduction

1. Although Sleipnir is described and often depicted as eight-legged, this picture leaves that detail to our imagination. My Odin conceit was first developed in "Under the Sign of Odin: Robert Bly's Wild Little Magazine," in *Robert Bly in This World*, edited by Thomas R. Smith with James P. Lenfestey (University of Minnesota Press, 2011), 55-84.

2. It so happens that Pegasus with his infrequent rider, Bellerophon, was on the cover of the first issue of *The Paris Review* in 1953, a magazine with which Bly's Harvard pals Donald Hall and George Plimpton were involved, and in which Bly had two poems published.

3. *Poetry* 91.5 (February 1958), 341.

4. So it appeared on the earliest Sixties Press stationery. For all bibliographic details of the magazine and press and related ephemera, see my *The Odin House Harvest: An Analytical Bibliography* (Red Dragonfly Press, 2015).

5. RB to DH, n.d. (September 1960). Bly had converted the former chicken coop to a space where he could work on his poetry and on the magazine. Secondarily, it also served as a very small guest house for visiting poets and helpers.

6. DH to RB, n.d. This was also a destination for poets from far and wide. See my "Odin House: A Literary Crossroads in the Middle of Nowhere," *Rain Taxi Review of Books* 15.1 (Spring 2010), 38-41.

7. Bly would occasionally, if temporarily, find himself in sync with some members of this crowd, such as Harold Rosenberg and Dwight Macdonald.

8. Reed Whittemore, *Little Magazines* (University of Minnesota Pamphlets on American Writers, no. 32) (University of Minnesota Press, 1963), 9. Pound was involved to some degree with *Poetry, The Egoist, The Little Review, Blast, The Dial, Criterion, The Transatlantic Review*, and *The Exile*.

9. Ezra Pound to Harriet Monroe, January 1915, in *The Letters of Ezra Pound, 1907-1941*, edited by D.D. Paige (Harcourt, Brace and Company, 1950), 48. Monroe was the founding editor of *Poetry*.

10. EP to The Alumni Secretary of the University of Pennsylvania, 20 April 1929 (in Paige, 225).

11. PB to RB, 6 February 1959.

12. MG interview with RB, 30 July 1999.

13. Was this an echo of T.S. Eliot's "a raid on the inarticulate" from "East Coker"?

14. "Introduction," *Black Mountain Review 1954-57* (AMS Press, 1969).

15. Almost all of this is now part of the Upper Midwest Literary Archives housed in the Andersen Library at the University of Minnesota, Minneapolis.

16. Snorri Sturluson, *Prose Edda*, quoted in Kevin Crossley-Holland, *The Norse Myths* (Pantheon Books, 1980), xxv.

17. Crossley-Holland, xxvi.

18. "With Robert Bly: An Interview," by Jay Bail and Geoffrey Cook, *The San Francisco Book Review* 19 (April 1971), no page nos. Reprinted as "The Evolutionary Part of the Mind: An Interview with Jay Bail and Geoffrey Cook," *Talking All Morning* (University of Michigan Press, 1980), 4, 6.

18. They include Bolvert, Grimnir, Gagnard, and Harbard.

19. Crossley-Holland, 27, 30, and 32.

Chapter 1

1. Ekbert Faas, *Towards a New American Poetics: Essays and Interviews* (Black Sparrow Press, 1978), 238.

2. MG interview with Christina Paulston, 4 June 2003.

3. GE to RB, 15 August 1958. GE to RB, 29 August 1958.

4. It is notable that all the translations are printed with the originals on the facing pages. The routine presence of the latter was to allow and even encourage readers to judge for themselves.

5. *"Modernist Poems from 8 Countries"* (Oslo: J.W. Cappelens, 1955).

6. The two exceptions over the course of the magazine will be identified as they appear.

7. LS to RB, 29 October 1956.

8. LS to RB, 7 August 1958.

9. LS to RB, 30 April 1961.

10. Its lines mostly consist of six syllables. (See Chap. Three on syllabics.)

11. RB to DH, n.d. For example, Reynolds had poems in *Poetry* 98.4 (July 1961) and *Paris Review* 26 (Summer-Fall 1961).

12. His third book, *A Roof of Tiger Lilies* (1964), would be the first to display plainly Bly's influence.

13. DH to RB, n.d.

14. RB to DH, 7 November 1957.

15. Snodgrass was at the University of Iowa from 1946 to 1955, receiving a B.A., M.A., and M.F.A.

16. Bly has written more recently that one's own generation leaves an indelible mark, like a tattoo. "All those of a given generation will have the same design." "Generations," *Ruminator Review* 1 (= *Hungry Mind Review* 53) (Spring 2000), 14.

17. A qualification appears in the notes on contributors: "In the Wax Museum this month there are three rather rhetorical poets.... Mr. Ginsberg is certainly the best. There is a fine review of 'Howl' in the *Black Mountain Review*, by Michael Rumaker. Nevertheless, the poem is written not in the modern tradition, but in the Longfellow tradition; and we think the attempt to write poetry with abstract words, as Mr. Winters in fact teaches, is a form of artistic suicide."

18. From Blake's preface to *Milton*, these words would often be used as a rallying cry in protests on college and university campuses a decade later.

19. McCormick was an aspiring novelist who was working as a cabdriver.

20. RB to DH, n.d. (1959).

21. MG interview with DH, 1 April 2000.

22. RB to DH, 1 November 1958.

23. Income from the venture was, in Bly's estimation, about $200. They were not even close to breaking even.

24. MG interview with RB, 30 July 1999.

25. RB to DH, 1 August 1958.

26. PW to RB & WD, 25 November 1958.

27. RE to RB, 2 October 1958. He also submitted a poem, which was apparently rejected, as another note followed: "'The state of poetry' must be in pretty good shape when there are 2 mags which limit themselves to a generation, or a decade, the *Paris Review* & you. It argues plethoric health and is a reasonable principle." RE to RB, 15 October 1958.

28. GP to RB, n.d.

29. LS to RB, 7 August 1958.

30. GS to WD, 26 July 1958.

31. WS to RB, 25 August 1958.

32. RB to WS, 23 September 1958.

33. WS to RB, 30 September 1958.

34. WS to RB, 18 October 1958.

35. JR to RB, 2 September 1958.

36. JR to RB, 18 November 1958.

37. JD to RB, 22 August 1958.

38. AH to RB, October, 1958.

39. DL to RB, n.d.

40. DL to RB, 3 March 1959.

41. RD to RB, 12 January 1959.

42. AT to CB and RB, 12 February 1959.

43. JW to RB, 22 July 1958. (in *A Wild Perfection: The Selected Letters of James Wright*, edited by Anne Wright and Saundra Rose Maley [Farrar, Straus and Giroux, 2005]).

44. JW to RB, 23 July 1958 (in *A Wild Perfection*.)

45. RB to JW, 1 August 1958.

46. JW to RB, 6 August 1958 (in *A Wild Perfection*.)

47. RB to DH, 8 August 1958.

48. RB to JW, 14 August 1958.

49. JW to RB, n.d. ("Friday Evening," mid- to late August 1958).

50. JW to DH, 14 or 15 (August) 1958 (in *A Wild Perfection*.)

Chapter 2

1. WR to RB, 25 June 1962. Ramshaw was then a professor at Colgate University.

2. The first is clear from two letters from Ramshaw; the second from "Going Out on the Plain in the Moonlight: An Interview with Cathy Lofsness and Kathy Otto, with Fred Manfred," *Talking All Morning*, 47. See also Deborah Baker, "Making a Farm: A Literary Biography," *Of Solitude and Silence: Writings on Robert Bly*, edited by Richard Jones and Kate Daniels (Beacon Press, 1981), 38-9.

3. MG interview with RB, 31 July 2001.

4. David Lehman, *The Last Avant-Garde: The Making of the New York School of Poets* (Doubleday, 1998), 48.

5. MG interview with RB, 31 July 2001. The identity of that "one of us" is not difficult to guess.

6. Robert Bly, "When Literary Life Was Still Piled Up in a Few Places," *A Community of Writers: Paul Engle and the Iowa Writers' Workshop*, edited by Robert Dana (University of Iowa Press, 1999), 39.

7. AM to RB, 28 July 1958.

8. MG interview with RB, 30 July 1999.

9. MG interview with DH, 1 April 2000.

10. *Harvard Advocate* 131.3 (December 1947).

11. His first issue as Pegasus (131.6 [May 1947]) had poems by Ashbery, Hall, Koch, and O'Hara. Indulging in more retrospective speculation, it may be a measure of the seriousness of his intentions that Bly did not involve himself with one of "mother" *Advocate*'s offspring, the *Harvard Lampoon*; nor, for that matter, with *Wake*, started in protest against the *Advocate*, with which Creeley, Hawkes, and Seymour Lawrence were involved. Yet both humor and protest would be central components of his magazine.

12. 132.4 (February 1949).

13. 132.5 (31 March 1949).

14. 132.6 (April 1949).

15. MG interview with RB, 25 July 2002.

16. "The Art of Poetry LXXIX," *Paris Review* 154 (Spring 2000), 43.

17. The Latin is from Horace, *Odes* 3.25 (word order slightly changed).

18. This and the following two quotations from Donald Hall, "Notes on T.S. Eliot," *Their Ancient Glittering Eyes* (Ticknor & Fields, 1992), 76-80.

19. Lehman, 137.

20. Ibid., 42.

21. Hall, "Notes on T.S. Eliot," 76.

22. MG interview with DH, 1 April 2000.

23. RB to DH, 24 September 1958. Bly would criticize Lowell more sharply in later years.

24. MG interview with DH, 1 April 2000. Not to mention Quixote's trusty horse, Rocinante.

25. 133.6 (June 1950). This was the "Commencement Issue," with Edward Gorey's cover illustration and Daniel Ellsberg listed on the masthead as president.

26. Bly says, "Because of Yeats, I wanted to bring history in." *PR* 154, 45. An accompanying note indicates that Bly "is now working on a play in verse on American subject matter." (He would continue writing plays, though his short story writing apparently ceased around this time.)

27. Printed in *The Boston Daily Globe* (21 June 1950).

28. RB to DH, 7 October 1960.

29. Robert Bly, *Selected Poems* (Harper & Row, 1986), 12. An entry in Bly's journal lists eight addresses in New York at which he lived from 1951 to 1953.

30. MG interview with DH, 1 April 2000.

31. RB journal, 1953, #24.

32. MG interview with DH, 1 April 2000. "Two Choral Stanzas" in *New Poems* 1 (Autumn 1952), and *PR* 1 (Spring 1953).

33. RB journal, 1954 (no day or month).

34. MG interview with RB, 30 July 1999.

35. MG interview with RB, 31 July 2001.

36. The others were Yvor Winters' at Stanford and Theodore Roethke's at the University of Washington.

37. Dana, 39-40.

38. RB journal, 31 May 1955.

39. MG interview with RB, 31 July 2001. When putting together *Silence in the Snowy Fields*, he decided that the poem held up well just as it was.

40. RB to DH, 15 June 1957.

41. Dana, 41.

42. MG interview with WD, 8 August 2000.

43. RB journal notes four visits in 1955. After 12 November he writes: "A great deal of talk, but no action."

44. MG interview with CP, 4 June 2003.

45. RB journal, 30 January 1956.

46. Some of them would eventually make their way into *The Light Around the Body* (1967).

47. MG interview with RB, 30 July 1999.

48. RB to DH, 24 September 1958.

49. RB journal, 8 December 1956.

50. RB to DH, 11 July 1957.

51. RB to DH, n.d. (late Summer 1957).

52. RB journal, n.d. (late 1956 or early 1957).

53. Later on, he would print this as a sort of gag, a standardized rejection slip. See Chap. Seven.

54. RB journal, 23 February 1957.

55. RB to DH, 15 June 1957.

56. RB to DH, 21 May 1957. Of course, he seems to have been wrong about this.

57. MG interview with RB, 30 July 1999. Also repeated in Robert Bly, "A Look Back: The Growth of Minnesota's Writing Community," *Minnesota Literature* 26.1 (September 2000), 1.

58. MG interview with CP, 4 June 2003.

59. RB to DH, 15 October 1957. Hall did not publish it.

60. WD to RB, 29 October 1957.

61. RB to DH, 29 October 1957.

62. RB to DH, 7 November 1957.

63. RB to DH, 23 November 1957.

64. RB to DH, 16 January 1958.

65. RB to DH, 16 January 1958. Bly wrote several plays in the 1950s and 60s.

66. RB to DH, n.d. (March).

67. RB to DH, n.d. (late March). His journal, 22 March, indicates the address of 109 E. 12th St.

68. The first was from Mrs. M.J. McGovern of New York. MJM to The Editors, 6 March 1958.

69. RB to DH, 17 April 1958.

70. RB journal, 14 May 1958.

71. RB to DH, n.d. (May 1958).

72. RB to DH, 7 June 1958.

Chapter 3

1. RB to DH, 24 September 1958.

2. RB to JW, 15 October 1958

3. RB to DH, n.d. (probably 21 September 1958).

4. D.C. Nolan to RB, 25 March 1959. Bly's brother-in-law, although disappointed, admitted they had made the right financial decision. JM to RB, 19 November 1958.

5. RB to JW, 9 October 1958.

6. RB to JW, 15 October 1958.

7. RB journal, 17 January 1959.

8. RB to DH, 20 February 1959.

9. "Fantastic! Wonderful man!" RB journal, 9 March 1959.

10. RB journal, 15 March 1959.

11. RB to JD, 5 May 1959.

12. JD to RB, 8 June 1959. Henry Hart, Dickey's biographer, says: "Dickey came around to Bly's point of view and joined his fight.... In urging Dickey to keep his eye fixed on real as well as unreal images, Bly helped Dickey cut the verbiage from his early poems. Bly also confirmed Dickey's belief that by translating foreign poems he could reinvigorate his own." *James Dickey: The World as a Lie* (Picador USA, 2000), 230.

13. GK to RB, 1 July 1959.

14. JW to DH, 17 September 1958 (in *A Wild Perfection).*

15. JW to DH, 19 November 1958 (in *A Wild Perfection*). Wright's personal situation—as he struggled with mental health issues and alcoholism—was precarious, however. He separated from his wife that spring. In June Bly wrote to Hall from Pine Island: "I have some bad news. When we got here, I called on Sunday Lib Wright, and she said Jim was in the hospital. We went up to see him, that is, Bill and I did, and found him at a rest home, somewhat subdued, as I guess shock treatment always leaves one, but very active in intelligence, translating, etc." RB to DH, n.d. (June 1959).

16. RB journal, week of February 8, 1959. Texts included *The Scarlet Letter, The Secret Sharer,* and *Heart of Darkness.*

17. RB to DH, n.d. (April 1959).

18. D.C. Nolan to RB, 20 February 1959, 25 March 1959. Ten parcels of 200

copies each were shipped (literally) on April 15.

19. RB to JW, 19 April 1959.

20. RB to JW, 15 October 1958.

21. WD to RB, 23 April 1959.

22. RB journal, week of April 26, 1959. A few earlier copies had been sent by air, the rest by ship.

23. $94.27 and $24.75.

24. $239.50, compared to an estimated $200 for the first issue. (Figures from Bly's records.)

25. JW to RB, 16 September 1958.

26. ED to RB, n.d. (1959).

27. GC to RB, 16 May 1959.

28. RB to DH, 29 November 1957. Bly possibly was remembering Kant and his conception of beauty, or the Bible, specifically *Proverbs* 11:22.

29. RC to RB, 9 May 1959.

30. RC to RB, 18 October 1959.

31. RC to RB, 4 December 1959. To my knowledge, Creeley did not submit anything of the sort.

32. RB to DH, n.d. (1959).

33. Faas with Maria Trombacco, *Robert Creeley: A Biography* (University Press of New England, 2001), 261.

34. We can only imagine Olson's reaction. A year later, Cairnie asked Bly—at Olson's request—to send Olson a copy of #2. GC to RB, 29 February 1960.

35. RB to DH, n.d. (March 1959). What really surprised Hall, and angered him, was that Bly "exercised the privileges of an editor and cut it here and there...." RB to DH, n.d. (early November 1958)

36. See the parody of this note by Noel Cobb in *The Sixties* 6.

37. JW to DH, 12 November 1958 (in *A Wild Perfection*).

38. RB to JW, 14 November 1958.

39. Ibid.

40. At one point he was working on a Crunk essay on Snodgrass: "I'm trying my hardest...to bring as much intuitive knowledge and understanding as possible into it. ... If only I could pull it off right!" He added in the same letter: "I feel that if I think enough about it I can probably come up with some kind of essay called 'What is Modern Poetry,' or some other switch." WD to RB, 16 January 1959 (= 1960).

41. RB to JW, 14 August 1958.

42. A few months later, therefore, Bly asked for it back. RB to JW, 9 October 1958.

43. JW to RB, 6 August 1958 (in *A Wild Perfection).*

44. RB to JW, 14 August 1958

45. Ibid.

46. JW to RB, 15 September 1958.

47. RB to JW, 19 September 1958. JW to RB, 11 October 1958.

48. RB to JW, 15 October 1958.

49. RB to JW, 12 November 1958.

50. RB to JW, 9 October 1958.

51. It may be useful here, as Bly occasionally mentions Pound, to give the latter his due. Pound likened poetry to condensation (in *ABC of Reading* [Yale University Press, 1934], 22). He also saw the similarity of poetic and sculptural technique (witness his work on Gaudier-Brzeska), in which the maker chips, cuts, shears away all that is extra, superfluous, artificial, just "words," to reveal the essence of the work, the kernel. This idea was central to Pound's Imagism, and to Bly's imagism.

52. RB to JW, 4 November 1958.

53. It appeared later in *The Lion's Tail and Eyes* and then, slightly altered, in *Silence in the Snowy Fields*.

54. JR to RB, 21 February 1958, is the first contact. RB to DH, n.d. (late May or early June, 1958): "Rothenberg is coming for tea tomorrow afternoon to talk about the book of Norwegian translations; I don't know yet if he wants it or not...." RB to DH, 8 June 1958, makes it clear that Rothenberg was also interested in publishing a book of Bly's own poems.

55. Kelly in *Trobar* 2 (1961), and Rothenberg in *Trobar* 3 (1961) and in *Poems From the Floating World* 1, 2, and 3 (1959-61).

56. MG interview with JR, 3 April 2004.

57. Faas, *Towards A New American Poetics*, 229.

58. In my view, Stephen Stepanchev, *American Poetry Since 1945: A Critical Survey* (Harper & Row, 1965), 175-87, was primarily responsible for lumping together these two rather disparate groups of poets. (See below, Chap. Ten.) Daniel Kane, *All Poets Welcome: The Lower East Side Poetry Scene in the 1960s* (University of California Press, 2003), has it wrong when he says that "Wright and Bly ended up associating themselves with the deep image as a coterie name and a specific aesthetic stance long after the original theoreticians had rejected the phrase as confining." (99) Kane also quotes Pierre Joris and Jed Rasula, both of whom, erroneously, even vindictively, suggest that Bly "co-opted" the deep image label. However, Rothenberg, who was in the thick of it, did not see it that way. (MG interview with JR, 3 April 2004.)

59. Fiedler's *Love and Death in the American Novel* (1960) would make this propensity clearer.

60. Note that in Bly's "Poems for the Ascension of J.P. Morgan" (1959) were five similar, though longer, excerpts of *realia*.

61. RB journal, November 1958.

62. Ibid., December 1958.

Chapter 4

1. JW to RB and CB, 28 April 1959.

2. JD to RB, 16 August 1959.

3. JD to RB, 19 August 1959.

4. JH to RB, 19 November 1959.

5. MG interview with RB, 25 July 2002.

6. BP to RB, 2 September 1959.

7. WSM to RB, 11 January 1960.

8. RB to JW, 3 January 1960. A short time later (17 February 1960) he writes to Hall, who is in England and about to go to Italy to interview Ezra Pound: "You might ask Pound what he thinks of *The Fifties*. Tate is so furious he can't speak."

9. DJ to RB, 15 July 1959.

10. RH to RB, 6 August 1959.

11. RB to DH, 20 March 1959. Kinnell recalls their first meeting in his poem "The Groans," *Walking Swiftly: Writings and Images on the Occasion of Robert Bly's 65th Birthday*, edited by Thomas R. Smith (Ally Press, 1992), 80-2. Bly later recommended Creeley as his successor.

12. RB to JW, n.d. (October 1959). Eshleman, then a graduate student at Indiana University, was a last minute replacement for Flores, according to RB journal, 24 October 1959.

13. RB to JW, 26 September 1959.

14. RB journal, 12 November 1959.

15. RB to DH, 19 November 1959. Roger Hecht, Kenneth Pitchford, Stanley Kunitz, Jackson Mathews, Oscar Williams, and John Hall Wheelock were all there, and a lively discussion ensued.

16. JD to RB, 6 December 1959.

17. JD to JW, November 27, 1959 (in *Crux: The Letters of James Dickey*, edited by Matthew J. Bruccoli and Judith S. Baughman [Alfred A. Knopf, 1999]).

18. JW to JD, 19 November 1959 (in *A Wild Perfection*).

19. RB to DH, 28 October 1959. The reading was on December 18. Bly wrote to Hall after the fact (n.d.: late January 1960): "The reading was explosive, with violent questions in coffee period, egged on by guess who. I finally got mad myself."

20. MG interview with RB, 25 July 2002.

21. RB to DH, 27 January 1960.

22. RB journal, 11 December 1959.

23. RB to DH, 3 July 1959.

24. RB to DH, n.d. (late January 1960).

25. RB to DH, 7 December 1959.

26. "Paper Editions has agreed to take 700 at 60%." RB journal, 9 December 1959.

27. "I gave 5 copies of #3 to McCosh, 5 to Shinder's down on Hennepin and 10 to Perine's at the University." WD to RB, n.d. (early 1960).

28. RB to DH, 17 February 1960. The initial press run was 1500 copies; the second was 750.

29. His reading included *Modern Man in Search of a Soul, Symbols in Transformation, Psychology and Alchemy*, and *Two Essays on Analytical Psychology*.

30. MG interview with RB, 25 July 2002. Bly dedicated a poem in *Silence in the Snowy Fields*, "Images Suggested by Medieval Music," to her and her husband.

31. RB to JD, 6 February 1960.

32. One might remember those "hot coals" from Bly's previously published "Poem in Three Parts." And nearly contemporary poems, published in *Botteghe Oscure* 25 (1960), 191-3, include the following images: "the sea," "dark knives," "the dark snow," "the dark house," "the black elephants of the flesh," "the bear," "the white horse," "dark clouds," "the dark world," "the dark leaves," etc.

33. RB to DH, 12 September 1959.　.

34. MG interview with JR, 3 April 2004.

35. RB journal, 26 August 1959. For a fuller account of this and other visits by other poets, see "Odin House: A Literary Crossroads," 38-41.

36. RB to JW, n.d. ("Friday"), but appears to be from early 1959.

37. Ibid.

38. RB to JW, 4 November 1958.

39. JW to RB and CB, 7 November 1958.

40. TG to RB, 2 October 1958.

41. These are presumably translated by Bly, as they both appear later, retitled and much altered, in *Twenty Poems of Pablo Neruda* (Sixties Press, 1967).

42. These are the lines as they appear in *Twenty Poems*, where Bly has retitled the poem as "Gentleman Without Company."

43. MG interview with RB, 13 January 2005.

44. MG interview with RB, 25 July 2002.

45. So says the note on Tuma in the back of this issue. See also MT to RB, 24 July 1958.

46. MT to RB, 24 July 1958.

47. MG interview with DH, 1 April 2000.

48. RB to DH, n.d. (May or early June 1958).

49. RB to DH, 15 September 1958.

50. Ignatow describes their first contacts in New York in the late 1950s, in "Reflections Upon the Past with Robert Bly," *Poetry East* 4/5 (Spring/Summer 1981), 197-206.

51. DI to RB, 16 May 1960.

52. DI to RB, 28 October 1960.

53. Duffy recalls: "one afternoon we spent an hour and a half looking up three-named poets in the Pine Island Public Library." MG interview with WD, 8 August 2000.

54. RB to DH, 14 January 1960.

55. *Partisan Review* (1959), 214-30.

56. Ibid., 224.

57. Ibid., 229-30.

58. LS to RB, 6 July 1959.

59. RB journal, week of 1 February 1959.

60. RB to JW, 2 December 1959.

61. CB to JW, 9 December 1959.

62. *Village Voice*, December 21, 1959.

63. *Village Voice*, March 30, 1960.

64. RB to DH, 14 January 1960. Carol says she told Podhoretz that they had heard he was Lionel Trilling's "pet poodle." CB to the Duffys, 12 January 1960.

65. RB to DH, 27 January 1960.

66. RB to JC, 27 January 1960.

67. RB to DH, 17 February 1960.

Chapter 5

1. Bly also tried to get Anthony Hecht in. RB to JW, n.d. (January 1960).

2. RB journal, week of 17 January 1960.

3. RB to JW, 6 February 1960.

4. RB to DH, 14 June 1960. There is more on this in my (as yet unpublished) "The Famous Herpetologist's Field Guide."

5. RB to DH, n.d. (April or May 1960).

6. RH to RB, n.d. (1960).

7. GK to RB, 12 March 1960.

8. JD to RB, 21 January 1960. Bowers was dropped from the list.

9. AH to RB, St. Joseph's Day, 1960.

10. GH to RB, 12 January 1960.

11. HK to RB, 6 April 1960.

12. JL to RB, 23 April 1960.

13. LT to RB, 17 January 1960.

14. DL to RB, 21 January 1960. Langton had a long career at San Francisco State University.

15. John Wain, "The Little Magazines: Men of the Moment," *The Observer* (10 April 1960).

16. RB to DH, 14 April 1960.

17. DM to RB, 22 January 1960.

18. EH to RB, n.d.

19. MR to RB, 12 January 1960.

20. HH to RB, 28 January 1960.

21. GF to RB, 24 January 1960.

22. RB to EW, 7 February 1960.

23. JW to RB and CB, 6 January 1960.

24. JW to RB, 18 Feburary 1960 (in *A Wild Perfection*).

25. RB to JW, 22 February 1960.

26. JW to RB, 28 November 1960.

27. RB to DH, 28 October 1959.

28. RB to DH, 23 September 1960. The so-called "anthology war" was well underway, as Allen's *The New American Poetry* had answered the first edition of *New Poets of England and America*, two books which had no poets in common. I have considered this in a little more detail in "Rays of Distant Bly Light from a Rare Stellar Convergence," *Michigan Quarterly Review* 54.2 (Spring 2015), 149-71.

29. RB to DH, 7 October 1960. Foster writes: "Robert Bly's new quarterly *The Fifties* was begun in the conviction that most poetry being written today is 'too old-fashioned.' ... And yet Bly fills *The Fifties* with many of the same old young poets assuming the same old solemnly poetic stances as before.... Real poetry is never going to be achieved by programs-for-real-poetry; or as Pound might have said, a jackass is still a jackass, whether Bostonese or liberated." Richard Foster, "Debauch by Craft: Problems of the Younger Poets," *Perspective* (Spring-Summer 1960), 16-17.

30. WD to RB, 10 February 1960. Duffy wrote: "That damn *Writer's Digest* has driven me into an Erasmus folly with its no good contributions. It amounts to at least 50-75 poems a day."

31. RB to DH, 6 August 1960.

32. RB to DH, 31 August 1960. "Louis has been a real help with this issue, and...thinks the magazine is getting solider, and is now all for harassing 'the old baskets'...."

33. *The Paris Review* 24 (Summer-Fall 1960), 153.

34. *Hudson Review* 12.4 (Winter 1960).

35. RB to GH, 8 August 1960.

36. RB journal, 6 December 1960.

37. There were several letters back and forth between 18 January and 15 February 1961. But Bly eventually dropped the matter.

38. "The Masculine versus the Feminine in Poetry: An Interview with William Heyen and Gregory FitzGerald," *Talking All Morning*, 211.

39. Dan Sullivan, "Minnesotans Publish Magazine To Boost Bright Young Poets," *St. Paul Sunday Pioneer Press* (13 December 1959).

40. Found in a clipping with no attribution.

41. *Rochester Post-Bulletin* (18 February 1960).

42. "A Couple of Literary Outlaws: An Interview with Robert Bly and William Duffy on the Founding of *The Fifties*," *Great River Review* 29 (Fall/Winter 1998), 47.

43. CB to CD and WD, 12 January 1960.

44. MG interview with CB, 29 June 2000. Carol offered her opinion with some regularity (as many letters make clear), and drew some prominent illustrations, but despite my prodding she refused to accept any credit for the putting forth of ideas, for the process of editing, and so on.

45. RB to JW, 1 July 1960.

46. Considering only American writers: Paul Bowles and William S. Burroughs were living there; Ginsberg, Gregory Corso, Truman Capote, and Tennessee Williams visited.

47. Kerryman to RB, 14 April 1961.

48. RB journal, Monday, 4 December 1961. Later, when Duffy's name disappeared from the table of contents (with issue #6), Rob Cuscaden, editor of *Midwest*, wrote (RC to RB, 19 June 1962): "I see where Duffy has taken the count; frankly, I'd shoot myself before trying it any way but alone."

49. RB to DH, n.d. (July 1961). This was a drawing of Carol's, adapted from Albrecht Dürer.

50. AS to RB, 10 January 1961. By this time Sexton and Wright were having an affair.

51. JW to RB and CB, 22 December 1958.

52. RB to DH, n.d.

53. This pseudonym is used very little, but it appears on the test dust jacket for the aborted Kerryman edition of *Forty Poems Touching on Recent American History*, where Cottonwood is named as the translator for the forthcoming Jiménez book.

54. RB to DH, n.d. (January or February 1959).

55. RB to DH, 22 February 1959.

56. WSM to RB, 12 January 1960.

57. He is not called Crunk for nothing. Virginia Christianson to RB, 21 February 1960: "Can there *really* be a critic with the unbelievably appropriate name—CRUNK? It's so good that it hurts my teeth—CRUNK."

58. A little later in his career, Bly would be a champion of *Dinggedichte* ("thing poetry") in Rilke and Ponge and in his own prose poems.

59. RB to DH, n.d. (Spring 1958).

60. WSM to RB, 9 May 1960.

61. LS to RB, 30 April 1961.

62. WSM to RB, n.d.

63. GK to RB, 12 March 1961.

64. RB to JW, 9 May 1959

65. RB to JW, 4 June 1960. Wright had written a year earlier: "Duffy…read me two new poems over the phone… Duffy's poems are stunningly good: original, fresh, the genuine stuff." JW to RB, 4 April 1959.

66. The poem first appears in a letter to Hall two years earlier. RB to DH, 8 August 1958. Much later, heavily revised and retitled "Waiting for the Stars," it was published in *Meditations on the Insatiable Soul* (HarperCollins, 1994). Carol Bly told me that the last two lines were her favorite of Robert's. They appear in a hanging rug she made, surrounding her image of an owl.

67. This section is introduced with a note: "In future issues we plan to print a group of short poems, of no more than four lines each, a group of love poems, and a group of poems to the moon. Poems may come from any country, and

be written in any style." Even though this doesn't pan out—Sexton and Snyder respond to the request—it is interesting in the context of Bly's lifelong output.

68. RH to RB, n.d. (1960).

69. RH to RB, 4 April (n.d., 1962?).

70. The editor, Theodore Weiss, was pleased: "Happy to receive your letter and deeply warmed by your generosity to the Hölderlin." He added: "What about starting a new magazine, a big one devoted entirely to serious reviewing?" Finally: "We look forward to your new issue as we do to your poems.... And have you received a copy of my book? ... Am—Orpheus and all!—eager to have your response to it." TW to RB, 16 December 1960. Weiss had been a target in #2's Wax Museum.

71. RB to DH, n.d. (August or September 1959).

72. RB to DH, 31 August 1960.

73. RB to DH, 23 September 1960.

74. RB to BD, 11 February 1961. Bly also sent a polite note to Marianne Moore on 12 January 1961, along with this issue. He said: "I am a great admirer of your own poetry, and I preferred to send this directly to you rather than have you hear it from someone else. There is no suggestion that you were aware of this rather odd policy of Miss Van Doren's. As an editor yourself, for a long time, of *The Dial*, I am sure you realize the necessity for these things to be brought out into the open, and for a protest to be made against this kind of editing, even though the protest may not be very effective." She responded (MM to RB, n.d.), thanking him and politely defending Van Doren, calling her "exceedingly scrupulous."

75. Bly's first and second books both have epigraphs by Boehme.

76. HR to RB, 20 December 1959.

77. His journals indicate such as early as 1956. RB to JW, 15 March 1959: "I have decided to start a little Spanish series, with the *Fifties*."

Chapter 6

1. LS to RB, 9 January 1961. JW to RB and CB, 13 December 1960.

2. MB to RB, 23 January 1961: "If anyone else is risking so much and succeeding so well today, they must be invisible and inaudible: the [Merwin] essay, I think, has the stature of *texte*." JH to RB, 21 January 1961: "All I can say is—keep on with it. I'm with you, or at least bringing up the rear somewhere."

3. AR to RB, 28 April 1961. The poems she sent were rejected however, an indication of how Bly refused to let friendship or collegiality impede the higher value of candid criticism.

4. AS to RB, 30 January 1961.

5. RH to RB, 4 January 1961.

6. RS to RB and WD, 21 June 1961. HN to RB, 6 October 1961.

7. SK to RB, 18 December 1960. MH to RB, 9 January 1961: "Thanks for your brave pioneering efforts." JHW to RB, 28 January 1961.

8. TH to RB, 24 April 1961.

9. HSM to CB and RB, 21 December 1960.

10. RB to JW, 30 March 1961.

11. RB to DF, 16 January 1961. The letter from Fitts to Bly is lost.

12. JL to RB, 31 January 1961.

13. JH to RB, n.d.

14. FS to RB, 21 January 1961.

15. PC to RB, 19 December 1960.

16. RB to PC, 2 December 1960.

17. PC to RB, 12 December 1960.

18. RB to DH, 6 August 1960.

19. SK to RB, 18 December 1960.

20. JHW to RB, 28 January 1961.

21. MG interview with RB, 25 July 2002.

22. *The Nation* (21 April 1961), 350-54.

23. For more on such supplantation, see my "Captain Robert Bly, Ortega y Gasset, and the Buddha on the Road," *The Kenyon Review* 35.4 (Fall 2013), 203-24.

24. With the exception of Hazel, all had been published or reviewed in *The Fifties/Sixties*. Clemenson, as already noted, was Wright's pseudonym.

25. NdG to RB, 8 May 1961.

26. JH to RB, 14 June 1961.

27. Hall, as usual, made many useful comments before printing. RB to DH, n.d. (late November or December 1960).

28. MB to RB, 10 October 1961. WSM to RB, 20 October 1961. AR to RB, 12 October 1961. DI to RB, 7 October 1961. DR to RB, n.d. JHW to RB, 11 October 1961.

29. JBM to RB, 30 September 1961. RC to RB, 26 October 1961.

30. Irvin Ehrenpreis, "Four Poets and Others," *The Minnesota Review* 2.3 (Spring 1962), 408.

31. VN to RB, 18 December 1961.

32. That symposium was written up by Columbia University's *The Morningsider* (17 January 1963).

33. JD to RB, 18 June 1963.

34. RW to RB and WD, 23 August 1961.

35. "Summary of the Proceedings in the Formation of the Association of Literary Magazines of America," *The Carleton Miscellany* 3 (Winter 1962), 70-80.

36. RB to DH, n.d. (November 1961).

37. Peter Michelson, "On *The Purple Sage, Chicago Review*, and *Big Table*," *The Little Magazine in America: A Modern Documentary History*, edited by Elliott Anderson and Mary Kinzie (Pushcart Press/*TriQuarterly*, 1978), 357. Bly resigned the next year. RB to DH, 22 October 1963.

38. For more in-depth examination, see my "Bringing Blood to Trakl's Ghost," *Antioch Review* 72.4 (Fall 2014), 636-54.

39. JW to RB and CB, 7 September 1960.

40. GK to RB (n.d.). WSM to RB, 19 December 1961. JH to RB (n.d.).

41. SB to RB, 15 November 1961.

42. H. Arthur Klein, "A Hold on Life," *The Nation* (9 February 1963). Conrad Knickerbocker of Kansas City wrote to Bly, 5 March 1963: "You should be well set up over *The Nation*'s review of the Trakl book. You will become rich and famous and take to strong drink and Ferraris."

43. Ehrenpreis, 407.

44. *The Chicago Literary Review* (January 1962).

45. Ulrich Weisstein, "Recent Translations of Twentieth Century German Poetry and Drama," *The German Quarterly* 37.4 (November 1964), 520.

46. RB to DH, 14 December 1962. Simon was a graduate student at Harvard when Bly was an undergrad.

47. *Hudson Review* 15.3 (Autumn 1962), 455-68 (with Trakl portion on 467). Once the book went out of print, there were plans—never realized—to do a corrected second edition. CB to JW, 17 January 1965.

48. RB to DH, 8 February 1961.

49. LS to HH, 7 August 1961.

50. DH to RB, 13 May 1960.

51. RB to DH, 30 April 1961.

52. *Poetry*, under Karl Shapiro's editorship, had published a number on postwar French poets in 1952, and in the later 50s, under Rago, translations of French poets regularly appeared. In July 1962, Rago would put out a bilingual issue devoted to Bonnefoy, translated by Kinnell and Mathews. Ignatow's *Chelsea* 13 (1963) was also a special French issue.

53. Bly's poetic sequence "Homage to Max Ernst" was written in 1964, and eventually published in *Kayak* 55 (1981).

54. Five of the twenty-two are ascribed to Charles Reynolds. RB to JW, 16 May 1961: "I have just translated today the first three pages of the Strindberg novel—*Where the Sea Begins*. Great!" RB to JW, 18 September 1958: "here are the Rilke translations that I promised you a month or more ago...."

55. The precise pairing of "Eliot and Pound" is repeated eleven times in this essay.

56. This is the first appearance of Chinese poetry in *The Sixties*.

57. John Haines, "Robert Bly: A Tiny Retrospect," *Of Solitude and Silence*, 175-78.

58. When Blodgett first submitted his poems, he said he was in a "psych ward" and asked that, should they take any of his poems, his name not be printed. EB to RB, 26 August 1959. Bly cut this poem, but Blodgett insisted that the frame of reference was essential. EB to RB, 3 December 1960.

59. It is also Duffy's last poem in *The Sixties*, and would open his section in *The Lion's Tail and Eyes*.

60. Hammer was an undergraduate at Yale, and this was his first publication.

61. RB to DH, n.d. (April or May 1959).

62. JL to RB, 25 September 1960.

63. JL to RB, 31 January 1961. Bly's name did not appear.

64. JL to RB, 28 February 1960.

65. JL to RB, 7 September 1961.

66. FM to RB, 26 April 1961.

67. Published as a Signet Classic in 1962, it would "bring in a total of $3,350 on the first printing." RB to DH, n.d. (October 1961).

68. RB to DH, 3 November 1961.

Chapter 7

1. An earlier version of this chapter was published as "Rude Awakenings: Rejections from *The Fifties, Sixties,* and *Seventies,*" *Great River Review* 52 (Spring/Summer 2010), 35-52.

2. As *The Fifties* 1 proclaimed, the magazine was based on the rejection of "old-fashioned" poetry.

3. WD to Jack Anderson, n.d. (1959?).

4. WD to Mr. Robbins, 5 May 1960.

5. RB to DH, 28 October 1959.

6. John Woods, "The Deep Image," *Westigan Review* 1.2 (Spring 1970), 27.

7. Nils Peterson, "'The Seeds of Longing:' Some Words About Robert," *Walking Swiftly*, 138.

8. Mr. Rogers to RB, n.d.

9. RB to Mr. Cuddihy, 4 May 1960.

10. WD to Jascha Kessler, n.d. (1960).

11. RB to Steve Feldman, 3 April 1970.

12. As quoted by Malanga in his response. GM to RB, 2 April 1962.

13. RB to AW, 10 May 1971.

14. RB to Mr. Payne, 3 June 1970.

15. WC to RB, n.d.

16. RB to M. Turner, and MT to RB, n.d.

17. As he told Hall. RB to DH, 4 November 1968.

18. WD to RWS, 4 April 1958.

19. RWS to RB, 30 November 1962.

20. RB to Mrs. Ed Hynes, 1 March 1960.

21. Mrs. Ed Hynes to RB, 10 March 1960.

22. Mr. Yates to RB, n.d. (1964/65).

23. Robert Marrow to RB, 4 August 1965.

24. Janie Phillips and Jean Reif to RB, n.d.

25. DN to RB, 25 November 1974.

26. Jay Nash to RB, n.d. (1960?).

27. Phil E. Wiedman to RB, 23 September 1960.

28. CO to RB, 28 April 1962.

29. T.C. Lengyel to RB, n.d. (1965).

30. Sol Newman to WD, 27 June 1960.

31. Nonee Nolan to RB, n.d. (1968).

32. *The Sixties* 6 (Spring 1962). Kuspit has had a long and productive career, especially as an art critic and professor. Bly prints his own response to this scolding: "Yes, Massah! Don't send me back to the Nawth!"

33. *The Sixties* 10 (Summer 1968).

34. BR to RB, 29 October 1963. Raffel made his mark primarily as a translator.

35. RB to NM, 13 February 1962.

36. O.W. Crane to RB, n.d.

37. *The Sixties* 10 (Summer 1968). Bly received another letter from Robert Fox identifying himself as the writer of this one: "I have no apologies for that. I show these poems to you for two reasons: first, because you alone have had the balls to introduce many fine foreign writers in translation, and second, because I am in wholehearted agreement with your statement in *The Fifties*." RF to RB, 17 March 1970.

38. MC to RB, 17 August 1973.

39. David Wade to RB, 16 September 1968.

40. Edward A. Campbell to WD and RB, 10 May 1960.

41. HM to RB, n.d. (1962?).

42. Lynn Lonidier to RB, n.d. (1963).

43. Elizabeth N. Sachs to RB, 5 January 1963.

44. SCS to RB, 29 September 1973.

45. FW to RB, n.d.

46. DAL to RB, 29 May 1964.

47. RB to Ruth Bodner, 6 July 1972.

48. RB to Mr. Morin, 3 April 1970.

49. RB to Mr. Linder, 26 December 1969. That last suggestion was an article of faith for Bly.

50. RB to Mrs. Latner, n.d. (1960).

51. SL to RB, 11 January 1970.

52. Larry Rubin to RB, 5 March 1960.

53. John Eshors to RB, n.d. (1970?).

54. HM to RB, 31 July 1961.

55. Sandy Taylor to RB, 14 January 1960.

56. RB to JD, 15 August 1958.

57. LZ to RB, 13 December 1958.

58. TE to RB, 13 December 1959.

59. Gil Orlovitz to the editors, 3 September 1958.

60. JW to RB, 18 September 1975.

61. CB to WD, 29 June 1960.

62. CB to RB, 6 July 1966.

63. TK to RB, 13 December 1972.

64. Alex Karanikas to MW, 6 June 1969.

65. MB to Kathryn, n.d. (c. 1970).

66. *Roots & Flowers: Poets and Poems on Family*, edited by Liz Rosenberg (Henry Holt & Company, 2001), 13-14.

67. RB to DH, 13 November 1972.

Chapter 8

1. RB to DH, n.d. (November 1961).

2. JW to RB and CB, 30 August 1961.

3. JW to WDS, 14 December 1960 (in *A Wild Perfection*).

4. JL to RB, 22 February 1962.

5. GK to RB, n.d.

6. JH to RB, 8 February 1962.

7. LS to RB, 19 December 1961.

8. This and the following quotations from "The Colonial School of Melican Poetry (or, 'Aw, man, I read those poems before...')," *Kulchur* 10.3 (Summer 1963), 83-84.

9. Jones' own Totem Press had published Olson's manifesto, *Projective Verse*, in 1959. His little magazine, *Yugen*, regularly printed the work of Olson as well as other Black Mountain, New York School, and Beat poets. He was also co-editor of *Floating Bear* and on the editorial board of *Kulchur*, both of which displayed similar inclinations.

10. RB to DH, n.d. (November 1961).

11. RH to RB, n.d. (1962).

12. Wright found this in Goethe's *Conversations with Eckermann*. JW to RB and CB, 10 March 1960.

13. JW to RB, 7 September 1960. Three poems in this group would be in the long-advertised anthology *Forty Poems Touching on Recent American History* (1971).

14. DC to RB, 1 September 1961.

15. Hiss was the civil servant who had been accused by Whittaker Chambers of being a Soviet spy and was brought before the House Committee on Un-American Activities.

16. JH to RB, 8 July 1963.

17. As the "Spanish Representative" and "foreign editor" of the Sixties Press, St. Martin helped with distribution in Madrid (as well as London and Paris).

18. JW to RB, 6 February 1960.

19. RB to JW, 22 February 1960.

20. JW to RB and CB, 28 February 1960.

21. JW to RB and CB, 30 August 1961.

22. "On the Occasion of a Poem: Bill Knott," *Collected Prose: James Wright*, edited by Anne Wright (University of Michigan Press, 1983), 311. (Originally published in *American Poets in 1976*, edited by William Heyen [Bobbs-Merrill, 1976].)

23. GS to RB, 10 March 1963.

24. RB journal, 21 December 1960.

25. This is by Noel Cobb, who had met Bly while an undergraduate at the University of Michigan. See Cobb "'Nearer Than Near, Closer Than Fingernails'" *Walking Swiftly*, 102-4.

26. Louis Simpson, *North of Jamaica* (Harper & Row, 1972), 210.

27. Jonathan Blunk, "The Sound That Comes from Character: An Interview with Louis Simpson on the Life and Poetry of James Wright," *The Georgia Review* 55.3 (Fall 2001), 449-74 (quotation from 456).

28. Bly tips his hat to the current issue of Theodore Weiss's *The Quarterly Review of Literature*, which was devoted to Montale. In 1975 he won the Nobel Prize in Literature.

29. Di Giovanni had communicated with Bly since the early days of *The Fifties*.

30. For more on this, see my forthcoming "The Morgan Mess, the Rosenberg Fiasco, and Bly in the Mix."

31. "Prose Vs. Poetry," *Choice* 2 (1962), 65-80.

32. RB Journal, 29 December 1959.

33. Kate and her husband Lars were downstairs neighbors in New York.

34. RB to DH, 27 September 1962.

35. RB journal, 29 September 1962. Official publication date was October 11.

36. DH to RB, 3 October 1962.

37. *The Critic* (August-September 1963), 85.

38. He continues: "It is hard to tell his poems from Bly poems. No man but Bly, as far as I know, has ever beheld his face. He is said to own a farm in Minnesota." *Burning Deck* 4 (1965), 22.

39. *Lillabulero* 1.3 (Summer 1967), 61-62.

40. "The Whole Lion," *The Review* (Oxford) 8 (August 1963), 55-8.

41. This and the several following quotations are from *Kulchur* 10 (vol. 3) (Summer 1963), 84-6. Bringing in the Marx brothers' "Duck Soup" is a nice touch.

42. With some understandable conflation and distortion (i.e., confusing Jones for Sorrentino, *Yugen* for *Kulchur*, and *The Sixties* 5 for *The Lion's Tail and Eyes*) Bly has recollected Wright's reaction in *Remembering James Wright* (Ally Press, 1991) 18-19, and "Introduction: James Wright's Clarity and Extravagance," *James Wright: Selected Poems*, edited by Bly and Anne Wright (Farrar, Straus & Giroux and Wesleyan University Press, 2005), xxxi.

43. RB to DH, 15 July 1963.

44. JR to RB, 30 July 1963.

45. JW to Michael Cuddihy, 15 September 1979 (in *A Wild Perfection*).

46. JW to RB, 2 March 1959.

47. JW to RB and CB, 17 March 1959.

48. JW to RB, 4 April 1959.

49. JW to RB and CB, 28 April 1959.

50. JW to RB and CB, 6 January 1960.

51. JW to Elizabeth Willerton Esterly, 7 July 1959 (in *A Wild Perfection*).

52. JK to RB, 7 May 1960.

53. RB to DH, n.d. (July 1961).

54. WB to RB, 1 March 1963.

55. JD to RB, 20 December 1963.

56. *Burning Deck* 2 (1963).

57. *Poetry* 105 (December 1964), 196-7.

58. *The Secant* 1.3 (June-July 1963).

59. *The Review* (Oxford) 8 (August 1963).

60. *Kulchur* 14 (vol. 4) (Summer 1964), 88-93. What Eshleman has in mind was the translation from Neruda's "Caballero Solo" in "The Necessity of Rejecting a Shakespeare Sonnet," *The Fifties* 3, which, as we have seen, was expurgated not by Bly but by the printer. Eshleman says: "If Bly did not care to face this in Neruda (if the printer refused, another poem could have been chosen), what can we possibly expect from him in Vallejo (whose sex is much more involuted than Neruda's)? Or for that matter, in any translation? As a poet?"

61. RB to NM, 13 February 1962.

62. RB journal, April 1961.

63. RB journal, 25 August 1961.

64. RB journal, September 1961.

65. RB journal, August 1962.

Chapter 9

1. Again, see my forthcoming "The Morgan Mess." Coincidentally, it was at a party at Harold Rosenberg's in January 1960 where Bly met Morgan for the first time.

2. RB journal, Saturday, 5 December 1959: "in the evening to a party…to meet Harold Rosenberg—a great hunk of New York rock with very intelligent, even brown, eyes."

3. As announced in *The Sixties* 4. Rosenberg was also quoted inside the front cover of that issue, and the essay "French Silence and American Poetry," in his book *Tradition of the New*, was referred to—in a positive light—in "Madame Tussaud's Wax Museum."

4. HR to RB, 20 May 1961. The magazine was eventually named *Location*.

5. DH to RB, n.d. (January or February 1963).

6. RB to DH, n.d.

7. RB to DH, 8 March 1963.

8. SG to RB, 18 March 1963.

9. LS to RB, 2 April 1963.

10. "A Wrong Turning in American Poetry," *Choice* 3 (1963), 33-47 He also planned to publish it separately under The Sixties Press imprint, as he had done with the *Broadsheet* and as he had briefly considered doing with "Prose vs Poetry." RB journal, November 1963.

11. JH to RB, 15 December 1963.

12. TM to RB, 20 January 1964.

13. RB to DH, 2 January 1963 (= '64).

14. RH to RB, 31 January 1964.

15. DH to RB, 5 June 1962.

16. LS to RB, 1 July 1962.

17. BM to RB, 7 May 1962.

18. BM to RB, 4 September 1962.

19. GH to RB, n.d.

20. NdG to RB, 9 November 1962.

21. RC to RB, 19 June 1962.

22. AG to RB, 30 January 1963.

23. GH to RB, 23 June 1964. A month later (26 July 1964), he asked again, and Bly gave him "Five Poems of Solitude."

24. HW to RB, 25 June 1963.

25. RH to RB, 4 June 1963. He refers to Eugene Jolas' legendary little magazine of 1927-1938.

26. RB to DH, 8 May 1963, and 10 June 1963.

27. RB to DH, 15 July 1963.

28. RB to DH, 8 January 1964.

29. RB to DH, 20 March 1964.

30. RB journal, 23 August 1963.

31. RB journal, October 1963.

32. RB to DH, 22 October 1963.

33. CK to RB, 30 October 1963.

34. RB to DH, 15 March 1964: "Lowell backed down at the last minute, and Robert Fitzgerald who is at Mt. Holyoke took his place; third was Spender. I like Spender a great deal! He has a wonderfully fresh mind, very open to ideas, and had moreover much more firmness and strength than I expected. We got along very well."

35. DR to RB, 13 May 1963.

36. JH to RB, 5 September 1964. Bly edited the manuscript and sent it to Hall (RB to DH, 26 August 1964): "I'm terribly interested to see what you think.... Then he can decide, on your advice, whether to submit it to Wesleyan, and, if so, when." *Winter News* was published in 1966.

37. *Kayak* 1 (Autumn 1964), 55-8.

38. LS to RB, 29 September 1963.

39. Jim McCormick to RB, 5 June 1965:"Laughable about the Irish printer refusing to set the Neruda poems; for a people who are supposed to laugh so much, our experience in Ireland taught us their laughter is always about the wrong things."

40. This is from the essay "First Principles."

41. See Marty Lammon, "Something Hard to Get Rid Of: An Interview with Robert Bly," *Ploughshares* 8.1 (1982), 11-23.

42. BK to RB, n.d. (1961).

43. RB to DH, 22 October 1963, indicates that Bly wanted Knott to have the chance to go to college. (Knott would dedicate his first book, *The Naomi Poems*, to Bly.)

44. BK to RB, n.d.

45. MG interview with RB, 23 May 2006. The first known letter from McGrath (then living on Long Island) to Bly, in which he responds to Bly's rejection or criticism of his poems, is from 1960.

46. RB to DH, 29 August, 14 and 24 September 1963. Bly had edited the selection.

47. JD to RB, 21 January 1960.

48. JD to RB, 8 September 1961.

49. JD to RB, 20 October 1961.

50. RB to DH, 22 August 1963.

51. DH to RB, 9 September 1963.

52. RB to DH, 24 September 1963.

53. RB to DH, 8 January 1964.

54. LS to RB, 20 January 1964.

55. This on the front flap of the dust jacket of *The Lion's Tail and Eyes*.

56. Compare this with Bly's verdict in "A Wrong Turning in American Poetry," 38, that Ransom and Tate's guiding impulse is "fear of revolution," and that "their holding position in poetry has more resemblance to the attitude of Governor Ross Barnett of Mississippi than most people would be willing to admit."

57. Hart, esp. 63-118, 159-71.

58. JD to RB, 10 May 1964.

59. The specious note calls him "one of the best pool players of the upper Midwest. He was the original for 'Minnesota Fats' in the recent movie [i.e., Jackie Gleason in "The Hustler"]."

60. MG interview with Don Olsen, 1999. Olsen had been a student of Tate's at the University of Minnesota. Among Bly's papers, in a notebook on his planned book of parodies, there is a copy of this drawing which has "Southern Agrarian," another indirect reference, written above "poet of the 'Twenties."

61. So Bly informs Hall. RB to DH, 21 April 1963.

62. DH to RB, 11 October 1963. JH to RB, 5 September 1964.

63. JH to RB, 5 March 1962.

64. RB to DH, 24 August 1962.

65. DH to RB, 2 September 1962.

66. JW to JD, 18 December 1960 (in *A Wild Perfection*).

67. JD to RB, 1 February 1961.

68. JD to RB, 24 January 1963.

69. RB to DH, 8 November 1963.

70. MB to RB, 20 August 1964.

71. BM to RB, n.d.

72. RB to DH, 6 January 1965.

73. RB to JD, 16 March 1965. JD to RB, 23 March 1965 (in *Crux*).

74. Robert Watson, *Poetry* 107 (February 1966), 332.

75. Richard Kostelanetz, "Flyswatter and Gadfly," *Shenandoah* 16 (Spring 1965), 92-5.

76. Hugo Williams, *The London Magazine* (October 1965), 101-4.

77. Kenneth Fields, "Strategies of Criticism," *The Southern Review* 48 (Autumn 1966), 968-9.

78. Christopher Wiseman, *Glasgow Review* (Autumn 1964), 42.

79. JD to RB, 16 July 1966 (in *Crux*).

80. JD to RB, 20 September 1966.

81. RB to DH, 3 September 1967.

82. RB to JD, 20 December 1967.

83. HSM to RB, 14 January 1961.

84. DI to RB, 21 June 1964.

85. Russell Banks, *Lillabulero* 3 (Summer 1967), 64-7.

86. Together with poems of Miguel Hernández, it would be reprinted by Beacon Press (as a "Seventies Press Book") in 1972.

Chapter 10

1. RB to DH, 10 December 1963. Officially, it was for the period September 1, 1964 to August 31, 1965.

2. RB to DH, 17 February 1964.

3. DH to RB, 28 February 1964.

4. Reprinted as: Ian Hamilton, "The Sixties Press," *A Poetry Chronicle: Essays & Reviews* (Faber & Faber, 1973), 122-7. Louis Simpson, *The Hudson Review* 16.1 (Spring 1963), 138: "There has been very little poetry in English that represents states of being. Wordsworth's is the only great poetry in English to have done so. Mr. Bly in his poems shows states of being."

5. RB journal, 20 April 1964.

6. LS to DH & KH, RB & CB, 7 May 1964.

7. JW to LS, 29 May 1964.

8. RB to DH, July 1964. Hall had arranged for Bly to continue in his place (RB to DH, 2 January 1964).

9. RB to DH, n.d.

10. RB typed note.

11. RB journal, 30 August 1964.

12. RB to DH, 25 September 1964.

13. RB to DH, 2 October 1964.

14. RB to DH, October 1964.

15. RB to DH, 4 December 1964.

16. RB to DH, October 1964.

17. RB to DH, 19 November 1964. Actually, the main disagreement was between Levertov and Hall, and it involved Dickey's forthcoming book, *Buckdancer's Choice*, as well. See Hart, 330-1.

18. RB to DH, 19 November 1964.

19. RB journal, n.d. (Fall) 1964 (on Kabir); 29 June 1964 (on Hamsun).

20. RB to DH, 9 September 1964.

21. RB to *TLS* editor, 27 March 1965.

22. RB to DH, 14 January 1965.

23. JH to RB 2 March 1965.

24. Kennan was widely known as a diplomat and historian.

25. RB to DH, 23 June 1965.

26. DH to RB, 17 March 1964.

27. RB to DH, 20 March 1964.

28. LS to RB, 24 March 1964.

29. JH to RB, 5 September 1964.

30. LS to RB, CB, DH, & KH, 7 May 1964.

31. RB to DH, 6 April 1964.

32. LS to RB, 1 April 1965. Robert Mazzocco, "Mixed Company," *New York Review of Books* 4.5 (April 8, 1965), actually reviews several books, including Hall's *A Roof of Tiger Lilies*. His exact words: "Among [Hall's] contemporaries, his affinities are with James Wright, James Dickey, Louis Simpson, and, especially, Robert Bly, the least mentioned but probably most talented of the group."

33. Stepanchev, 180. About Bly in particular, he says: "It is evident that Robert Bly's theory and practice cohere." (187)

34. We have seen, in Chap. Three, that Bly and Rothenberg were on the same wavelength only briefly.

35. Here's one: "That was a good issue, but why the hell didn't you get someone who knows some Spanish to translate those poems by Vallejo and Neruda? ... Well, keep trying." J. Palley to RB, 29 May 1964.

36. RB to DH, 22 January 1964.

37. RB to DH, August 1964. Hamburger first wrote Bly on 14 March 1960.

38. RB to DH, 20 October 1964 (in Paris).

39. DH to RB, 30 September 1965. Not surprisingly, delays sometimes caused Bly to forfeit poems that he wanted to publish. Haines wrote: "'Dream of The Lynx' has been taken, along with a few others. You should have spoken sooner! You've had nearly two years!" JH to RB, 5 September 1964.

40. RB to DH, 10 January 1966.

41. Kerryman to RB (invoice), 18 May 1966. Again, this was five years later than originally projected. Bly instructed Kerryman to mail subscribers's copies in time for college students to get them before summer break. RB to DC Nolan, 12 April 1966.

42. As indicated in Bly's response. RB to DH, 2 February 1966.

43. LS to RB, 21 January 1966.

44. *News of the Universe* would be the title of a large anthology edited by Bly and published in 1980.

45. We might note that Barney Rosset's *Evergreen Review* 5.21 (November-December 1961) was a special "German Culture" issue.

46. The other translators were Wright, Rothenberg, Arianne Schultz, George Arman, Dallas Wiebe, Ruth and Matthew Mead, and Joanna Campbell, on whom this note: "She has published poems in the anti-war issue of *Coastlines*, and in *Poetry Northwest*. Her translation of Eich's story *The Stiltswalker* appeared in *New Directions* 18." All this was true, but her real name was Carol Bly. An advertisement for the Meads' translation of Bobrowski's *Shadow Land* is laid in this issue.

47. JD to RB, 4 March 1962.

48. JD to RB, 13 June 1962.

49. JD to RB, 2 July 1962.

50. JD to RB, 18 June 1963.

51. RB to DH, 15 July 1963.

52. RB journal, 30 October 1965.

53. RL to RB, n.d.

54. GH to RB, 3 March 1962.

55. Bly had spent some time with Hamburger and Middleton while in England; he liked them both (especially Hamburger, who helped with the German section of #8), but he was unimpressed with the latter's ideas. RB to DH, 2 October 1964. Bly had quoted Hamburger in *Twenty Poems of Georg Trakl.*

56. Bly's choice of Arp was illuminated by a recent serendipitous occurrence: "The other night I found by accident Jean Arp's gallery here in Paris, and walked in. ... As I gradually looked around, ... here were three of his sculptures.... Staggering things! It's wonderful to see great things like that near, one or two feet away! and not in a museum, not owned by somebody's superego. They were really beautiful. ... Imagine Arp still working, at his age, and so well. I was overjoyed, still am." RB to DH, October 1964.

57. DH to RB, n.d. (November 1965).

58. RB to DH, 21 November 1965.

59. In 1967 Bly published a review of Lowell's book *Near the Ocean.* He called it "an almost total loss." Again, Bly's disappointment is great because of Lowell's

past greatness. "One of Lowell's finest acts was his refusal even to appear to support the Administration's foreign policy by accepting White House hospitality a few years ago. Yet it is clear that something of the lies and emptiness now penetrating American ground has seeped into the book." ("New Lowell Work, 'Near the Ocean,' Far From His Best," *The Minneapolis Star* [August 16, 1967], 12B.)

60. Gunderson was a Philosophy professor at the University of Minnesota, and a poet.

61. "From a paper read at the 1963 convention of the National Council of Teachers of English at San Francisco, published in *College English*, March, 1964."

62. RB to DH, 16 August 1962.

63. RB to DH, 8 January 1964.

64. RB to DH, 17 February 1964.

65. RB to DH, 20 March 1964.

66. The copyright page says: "Printed in the Netherlands." While Bly was in England, having decided that it was time to bid Kerryman *adieu*, he made a connection with the printing firm Drukkerij G.J. Thieme, in Nijmegen. Patrick Bowles, the "Paris editor" of the *Paris Review* (which had used this printer for eight or nine years), wrote Bly a letter of introduction. (PB to P.J. Van Zee, 20 June 1964.) Larry Bensky, Bowles' successor, then acted as middleman. (LB to RB, 25 February 1965.) In January 1966, Bly wrote the printer "Thank you for your patience with our delay. The delay centered around a single word in an Apollinaire poem, 'ganique.' No French professor in France or the USA could find the meaning of this word. It turned out to be a Finnish word." RB to Van Zee, 22 January 1966. Bly had written Roger Shattuck, author of the recent book *The Banquet Years: The Origins of the Avant-Garde in France*, in which Apollinaire figures prominently. (RB to RS, 28 September 1965.) Shattuck put him on the trail to the answer. RS to RB, 26 October 1965: "I don't know. Nor does anyone else here. ... I've always figured it was Finn or Lapp ....there's one guy who probably knows, Professeur Décaudin, Faculté des Lettres, Toulouse, France. Tell him I sent you."

67. These quotations are from the front flap of the dust jacket.

68. RC to RB, 10 August 1966.

69. CS to RB, 5 September 1966.

70. MR to RB, 28 August 1966.

71. Margaret Randall, "Some Books," *El Corno Emplumado* 21 (January 1967), 111.

Chapter 11

1. LS to RB, 1 April 1965.

2. RB journal, November 1965. On November 27, 35,000 protesters circled the White House and then marched to the Washington Monument for a rally.

3. MG interview with RB, 3 September 2006.

4. LS to RB, 26 November 1965.

5. JH to RB, 18 December 1965.

6. This version from *The Light Around the Body* (1967) is much revised from its first appearance in *Poetry* 108.6 (September 1966), 387, where it had a slightly different title.

7. In addition to the political poems that had regularly appeared in *The Fifties* and *The Sixties*, Bly had contributed to, for example, the "Political Poetry" section (edited by Ignatow) of *Chelsea* 8 (1960) ("Merchants Have Multiplied"), and to the "Anti-War Issue" of *Coastlines* 19 (1962) ("On Listening to Stevenson and Kennedy Lie about the First Cuban Invasion").

8. *Selected Poems* (Harper & Row, 1986), 62.

9. This is the final version in *A Poetry Reading Against the Vietnam War* (The American Writers Against the Vietnam War, 1966).

10. RB to DH, 2 February 1966.

11. Earlier, on September 24, there had been a "Sing-In for Peace" at Carnegie Hall, at which some sixty performers, mostly folk singers, played to an audience of over 5,000. This event included actors, playwrights, novelists, critics, and these poets: Alan Dugan, Kinnell, Kunitz, Levertov, Lowell, Walter Lowenfels, Joel Oppenheimer, Muriel Rukeyser, and Robert Penn Warren.

12. The organizer (Stanley Kauffmann, the *New York Times*' drama critic) was not taking any more poets. GK to MG, 23 April 2007.

13. Bly had met Ray, then at Cornell University, a few years earlier, and had helped him with his anthology, *For the Hungarian Revolution*. Ray said: "it was his idea to turn the event into an anti-war reading." DR email to MG, 11 October 2006.

14. RB journal, 18 March 1966. The eminence of *The Sixties* undoubtedly aided in gathering such a group so quickly. Group members agreed to read for free, but their travel expenses were paid.

15. "Poets Hold 'Read-In' in Oregon To Protest U.S. Role in Vietnam," *The New York Times* (6 March 1966).

16. Norma Hober, "Bly Tells of Poetry Read-Ins," *Montana Kaimin* (University of Montana, Missoula), 68.4 (10 March 1966).

17. RB journal, 18 March 1966.

18. JH to RB, 26 March 1966.

19. MG interview with RB, 30 July 1999.

20. GK to RB, 27 March 1966.

21. AR to RB, 6 April 1966.

22. RB to DH, 18 April 1966. This, however, did not take place until October 2.

23. From Bly's scrapbook of clippings, "Vietnam War Readings," it is clear that he participated in the following read-ins that spring: Portland State University, 4 March; Reed College, 5 March; University of Washington, Seattle, 5 March; University of Wisconsin, Milwaukee, 15 April; University of Chicago, 16 April; Harvard University, 3 May; Columbia University, 4 May; Union College, 5 May (11:30 a.m.); SUNY Binghamton, 5 May (4 p.m.); Cornell University, 5 May (8 p.m.); Queens College, 6 May; Trinity College, 7 May; Oberlin College, 7 May; University of Pennsylvania, 8 May; New York University, 10 May; Wisconsin State College, Oshkosh, 11 May; St. Cloud State College, 14 May (3 p.m.); Uni-

versity of Minnesota, Minneapolis, 14 May (8 p.m.); Macalester College, 15 May.
Also, the list of American Writers against the Vietnam War kept growing.
By May 14 it included: William Alfred, Marvin Bell, Bly, Paul Carroll, Bruce
Clemens, Creeley, George Deaux, Alan Dugan, F.W. Dupee, Ferlinghetti, Stuart
Friebert, Ginsberg, Mitchell Goodman, Paul Goodman, Allan Grossman, Hall,
Hecht, Hitchcock, Daniel G. Hoffman, John Hollander, Donald Justice, Ilona
Karmel, X.J. Kennedy, Kinnell, Knoepfle, Robert Kroetsch, Kunitz, Richmond
Lattimore, Levertov, Robert Lifton, Logan, Lowell, Walter Lowenfels, Lenore
Marshall, Robert Mezey, Anais Nin, Conor Cruise O'Brien, Orlovsky, Ray,
Rexroth, Rich, I.A. Richards, Dennis Schmitz, Sexton, Shapiro, Philip Silver,
Peter Simpson, Louis Simpson, Snodgrass, Susan Sontag, Barry Spacks, George
Starbuck, Lucien Stryk, May Swenson, Wilbur, Malcolm Willson, Wright, David P. Young, and Marguerite Young.

24. HB to RB, 26 March 1966. The others included Dugan, Richmond Lattimore, Lenore Marshall, Daniel Hoffman, Mitchell Goodman, Lowenfels, George Deaux, Eric Sellin, and Robert Mezey.

25. *The Philadelphia Inquirer* (9 May 1966).

26. RB journal, 24 May 1966.

27. DR to RB, 31 March 1966. Morse had led the attempt to repeal the Gulf of Tonkin resolution in the Senate on March 1, an effort which was defeated, 92 to 5.

28. GK to RB, 27 March 1966.

29. The extant typescript has Reynolds, but Campbell won the day.

30. HG to RB, 8 April 1966. Gantt made arrangements with the Tutrone Printing Company.

31. RB to David Tutrone, 20 April 1966.

32. RV to CB, 28 April 1966.

33. MG interview with RB, 31 July 2001. In the end, a slip was pasted on the copyright page: "The blacked out spaces are in mourning for the poems of E. E. Cummings, for which permission was refused by Harcourt Brace." It led many to assume (erroneously) that the publishing house wanted to dissociate itself from an antiwar publication. For details on the expurgated portions, see *The Odin House Harvest*, 51. Published by The American Writers Against the Vietnam War and distributed by the Sixties Press (which actually held the copyright), the edition was 3000 copies. To bolster their effort, "Poetry of the Read-In Campaign," with excerpts from the book, appeared in *The Nation* (30 May 1966), 653-5.

34. DR email to MG, 11 October 2006.

35. JR to RB, 14 June 1966. This issue of *Some/thing* became famous for its cover, designed by Andy Warhol.

36. BK to RB, 16 October 1966.

37. SB to CB, 16 August 1966. He adds: "What ever happened to that book of American poems [*The Continent Rising from the Sea*] that Robert was going to publish with my 'All the sad young men are looking for papa' in it?"

38. Louis Lipsitz, *Lillabulero* 1.2 (Spring 1967), 31-4.

39. *London Bulletin (Bertrand Russell Peace Foundation)* 1 (August 1967), 4.

40. "The Poet as Responsible," *Northwest Review* 9 (Fall/Winter 1967-1968), 116-18.

41. RB to JH, 8 July 1966.

42. JH to RB, 12 July 1966.

43. RB journal, 15 July 1966.

44. JH to RB, 20 July 1966.

45. GH to RB, 11 November 1966.

46. They would reconcile some years later.

47. RB to DH, 29 July 1966.

48. DI to RB, September 1966. Bly participated in an antiwar reading there in the spring of 1967.

49. RB journal, 4 October 1966.

50. "The American Outsider," *The Nation* (14 November 1966), 517-19.

51. HY to RB, 2 June 1966.

52. RB journal, 14 December 1966.

53. "25 of us went out on a platform-truck with sound equipment and a gigantic billboard with a two-headed Johnson on it (second head emerging from his buttocks) and hit 5 locations with songs, poems and a skit by the Pageant Players last Friday. We will do this hopefully 3 times during the Angry Arts week and hope to have you with us on the truck. ... I hope all is well with your planning the Napalm Reading. I haven't invited anyone yet, so the list is still all yours." CE to RB, 16 January 1967.

54. Carol Grosberg to "Dear Artist," 24 March 1967. The report from the Angry Arts coordinator said: "62,000 people saw 40 performances in theaters and churches, —10 plays, 17 concerts, 9 film showings, a poetry reading, 3 panel discussions and one seven hour Vietnamese Life Project."

55. Curtis Harnack, "Week of the Angry Artist..." *The Nation* (20 February 1967), 245-8.

56. This was headed by Bly, Galin (the founder), Wright, Zweig, and Frederick R. Karl, with Lowell, Trilling, Levertov, Kinnell, Simpson, Burnshaw, Leon Edel, Gardner, Hall, and Joseph Heller listed as members.

57. Harnack, *The Nation,* 246.

58. DL to RB, 5 March 1967.

59. Apparently, Hall had agreed to bring up the idea to Harper & Row. RB to DH, 10 January 1967.

60. RD to RB, 7 December 1966. Duncan's life partner, Jess, was an important collage artist.

61. GS to RB, 19 June 1967.

62. GS to RB, 31 May 1967.

63. Including: *Quixote* ("The Peace Issue") 1.7 (June 1966); *Some/Thing* 3 ("A Vietnam Assemblage") (2.1) (Winter 1966); *The 1968 Peace Calendar: Out of the War Shadow* edited by Denise Levertov (War Resisters League, 1967); *Poems: Artists and Writers Protest Against the War in Vietnam* edited by Jack Sonenberg (Profile Press, 1967); *Where is Vietnam? American Poets Respond* edited by Walter

Lowenfels (Anchor Books, 1967).

64. "I don't know him or anything about him, except that he wanted to be in the book, and gave permission to use the extract I selected. Had you written me before the anthology went to press, I could have excluded him. I don't want a Dickey to stand between our friendship and our common views on peace and poetry." WL to RB, 11 June 1967.

65. "On Political Poetry," *The Nation* 204.17 (24 April 1967), 522-24. In expanded form, this was to be the introduction to *Forty Poems Touching on Recent American History*, projected for publication by the Sixties Press later that year.

66. RS to RB, 2 August 1967.

67. RB to DH, 16 September 1967: "We're $4000 in debt, but I'm going to do the California circuit in November, and try to get $2000 from that, so we'll be a couple of weeks late getting to Ann Arbor.... Then I hope to get $1500 from Dickey [for rights to *The Suspect in Poetry*—which didn't work] and maybe a $500 or $1000 advance either for a children's book, or a book of essays [neither of which happened]."

68. RB to RS, 12 September 1967.

69. RS to RB, 17 September 1967.

70. CK to RB, 18 September 1967.

71. RB to CK and RS, 28 September 1967.

72. RB to DH, 16 September 1967.

73. According to the National Mobilization Committee to End the War in Vietnam.

74. One useful account is Norman Mailer's *Armies of the Night* (1968).

75. See Joseph A. Loftus, "Guards Repulse War Protesters at the Pentagon," *New York Times* (22 October 1967), 1/58.

76. GK to RB, 15 November 1967.

77. See Homer Bigart, "264 Seized Here in Draft Protest," *New York Times* (6 December 1967), 1/8.

78. Press release from the Lutheran Church in America Commission on Press, Radio and Television (16 November 1967). William Sloane Coffin, chaplain at Yale University (and founder of Clergy and Laity Concerned about the Vietnam War), may have been a model for Bly here.

79. DH to RB, 27 September 1967.

80. *The New York Review of Books* 9.11 (21 December 1967), 220. To this letter was appended his initial refusal, the responses of Stevens and Kizer, and his original rejoinder.

81. "Antiwar Poet Refuses U.S. Gift," Bob Lundegaard, *The Minneapolis Tribune* (15 December 1967), 19.

82. KB to RB, 17 December 1967.

83. WH-M to RB, 12 December 1967.

84. CB to William Bentinck-Smith, Assistant to the President, 16 May 1969. This, she says, was her proudest moment with the magazine. MG interview with CB, 29 June 2000.

85. "You won! Absolute secrecy! Congratulations! Don't tell anybody, even Jim Wright. Please! They'll know it was me. The award, when you'll make a speech, is March 6th, so stay an extra week with Louis or something. I'll be there with you. YAHOO!!" DH to RB, n.d. (late 1967).

86. PJ to RB, 3 January 1968. He added: "We trust that you can postpone your departure until March 8, so that you can be present to accept the $1,000 award in Philharmonic Hall, Lincoln Center, at 5:30 P.M., Wednesday, March 6; appear at a press conference preceding the awards that day; and take part in what we hope will be a television 'special' for all six winners on March 7."

87. CK to RB, 28 February 1968.

88. Isabel Wilder accepted the award on her (absent) brother's behalf. As stated above, Kennan was one of the dedicatees of *A Poetry Reading Against the Vietnam War*. Howard Hong had been on the faculty of St. Olaf College when Bly was a student there.

89. The year before, Mitch Goodman and a hundred or so others had walked out because Vice President Hubert Humphrey was the principal guest speaker.

90. "The National Book Awards," *The Nation* (25 March 1968), 413.

91. Martha MacGregor, "The Week in Books," *New York Post* (9 March 1968).

92. Kozol aligned himself with what Bly had just done, and said he was giving his $1,000 prize money to community leaders in Boston's South End ghetto.

93. "The National Book Awards," 413.

94. His introduction to the imminent Neruda book is printed in full, together with the poem "Lies" and Paul Zweig's review of *The Light Around the Body*, titled "A Sadness for America."

95. AM to RB, 9 March 1968.

96. SM to RB, 24 March 1968.

97. GK to RB, 8 May 1968.

98. BM to RB, n.d.

99. WS to RB, 16 March 1968.

100. DI to RB, 11 April 1968.

101. PL to RB, 6 November 1968.

102. LM to RB, 20 January 1969.

103. His allusion was to Yeats' "The Scholars": "Lord, what would they say / Did their Catullus walk that way?" LS to RB, 3 May 1968.

104. David Ignatow, "Robert Bly," *The One in the Many: A Poet's Memoirs* (Wesleyan University Press, 1988), 110-11.

105. "Yes, it was a great evening in New York. I feel we got closer to knowing each other than we'd done, and I liked that. ... Congratulations on doing it, Robert.... You're kind and generous to say that what I suggested really did help." WSM to RB, 29 April 1968.

106. JH to RB, n.d. (1973).

107. This is quoted in a (carbon copy) letter from Florence Howe to Joan Baez, 24 March 1969.

108. The list includes: Daniel Berrigan, Ted Berrigan, Henry Braun, Paul Car-

roll, Creeley, Ed Dorn, Duncan, Eshleman, Ferlinghetti, Ginsberg, Hall, Ignatow, Kinnell, Etheridge Knight, Knott, Levertov, Lipsitz, Merwin, Carl Rakosi, Rexroth, Rich, Ridland, Rukeyser, Rutsala, Ed Sanders, Simpson, Snyder, Stafford, Starbuck, Diane Wakoski, C.K. Williams, and Jay Wright.

109. Sarah Dale, "Draft Resistance is Poetry Theme," *The University Daily Kansan* (11 April 1969).

110. All the above information in a letter (with appended schedule) from Florence Howe to RB (and all participants), 15 April 1969.

111. TB to RB, 16 April 1969.

112. FH to RB, 22 July 1969.

113. DH to CB, 21 November 1969. There also came another opportunity for Bly to turn down money. "You have been selected to receive a National Endowment for the Arts award [of $250]...for your role in selecting for your magazine...'The Bear' by Galway Kinnell." Nancy Hanks to RB, 3 December 1969. Bly replied: "I prefer not to accept this money. Refusing government money is a small thing, like participating in a peace march; yet I believe the war will eventually end from the weight of a massive collection of these details." RB to NH, 7 December 1969. The NEA simultaneously awarded Kinnell $500 for the same poem. He accepted, indicating that he did so only to donate the money to Resist (a federal offense). His letter, and acceptance of his donation by Florence Howe, was in *NYRB* 14.11 (4 June 1970).

114. "Bly had written several plays during the 1950s and 1960s. He had some copies of this printed privately, but it was also published in *Chelsea* 24/25 (October 1968). For more details, see *The Odin House Harvest*, 58. The play was performed at the University of Kansas, and in Cincinnati a couple of years later. RB to DH, 20 May 1969."

115. *The Nation* (25 March 1968), 417.

116. MG interview with RB, 30 July 1999.

117. LF to RB, n.d.

118. HG to RB, 12 January 1970.

119. Ferlinghetti let Bly decide, adding: "In any case, ask them to make a note in the LP giving your copyright and City Lights Books as publishers of it." LF to RB, 14 December 1970. The flyer, which also had a quotation from Leo Tolstoy, came from the Institute for the Study of Nonviolence, an organization overseen by Baez and her husband, David Harris. More details in *The Odin House Harvest*, "64-66."

120. GK to RB, 7 June 1970.

121. JL to RB, 28 November 1970.

122. JHW to RB, 8 November 1970.

123. DI to RB, 19 January 1971.

124. *Selected Poems*, 63, 194, 195, 197.

125. Martin Dodsworth, "Bookmarks," *Prairie Schooner* 45 (Spring 1971), 92-3.

126. Richard P. Sugg, *Robert Bly* (Twayne Publishers, 1986), 73.

127. RB to DH, 2 May 1970. Bly refers to a book published that year by Al-

bert Szent-Györgi, who won the Nobel Prize in Physiology or Medicine in 1937 for his role in identifying Vitamin C.

Chapter 12

1. RB to JD, 28 June 1966.

2. RB to DH, 4 July 1966.

3. Louis Simpson, *A Revolution in Taste: Studies of Dylan Thomas, Allen Ginsberg, Sylvia Plath, and Robert Lowell* (Macmillan Publishing Co., 1978), 156.

4. AS to RB, 2 October 1966.

5. CH to RB, 12 December 1969.

6. CE to RB, 17 January 1967.

7. JH to RB, 4 July 1966.

8. PC to RB, 6 June 1966.

9. GH to RB, 25 January 1966.

10. GW to RB, 31 May 1966.

11. RB to TB, 7 December 1966. Strictly speaking, Snyder's Crunk had been Wright.

12. William E. Stafford, "A Poetry Happening," *English Journal* 56.7 (October 1967), 951-2.

13. RB to DH, 8 December 1966.

14. GS to RB, 25 December 1966.

15. GS to RB, 10 March 1967.

16. Ignatow did the introduction. RB to Harry Gantt, 12 December 1967.

17. HG to RB, 15 July 1966. Bly also asked him about the possibility of reprinting *The Fifties* 1.

18. RB to HG, 15 March 1967.

19. HG to RB, n.d. 3000 copies was a new high.

20. HSM to RB, 4 March 1960.

21. JW to RB and CB, 15 April 1960.

22. Hall had recently written: "Denise was just in Detroit reading beautiful poems.... She loves you again because of napalm & all!" DH to RB, 28 March 1967.

23. DL to RB, 31 October 1967.

24. RD to DL, 16 August 1967. This is letter 402 in *The Letters of Robert Duncan and Denise Levertov*, edited by Robert J. Bertholf and Albert Gelpi (Stanford University Press, 2004).

25. DL to RD, 31 August 1967 (letter 403, Bertholf & Gelpi).

26. DR to RB, 30 September 1967.

27. AA to RB, 9 February 1968. It did prove costly to the Ray-Ammons relationship. DR email to MG, 24 October 2006.

28. Patrick Herriges says he "proofed" this Blue Toad award. See "My Home-

town," *Walking Swiftly*, 41.

29. RB to DH, 21 November 1965.

30. JD to RB, 14 November 1965.

31. First Hall, and then Levertov, on the editorial board of Wesleyan University Press, served as editor of Dickey's book. For the various entanglements, see Hart, 330-2.

32. PC to RB, 6 June 1966.

33. RB to JD, 28 June 1966.

34. JD to RB, 16 July 1966 (in *Crux*).

35. DI to RB, 18 June 1966.

36. DI to RB, 14 September 1966.

37. DH to RB, 10 April 1967.

38. DH to RB, n.d.

39. Hart, 344.

40. Ibid.

41. *Kayak* 12 (1967), 45-9.

42. "On *Kayak*," *The Little Magazine in America*, 445.

43. The following quotations are from "Letters," *Kayak* 13 (January 1968), 12-21.

44. BM to RB, 31 December 1967.

45. JH to RB, 9 January 1968.

46. GH to RB, 15 January 1968.

47. BP to GH, 22 January 1968. Peters sent Bly a copy of the letter.

48. JW to RB & CB, 30 August 1961.

49. HSM to RB, 20 October 1963.

50. "The Art of Poetry LXXIX" (Bly interview by Francis Quinn), *The Paris Review* 154 (Spring 2000), 55.

51. RB to DH, 25 September 1964.

52. "The Art of Poetry LXXIX," 55.

53. RB to DH, 20 April 1965.

54. The interview took place not in London but in New York, and a year later. RB to DH, 14 July 1966.

55. MB to RB, 19 April 1968.

56. PL to RB, 6 November 1968.

57. BG to RB and JW, n.d.

58. DD to RB, 25 January 1969.

59. DS to RB, 17 October 1968.

60. *The Times Literary Supplement* (14 November 1968), 285.

61. Richard Howard, *Poetry* (February 1969), 348-9.

62. *El Corno Emplumado* 28 (October 1968), 140.

Chapter 13

1. RB to DH, 3 September 1967

2. RB to DH, 28 April 1968.

3. MG interview with RB, 17 January 2007.

4. It would, however, end badly. For Bly's part in the story, see Ed Sanders, *The Party: A Chronological Perspective on a Confrontation at a Buddhist Seminary* (Poetry, Crime & Culture Press, 1977), and Tom Clark, *The Great Naropa Poetry Wars* (Cadmus Editions, 1980). See also "Rays of Distant Bly Light."

5. RB journal, 1968, *passim*.

6. TP to RB, 28 July 1968.

7. RB to DH, 19 June 1968.

8. HK to RB, 10 May 1968. Obviously, he would not have accepted in any case.

9. WSM to RB, 3 August 1968.

10. PC to RB, 11 August 1967.

11. PC to RB, 5 February 1969. The Italian reference is from Eliot's dedication of *The Waste Land* to Ezra Pound, a phrase Eliot took from Dante.

12. DI to RB, 11 April 1968.

13. She also submitted: "i know you don't dig my work overly, but reading this number moves me to send again...feel free, etc." MR to RB, 14 August 1967.

14. JL to RB, 19 August 1967.

15. RB to RB, n.d.

16. JC to RB, 8 August 1967.

17. DC to RB, 10 August 1967.

18. JW to RB, 14 November 1967.

19. GS to RB, 16 January 40068 [*sic*].

20. ARA to RB, 9 February 1968.

21. KR to JL, 18 August 1967 (letter 126 in *Kenneth Rexroth and James Laughlin: Selected Letters,* edited by Lee Bartlett [W.W. Norton & Company, 1991], 243).

22. KB to RB, 5 October 1967.

23. PL to RB, 29 September 1967.

24. DH to RB, n.d.

25. DH to RB, n.d. (August or early September 1967).

26. RB to DH, 3 September 1967.

27. WW to RB, 18 August 1967.

28. DR to RB, 30 September 1967.

29. POA to RB, 20 September 1967

30. NL to RB, 19 August 1967.

31. MK to RB, 14 September 1967.

32. JJ to RB, 6 November 1967.

33. PS to RB, 1 June 1969.

34. Richard Tillinghast, "Robert Lowell on Native Ground," *Virginia Quarterly Review* 71.1 (Winter 1995), 86-100.

35. WSM to RB, 19 September 1967.

36. CR to RB, 4 March 1969.

37. RF to RB, 29 August 1967.

38. PC to RB, 11 August 1967.

39. BG to RB, 22 September 1969.

40. DD to RB, n.d.

41. OB to RB, 12 April 1968.

42. HG to RB, 14 May 1968.

43. Translated into the facing Spanish by A.M. Garibay, and into English by Marijane Allen. In the previous issue, Bly had promised "Inca poems" – but Nahuatl is Aztec.

44. Olsen, under the imprint of his Ox Head Press, had done Bly's *Ducks* and *Chrysanthemums*.

45. DI to RB, September 1966.

46. DI to RB, 24 August 1968.

47. Harry Greenberg, "An Interview with Bill Knott (1940-1966)," *Some* 4 (Summer 1973), 41.

48. Surely this is a response to the 1968 letter from C.O.P., the Committee on Poetry, signed by 16 poets, that said: "We herald to literary persons: get on the ball for LeRoi Jones, or else get off the poetic pot."

49. He was thinking along these lines as early as 1967. He wrote in his journal, 27 June: "There have been 10 issues of the *Fifties* and *Sixties*—etc.—there will be 10 issues of *the Seventies*. Then a little explosion, in which the red pig will disappear into outer space & be lost to human eyes…enough of the pure water we have ourselves tried to drink."

50. BH to RB, 15 October 1969.

51. SK to RB, 31 October 1968.

52. More details are in *The Odin House Harvest*, 60-63.

53. RB journal, 6 August 1964.

54. RB to TB, 10 January 1967.

55. TB to RB, 28 March 1967.

56. TB to RB, n.d. (April).

57. TB to RB, n.d. ("Tuesday noon").

58. RB to TB, 30 May 1967.

59. RB to DH, 16 October 1967.

60. GJF to RB, 11 November 1967.

61. On an envelope from REA Express, dated 10 April, Bly has written "Total Cost $1100 for 3000 copies."

62. This translation differs in several respects from the later revised version

published in *The Winged Energy of Delight: Selected Translations* (HarperCollins, 2004), 97.

63. See, for example, the anthology *Naked Poetry: Recent American Poetry in Open Forms*, edited by Stephen Berg and Robert Mezey (Bobbs-Merrill, 1969).

64. PL to RB, 6 November (1968).

65. "In the hands of Robert Bly, a first-rate poet himself, the translations of both the verses and the prose-poems (particularly, among the latter, 'Walt Whitman' and 'In the Subway') are brilliant." *Long Beach Press-Telegram* (10 December 1969).

66. JC to RB, 11 June 1969.

Chapter 14

1. *TPJ* 2.2 (Winter 1969).

2. XJK to RB, 21 October 1970.

3. CR to RB, 31 March 1969.

4. BG to RB, 17 June 1969.

5. GF to RB, 9 May 1969.

6. WM to RB, 8 July 1970.

7. Vivian & Gary Flake to RB, 28 August 1970.

8. CB to RB, 24 February 1970.

9. DW to RB, 23 July 1971.

10. RB to DH, 2 October 1969.

11. Ginsberg typed his "Car Crash" poem in the chickenhouse while Bly and Orlovsky planted poplars together. Ginsberg's poem, "Reflections in Sleepy Eye," dictated on the way to the farm, was dedicated to Bly. More details on these in my forthcoming "Allen & Peter & Robert." DI to RB, 28 June 1969. WSM to RB and CB, 3 June 1971. For other visitors, see "Odin House: A Literary Crossroads."

12. RB to DH, 5 January 1970.

13. LS to RB, 22 September 1970.

14. RB journal, 30 July 1970.

15. MB to RB, 2 May 1970.

16. For a fuller account of Bly's California experience, see my "A Hole in the World: Robert Bly's Point Reyes Chronicle," *Catamaran Literary Reader* (16) 4.4 (Winter 2016), 55-60.

17. The Evolutionary Part of the Mind: An Interview with Jay Bail and Geoffrey Cook," *Talking All Morning*, 4, 6.

18. DJ to RB, 30 September 1971.

19. For more on the following two incidents, see "Captain Robert Bly...."

20. RB to Brian Konnersman, 24 March 1971.

21. Jerry Gorshine to RB, 30 March 1971.

22. Sent in the summer of 1971, "Letter to Robert Bly" appears in *Arsenal:*

Surrealist Subversion 2 (Summer 1973), 21.

23. An eyewitness account by Douglas Macdonald, "The Great Bly Reading: From Fits to Ecstasy," *Two Hands News* 6 (December 1976), 1.

24. Jeff Poniewaz, *The Surrealist Assassination of Robert Bly*, n.p., 1978.

25. For more details of their friendship and their working relationship, see my "Tranströmer and the Badger," *Antioch Review* 70.2 (Spring 2012), 264-76. See also *Airmail: The Letters of Robert Bly and Tomas Transtömer*, edited by Thomas R. Smith (Graywolf Press, 2013), in which appear most of the letters below.

26. TT to RB, 23 March 1965 and 30 October 1965.

27. TT to RB, 30 January 1966.

28. TT to RB, September 1966.

29. TT to RB, 15 January 1967. While Transtömer was always ready to offer help and suggest alterations, Bly tried hard to get it right before sending them along. Christina Paulston helped, as she had previously (with Ekelöf). CP to RB, 25 March 1965.

30. RB to TT, 18 March 1966; TT to RB, 20 July 1966.

31. RB to TT, 10 April 1966. That book was published as *Friends, You Drank Some Darkness* (Beacon Press, 1975).

32. So reads Bly's inscription in the copy Bly presented to St. Martin.

33. RB to TT, 24 June 1969.

34. EB to RB, 19 January 1970.

35. RB to TT, 29 July 1970. This book was *Night Vision* (Lillabulero Press, 1971).

36. TT to RB, 11 August 1970; RB to TT, 14 September 1970; EB to RB, n.d.; RB to TT, 23 October 1970.

37. RB to TT, 10 December 1970.

38. EB to RB, n.d.

39. TT to RB, 18 April 1971. The run-on lines in the English text are not indented as in the Swedish.

40. TT to RB, 25 September 1971.

41. RB to TT, 30 September 1971.

42. RB to TT, 23 October 1970.

43. RB to TT, 3 September 1971.

44. TT to RB, 25 September 1971.

45. Most of the introduction appeared first in *Field* 1 (1969).

46. TT to RB, 27 February 1970.

47. Philip Dacey, *Crazy Horse* 9 (December 1971), 15.

48. LF to RB, 25 February 1972.

49. RB journal, 12 June 1971. He calls it "the Dragon Smoke issue." Other working titles included "The Red Pig of Association" and "A Poetry of Leaps."

50. RB to TT, 22 July 1971.

51. CB to Stephen Braitman, 10 August 1971.

52. John Melcher to RB, 8 February 1972.

53. For details, see *The Odin House Harvest*, 28-39.

54. Both Teter and Burke would be involved with subsequent publications of Bly's. The earliest reaction to the issue is from DI to RB, 27 March 1972.

55. An earlier version, in *Stand* 9.1 (1967) 10-12, was reprinted in Berg and Mezey, *Naked Poetry*, 161-4.

56. He used the term in: "Some Thoughts on Lorca and René Char," *The Fifties* 3 (1959), 7; "Prose vs. Poetry," *Choice* 2 (1962), 67; and "On Political Poetry," *The Nation* (24 April 1967), 522-3, a shortened version of "Leaping Up into Political Poetry," *London Magazine* 7 (Spring 1967), 82-7, which was also the introduction for *Forty Poems Touching on Recent American History*.

57. So he says in "Poetry of Steady Light." This poem too is in *Twenty Poems*, with some changes, mostly line breaks.

58. The identification of Jesus with the Essenes is not widely accepted by New Testament scholars.

59. Attentive readers may recall Bly's suggested resolution for young poets back in *The Fifties* 2: "I promise I will neither write nor read another poem on the death of Orpheus as long as I live."

60. So Bly repeats part of the epigraph to *The Sixties* 9. Bly had met Andrei Voznesensky in Vancouver in 1971. See "A Hole in the World" for more on that.

61. Snyder had sent this a couple of years earlier. Later, he wrote: "Are you going to do *Seventies*? I've heard conflicting rumors. If not, I'll send 'The Way West' on elsewhere. But I hope you keep it going." GS to RB, 1 June 1971.

Chapter 15

1. TT to RB, 1 May 1972.

2. GO to RB, 23 September 1972.

3. DL to RB, n.d.

4. RE to RB, 14 April 1972.

5. RE to RB, 30 May 1972.

6. WS to RB, 9 June 1972.

7. AM to RB, 11 December 1972.

8. DH to RB, 21 April 1972.

9. EK to RB, n.d.

10. SP to RB, 5 June 1972.

11. CF to RB, 27 May 1972.

12. GH to RB, September 1972.

13. BG to RB, 30 March 1972.

14. RS to RB, 17 December 1972.

15. BR to RB, 26 September 1972.

16. TM to RB, n.d.

17. JC to RB, 8 September 1972.

18. BC to RB, n.d.

19. AG to RB, n.d. (1972).

20. GP to RB, 29 June 1972.

21. RB to DH, 26 June 1972.

22. MB to RB, 31 March 1972.

23. JH to RB, 24 April 1972.

24. TM to RB, 22 September 1972.

25. JA to RB, n.d.

26. NT to RB, 27 April 1972.

27. ER to RB, n.d.

28. PM to RB, 7 March 1973.

29. JL to RB, 14 March 1972.

30. JH to RB, 24 April 1972.

31. These books were published between 1971 and 1977: in 1971, *The Fish in the Sea is Not Thirsty* (Kabir), and *The Sea and the Honeycomb* (expanded); in 1972, *Bashō, Ten Sonnets to Orpheus,* and *Neruda and Vallejo: Selected Poems;* in 1973, *Jumping Out of Bed, Sleepers Joining Hands,* and *Lorca and Jiménez: Selected Poems:* in 1974, *Point Reyes Poems;* in 1975, *Kabir: 28 Poems, The Morning Glory, Friends, You Drank Some Darkness, David Ignatow: Selected Poems* (as editor), *Old Man Rubbing His Eyes,* and *Leaping Poetry;* in 1977, *The Kabir Book: Forty-Four of the Ecstatic Poems of Kabir* and *This Body is Made of Camphor and Gopherwood.*

32. See John Rosenwald, "Small Engine Repair: Thirty-Five Years of the Annual Conference on the Great Mother and the New Father, Organized by Robert Bly," *Robert Bly in This World*, 120-48. These annual conferences are still going.

33. So reads the press release, published as "Minnesota Writers' Publishing House," *North Country Anvil* 3 (December-January, 1972-73), 73-78, and in altered forms as "Starting a Cooperative House," *American Poetry Review* 3 (March/April 1974), 12-13, and in *Urban Review* 7.4 (1974), 327-30. See Charlie Waterman, *Minnesota Writers' Publishing House Newsletter* 1 (June 1975), 1-2.

34. RE to RB, 11 March 1973. See also Scott Chisholm, "Resistance and Privacy: An Interview with Robert Bly," *Stone Drum* 1.1 (Spring 1972), 16-30.

35. Franz Allbert Richter and Lewis Hyde, "An Interview with Robert Bly," *The Lamp in the Spine* 3 (Winter 1972), 62.

36. RPD to RB, 11 November 1972.

37. HV to RB, 1 September 1973. Another allusion to Yeats's "The Scholars."

38. HV to RB, 30 September 1974.

39. HV to RB, 19 September 1975.

40. DH to RB, 26 December 1973. This, incidentally, is similar to a comment made more recently by Robert's ex-wife Carol. MG interview with CB, 29 June 2000. "Robert did three very important things: his own poetry, introducing South American poets, and so on, to a wider audience, and bringing politics into it. He should have been given the Nobel Prize for that."

41. WS to RB, 25 October 1974.

42. BK to RB, n.d. (1974?).

43. LS to RB, 18 April 1975.

44. DH to RB, 21 February 1974.

45. GO to RB, 2 February 1976. It should be noted that Orr's disgruntle-ment—based primarily on Bly's failure to follow through on a promised 'young poets' anthology, and Orr's acute awareness of the disappointment of those poets whose work had been accepted for it—was short-lived.

46. DH to RB, 24 February 1975.

47. See "I Came Out of the Mother Naked," Bly's essay in *Sleepers Joining Hands* (Harper & Row, 1973), 29-50.

48. RB to MT, 27 April 1975.

49. MP to RB, 30 July 1973.

50. For details, see "Rays of Distant Bly Light...."

51. LH email to MG, 13 August 2007.

52. RB journal, 1 September 1971.

53. LH to CB and RB, n.d.

54. LH to RB, 10 December 1973.

55. LH to RB, 29 June 1975.

56. HSM to RB, 28 September 1976.

57. He chose the New England Free Press in nearby Somerville. More details in *The Odin House Harvest*, 73-75.

58. RB Journal, 6 October 1977.

59. Robert Bly, "The Man Who Stayed Behind," *New York Times Book Review* (30 October 1977).

60. The book was not widely reviewed, but it sold well. One example: John Crispin, *World Literature Today* (Summer 1978).

61. RB to TB, 14 March 1972. Bilodeau had reclaimed his birth name of Baland. He had been similarly involved with the ill-starred *Forty Poems of Juan Ramón Jiménez*.

62. HN to RB, 27 January 1973. Einar Bergh, of the Norwegian Information Service in the United States, also wrote to Bly on June 5, 1975 about his "excit-ing" plans to bring Jacobsen to the U.S.

63. GN to RB, 5 March 1973.

64. LJ to MG, 11 July 2005. Artcraft Press, Inc., of Minneapolis, did the typesetting and makeup.

65. Bly wrote in his own copy: "Arrived May 5, 1977." This book also had a second printing, although not acknowledged on the copyright page, in Bly's let-ters, or in any journal entries. See *The Odin House Harvest*, 73-75.

66. A portion of this introduction first appeared in *The Sixties* 10 (1968).

67. "Rolf Jacobsen's Twenty Poems," *Nordisk Tidende* ("America's Leading Norwegian Newspaper") (2 March 1978).

68. "On Rolf Jacobsen and Peter Everwine," *Three Rivers Poetry Journal* 15/17 (1980), 83-4.

69. A few of these have already been mentioned in passing. Most of this information is scattered in Bly's papers—thus the lack of citations—and much of it difficult to date more than approximately.

70. Bly originally thought *The Seventies* would continue the numbering from *The Fifties* and *The Sixties* and therefore start with #11. Later he started with #1.

71. HSM to RB, 30 September 1965.

72. RB to DH, 27 February 1962.

73. DH to RB, n.d. (in 1962 folder; this might precede the above letter).

74. RB to DH, n.d. (February 1960).

75. RB to DH, n.d. (Spring 1960).

76. PB to RB, 31 December 1957.

77. RB to DH, 20 March 1964.

78. DH to RB, n.d. (1964).

79. RB to D.C. Nolan, 18 March 67.

80. DCN to RB, 27 October 1967.

81. Roger Straus to RB, 27 October 1967.

82. JC to RB, 11 June 1969.

83. *The San Francisco Book Review* 19 (April 1971), 13.

84. For details of publications of the Eighties / Nineties / Thousands Press, which include five books and one last stab at the magazine, see *The Odin House Harvest*, 75-78. These are all fine and interesting publications in their own right, but the energy had left the wine (to borrow an expression from a later Bly poem), the backbone of a distinct program had weakened inevitably as Bly's ever-fierce attention became focused elsewhere.

Acknowledgments

I want to express my deepest gratitude to Robert Bly, whose abundant generosity and full cooperation all through this book's long gestation has been the most important.

Thanks much to Paul Feroe for the initial exhortation that I undertake this book. For various other kinds of help and encouragement along the way, I am thankful to Ruth Bly, Mike Hazard, Scott King (*requiescat in pace*), Jim Lenfestey, Eric Lorberer, and Thomas R. Smith.

I am also very grateful to my editor/book designer, John Toren, and my publisher, Norton Stillman, for seeing this book into print.

While the bulk of my original research was done when Bly's correspondence, personal journals, and other papers were still in his hands, I am grateful for subsequent help from Cecily Marcus and the staff of the Upper Midwest Literary Archives at the Elmer L. Andersen Library at the University of Minnesota, where those papers are now held.

Quotations from Robert Bly's correspondence (letters sent and received), journals, interviews, essays, and some poems and translations are reprinted with his generous consent.

For Robert Bly's letters to Donald Hall, thanks also to the Donald Hall Papers, 1928-2018, MC 53, Milne Special Collections and Archives, University of New Hampshire Library, Durham, NH, USA.

Permission to use the excerpts from letters of Robert Creeley has been granted by The Permissions Company, LLC, on behalf of Penelope Creeley.

For Donald Davie's comments, copyright © the Estate of Donald Davie, by permission of Carcanet Press, Manchester, UK.

For quotations from the letters of James Dickey, thanks to the heirs of James Dickey and Raines & Raines.

Quotations from the letters of Robert Duncan, copyright © 2021 the Jess Collins Trust, reproduced with permission.

Permission to quote from unpublished letters of Richard Eberhart is granted by the Richard Eberhart Estate.

Quotation from a letter of Allen Ginsberg, copyright © by the Allen Ginsberg Estate, used by permission of the The Wylie Agency LLC.

Quotations from the letters of Donald Hall are reprinted by arrangement with the Estate of Donald Hall and the Strothman Agency.

"James Laughlin to Robert Bly," copyright © 2021 by Leila Laughlin Javitch, Amelia Laughlin, and Walker Laughlin. Reprinted by permission of New Directions Publishing Corp., acting as agent.

Quotations from the letters of W.S. Merwin, copyright © by W.S. Merwin, used by permission of The Wylie Agency LLC.

"Cynthia Ozick to Robert Bly," copyright © by Cynthia Ozick.

"Adrienne Rich to Robert Bly," copyright © 1961, 1966 by Adrienne Rich. Reprinted by permission of The Frances Goldin Literary Agency.

Quotations from the letters, poems, essays, and translations of James Wright are reprinted by the permission of Anne Wright.

And thanks to the following individuals—poets, writers, their relatives and literary executors—for permission to use quotations of unpublished (and, in a few cases, published) letters and other writings: Tim Baland, Joan M. Blackburn (on behalf of Paul), Bridget Bly (Carol), Laura Boss (Michael Benedikt), Bobbie Bristol (Galway Kinnell), Michael Brownstein, Maryrose Carroll (Paul), Alison Cassidy (Paul MacLean), Jane Dalrymple-Hollo (Anselm Hollo), Tammy Dobos-Simonton (R.P. Dickey), William Duffy, Caryl Eshleman (Clayton), Robert Fanning (Bill Knott), Carolyn Forché, Paul Garon (Chicago Surrealists), Elizabeth Glaze (Andrew), Penina Graubart (David Ignatow), the family of Jim Harrison, Helen Hecht (Anthony), Edward Hirsch (Philip Levine), Richard Howard, Lewis Hyde, Donald Junkins, X. J. Kennedy, Ted Kooser, Mary Lacey (Denise Levertov), John Logan, Jr. (John, Sr.), the estate of Archibald MacLeish, Sebastian Matthews (William), Thomas McGrath, Jr. (Thomas, Sr.), Elizabeth McKim (Etheridge Knight), Thomas Meyer (Jonathan Williams), Daniel Meyers (Bert), Michele Mortimer (Stanley Kunitz), Daniel Nordby (Carl Rakosi), Kathleen Norris (David Dwyer), Gregory Orr, Christina Paulston, Tom Pickard, the George Plimpton Estate, Margaret Randall, David Ray, Barbara Riddle-Dvorak, Steven B. Rogers (John Haines), Jerome Rothenberg, Lawrence Sikora (Russell Edson), Marjorie Simon (George Hitchcock), Matthew Simpson (Louis), Gary Snyder, Christopher Sorrentino (Gilbert), Kim Stafford (William), Dabney Stuart, Helen H. Tate (Allen), Paul Trachtenberg (Robert Peters), Monica Tranströmer (Tomas), Helen Vendler, Diane Wakoski, and Geneviève Zweig (Paul).

For the right to reprint published poems, I acknowledge as follows:

Robert Bly, "Restless in the Fall Afternoon" (revised and retitled "Waiting for the Stars"), "Sleet Storm on the Merritt Parkway," "At a March Against the Vietnam War (Washington, November 27, 1965)," "Johnson's Cabinet Watched by Ants," and "The Teeth Mother Naked at Last," from *Collected Poems.* Copyright © 2018, 2011, 2005, 2001, 1997, 1994, 1985, 1981, 1979, 1977, 1975, 1973, 1972, 1967, 1966, 1965, 1964, 1963, 1962, 1961, 1960, 1959, 1953 by Robert Bly. Used by permission of W. W. Norton & Company, Inc.

Allen Ginsberg, "Car Crash" from *Collected Poems, 1947-1997, Allen Ginsberg.* Copyright © 2006 by the Allen Ginsberg Trust. Used by permission of HarperCollins Publishers.

David Ignatow, "The Question" from *Against the Evidence: Selected Poems 1934-1994.* Copyright © 1993 by David Ignatow. Published by Wesleyan University Press and reprinted with permission.

Rolf Jacobsen, "Guardian Angel" from *The Winged Energy of Delight: Selected Translations by Robert Bly.* Copyright © 2004 by Robert Bly. Used by permission of HarperCollins Publishers.

Juan Ramón Jiménez, "I Am Not I," "At First She Came to Me Pure," and Federico García Lorca, "Rundown Church, from *Lorca & Jimenez: Selected Poems* by Robert Bly. Copyright © 1973, 1997 by Robert Bly. Reprinted by permission of Beacon Press, Boston

Gregory Orr, "Silence" from *The Caged Owl: New and Selected Poems.* Copyright © 2002 by Gregory Orr. Reprinted with the permission of The Permissions Company, LLC on behalf of Copper Canyon Press, www.coppercanyonpress.org.

Louis Simpson, "American Poetry" and excerpts from "The Inner Part" from *The Owner of the House: New Collected Poems 1940-2001.* Copyright © 2001 by Louis Simpson. Reprinted with the permission of The Permissions Company, LLC on behalf of BOA Editions, Ltd., boaeditions.org.

Henry Taylor, "And Robert Bly Says Something, Too," "Mr. James Dickey in Orbit" from *The Horse Show at Midnight and An Afternoon of Pocket Billiards.* Copyright © 1992, Louisiana State University Press.

Tomas Tranströmer, "After a Death," translated by Robert Bly, from *The Half-Finished Heaven: The Best Poems of Tomas Tranströmer.* Copyright © 2001 by Tomas Tranströmer. Translation copyright © 2001 by Robert Bly. Reprinted with the permission of The Permissions Company, LLC on behalf of Graywòlf Press, graywolfpress.org.

John Wieners, "Two Years Later." Copyright © 1972, 2021, The Literary Estate of John Wieners, Raymond Foye Executor.

———

Every effort has been made to locate and contact copyright holders in order to obtain the appropriate permissions to quote from published or unpublished material.

———

I am deeply indebted to the personal care and professional expertise of Drs. Kayan, Roohani, Delgado, and Tarrel, neurologists all.

———

Ultimate thanks, in all ways and always, to Sarah Campbell.

Index of Personal Names
(italics indicate photo)

Whalen, Philip, 14, 18, 20, 298
Wheelock, John Hall, 70, 96, 99, 112, 216, 312
   n. 15
Whitman, Walt, 12, 22, 25, 29, 53, 100, 109, 111,
   113, 140-1, 150, 151, 179, 190, 196-7, 200,
   216, 234, 295
Whittemore, Reed, 102-3, 164, 298
Wieners, John, 278, 295, 298
Wilbur, Richard, 18, 29, 33, 58, 81, 100, 142,
   173, 175, 231, 232, 294, 298, 332 n. 23
Williams, Jonathan, 18, 239-40
Williams, William Carlos, 3, 21, 29, 30, 34, 38,
   45, 56, 62, 70, 73, 74, 76, 99, 224
Wilson, Edmund, 18, 102, 121
Wilson, Mark, 130
Winters, Yvor, 16, 81, 100, 108, 112, 169, 294,
   305 n. 17, 308 n. 36
Witherup, William, 241, 295
Wordsworth, William, 117, 174, 185, 251, 270,
   327 n. 4
Wright, Charles, 295
Wright, James, 8, 17, 21-4, 41, 43, 44, 47-51, 52,

56, 57-8, 61-2, 64, 66, 73, 76, 79-80, 86, 90,
92, 95, 97, 98, 101, 103-5, 128-9, 132-3,
135-6, 139-41, 142, 143, *144,* 145-7, 148,
149-51, 155, 157, 158, 168, 174, 177-8,
181-4, *194,* 195, 197, 200, 212, 219, 222-3,
228, 233-5, 239, 268, 295, 297, 298, 309 n.
15, 316 n. 50, n. 65, 328 n. 32, 332 n. 23,
333 n. 56
Wylie, Andrew, 117

Yeats, W. B., 29, 31, 33, 45, 69, 135, 150, 160,
169, 187, 189, 245, 253, 286, 296, 307 n.
26, 335 n. 103
Young, David, 295
Young, Marguerite, 33, 34, 40, 332 n. 23

Zdonek, Raymond, 276
Zea, Carlos de Francisco, 48, 95, 252
Zukofsky, Louis, 20, 45, 128, 240, 294
Zweig, Paul, 175, 199-200, 212, 246-7, 248, 333
n.56, 335 n. 94

The author (left) with Robert Bly

Mark Gustafson, born and raised in Chicago, has been a classics professor focusing on historiography, religions, late antiquity, and ancient tattoos. He first encountered Robert Bly's poetry a half-century ago, and spent the next twenty years attending readings and scouring used book stores for Bly's more obscure publications. While living in Bemidji he arranged an introductory visit with Bly at Kabekona Lake. A mutual friend then suggested that Gustafson write a book on Bly's magazine and press and made the same suggestion to Bly. Eventually, Gustafson had his own key to Bly's house in Moose Lake, and thus open access to his collected papers.

In 2012, Red Dragonfly Press published his *The Odin House Harvest: An Analytical Bibliography of the Publications of Robert Bly's Fifties, Sixties, Seventies, Eighties, Nineties, and Thousands Press*—a companion to the book you're holding in your hands. In 2015, it appeared in a revised trade edition.

Essays in *Antioch Review, Catamaran Literary Reader, Great River Review, Kenyon Review, Michigan Quarterly Review, Rain Taxi Review of Books,* and *Robert Bly in This World* (University of Minnesota Press, 2011) grew out of the research for both of these books.

While still engaged in a massive biographical project on the many lives of Robert Bly, Gustafson's next book will consider the early decades of Minnesota's vaunted literary ecosystem, and especially Bly's leading role in its development.

Gustafson lives in Minneapolis but is happiest at his rustic cabin on Leech Lake in northern Minnesota.